Animal welfare
in Australia

ANIMAL PUBLICS

Melissa Boyde & Fiona Probyn-Rapsey, Series Editors

Other titles in the series:

Animal death
Ed. Jay Johnston & Fiona Probyn-Rapsey

Animals in the Anthropocene: critical perspectives on non-human futures
Ed. The Human Animal Research Network Editorial Collective

Cane toads: a tale of sugar, politics and flawed science
Nigel Turvey

Engaging with animals: interpretations of a shared existence
Ed. Georgette Leah Burns & Mandy Paterson

Fighting nature: travelling menageries, animal acts and war shows
Peta Tait

Animal welfare in Australia

Policy and politics

Peter John Chen

SYDNEY UNIVERSITY PRESS

First published by Sydney University Press
© Peter John Chen 2016
© Sydney University Press 2016

Reproduction and Communication for other purposes
Except as permitted under the Act, no part of this edition may be reproduced, stored in a retrieval system, or communicated in any form or by any means without prior written permission. All requests for reproduction or communication should be made to Sydney University Press at the address below:

Sydney University Press
Fisher Library F03
The University of Sydney NSW 2006
AUSTRALIA
Email: sup.info@sydney.edu.au
sydney.edu.au/sup

National Library of Australia Cataloguing-in-Publication Data

Creator:	Chen, Peter J. (Peter John), 1972– author.
Title:	Animal welfare in Australia : politics and policy / Peter John Chen.
ISBN:	9781743324738 (paperback)
	9781743324745 (ebook: epub)
	9781743324752 (ebook: Kindle)
	9781743325025 (ebook: PDF)
Series	Animal Publics.
Notes:	Includes bibliographical references and index.
Subjects:	Animal welfare—Government policy—Australia.
	Animal welfare—Political aspects—Australia.
	Animal welfare—Moral and ethical aspects—Australia.
	Human–animal relationships—Australia.
	Australia—Politics and government.
Dewey Number:	636.0832

Cover image: Hand feeding sheep in feedlot at Connemara Station, Tarcutta, New South Wales. Photographer: Carl Davies. CSIRO Science Image, http://scienceimage.csiro.au. Used under CC Attribution 3.0 Unported (CC BY 3.0).
Cover design by Miguel Yamin

Contents

Acknowledgements	ix
List of figures	vii
List of acronyms	xi
Nomenclature	xiii
Introduction	xv
Part 1	1
1 History	3
2 Ethics	21
Part 2	37
3 Attitudes to animals	39
4 In the media	85
5 Mapping the policy domain	123
Part 3	149
6 Animal protectionism	151

7	Animal-using industry	223
8	Political and administrative policy elites	275

Conclusion — 319

Appendices

Appendix A: Research methods	323
Appendix B: Major ethical positions regarding animals	326
Appendix C: Australian animal protection organisations – a sample	
Appendix D: Animal-using industry in Australia – representative bodies and their relationships with policy-makers	334
Appendix E: Timeline of animal welfare policy in Australia	338
Appendix F: Significant legal instruments	350
Appendix G: Top Google queries relating to the 10 most frequently searched-for animals	360

Reference list — 365

Index — 401

List of figures

Figure 1.1. Frequency of 'vegetarian' in English-language books.   15
Figure 3.1. Australian annual per capita meat consumption, 1962–2010.   41
Figure 3.2. Recreational activities employing animals.   43
Figure 3.3. Animal used in research and teaching in Australia, by type.   45
Figure 3.4. Victorians' perceptions of the importance of animal welfare.   52
Figure 3.5. Importance of animal wellbeing, by type.   53
Figure 3.6. Comparative egg sales as ethical consumption.   61
Figure 3.7. Awareness of issues affecting animal wellbeing.   62
Figure 3.8. Perceived adequacy of welfare laws in Australia.   67
Figure 3.9. Australian stockpersons' perceptions of animals' capacity to experience pain 'like humans'.   73
Figure 4.1. Number of issues mentioned in newspapers, 2005–2014.   88
Figure 4.2. Number of events mentioned in newspapers, 2005–2014.   89
Figure 4.3. Regional variations in event reporting from the national average (percent), 2005–14.   101
Figure 4.4. Animals on Australian free-to-air television.   107
Figure 4.5. Representations of animals on Australian supermarket shelves.   113
Figure 4.6. Representations of farmers and farming on Australian supermarket shelves.   115
Figure 6.1. Animals processed by Australian RSPCAs, 2004/5–2013/4.   196
Figure 6.2. Public support for different activist tactics.   205
Figure 7.1. McInerney's 'conflicts between animal welfare and productivity' model.   237

Acknowledgements

I must thank Professor Marian Sawer for her encouragement and advice in the development of the manuscript at its inception, and Professor Fiona Probyn-Rapsey for the opportunity to add this volume to the Animal Studies series. Agata Mrva-Montoya and Denise O'Dea from Sydney University Press have been essential to the realisation of this project and have my gratitude for their attention and focus.

During the development of the research project I received generous assistance with access to documents and databases from a variety of organisations and individuals. Thanks go to the Animal Health Alliance, Anne Clarke of the RSPCA ACT, Gordon Phillips of the Queensland Office of Fair Trading, and Lynda Stoner of Animal Liberation New South Wales. I am indebted to Karo Tak for her introduction to, and insight on, the Sydney veg*n community; as well as to Malcolm France, for input into my research design for a survey of animal welfare officers.

Final drafting was completed under the auspices of the Special Studies Program of the School of Social and Political Studies of the University of Sydney. The program provides time for the contemplation of larger writing projects. I'm also very grateful to the School of Politics and International Relations of the Australian National University, at which I was a visitor in 2014–2015.

The book was written exclusively on the land of the Gadigal people. With love: JF.

Frequently used acronyms

AA	Animals Australia
AAS	Animal Attitude Scale
AAWS	Australian Animal Welfare Strategy
ABS	Australian Bureau of Statistics
ACCC	Australian Competition and Consumer Commission
ACT	Australian Capital Territory
AIO	Animal-using Industry Organisation
AL	Animal Liberation
ALF	Animal Liberation Front
ALP	Australian Labor Party
APO	Animal Protection Organisation
AWL	Animal Welfare League
AWO	Animal Welfare Officers
COAG	Council of Australian Governments
LNP	Liberal National Party (Queensland)
LSRA	Liberation, Strong-Rights, Abolition
MLA	Member of the Legislative Assembly
MLC	Member of the Legislative Council
MP	Member of Parliament
n.d.	Not dated
NFF	National Farmers' Federation

NSM	New social movement
NSW	New South Wales
PETA (Aus)	People for the Ethical Treatment of Animals (Australia)
PETA (US)	People for the Ethical Treatment of Animals (USA)
QFF	Queensland Farmers' Federation
RSPCA	Royal Society for the Protection of Animals
s.d.	Standard deviation
SFO	State Farming Organisation
SFP	Shooters and Fishers Party
SMO	Social movement organisation

Nomenclature

Throughout, the term 'animal' is used to describe non-human animals, as defined in Chapter 1. Preference tends to be given to the term 'companion animal' over 'pet'; the former term is favoured by many animal protection organisations and the Australian Companion Animal Council.

Following Guither (1998, 9) and others, I tend to employ the phrase 'animal protection' to cover the full spectrum of attitudes of animal advocates and welfare providers, including (but not limited to) welfare and abolitionist perspectives. Guither defines 'animal welfare' as 'all efforts to prevent cruelty, improve humane treatment, reduce stress and strain, and monitor research with animals'. While this clashes with the tendency of some abolitionist authors to use the term 'welfarist' and 'protectionist' interchangeably, it appears to be the most useful convention. 'Animal welfare', therefore, is used to describe the dominant policy paradigm in the Australian context: a focus on debates about how animals should be treated, but within an overarching norm that sees them legally and ethically subordinate to humans. In this way, animal welfare is different to its human counterpart (Haynes 2008).

In discussing vegetarians and vegans I have sometimes used the word 'veg*ns', an umbrella term for both groups (I discuss the distinction between the two, as well as other abstainer communities, in Chapter 3).

In general, organisations in this book are named using their current organisational name; this is extended to acronyms.

Biblical verses are sourced from the King James Version. Quranic verses are sourced from the Pickthall translation.

Introduction

The direct inspiration for this book was the temporary cessation of live animal exports to Indonesia in late 2011. This decision of the Gillard Labor government directly followed the broadcast of footage of slaughterhouse practices in Jakarta. In response to this footage, the websites of activist organisations crashed due to dramatic surges in traffic (AAP 2011a), and members of Parliament reported being deluged with calls about the show. Popular concern led some government backbenchers to advocate that the live-export industry be phased out, while competing legislative proposals emerged from the Australian Greens and independent senators to ban or restrict the practice. In the following two years, successive reports of animal mistreatment in Egypt and Pakistan sparked further unrest (Rout and Crowe 2012).

A few years before these live-export scandals, PETA (USA) had led an influential campaign against the practice of mulesing in Australia, focusing particularly on the lack of pain relief during this invasive procedure. In response, in 2004 the wool industry had agreed to invest in research that would allow mulesing to be voluntarily phased out (mulesing is defined by the Primary Industries Council as the surgical removal of well-bearing skin from the tail and breech area of a sheep, and is performed to prevent insect infestation; Primary Industries Ministerial Council 2006, 17). Between these two controversies, by 2014 it appeared that a significant shift in the political balance over animal welfare standards had emerged in Australia.

Since then, however, it is possible to see a shoring up of the pre-existing status quo towards policy regarding the treatment of animals. The government's decision to temporarily halt live export negatively affected the operations of exporters and tested Australian–Indonesian relations, with wider implications for co-operation between the two nations that spilled over into debates about border protection and asylum seekers. However, exports resumed in 2013 and the live-export sector has since benefited from free-trade negotiations that look set to grow this agricultural subsector in Australia dramatically. In the same period, key members of the sheep industry abandoned their commitment to PETA to phase out mulesing in favour of a longer-term strategy of research and breeding (Jepson 2012). And although animal welfare activists have enjoyed other victories, such as a 2014 ban on the use of cages for chickens and pigs in intensive production in the Australian Capital Territory, this occurred only after the last of these industries had been paid by the ACT government to leave the jurisdiction.

The policy landscape may shift, but one thing is constant: Australians' attitudes to animals are complex and contradictory. In 2013 Australians directly consumed hundreds of millions of animals as meat while lavishing money and affection on their companion animals, 25 million of whom reside in 5 million (or 66 per cent of) Australian households (Animal Health Alliance 2013). Australians spend $8 billion annually on this subclass of favoured animals – four times the total amount individuals gave to charitable causes (McGregor-Lowndes and Pelling 2013).

Another case that unfolded during the writing of this book captures this complexity. In 2014, following a slight rise in the small number of shark attacks (AAP 2014), the Western Australian government implemented a program of shark culling. In response, the public rallied to the largest pro-shark protests in Australian (and possibly international) history (ABC 2014). That sharks, the focus of a common, visceral phobia that is often seen as being hardwired and is far beyond a rational estimate of the actual risk of attack (Ritter et al. 2008, 47), mobilised so many, shows how complex our political relationship with animals can be. Millions of domesticated animals go to their deaths

Introduction

annually in Australia largely unremarked, yet a small number of sharks prompted vigorous protests. These events demonstrate the difficulty of policy-making around animal welfare and protection issues. Add a scarcity of scholarship on policy-making pertaining to animal protection in this country, and the political response to animal protection issues in Australia cannot be readily explained or understood.

The status quo

Where do animals fit in the Australian political landscape? If, as the philosopher Jean-Paul Sartre argued, we are the sum of our actions, then the overwhelming majority of Australians would appear to support the idea that non-human animals should be subordinated to human desires. This status quo is what Joy (2010) calls 'carnism': an ideology that normalises animal use whether or not it is necessary for human survival. In giving a name to the ideology of animal use – just as those who avoid animal products are called vegetarians or vegans – Joy highlights a previously 'unmarked category'. That we usually have no names for such categories reflects the tendency for the characteristics of the powerful (be that whiteness, maleness or adherence to a 'normal' diet) to neither have, nor need, a specific designator. This is an irony that sees the privileged as invisible, with only deviations from the norm marked out by special terminology.

The assumption that the status quo is simply 'normal' conceals the power relations behind it. In the case of humans and animals, the persistent subordination of the species with which we share the planet is driven by two forces. The first is inertia. The consumption of animals and animal products often occurs in the most intimate of settings, and forms the pattern of our daily lives and habits. Here Bourdieu's (1990) notion of *habitus* is useful: the dispositions and preferences individuals acquire through formal and informal socialisation. These are powerful predictors of human behaviour because they are recreated inter-generationally and over time come to constitute 'our culture'.

The second is the political economy that alienates many of us from the source and character of the products and services we consume. Over the past hundred years, development has been marked by a shift in employment towards specialisation and away from primary production. The effect of this is to obscure how goods and services are produced. While this is clear in the psychological avoidance many people demonstrate regarding where their consumer products come from, it is also demonstrated across the economy, from labour standards to the 'outsourcing' of industrial pollution to developing nations (Shell 2009).

And yet this culture of domination is neither absolute nor unchallenged. Almost as long as our species has claimed the status of 'civilisation' there have been those who have questioned the status quo. Pythagoras' (c500 BCE) followers are commonly associated with religious vegetarianism (Walters and Portmess 2001, 15), and the 'Pythagorean diet' was a common term for vegetarianism as recently as the 19th century. Over the past 200 years, movements have waxed and waned that challenged the environmental, health, spiritual, and ethical appropriateness of our use of animals. Since the 1970s a renewed set of political movements has refreshed and rearticulated a range of challenges to the political economy of carnism. Promoting incremental or radical alternatives to established human–animal relations, these groups have opened up a new political dialogue around social and industrial animal use.

Yet most individuals in our society maintain a complex and ambivalent relationship with animals, based on often quixotic criteria. The intimacy and affection that some species are afforded is matched by an apparent ruthlessness towards others; animals with complex mental states and social capacity are treated as little more than machines, re-engineered to move from birth to plate in a way that is standardised, homogenised and designed to reduce observable diversity and individualism (Probyn-Rapsey 2013, 240–1).

While these inconsistencies often frustrate activists, the shifting and contradictory attitudes of the public towards animal protection also confuse those in animal-using industries. Many in industry see urban-based activists as mawkish and out of touch with the realities of animal husbandry, and are frustrated by the gap between the stated concerns of their customers regarding standards of animal treatment and their willingness to pay higher prices for food and other products (Phillips and Phillips c2010, 161). Concern for animal welfare can be sporadic, appearing seemingly randomly and – as was the case with mulesing – from both domestic and international sources.

These contradictions, and a range of other factors, make the policy process surrounding animal protection difficult to understand and hard to control. The wide range of contexts in which human and animal interests intersect and clash make simplified policy responses impossible, with oversight and administration often spanning multiple boundaries (jurisdictional, administrative, and paradigmatic). The fragmented nature of the animal agriculture and animal protection communities means that participants often have a limited view of the policy process. Elected officials who are placed between competing demands are often not engaged in protection issues on a systematic or ongoing manner. With the devolution of many standards-setting and monitoring activities into industry, public servants have only partial engagement with the scope and implications of welfare legislation.

The objective of this book, and the primary research behind it, is to better understand the policy-making process surrounding animal protection in Australia. The importance of this task is apparent to many animal activists: given the pervasiveness of animal use in Australia, they recognise the incredible scale of the practices they wish to abolish or alter. From the industrial perspective, events like the temporary suspension of live exports to Indonesia have alerted many to the importance of engaging with policy debates in this area (a $1 billion class-action lawsuit was launched by affected industries in late 2014; Neales 2014, 6). While activists are interested in the policy processes that would allow them to cement policy 'wins', industry representatives are concerned with making the policy process both more amenable to their interests and more predictable.

The scope and methods of this book

The field of animal–human relations is a growing area of academic study, both within Australia and internationally. It is intensely interdisciplinary in nature, incorporating the social sciences (political science, sociology, anthropology, geography), humanities (philosophy and ethics, arts, cultural studies, history), psychology, law, economics and political economy, medicine, veterinary science and biology. Given this, this book draws on contemporary academic debates, but does not attempt to critically engage with all of them. This includes questions regarding political philosophy and ethics, technical debates about sentience and the threshold of self-awareness, and the science of animal-welfare standards.

This approach is deliberate. A focus on policy-making has permitted greater access to policy domain participants than would have otherwise been possible. As is discussed later in this volume, some industry participants are sceptical about the motivations of academics interested in this area. Additionally, research on animal-protection politics in Australia to date has tended towards normative ethical orientations (the most obvious examples being the work of Australian ethicist Peter Singer and his successors and interlocutors), political sociology research into animal-rights activism (see, for example: Munro 2005a; Munro 2001a), applied political philosophy (see O'Sullivan 2011) and an emerging but very active focus on animal law (see Cao 2010; Bruce 2012a; Sankoff et al. 2013) (also discussed later in this volume). While Australian policy scholars have written widely on rural policy and political interest articulation (see Botterill 2003; Halpin 2004), this has focused on industry policy in the conventional sense of the term, with an emphasis on market promotion and development (Freedman 1997), rather than on animal-protection issues.

The research strategy underlying this volume – unpacked in detail in Appendix A – is a mixed methods approach. This approach, drawing on a wide variety of data sources, is ideal for a study that aims to provide a broad overview of a diverse policy-making field. The study of policy processes is not normative in nature, and this represents both a strength and a weakness. The study aims to explain how power structures produce public policy outputs and outcomes. This permits the identification of tendencies, trends and regularities, and therefore sits at the meso-level of analysis, between excessive attention to singular cases and gross national generalisations.

The book is divided into three parts. Part 1 provides a historical perspective, which is essential to understanding the status quo. How have current patterns of animal regulation and use developed over time? Political interest in animal protection waxes and wanes, and global forces have played a significant role in shaping the domestic animal industry and animal activism. The history of ideas about the relationship between humans and animals, both how we define what it is to be one or the other, and what moral significance we attribute to these classifications, is also important. Major currents in religious, moral and ethical thought are outlined as a means of understanding how our thinking about animals has (or has not) developed.

Part 2 provides a broader view of the current situation. I consider the Australian public's ideas about animals through the lens of public behaviour and opinion, and how popular media both shape and reflect our attitudes. The concept of a policy domain is introduced as an analytical tool with which to map out the major policy actors involved. In the case of animal protection in Australia, policy tends to be produced via a network of highly attenuated and disconnected policy-making structures, with critical input from non-government and industry organisations. After mapping the policy domain, in Part 3 I examine three crucial actors within it: activists, industry representatives and policy-making elites. I consider who these actors are, how they influence policy, and where and how they come into conflict with one another.

As we shall see, the low salience of animal welfare and protection has tended to produce a policy vacuum in Australia, and this sustains the complex, disconnected and conflictual character of much animal-protection policy in this country. Given the rising salience of the issue for a range of stakeholders, however, the time seems right for a volume exploring how Australia regulates relations between humans and non-human animals. Scholarship has the potential to significantly contribute to our understanding of these policy processes, and to help stakeholders to navigate the complex and often contradictory policy landscape.

Part 1

1
History

This chapter provides a short history of the relationship between humans and animals in Australia. The history of this area is significant in shaping the conditions participants in the policy process face today: this includes the material conditions of animal production systems, the industrial mix and structure of animal industries, cultural expectations about what is normal and appropriate, and policy paradigms and legal frameworks. From a social-constructivist perspective, this history conditions the expectations and understanding of participants in the policy process. From a rational-actor viewpoint, historical forces shape the distribution of politically relevant resources. From an institutional point of view, history ties particular forms of politics to particular parts of the constitutional-legal system (Stewart et al. 2008, 44). This chapter will demonstrate that our current 'naturalised' relations with animals are the product of cultural factors and policy decisions made by successive governments, and that the current 'advocacy explosion' around human–animal relations is not unique in the history of modern Australia.[1]

---

1 A timeline of human–animal relations in Australia is provided in Appendix E.

Human and animal relations in Australia

Before Europeans

While it is extremely difficult to generalise about Indigenous cultures, Aboriginal and Torres Strait Islander peoples – as established hunters and gatherers in a landscape of which they had very detailed and local knowledge – maintained a view of their physical environments as a complex set of inter-related connections between animal, human, plant and geological features. In this animals played a role in social and spiritual life as food, as companions, and as totemic signifiers.

Crook (2008, 4) considers it unlikely that Australia's Aboriginal people engaged in vegetarianism, and so the use of animals is likely to have been a social and cultural norm in what is now Australia. While European-style farming practices were not established in Australia until the start European occupation (with the exception of the Gunditijmara people, who engaged in eel farming in natural and artificial waterways) (McNiven and Bell 2010), animal-use practices included extensive fishing in mainland coastal areas and wetlands, hunting, and fire-stick agriculture associated with ecological management. As in contemporary Australian society, the production and consumption of meat was gendered. Farrer (2005) argues that women's gathering contributed the majority of Aboriginal diets. This means that Aboriginal people probably consumed considerably less meat per capita than the first European arrivals.

This said, it is likely that Aboriginal people had a less utilitarian or instrumentalist view of animals than did Europeans at the end of the 18th century: animals were not valued simply in terms of their contribution of meat and skin to humans. As long-term managers of the environment, Aboriginal people had an interest in ensuring that plants and animals used as food and medicine, and as part of spiritual practices, were sustained. This was part of a wider duty to country that informed cultural knowledge and beliefs. This knowledge included an understanding of animal behaviour, as well as limits on animal exploitation to ensure sustainability (the maintenance of 'good country'; Rose 2011, 26).

1 History

As part of this complex system of practical knowledge and spiritual beliefs, Indigenous people adhered to a range of prohibitions regarding animals, including specific restrictions on the consumption of personal totem animals, as well as generalised restrictions on hunting and foraging in areas of spiritual importance. Attributing life to a wide range of environmental elements, Indigenous people recognised the consciousness of plants and animals, even if human physical needs required their use as food, clothing and tools (Rose 1996, 8–9, 23). Animals were considered to have a high level of consciousness and even human characteristics (humour, greed, etc.), reflecting cross-species kinship.

Farm politics after 1788

With the colonisation of Australia, European attitudes to animals were transplanted. The settlers were largely uninterested in local understandings of the environment beyond identifying water supplies and potential farmland. The immediate concern of the new arrivals was to ensure enough food and muscle power to survive in an alien environment, one that appeared quite unsympathetic to their established agricultural production practices (the first stock animals brought to the colony, cattle and sheep, were lost or died, requiring a number of further attempts to establish productive herds; Henzell 2007). Colonial government policy (both domestically and in Britain) focused on the establishment of self-sustaining colonies, both to provide sustenance for the new inhabitants and to raise capital to pay for colonisation.

The most obvious example of this initial policy focus was the development of the Australian wool industry from the 1820s (Davidson 1981, 6–7), which, unlike meat (which at the time could not be exported), would find a market in England. Herding of sheep (for wool export and for domestic consumption) and cattle was significant in facilitating the expansion of colonial land occupation away from the points of initial settlement, as these animals were 'portable larders'. In a country where crops were initially difficult to grow, where horse-power and labour were limited, and where there was only a small regional market for exports, herding in the large savannah-like areas west of the Dividing Range made commercial and political sense.

The role of government in encouraging animal agriculture in colonial Australia, therefore, tended to focus on fostering pastoralism and the distribution of lands. Land distribution shaped agricultural practices and colonial politics. Attempts at the monopolisation of lands around the initial settlements further encouraged outward expansion and pastoralism (Pearson et al. 2010). While those with extensive landholdings were often politically powerful (the 'squattocracy'), the comparative shortage of labour in the colonies tended to mitigate against the power of landholders after the end of transportation mid-century. The most obvious example of this was the political preference for 'closer settlement' (from about 1860 in New South Wales, Queensland, and Victoria): policies aimed at the creation of smaller blocks leased by yeoman farmers (Pearson et al. 2010; similar attempts were undertaken in the early 20th century with various 'soldier-settler' farming schemes).[2] The development of the labour movement in the late 19th century from within the shearing workforce demonstrated the comparative power of labour when compared with its European counterparts.

Other areas of state investment supported new agricultural practices. Local governments were involved in setting up slaughter-houses to supply local meat and to create jobs. Dairying received a considerable boost following investment in road and rail transport with the prosperity of the late 19th century (Peel 1973, 55). Dairying was also seen as an effective way to produce smaller family-focused farms in line with the closer settlement movement; this is one of the reasons why deregulation occurred in dairying later than in other agricultural sectors. With federation, state-sponsored agricultural research fell under the remit of the Council for Scientific and Industrial Research (CSIRO, established in 1926), with an emphasis on animal breeding for local conditions, new food production practices, and pest control. This was not without resistance from state-based authorities, but the need to ensure the supply of safe and reliable foodstuffs during the Second World War assisted in promoting the role of the national applied-research organisation's involvement in agriculture and food technology (Farrer 2005).

---

2 These policies were resisted through a variety of means both legal (e.g. political lobbying) and illegal (e.g. the 'dummying' and 'peacocking' of smaller licences by established landholders).

1 History

Meat and the new Australian identity

While a taste for meat eating was inherited from the British (regarded in the 18th and 19th centuries as among the largest consumers of meat and alcohol in Europe; Santich 1995), the consumption of meat was a formative part of the Australian experience. New settlements were highly regulated by the government, and the provision of a basic ration including regular meat encouraged meat production and established the expectation of meat in a working man's diet (a norm that can be seen in the 1931 'Beef Riot' in Adelaide, prompted by the substitution of mutton for beef in the unemployment ration). Meat was both plentiful and cheap when compared with England. This, plus the relative scarcity of other foodstuffs such as vegetables and processed foods, meant meat and simple breads made up the backbone of the diets of people working on sheep and cattle stations. Meat was commonly eaten at every meal in the colony, compared with once or less per day by labourers in the home country (Santich 1995).

The bountiful supply of meat among all classes in the colonies was observed by travellers, and became a selling point for inbound migration following the end of convict transportation, using slogans such as 'Meat three times a day' (1847; Ankeny 2008, 20). In colonial Australia, meat could be cheaper than bread. Attempts to moderate this monotonous meat diet were encouraged from the 1850s, but this was mitigated against by the high cost of fruit and vegetables, by cultural preferences (still seen today in the tradition of the summer Christmas roast), and by dietary theories that muscle output (labouring) required muscle input (meat). This remains a popular trope in advertising.

Farm policy after the Second World War: protection to free trade

The development of an effective agricultural sector that could both meet the needs of Australians and provide material for export was part of a long process of nation building from the colonial era into the 20th century. With federation in 1901 the new Commonwealth government found itself with limited constitutional powers to act systematically to produce agricultural policy. State and territory-based policy-making had produced a raft of initiatives governing land distribution and allocation, with the most significant policies developed around the management of animal diseases. This included the formalisation of stock routes and disease districts to control and prevent the spread of illnesses, including the use of some levies for disease mitigation.

The Second World War significantly altered the involvement of the Commonwealth in farm policy. First, the introduction of price and export controls, as well as rationing, saw the elevation of farming from a means of national development to one of national survival. The impact of the war on global production and trade had implications that lasted into the 1950s and beyond, and successive Australian governments attempted to manage the anticipated demand surge and input scarcity that had been observed following the First World War (Hefford 1985).

Under the Liberal–Country governments of the 1950s and 1960s, this led to the development of a complex array of farm policies that encouraged investment through favourable tax concessions and direct subsidies for inputs (particularly chemical fertilisers and fuel; Godden 2006: 154), built infrastructure (irrigation and the 'beef roads' of the 1960s), provided disaster and drought assistance (Botterill 2003), established marketing assistance and export control, supported industry rationalisation through exit grants, and implemented price-control mechanisms in a number of farm sectors (wheat, dairy and wool).

From the 1970s this type of 'protection all round' policy began to give way to the language of economic rationalism: policies became increasingly subject to formalised review based on strict application of market efficiency (Botterill 2005). In addition, government support had been subject to considerable ad hoc decision-making, creating political problems in managing the agricultural portfolio. While this shift in policy orientation elicited political resistance from some in protected agricultural sectors, the declining size of the agricultural industry (both in terms of the number of jobs involved, and as a proportion of GDP) reduced its political power (Martin et al. 1989, 7–9). This period coincides with the formation of the National Farmers' Federation, a recognition that the Country/National Party and the political class as a whole could no longer be relied on to automatically ensure the interests of farming industries.

While the wool and dairy industries retained – for a time – some degree of pre-1970s protectionism, minimum price guarantees for wool ended in the early 1990s and dairy followed a decade later. Today, industry support is less explicitly protectionist: direct industry support is provided in the form of public–private research funding through the Co-operative Research Centres (CRC) program (Godden 2006). CRCs are not, however, unique to the agriculture sector. More specific support can be found in ongoing biosecurity measures that limit the import of some animals and animal products, ostensibly because of the risk of importing disease. Under these arrangements, import permits are required for food products, with a range of restrictions based on the type of import, its source and its processing prior to arrival. Thus, chicken meat can be imported only from New Zealand, whereas there are fewer restrictions on pork. While these controls are presented as being purely for quarantine purposes, their commercial impact on producers and in international trade negotiations makes the overarching regulatory process, as well as the determination of individual cases, highly political at times.

Agricultural policy has thus shifted away from being a 'gift' bestowed on industry by policy-makers, and towards administrative standardisation and parity with other welfare programs. While farming remains to some extent a special and politically sensitive area due to the remaining influence of the National Party, agriculture has been subject to a move to standardise treatment across and between different sectors. While farming organisations, like many producer groups in pluralist democracies, have the advantage of access to policy-makers, we can see a narrowing of focus in agricultural policy-making over recent decades, and deliberate attempts to structure relations between the state and industry through a narrower range of representative bodies. This has implications for the political capacity of agricultural industry groups: they face a trade-off between achieving 'insider' status and accepting a narrower canvas on which to develop policy (Walmsley 1993, 46–7).

In defence of animals: animal protectionism in Australia

The last two centuries have thus seen major and ongoing changes in animal-related industries. During the same period, Australians' attitudes to the animal world have undergone a revolution. Croft (1991), for example, demonstrates how settlers attempted to grapple with native animals' place in their biological and social schema while at the same time reproducing agricultural norms and practices from 'home'. Animals such as the kangaroo have variously been food, scientific curiosities, sporting trophies, economic commodities, pests, national emblems and subjects of conservation by settlers and settler governments. What the new arrivals did not endeavour to do, however, was to systematically emulate the pre-existing patterns of food production and consumption of Indigenous people (Farrer 2005).

It would be a mistake to assume, however, that the Australian animal protection movement is a wholly new phenomenon. Attempts to change our attitudes to animals can be found less than 50 years after the arrival of the First Fleet, in the passage of the first animal welfare legislation in Tasmania in 1837. Overall, however, the development of assertive animal protection organisations (APOs) came quite late in the colonial era, and the subsequent history of animal protection politics is marked by an interesting abeyance or slowdown of activity for at least 40 years, between the 1920s and the 1960s.

Early influences from afar

One of the key influences in the formation of formal animal protection laws in pre-federation Australia was the Royal Society for the Protection of Animals (RSPCA) in England. It was not the first organisation of its kind, but the lack of enabling legislation to permit prosecutions had led to the rapid demise of earlier groups and societies. Established in 1824, the RSPCA was formed in response to the passage of Richard Martin's *Cruel Treatment of Cattle Act* two years before. This legislation prohibited the cruel and improper treatment of 'Horses, Mares, Gelding, Mules, Asses, Cows, Heifers, Steers, Oxen, Sheep, and other Cattle'. This provided the foundation for the expansion of anti-cruelty laws in the United Kingdom, particularly against animal fighting and baiting, which were added to the legislation in 1835 (Kalof 2007, 137–8). Legislation for the regulation of knackeries followed in 1843, and the licensing of vivisection in 1876. It was also significant in placing animal welfare within the paradigm of the criminal code. At first, the laws were personally prosecuted by Martin, who hired investigators to bring charges against offenders (Fairholme and Pain 1924, 30–40). The RSPCA assisted, but its capacity was limited, and the state was soon drafted into assisting with policing. London metropolitan police and military personnel, for example, were deployed to suppress bull-running (a type of baiting) in 1838. (It is important to note that these laws only applied to non-owners. As in other areas, there was a tendency for early anti-cruelty laws to focus, explicitly or implicitly, on the regulation of working-class people.)

It is interesting that legislation was promoted by individuals rather than associations prior to 1822, demonstrating the difficulty of advancing a legislative agenda for the protection of animals from cruel and unusual treatment (such as attempts to ban bull-baiting at the turn of the century, and more general-purpose legislation in the early 19th century, proposed by Lord Erskine). While welfare legislation in the English-speaking world predates Martin's Act (following Proverbs 12:10, the Massachusetts Puritans formally prohibited 'Tiranny or crueltie' against domesticated animals in 1641, although like Martin's Act this reflected practical and economic concerns, rather than a blanket concern for non-human animals), the passage of this legislation in the 'mother of parliaments' served as a model that was influential in the passage of similar legislation and the emergence of similar organisations in Australia.

Colonial activists

The development of animal welfare activism in Australia has a number of interesting sources. The first is the transfer of ideas from the United Kingdom to Australia by informed locals keeping up with news from home, and by 'new chums'. The first APO was the Victorian Society for the Protection of Animals (VSPCA), established in Melbourne in 1871, some six years after the introduction of specific anti-cruelty laws in that colony. This group was quickly followed by similar associations in the other colonies, demonstrating the spread of these ideas across the continent at this time.

While the SPCAs in Australia were formally independent, other activist organisations had a direct relationship with groups and movements in the home country. The British Union for the Abolition of

Vivisection (BUAV) is a good example of the type of international organisation active during the 19th century. British anti-vivisection had an international focus from its beginnings. As Murrie (2013, 259) notes, early concerns in England focused on vivisection by French scientists, who were leaders of the practice. Concerned about the rapid expansion of vivisection among scientists, the BUAV engaged in public debate about protection laws and helped to spread information about issues and legal developments around the world. It remained active in Australia through to the 1980s, and still exists in a small form today.

While these specific abolitionist and welfare groups tended to focus on the reduction of animal suffering, their origins lie in an array of religious social reformist organisations active during the 19th and early 20th centuries. Christian temperance and abstinence groups (the largest social movement of the 19th century; Allen 2013, 150) came together with a range of nonconformist denominations (Christian Spiritualists, Theosophists, Seventh-Day Adventists and others) in the promotion of dietary reform. This reform often focused on the advocacy of vegetarianism, albeit largely for the urban classes, removed as they were from manual labour. Rejecting the conservative notion of 'the fall' in favour of a view of human progress and perfectibility through personal discipline (Smith 1965) and (for some) scientific inquiry, they were active proselytisers of alternative diets and progressive social causes including early feminism and expanded democratic participation.

The role of nonconformist religious groups is important in pre-federation Australian animal history as they drew inspiration from a wide range of countries (including Germany, the United States and India) and included influential figures willing to advocate publicly for their causes. The VSPCA, for example, was promoted by the future prime minister Alfred Deakin when he was in colonial parliament. Part of the appeal of the movement to political elites was its focus on the conduct and discipline of the working classes (particularly regarding alcohol use, but also in the promotion of healthy living more broadly), therein supporting the development of a disciplined and sober workforce suitable for a modern, industrialising economy (Allen 2013, 153). Like the temperance movement, these movements were also significant for their inclusion of women as founders and in senior leadership roles.

1 History

Declining concern for animals

While the SPCAs would continue their work to the present day, the outbreak of the First World War marked the start of the decline of many groups within the movement. The high-water mark of the temperance movement was the introduction of 6pm closing of hotel bars and pubs in 1916 (coinciding with the need for social discipline during wartime; Allen 2013, 162). However, while it might be possible to blame the two wars and interwar depression for the waning of interest in social-improvement organisations, there appear to be more complex reasons for the decline of these groups (Guither 1998, 4–5).

The movements that supported dietary reform in Australia appear to have fallen in popularity by about 1908, with all of the Australian vegetarian societies (formed in the last decades of the 19th century) having wound up by that year (Crook 2008). In part, these groups were victims of their own internal inconsistencies: Spiritualism – one of Deakin's keen interests – also promoted rationalism via scientific inquiry, and thereby encouraged the scientific debunking of the very frauds it featured in many of its public performances (Smith 1965, 259). While these groups were active promoters of dietary reform, this too came under challenge from the medical profession and state departments of health, who had by now established a greater claim to scientific authority. In addition, Thompson (2002, 57) argues that nonconformist churches suffered considerably with the rise of British patriotism in the lead-up to war. Many Protestants shifted towards the more socially conservative and politically acceptable Church of England as an expression of patriotic Christianity.

After the First World War health promotion moved firmly into the hands of the expanding health departments. Following the establishment of a national dietary survey in the late 1930s, the first comprehensive diet for 'national survival' was published, aiming to address perceived deficiencies both in total caloric intake and in the consumption of milk and eggs specifically.[3] These guidelines became

---

[3] This difference between and emphasis on dietary advice and other aspects of animal use within the wider movement may explain the longer lifespan of the BUAV, which peaked in the 1940s (when measured in terms of the number of active branches internationally).

entrenched through rationing during the Second World War, further moving the regulation of diet into the hands of the state (Santich 1995). Importantly, this type of dietary advice was influenced by eugenics thinking at the time, which, in Australia, had a strongly racialised component. This has significance in later debates over live export and issues of national identity, as we will see in coming chapters. Overall, it appears that a wide range of factors external to, as well as within, the 19th-century food reform movement led to its rapid decline in the early 20th century, and to its failure to revitalise significantly until the late 1960s. As Figure 1.1 illustrates, in the first era of popularised diet alternatives, published book references to 'vegetarian' rose rapidly in the last quarter of the 19th century before flattening out after the First World War. They did not begin to increase significantly again until the 1980s. Given the international nature of the movement from the 19th century, it is not surprising that this is not a uniquely Australian phenomenon.

During the intervening period, animal protection issues remained largely the preserve of the various state-based SPCAs and smaller, specialised bodies. Competing welfare organisations formed during this period at times placed pressure on the SPCAs over their service provision and lobbying efforts (Pertzel 2006). Over time, these organisations shifted the balance of their attention towards companion rather than industrial animals. This shift had structural and cultural origins. Structurally, the start of the 20th century saw the bifurcation of animal welfare regulation. Through the introduction of specific exemptions from cruelty laws for particular farming practices, animal welfare regulation was effectively divided into two types: the decriminalisation of farming practices seen as necessary for production, and the ongoing application of general anti-cruelty criminal law to non-farmed animals (White 2008). Culturally, Australia was becoming increasingly urbanised and animal organisations followed this trend. With a tendency to attract patronage from social and political elites, these organisations developed into the acceptable face of animal welfare promotion (their designation as *royal* societies from the 1930s considerably assisted in cementing these organisations' social respectability; Budd 1988, 94), working with governments and benefactors to build infrastructure and slowly increase their levels of staffing. Nevertheless,

1 History

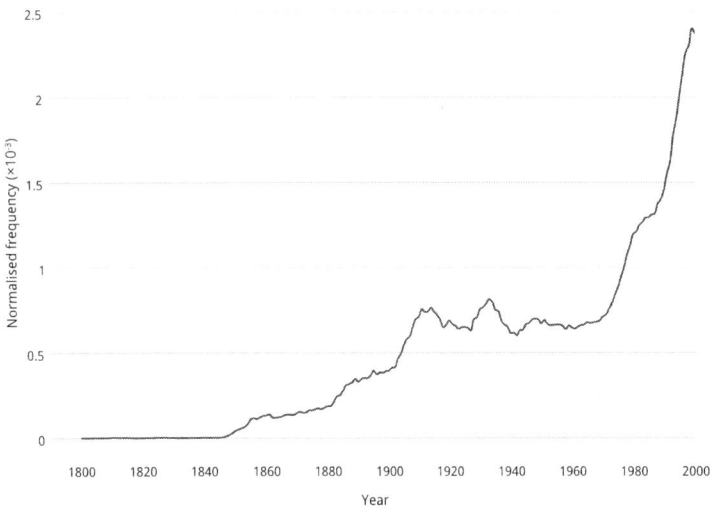

Figure 1.1. Frequency of 'vegetarian' in English-language books published in Britain, 1800–2000. Drawn from data provided by the Google Ngram Viewer (books.google.com/ngram). US publications (not shown) reveal a very similar trend.

an affinity between the increasingly respectable RSPCAs and the more radical abolitionist anti-vivisectors remained. White's 1937 volume on the history of the RSPCA in Queensland praises 'the extremists' (120) of the BUAV and others just prior to the outbreak of the Second World War, even as it tends to focus on more incremental reforms in Australia, such as the adoption of more humane slaughter technologies. This period saw the slow consolidation of legislation focused on the prosecution of cruelty, with an emphasis on the provision of services to animals in need and on resolving social problems, such as an excess of stray companion animals, through the operation of pound services and various dog and horse 'homes'.

A 'second wave'?

While the persistence of anti-vivisection activism during the mid-20th century demonstrates that more radical views about animal treatment never completely vanished, the 1960s and 1970s saw a renewed interest in animal politics, challenging the primacy of humans. Between the first and second waves, working animals largely disappeared from city streets across Australia, as developments in automotive technology flowed through from the war to the peace-time economy (Budd 1988, 20). Tractors outnumbered horses by 1946, demonstrating the rapidity of this transition.

Significantly, the direct visibility of the ill-treatment of horses by working-class men (particularly the infliction of exhaustion through overloading) served as a primary driver of urban mobilisation in the 19th and early 20th century. A typical account appeared in the *Sydney Morning Herald* on 27 March 1887:

> An 'Eye-witness' writes to say that a disgraceful scene of cruelty took place in Palmer Street, Wooloomooloo, on Saturday night, lasting from half-past 11pm till quite half-past 12. A drunken man in charge of a butcher's cart and horse most fearfully ill-used the poor animal, which was to all appearance thoroughly tired out, felling the poor beast to the ground four different times, and beating it with the butt-end of the whip. There were two other men with him, evidently his companions, who stood and yelled, and seemed to glory in the scene.

After the Second World War, city-dwellers' exposure to animals shifted considerably towards companion animals and animals exhibited in shows and zoos.

The re-emergence of the movement in the 1960s and 1970s tends to be associated with other 'liberation' movements attacking social orthodoxies (black liberation, women's liberation, gay liberation) (Townend 1981). As Sandøe and Christiansen (2008) argue, this mirrors the association of Richard Martin's Act with the abolition of slavery in the UK in the 19th century. As we will see in Chapter 6, while it is possible to identify two distinct 'waves' when looking at the formation of new groups and the mobilisation of public opinion, a clear distinction between them as 'welfare' and 'rights' movements is quite false.

1 History

Certainly, however, this period did see the creation of new, distinctive groups who increasingly used the language of animal 'rights'.

While the direct catalyst for the new liberation organisations in Australia was the publication of the Australian academic Peter Singer's *Animal liberation* (1975), this was just one example of a new literature on the industrial production of animals in post-war agriculture. The start of renewed interest in animal welfare issues by the wider public was associated with the publication of an exposé of intensive agricultural production by Ruth Harrison in *Animal machines* (1964). Reflecting a social norm that had seen wide-scale automation and de-population of agricultural industry, Harrison's work (introducing the term 'factory farming' into the animal rights lexicon) appraised readers of the reality of modern farming practices and the implications of the adoption of scientific management in agricultural production (1964). *Animal machines* informed Singer's writing, and the 1970s saw the formation of organisations in NSW (1976) and Victoria (1979) that took their names directly from Singer's book.

The significance of these small organisations lay less in their initial influence than in the introduction of a radical ethical challenge to the treatment of animals. The second wave was not simply an increase in political organisation around animal protection and welfare issues, but a challenge to the basic premise on which Australian animal welfare laws rested.[4] Importantly, it was at this time that the specific exemptions to cruelty charges enjoyed by rural producers since the early 20th century were transformed into generic exemptions for 'accepted farm practices', a change that reflected wider policy-making trends and served to reduce the impact of the new radical groups (see Chapter 8).

---

4   The distinction may be less significant than some have argued. Certainly parts of the anti-vivisection movement were abolitionist in their objectives in the late 19th century. However, the anti-vivisection movement tended to focus on scientific practices, rather than seeking a more universal application of their moral concerns.

Conclusion

The history of human–animal relations in Australia is a political one. The capacity of the emerging Australian state to impose its will on the continent has been shaped by environmental realities, as well as by the political economy of the new colony. The British colonial project needed animals to survive and to form a microcosm of the agricultural system found in England. The colonists' willingness to ignore or discount all that had come before reflected a political desire to deny a human history to the new continent. As the Australian system of state-sponsored agricultural development emerged, the use of animals became crucial to national development and to the establishment of family-based farms as a core economic unit. This history remains inscribed on the landscape of Australia, both physical and political. Animal agriculture was key to establishing the success of the new nation as a self-sustaining colonial enterprise. This provided regional and rural interests with political influence and enabled them to promote and protect agriculture. Even once farming was no longer the primary source of Australian wealth, this history was retained in the institutionalisation of agricultural interests in government departments, and in the wide range of private interest groups and associations active in policy debates.

The history of animal welfare and protection policy has similarly been shaped by Australia's willingness to import ideas from overseas. The migration of political radicals, free-thinkers and social dissenters to the colony served to more rapidly distribute some of the new challenges to the status quo. In the end, however, the economic and geopolitical realities of the emerging nation came to dominate. It is interesting, therefore, that the second wave of dissenters emerged from the work of an Australian (albeit heavily influenced by thought in the UK) during a time when the dominance of traditional agricultural practices was subject to considerable economic and political upheaval. This political opportunity allowed a radical challenge to the status quo and a new critique of conventional practices. With the traditional power of rural voices in decline, these political currents were not shut down in the way that they had been 70 years prior, when an expanding state–agricultural partnership had been able to dominate public discourse more effectively. This second wave has led to the intensification of challenges to the status quo, with the activism of the 1970s giving way to a greater diversity of ethical challenges to established patterns of human and animal interaction. In the next chapter, I examine a range of perspectives on the ethics of humans' relationship with animals.

2
Ethics

While this volume does not aim to make normative claims, at the heart of this policy issue are contested claims about how humans should relate to non-humans. Public policy's apparent focus on technical decisions about resource allocation and administrative procedures only loosely conceals its core interest in the mediation of competing values (Considine 1994, 3). While many motivations are discussed in the following chapters – economic, political, strategic – it is important to understand where the various actors stand in relation to contemporary debates about human–animal ethics. Therefore, in this chapter I outline some significant currents of thought about the ethics of human–animal relations. No single group 'owns' an interest in animal ethics; rather, all the political actors discussed in this volume, including members of the general public, make decisions based on ethical assumptions. Significantly, however, the vast majority of actors may not be able to explicitly articulate their own ethical position regarding animals. In examining our society's approach to human–animal ethics, we therefore need to begin with some basic questions: What is the locus of our concern? That is, to whom do we extend ethical consideration? How do we assess their interests? And how do we balance these interests against competing priorities and ethical concerns?

What are animals?

Before we can consider the variety of ethical perspectives on animals, it is important to understand what we mean when we talk about 'animals'. This is necessary not only to define the terrain of analysis, but also in order to recognise the limits of our current knowledge. La Barbera (2012, 1) observes that 'animal' is an ontological category: it helps us to define a socially meaningful class of entities. This is more than simply an esoteric discussion, as the scientific classification of animals by humans informs what social, legal and political status they are afforded. Inclusion or exclusion from the category of 'animal' leads to a range of different treatments, both under law and in the minds of thinkers about animal ethics.

By classifying the world, human beings have attempted to order the complex environment in which we live, and so to exert a measure (real or perceived) of control upon it (Crowson 1970, 1–2). As scientific understanding of the natural world has increased, there has been a paradoxical firming and loosening of the boundaries between different types of living things. Developments in evolutionary biology and genetics have enabled more definitive identification of living things. At the same time, however, a basic definition of what constitutes 'life' remains elusive, particularly as science explores deeper questions about sentience and mental states: at what point can an entity be said to possess the type of self- and situational awareness that humans see as morally significant? In the study of policy and politics, a similar focus on classification and definition has become increasingly important, as scholarly interest has shifted from questions of how and why power is mobilised to a focus on evidence-based political and administrative decisions: in making political decisions of ethical import, can we employ a formal and impartial set of criteria? In both biological and political terms, then, how we define and categorise 'animals' both reflects and informs our ethical perception of them.

2 Ethics

The European tradition

The most eminent scientific treatise on animals in the European tradition emerged from ancient Greece. Aristotle undertook significant efforts to identify and classify animals, a body of work that remained highly influential throughout Europe and western Asia into the late Renaissance (Asimov 1965). Aristotle focused on categorisation based on physiological similarity, and his influence can be seen in the rise of Linnaean classification during the scientific revolution. Importantly, the Aristotelian approach also incorporated a moral hierarchy, ascending from plants to animals and finally to humans, that was based on the complexity of the soul. In this model, only humans possessed the high-order values of rationality – a distinction implicitly retained in the metaphor of 'lower' and 'higher' forms of life in post-Darwinian thinking (Prothero 2007, 125).

In his *Systema naturae* (1735), Carl Linnaeus codified the various classification systems that had emerged from a mixture of classical Greek natural philosophy and from the Platonic idea that the observable natural world consists of approximates of perfect archetypes or 'forms'. Animals sat in an exclusive category (kingdom) that was distinct from other biological entities (plants) and from non-living matter (minerals). Moving away from Aristotle, and in a direct challenge to religious orthodoxy, Linnaeus placed humans in a biological category alongside apes, based on physical rather than behavioural similarities. Over time, Linnaeus' neat classification system has broken down, beginning with the discovery of microbial life (1676) and later with the ambiguous status of infectious agents such as viruses (Xue et al. 2012) and prions. More recently, the discovery of a range of organisms that have both animal and plant characteristics has further muddied such neat divisions (Ebdrup 2012). In the 20th century, reflecting the influence of Darwin, Linnaean classification was superseded by a 'cladistic' approach, in which organisms are classified according to their evolutionary relationship rather than physical similarities.

The upshot has been a move towards an inclusive definition of animals based on a minimum set of shared characteristics. Inherently, this excludes categorical discrimination based on the extent to which a specific trait (say, self-awareness) is displayed. Today, animals are generally defined as having five characteristics (Holland 2011, 1–3):

1. They are living things: they live and die, and are part of a process of reproduction.
2. They are multicellular organisms.
3. They consume other organisms (living or dead) to live.
4. They sense their environment and are able to move for at least part of their life cycle.[1]
5. They possess strong and flexible epithelial cells, which are critical in their embryonic development and to the development of the anatomical complexity exhibited by many animals.

In the development of the biological sciences, therefore, the notion of an 'us and them' distinction between humans and other animals has been collapsed by successive waves of analysis and classification. While humans may exhibit traits at the extreme end of a measurable spectrum (for example, rational planning and complex tool-use), similar traits are observed within the animal kingdom. This highlights the subjectivity of moral hierarchies based on any one trait, as well as the difficulty of picking a neutral benchmark against which to compare different types of animals for the purpose of making ethical judgements about their worth.

This latter point is particularly acute when animals come from different phylum (major subclassifications of the animal kingdom), and so have radically different bodyplans due to early evolutionary divergence. This can make simple definitions of 'intelligence', 'consciousness' and other characteristics difficult to pin down. Echinoderms (starfish), for example, lack the type of brain common to most animals, but sense their environment through eye-spots and a distributed net of neurons. With this 'brain' they independently control each of their arms to move and catch prey. Insect colonies, meanwhile, collectively display complex environmental sensing and organised response (Miller 2007); this is only revealed as a kind of non-human intelligence if the notion of intelligence is not tied to the individual brain.

Science has often been seen as a useful means of resolving questions about the moral significance of different animals. In reality, however, this is rarely true. While scientific research has facilitated

---

[1] The static adult oyster, for example, has a motile larval stage following fertilisation.

comparisons of closely related species (for example, in recent developments in assessing the intelligence of chimpanzees), beyond simple direct comparisons scientific research more often serves to highlight the impossibility of understanding the subjectivity of different species. Scientific research itself also has practical implications for animal welfare and has been the subject of ethical debates; in the 19th century, for example, the drive for greater scientific understanding of animal biology saw the rise of unregulated vivisection without anaesthesia (Murrie 2013, 259-60). In considering the ethics of human–animal interaction, then, science does not provide us with easy answers; instead, philosophical and political thinking must also come into play.

What concern do we owe animals?

Classical perspectives

While science has undermined the primacy of Aristotelian binomial classifications as absolute categories, they remain important in the popular imagination. This is largely thanks to their useful heuristic value, but is also a result of the long-standing dominance of these categories, which are rooted in some of the earliest natural philosophy. Given the closeness of people in classical societies to agriculture and the natural environment, it is not surprising that the study and treatment of animals has a long philosophical tradition.

For the Greeks of the classical era, the dominance of Platonic forms had wider implications than simply the development of classification. Aristotle specified the degree to which living things could be seen to have 'souls': plants had a simple soul (they live but do not feel), animals a more developed soul (they feel but do not reason), and humans the highest soul (we reason) (Nordenskiold 1946, 36). This approach was not limited to thinking about the natural world. Aristotle explicitly linked the natural order to the political one, arguing in *Politics* (c350 BCE):

> Plants exist for the sake of animals, and the other animals exist for the sake of man: domestic animals for his use and food; wild animals

– if not all, then most of them – for his food and other needs, such as clothing and tools. (In Pellegrin 1986, 160)

This instrumental view is based on a number of perceived characteristics of animals: first, that unlike the cultural development of humans, their nature is 'fixed' and therefore the current social order of human dominance can be seen as a natural part of life (an idea associated with a conservative worldview); and second, that animals lack rationality beyond a necessary 'practical wisdom' (Newmyer 2011, 9, 74), which excludes them from human considerations of justice. This position was contested by the stoics, who denied animals any reason (and therefore any ethical consideration) and who saw the affordance of justice to animals as a diminution of that which could be afforded to humans, revealing an early concern with ethical relativism (Newmyer 2011, 108–9). The stoic Cicero (1896, xcii) argues in *On the nature of the gods* that 'In the first place the universe itself was made for the sake of gods and men, and the things that are in it were prepared and devised for the advantage of men'. Overall, the slightly more generous view of animals of the heirs of Aristotle tended to dominate the ancient world: animals were seen to exist 'for man', but were held to have some characteristics that might not entirely instrumentalise their use.

The major Abrahamic religions[1]

The influence of this perspective on European thought remains today, and the work of Aristotle and his followers dominated the early and middle Christian period, with mediaeval scholasticism explicitly encouraged to focus on the heavenly realm; on worldly matters, they were encouraged to adopt the views of classical writers with limited revision (Asmov 1965). For the most part, the Aristotelean view of the pre-ordered nature of human–animal relations was compatible with Judaeo-Christian philosophy.[2]

---

1 This section presents a comparatively conservative perspective of these faiths' attitudes towards animals. For a more expansive interpretation regarding the prohibition of animal use in these traditions, see Kemmerer (2012).

2 Ethics

While the key Jewish and Christian texts contain a range of dietary restrictions prescribing what foods can be eaten and how they should be prepared, both religions broadly give humans dominion over all living things as food.[3] This notion of control or 'stewardship' has been subject to some theological debate. Callicott (1994, 24) considers it a care-taking role, one that goes beyond exploitation to entail greater ecological responsibility for retaining and sustaining God's creation. Since the 19th century, passages of the Bible have been used to promote vegetarianism,[4] and there has been a biblical motivation behind some contemporary conservationism (Basney 2000).

While the Bible has little to say specifically about the treatment of animals, there are some indications that unnecessary cruelty was not regarded as the act of a 'righteous person' (Proverbs 12:10).[5] Similarly, care for animals can be seen as engaging in due regard for part of God's creation (Genesis 1:25). Overall, however, the Bible is clear in making a distinction between humans and the natural world (Genesis 1:26–28), a hierarchy of ownership and control that is not automatically in alignment with contemporary environmental thinking about the inseparability of humans from their environment (Hayward 2011, 6). Thomas Aquinas and Immanuel Kant (1963, 239–41)[6]

---

2 A good example of early Christian vegetarianism (near veganism) was the Cathars of the 11th to 13th centuries. Following a dualist view of God, this sect refused to eat animal products because they originated in copulation. The Cathars were deemed heretics by the Catholic Church as it attempted to exert greater centralised control.
3 Genesis 9:2, 3: 'And the fear of you and the dread of you shall be upon every beast of the earth, and upon every fowl of the air, upon all that moveth upon the earth, and upon all the fishes of the sea; into your hand are they delivered. Every moving thing that liveth shall be meat for you; even as the green herb have I given you all things.'
4 For example Genesis 1:29: 'And God said, Behold, I have given you every herb bearing seed, which is upon the face of all the earth, and every tree, in the which is the fruit of a tree yielding seed; to you it shall be for meat.'
5 Similarly, the Quran includes passages that limits the use and ill-treatment of animals, such as 3:38: 'There is not an animal in the earth, nor a flying creature flying on two wings, but they are peoples like unto you. We have neglected nothing in the Book (of Our decrees). Then unto their Lord they will be gathered.'
6 Kant states: 'Tender feelings towards dumb animals develop humane feelings towards mankind' (240).

both objected to cruelty towards animals because of concerns that such cruelty could lead to cruelty between humans (Harwood 1928, 13, 40): thus, it was still an essentially anthropocentric concern. (This is the same reason why only slaves were permitted to butcher animals in Thomas More's *Utopia* in 1516. Similarly, William Hogarth's instructive 1751 engravings, *The four stages of cruelty*, depict a narrative of decline starting with childhood cruelty to animals.) This type of argument is not reserved to obscure biblical debates, but can be found in mass-produced Christian publications distributed across Australia for a general audience (for example *The Watchtower*, published by the Jehovah's Witnesses, May 2015).

In line with this instrumentalist perspective, René Descartes (1637) argued for a mechanical view of the universe. In building a general theory of the behaviour of the world without the need for divine intervention, animal action is akin to reflex. If animals are seen as complex machines without consciousness, no soul need be present to explain their behaviour. In creating this dualism between the physical brain and the higher-order mind, Cartesianism disassociated the similarities of humans and other animals in a way that diverged fundamentally from the Aristotelian tradition (Descartes et al. 2007, 60). Animals, as automata like the clockwork entertainments of his time, became objects that could be possessed (La Barbera 2012, 28), a perspective that the followers of Linnaeus and Darwin would end up struggling against.

This distinction between higher-order mental characteristics (reason, recognition of the rights of others, sentience) provided the basis for the distinction between humans and animals in the various strands of political contract theory (Hobbes, Locke, Rousseau). Indeed, contract theories often define humanity in direct distinction to the animality of 'states of nature', albeit with different understandings of what the natural state looked like, and therefore different normative implications. Thus the political philosophy that stems from these views tends to focus on the capacity of humans to enter into contracts that govern their interactions – that is, their capacity to be agents, and therefore to demonstrate 'moral agency'. Similarly, David Hume argued that justice is only possible between those of equal standing able to engage in a mutual agreement to establish a set of rules to distribute resources fairly. This type of thinking was an extension of the focus on rationality as the key difference between animal and human, and had implications for the expectation – central to these theories – that protection from violence is the fundamental purpose of political society.

Alternatively, early proponents of virtue ethics attributed moral significance to this very lack of rationality: animals could not be seen to engage in sin, as they lack an understanding of what sin is. They could thus be seen as innocents: animals could not sin, but could be sinned against by humans. As the anti-vivisectionist Francis Power Cobbe put it, they are 'incapable of offence' (1884, 5). This perspective implies a duty of restraint by humans towards animals, who, by their nature, were not required to demonstrate a reciprocal concern for humans.

The development of the welfarist model

The limits of these traditional attitudes to animal welfare became politically significant in England in the 18th century. Shevelow (2008) observes that in the late 1700s reports of sadistic acts of animal cruelty and the enduring popularity of blood sports were appearing in the new media of public newspapers. Particularly gruesome acts – such as the Manchester butchers who cut the feet off sheep before driving them through the centre of town (213), or the man who tore out the tongue of his horse (Fairholme and Pain 1924, 13) – elicited concerns that such acts reflected poorly on a civilised Christian community, and appeared to be beyond sanction under a legal system based on classical views of animals as property (whether of private individuals in the case of domesticated animals, or of the state in the case of wild animals). Progressive clergy began actively to promote a more benign view of Christian dominion with relation to stock animals.

Armstrong and Botzler (2008, 4–5) argue that the widening acceptance that animals had more complex mental states strengthened calls for improvement in the treatment of animals. At this time Jeremy Bentham's utilitarian philosophy focused on the abrogation of unnecessary suffering through public policy and not simply private morality (*Principles of morals and legislation*, 1781). The development of early animal-welfare legislation reflected progressive thought of the time, rather than simply the idiosyncratic legislation of highly motivated individuals.

While the culmination of this new pressure for reform, Martin's *Cruel Treatment of Cattle Act*, could be seen as a significant break with the past, it focused narrowly on a specific type of valued animal and did not extend to the owners of animals. This reflects both political pragmatism (Martin had learned the lessons of previous failed legislative attempts) and a continuation of thinking that stretched back to Aristotle. This connection is clear in the implicit hierarchy of animals based not on their implicit capabilities or capacities but on their functional relationship to human beings. Thus, while authors such as Francione (2000) argue that Benthamite ideas drove the development of contemporary animal-welfare laws, in reality these laws were the codification of competing approaches to determining the moral status of animals. They drew on utilitarian assessments of the relative capacity of animals to experience pain and suffering (1907, s122), historically contingent views of the value of animals to humans, and debates about animals' mental and cognitive capacity and their relationship to human reason.

The most significant of the latter perspective has been the use of evolutionary theory to look at genetic relationships between species, with a recognition that simple and complex animal forms exist along a continuum. In *Descent of man* (1871) Darwin makes this clear, stating:

> If no organic being excepting man had possessed any mental power, or if his powers had been of a wholly different nature from those of the lower animals, then we should never have been able to convince ourselves that our high faculties had been gradually developed. But it can be shewn that there is no fundamental difference of this kind. We must also admit that there is a much wider interval in mental power between one of the lowest fishes, as a lamprey or lancelet, and one of the higher apes.

In making this connection, the Darwinian evolutionary thought that would be so powerful in shaping the natural and social sciences would promote thinking about animals along a continuum of capacity and subjectivity.

While Darwinism introduced new possibilities for the political treatment of animals based on grounds other than the instrumental, it remained heavily anthropocentric. Thus Bailey (2011) sees the common distinction between 'higher' and 'lower' animals in European philosophy as grounded not in a deeper categorical distinction based on phenomenological insight, but more simply in an intellectual justification of anthropocentric delineation based on the relative similarity of some animals to humans. This approach privileges primates based on their closeness to humans (both structurally and behaviourally), while overlooking animals whose very different physiologies may reflect their different environments. Cephalopods (octopuses), for example, exhibit sophisticated intelligence and the capacity for tool use, but have been neglected for many years owing to their very different nervous systems (Spedding 2000, 33) and their marine habitat.

Challenges to the welfare model

The radical second-wave animal protection organisations both responded to and promoted new ethical frameworks for considering human–animal relations. While the publication of Singer's *Animal liberation*[7] directly encouraged the formation of second-wave groups in Australia, we should not assume that the movement seeks to implement a specific academic ethical position. In the UK, for example, new activist practices associated with animal rights (such as the Hunt Saboteur movement, which started operations in the 1960s) pre-date and significantly informed academic debates regarding human–animal relations. Reaching a critical mass in the 1980s, the initial codification and development of ethical perspectives by people such as Singer have generated a wide array of responses from different ethical perspectives.

Since the 1980s academic ethicists have applied every significant school of thought to the question of human–animal relations. Major debates have focused on the appropriate decision-making framework within which to assess ethical questions, the main models being Singer's consequentialist (or 'ends') perspective, which highlights choice outcomes, Tom Regan's deontological ('rules') focus on animal rights, and Rosalind Hursthouse's application of virtue (or 'character') ethics.

---

7   *Animals, men and morals* (Godlovitch et al. 1971) should perhaps be flagged as the first work of significance, in that it led directly to the development of Singer's volume. As is commonly the case, individuals associated with the crystallisation and popularisation of ideas seldom work in an intellectual vacuum.

Singer and Regan's theoretical differences highlight competing perspectives on how to determine the nature of animals as moral subjects (what Regan calls 'moral patients'). This in turn reflects differences in how ethical decision takers might assess the characteristics of animals in any moral calculus of their relative value. Commonly, this rests on contested notions of which animals exhibit sentience, which is itself a contested concept: some thinkers emphasise consciousness and self-awareness, while others stress the 'emotional need to seek satisfaction and avoid suffering' (Webster 2011, 7).

This draws philosophy and biological sciences into dialogue. Once, only animals with vertebrae were considered significant moral subjects;[8] increasingly, as scientific studies have looked at a wider range of complex cognitive relationships, invertebrates have been included. This type of research includes behavioural studies, as well as biological research into attributes such as the presence of pain-sensing nociceptors, or comparative brain size to body weight. Shifting away from narrow comparisons with human anatomy has thus been important in advancing arguments for the moral standing of invertebrates without human-like central nervous systems.

In focusing attention on sentience as a tool to determine the moral obligation of humans to animals, Singer importantly popularised the concept of 'speciesism': the arbitrary valuation of other animals based on an irrational preference for members of one's own species, a practice Singer equated with racism and sexism. While this represented an explicitly political claim at the time – situated as it was in the context of the 1970s – the move highlighted the enduring centrality of humans as the privileged referent, even within animal welfare debates.

Hursthouse, meanwhile, focuses on the perspective of a 'virtuous person', asking what type of choices a moral actor might make. This approach shifts attention away from the subject to the agent of moral choice, and in attempting to de-emphasise the potential for future biological science to resolve current ethical debates represented a departure from the dominant discourse.

---

8   The ability of fish to experience pain remains contested, however, with significant types of nociceptors absent or present in very low numbers relative to other vertebrates (Rose et al. 2014).

Feminist care ethics have also been systematically applied to the question of animals. This approach, centred on the cultivation of positive relationships, challenges liberal and individualist assumptions to consider ethical choices in the context of ongoing interactions between humans and animals; it draws less on 'scientific' attributes and more on alternative drivers of behaviour such as emotion and empathy. In this way it is informed by standpoint feminism, but also has origins in the critical stance of the 19th-century anti-vivisection movement towards the instrumental rationality of biologists (demonstrating both the complex relationship between theory and practice as well as the parallel strands running concurrently throughout the 19th and 20th centuries). It also shares some ideas with Singer's focus on liberation and speciesism. But in moving away from the dominant consequentialist and rules-based perspectives, it rebuffs Singer's emphasis on crafted standardised sets of 'decision rules' to be applied universally as part of a masculinist ethical tradition that does not give due consideration of emotional states and situational relationships.

The legacy of anti-vivisection is also evident in the work of Gary L. Francione, which emerged in the 1990s. Francione is highly critical of both Singer and Regan for what he describes as a continued re-validation of traditions of animal use and anthropocentrism via their implicit and explicit comparisons of animal and human characteristics, as well as an inherent pragmatism that focuses on incremental change over radical abolition. While acknowledging that these thinkers present new ideas about animal ethics, Francione sees utilitarianism and strong rights positions as sustaining animals' subordinate status in society. Describing these positions as 'new welfarism' to reduce the political and ideological distance between the 19th-century welfare movement and the early second wave, Francione argues that they continue to treat animals as property or slaves, and so undermine the prospect of meaningful changes to human–animal relations. In rejecting this approach, he argues that slavery cannot morally be reformed, only abolished. This mirrors 19th-century splits among anti-vivisectionists, between those who completely rejected the practice (abolitionists) and those who supported the moderation of vivisection through regulation and the use of anaesthesia (Murrie 2013). As we will see in later chapters, this welfare versus abolition debate currently defines interactions between animal activists in Australia today.

Defending the status quo

As foreshadowed, one notable absence from the discussion above is a significant modern defence of the behavioural status quo. This absence is interesting and provocative. Keane (2009, 26–7), for example, observes that the slave-owning societies of antiquity were notable in their production of philosophical critiques of slavery, but did not produce a substantive defence of the institution. The justifications of slavery produced on the eve of the US Civil War, he argues, reflected the imminent death of an institution that could survive only when it was taken for granted. This 'house of cards' argument is reflected in Joy's (2010) decision to name carnism. Similarly, Lupton (1996, 124–5) sees the reluctance to name and defend the status quo as a psychological defence: it allows meat-eaters to avoid explicitly acknowledging how meat is produced. Death is an implicit 'absent referent' that the contemporary consumer actively avoids. I will explore this topic further in Chapter 4.

Some formal defences of the status quo do exist.[9] One example is Scruton's (1998) *Animal rights and wrongs*. An Australian example is Leahy's (1994) *Against liberation*. Responding particularly to the work of writers such as Singer and Regan, these volumes argue that proponents of animal rights overstate the similarity of animals to humans and understate the differences. For both authors, animals are 'primitive beings' that lack self-awareness, language, rationality and higher-order capacities to organise. In addition, only human society develops the moral capacity of subjects through its cultivation of an awareness of rights and responsibilities; this makes humans more significant moral subjects.

Leahy and others argue that as a result of this basic difference, animals are rightly available for human use, and are rightly lower in our hierarchy of concern. This is regulated by two factors: our 'naturally

---

9 Since the 1970s a number of defences of animal experimentation have been produced, but these are often based on an explicit assumption of high-welfare experimentation (see, for example, Fox 1986).

humane' character, and laws prohibiting excesses by social outliers. In democratic societies, Leahy argues, political and legal institutions ensure that humane standards are upheld. The status quo, therefore, is not arbitrary, but reflects a collective intelligence codified in law.

Elements of this argument have been employed in more popular (and more populist) texts. The best example is Michael Pollan's (2006) *The omnivore's dilemma*. Widely read and cited (Williams and Germov 2011), Pollan's work popularises many of the same arguments contained in *Against liberation* concerning the subordinate status of animals.[10] Pollan, however, rejects the argument of democratic conservatism, contending that modern food systems reduce the transparency of production systems, subverting our natural affinity for the animals we use. In his call to reconnect with the origins of food to produce a more ethical omnivorism, Pollan aligns with the pro-carnist ethics that Johnston and Baumann (2010, 154–6) identify in the popular food-appreciation movement. In their consideration of 'foodies', Johnston and Baumann argue that, while foodies prioritise personal hedonism over other ethical concerns, they often express an interest in obtaining ingredients from high-welfare meat production (what critics disparage as 'happy meat'; see Image 5). Such consumers may pride themselves on not shying away from the realities of farming practices, unlike less discerning customers. As Johnston and Baumann point out, the idea that ethically produced meat also tastes better entails a logic of win-win for foodies: more ethical treatment of animals pays off with greater enjoyment at the table.

Conclusion

Humans have a long history of contemplating our relationship with, and ethical duty to, animals. This has produced an array of ethical and moral positions, some based on received wisdom and others derived

---

10 'Popularises', however, may be overstating the influence of these volumes. In the period 2006–2014, Pollan's book sold 9,686 copies in Australia. In contrast, *Our family table*, a cookbook by the winner of the first Australian *MasterChef* series, sold 138,603 copies in its first six months (Nielsen Bookscan, unpublished data extract).

from first principles. Combined, these now occupy a large conceptual space, including religious law and various normative ethical schools of thought. In recent years, an ethical defence of the status quo has been added to this expanding body of literature. (A summary of the main ethical traditions regarding human–animal relations is provided in Appendix B.) These theories do not simply indicate what type of human–animal relations are acceptable; they also focus on different aspects of animality in order to delineate between different types of treatments.

While the extent to which these different perspectives form the basis of political action is discussed more in later chapters, it is clear that some political actors in the Australian context are directly informed by their engagement with the literature on human–animal relations. Animal Liberation organisations across Australia, for example, were directly inspired by Peter Singer's book. Over time, some of these organisations have moved away from Singer's utilitarianism towards different philosophies as a result of engagement with a widening literature. The relationship between these debates and the general public, however, is less clear: discussions of animal welfare issues in the popular media rarely, if ever, introduce the arguments of ethicists in support of a moral position. Even popular volumes that introduce ethical conundrums are massively outsold by books promoting – largely through cooking and consumption – the human–animal status quo. If, as Leahy might argue, it is right and proper for legislation and popular opinion to influence each other in the quest for an acceptable ethical position on animals, we need to understand the position of animals in the public eye. We turn to this in Part 2 of the book.

Part 2

3
Attitudes to animals

This chapter focuses on how animals are perceived by the Australian public. In generalising about 'public opinion', I recognise that it is a fraught term in the social sciences: each element of the phrase (both 'public' and 'opinion') is contested, and the connection between popular opinion and governmental action is similarly complex. 'Public opinion' can be used as a popular shorthand to describe every member of a given society, or in more specific and technical ways that focus on *realpolitik*: majorities, sizable minority groups, or small but influential groups (Wilson 2013, 276). As Splichal argues (2012, 25–32), this highly contested concept has shifted from a comparatively simple notion of public opinion as a single and expressible 'average' position on matters of clearly delineated public interest, to a fragmented, ambiguous notion encompassing majority and minority opinions and multiple publics and counter-publics (Fraser 1990). Often – particularly on complex or abstruse policy issues – the public has no opinion, but generates one only when prompted by pollsters or researchers, constrained by the limits and prejudices of their knowledge and the survey instruments of the interrogator (Bourdieu 1979). For our purposes, public opinion comprises a range of elements: respondents' level of knowledge about an issue; how the issue is understood (that is, how respondents perceive the key elements of an issue, its causal drivers and the relationships between its actors); personal preferences about the issue; the status of the issue as either public or private (is it an issue the public expects governments to address?); and the issue's 'salience', or importance to the public relative to other issues. Acknowledging these limitations, in this chapter I employ the best evidence available to describe where the majority of Australians stand on the issue of animal wellbeing. I ask: How do they act? Do they care about animal protection? What do they think about particular issues and debates? Do they want government action, or are they happy with the status quo?

For policy research, establishing public opinion is useful for a number of reasons. Understanding the relationship between public opinion and policy can tell us about the democratic responsiveness of the policy domain. Where opinion and policy are closely indexed, the policy domain is likely to be populist and to be structurally open to popular opinion and/or participation. Where opinion and policy are misaligned, the cause is commonly powerful entrenched interests resistant to popular participation (Kingdon 1995), or disorganised social interests unconnected to policy-makers (such disorganised interests are known as 'latent interests' or 'potential groups'; Truman 1951, 168). Where politics matters to sufficiently large and motivated groups in the community, but entrenched interests are powerful, elites are likely to engage in purely symbolic or rhetorical responses to public concerns (Cohen 1997, 26). If public opinion is aligned with particular organised interests, this may convey information about those interests' political resources, both tangible (such as their ability to fundraise, mobilise and recruit) and intangible (such as their perceived political legitimacy) (Giugni 2004, 124–5). Finally, where policy requires public participation (for example, where policy regulates the public, or conveys exhortations to voluntary behaviour), the alignment of popular opinion with the objectives and design of the policy can be critical to the policy's success (Ammon 2001, 145).

As we will see, it would be a mistake to approach the population of Australia as a homogeneous group. On the question of animals and their treatment, 'average' attitudes and aggregate behaviours overstate the degree to which public opinion is stable. While some aspects of popular opinion can be clearly identified, other public attitudes remain pre-conscious and unarticulated. Understanding popular dispositions towards animals and their welfare nevertheless provides a context for

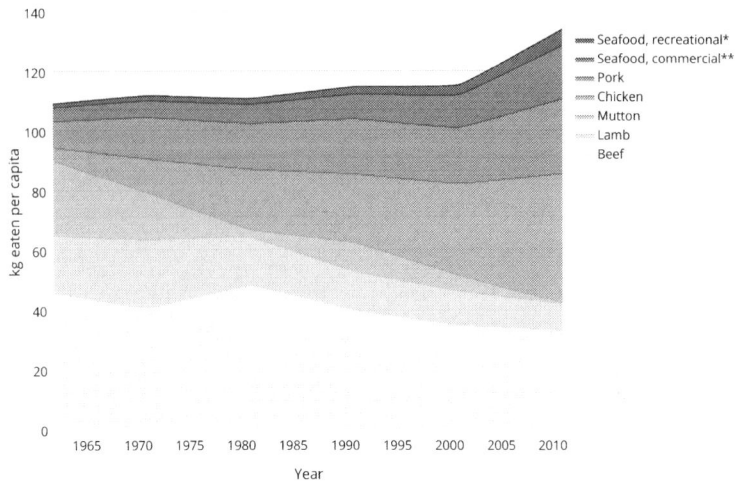

Figure 3.1. Australian annual per capita meat consumption, 1962–2010. Redrawn from base material provided by Wong et al. (2013). *Based on estimates made in NSW in 2000–2001 (Lyle and Henry 2002), an additional 30 percent by weight can be added for recreational fishing catch. **Estimated from ABS (2000).

understanding political action and policy-making. Looking at both the behaviour and the attitudes of Australians, in this chapter I will consider what is at stake in debates about animal use, and to what extent current public policy reflects popular opinion.

How we love animals

On our plates

Australians like to eat animals; we are one of the largest consumers of meat in the world per capita, consuming almost twice the average of consumers in the United Kingdom (Franklin 2006, 223). This has cultural, historical and geographical origins. Since colonisation, meat has been a major feature of the Australian diet (Crook 2008, 7). (For

	Beef	Lamb	Mutton	Chicken	Pork
Year	2012–2013	2013	2013	2010	2011–2012
Number	2,574,000	9,614,600	384,584[1]	498,660,466	6,171,483
Recalculated from	MLA 2013a	ABS 2014; MLA 2013b		ACMF 2011	Australian Pork 2012

Table 3.1. Annual number of animals consumed by Australians

some observers in the 19th and early 20th century, this level of consumption was tied to the coarseness of Australian culture, reflecting a tendency to see meat consumption as something spiritually pure individuals should avoid.) While recent decades have seen a shift away from particular types of meats (in particular, away from red meat and towards chicken), our appetite for meat has continued to grow (see Figure 3.1): during the past 50 years, the quantity of meat consumed per person has steadily increased. Our population of 23 million now consumes over half a billion animals per year (see Table 3.1). This equates to 22 animals per person, per year.

In addition to animals consumed as meat, Australia houses 16.5 million chickens as 'layer hens' to produce most of the 4.7 billion eggs consumed annually (Australian Egg Corporation Limited 2014).[2] For every female layer produced, a male chick is discarded, either by gassing with carbon monoxide or by manual crushing. Based largely in Victoria, 1.7 million cows produce 9.2 billion litres of milk in Australia annually (Dairy Australia 2015), 40 percent of which is destined for export. To produce this ongoing stock of lactating animals, 900,000 calves are produced each year; these are either destroyed soon after birth or reared for their meat and skin (Turner n.d., 192–3).

---

1   The figure for mutton is an over-estimate, as much of this is diverted to pets, rather than consumed by humans.
2   A greater volume of eggs is imported than exported, but eggs are also exported as components of value-added products, making the exact figure difficult to estimate.

3 Attitudes to animals

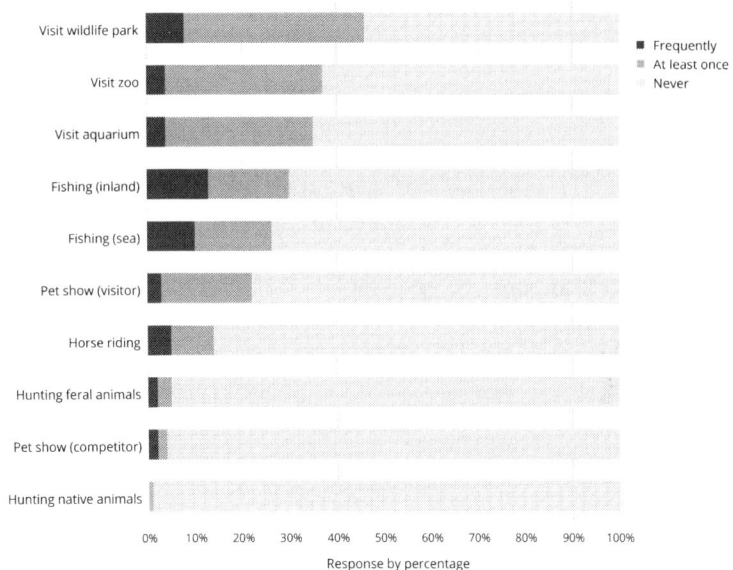

Figure 3.2. Popularity of recreational activities employing animals, as measured by frequency of participation. Compiled from Franklin (2007; $n = 2,000$).

On the track, on display, in the lab

In addition to the half billion animals we eat every year, animals are also 'consumed' by humans in a range of other ways, including for entertainment. In 2012–2013, 12,684 horses worked in the racing industry in Australia.[3] Horse racing and breeding directly produce well over 4,500 'waste' animals per year, most of which go to slaughter.[4] Dog racing in Australia employs about 13,000 'named' dogs (greyhounds are named at the start of their racing careers, usually when they are about a year old), while wasting 8,100 dogs per year.[5] Approximately 83,000

---

3 This assumes that all registered horses are actually engaged in racing (ARB 2013).
4 At minimum. This figure, estimated by Hayek (2004, 88), only includes the direct wastage of horses from the industry and does not include those horses deemed unproductive after auction.

'working dogs' are used in agriculture and entertainment (Duckworth 2009). Australia is home to 95 zoos and aquaria, the largest of which hold thousands of animals for display and breeding purposes, only a small proportion of which are produced for the purpose of rejuvenating wild stocks. These staged exhibits are popular with the public, but are minor components of the overall recreational mix of Australians (see Figure 3.3). Rodeos report 22,000 animal 'usages' a year,[6] recording approximately six injuries and four untimely animal deaths annually (Australian Professional Rodeo Association n.d.). Australia is home to eight circuses that employ a wide range of animals (commonly horses, dogs and exotic animals), while international animal circuses such as the Great Moscow Circus tour regularly and are still popular.

When it comes to directly killing animals for food or pleasure, Finch et al. (2014) estimate that there are between 190,000 and 332,500 active recreational land hunters in Australia. As we can see in Figure 3.2, however, fishing is significantly more popular than land hunting as a recreation.

The number of animals used in research and teaching is difficult to estimate, with published figures ranging from 2.4 million per annum (Meng 2009, 50) to 6.5 million (Humane Research Australia 2014). Knight (2013, 12) notes that Australia is one of the top five users of animals in research globally. Part of the difficulty in estimation comes from differences in definition: lower estimates tend to exclude animals consumed to provide tissue, stock maintained as reservoirs of generic material, animals used in observation, and surplus animals that are euthanised (Taylor et al. 2008). In the historical context of anti-vivisectionist politics, this stems from a delineation between different types of animal research based on the extent of suffering involved, and/or the invasiveness of the experimentation. Thus the higher figure is likely more accurate if we are interested in the total numbers of animals

---

5 Duckworth (2009) cites between 15,000 and 25,000 dogs wasted per year based on disparities between the number of litters and the number of dogs finally named. Calculated from Greyhounds Australasia (n.d.); McDonald (2012).
6 A usage is not an individual animal, but refers to each time an animal is used in an individual event. The actual number of individual animals employed is lower than this figure. This, however, does not include usages outside of competitions (e.g. practice usage).

3 Attitudes to animals

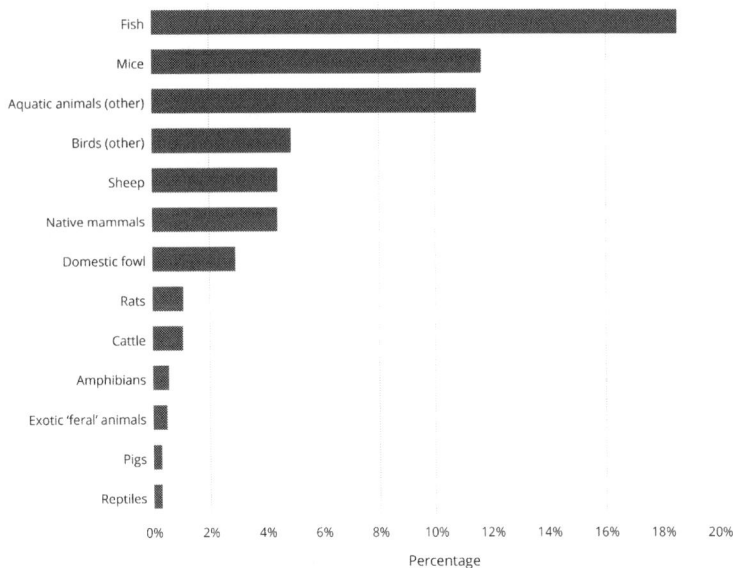

Figure 3.3. Animals used in research and teaching in Australia, by type. Redrawn from Humane Research Australia (2014).

used, but should be reduced by approximately half if we are interested only in use that ended in an animal's premature death. A breakdown of animal use is provided in Figure 3.3, with sea animals and rodents the animals most widely employed for research, thanks in part to their rapid breeding cycles, the ease of handling them and the low cost of maintaining them.

In our homes

Of the animals we commonly come into contact with, we pat the ones we don't eat. In 2013, Australians owned 25.2 million companion animals. While fish are the most numerous, dogs and cats are the most commonly found in Australian households, as illustrated in Table 3.2. There are more pets in Australia than people.

	% of households	Total companion animals (millions)	Rate per 100 persons
Dogs	39	4.2	18.2
Cats	29	3.3	14.3
Fish	15	10.7	46.3
Birds	13	4.8	20.8
Other	7	2.2	9.5
Total	**63**	**25.2**	**108.9**

Table 3.2. Australian companion animal ownership, by type. Recalculated from Animal Health Alliance (2013).

The use of the term 'pet' is a contested one, however, with the alternative term 'companion animal' increasingly commonly used.[7] This distinction has political implications: it delineates between a view of animals as possessions, and one that focuses on their relational status with humans. The difference between possession and companion, however, tends to depend on the type of animal. While only one-quarter of birds are purchased as companions, around 70 percent of dogs and cats are acquired primarily for this purpose (Animal Health Alliance 2013). Thus, this categorisation homogenises a more complex pattern of human–animal relationships in which humans show a greater ethical concern for some animals than for others. According to Franklin (2007), cats and dogs occupy a special position in many Australian homes as companions or 'family members' (approximately 85 percent of households use the latter description). Reflecting the level of care many people feel for these animals, the pet industry in Australia is now an $8 billion sector. The Australian pet-food industry – that is, the slaughter of animals to feed companion animals – is valued at $3 billion per annum (Animal Health Alliance 2013). Pet food displays strong price inelasticity (that is, demand tends to remain static regardless of price changes) in the same way that demand for baby food is resistant to economic downturns.

---

7 The term entered publication in the late 1960s, but did not become frequently used until the mid-1990s (Google Ngram Viewer).

	General community		
	Overall	**Male**	**Female**
AAS Score	67.6	63.8	69.5
s.d.	9.3	8.7	9.1
n	550	186	364

Table 3.3. Animal Attitude Scale, population average. Signal and Taylor (2006).

How we see animals

From the preceding section, it is clear that animals in Australia occupy a paradoxical position: they are treated as intimates, or as commodities. Many of our social norms about the treatment of animals depend on how different species are valued and perceived. I will now examine popular attitudes to the treatment of animals in Australia: just what is the public view of animals and their interests?

Do we care?

At the same time as they use and enjoy animals and their body parts, Australians have a low tolerance for what they perceive as animal mistreatment. This means that Australians' attitudes towards animals are complex and at times paradoxical. Table 3.3 provides an overview of the Australian population's attitudes towards the wellbeing of animals. This table employs a modified version of the Animal Attitude Scale (AAS) initially developed by Herzog et al. (1991) and adapted for Australia by Signal and Taylor (2006). The AAS is a 100-point continuous measure[8] pertaining to specific and general human–animal interactions, which is used to assess respondents' attitudes to the use and treatment of animals by humans. The higher the AAS score, the greater the individual's reported support for animal welfare. In

---

8 Derived from 20 Likert scale questions: the familiar Strongly Disagree, Disagree, Neither Agree nor Disagree, Agree, or Strongly Agree-type ordinal categorical qualitative scale popular in social research.

Strongly agree	Agree	Neutral	Disagree	Strongly disagree
36.6%	42.5%	17.0%	2.8%	1.2%

Table 3.4. Response to the statement: 'Animals are capable of thinking and feeling emotions'; $n = 1,041$. Humane Research Council (2014), 14.

Table 3.3 we can see that popular concern for animal welfare is modest in Australia, sitting two-thirds along the range between least and most concern. While gender is commonly cited as a factor in empathy towards animals (and is reviewed later), the variation *within* genders is greater than the difference *between* them on the AAS.[9]

Unpacking this overall indicator with some more recent data illuminates consistencies and inconsistencies in the collective attitudinal schema. First, Australians largely see animals as having the capacity for thought and emotion, as illustrated in Table 3.4. This appears to coincide with the sense that animals need protection from mistreatment by humans (Table 3.5). Referring back to the range of ethical positions mapped in Appendix B, it would appear that one-third of Australians subscribe to either a liberationist, strong animal rights or abolitionist perspective (Singer, Regan or Francione); two-thirds support either the status quo (as defended by Michael Leahy) or a weak animal rights position (as articulated by Mary Ann Warren and discussed below); and a small minority (about 4 percent) subscribe to the strongly anthropocentric views articulated by Descartes, Ryder and Kant.

For whom or what do we care?

It is interesting to see the stated willingness of nearly one-third of the public to attribute considerable rights to animals, given the behavioural statistics presented in previous chapters. This suggests either that a sizeable minority of Australians routinely engage in behaviours to

---

9 A distinction should be made here concerning the extreme mistreatment of animals: males are disproportionately perpetrators of abuse, while women are more likely to be involved in animal hoarding (Tiplady 2013, 22, 24).

3 Attitudes to animals

Statement	Agree
Animals deserve the same rights as people to be free from harm and exploitation	30%
Animals deserve some protection from harm and exploitation, but it is still appropriate to use them for the benefit of humans	61%
Animals don't need much protection from harm and exploitation since they are just animals	4%
Don't know	5%

Table 3.5. Attitudes to animal treatment; $n = 1,000$. Essential Media Communications (2012).

which they morally object, or that they lack a coherent understanding of the language of ethics and its relationship to their own behaviour. This question can be resolved, to some degree, with the slightly older data presented in Table 3.6.

This also partially resolves the question of whether Australians subscribe to Leahy's notion that the ethical treatment of animals should be informed by consensus practice (the wisdom of the crowd in setting ethical norms), or to Warren's view that animals, as lesser beings who are subject to our care, should receive a level of treatment based on an independently determined definition of their ethical rights. The level of moral protection that the majority of Australians believe we should accord to animals mirrors everyday animal use. Thus, while significant numbers of Australians state that they support human-equivalent rights for animals, they make exceptions by excluding both the processing of animals into meat and pet ownership. This reveals an internal cognitive inconsistency between our stated higher-level values and practical lived experience. It also displays a high level of anthropocentricism: human interests are prioritised over those of animals.

This means that not all animals will be treated equally, even if they share characteristics that in ethical metrics would make them equivalent moral patients, such as cognitive ability, a capacity to suffer, or in-species sociability. (O'Sullivan 2011, 28–31). As we saw in Chapter 1, there is a historical tendency towards idiosyncratic interest in animal protection. This may have its origins in the general human tendency to create

	Strongly agree	Agree	Disagree	Strongly disagree	No opinion/ Don't know
It is quite acceptable to eat meat so long as animals are reared and killed humanely	26%	67%	5%	1%	1%
Animals should have the same moral rights as human beings	15%	40%	34%	6%	20%
Keeping animals as pets is unnatural and demeaning to both parties	2%	8%	48%	38%	4%

Table 3.6. Attitudes towards animal treatment; n = 2,000. Compiled from Franklin (2007).

hierarchies and to put things and organisms into a moral order. From a sociological perspective, Arluke and Sanders (1996, 18) attribute this to the long tradition of hierarchical ordering discussed at the start of Chapter 2, and propose that people have traditionally delineated between 'good' animals (those used as pets or tools) and 'bad' (those seen as vermin, freaks or demons). From a policy perspective, early state intervention concerning animals often reflected class distinctions: some social groups were seen as more likely to engage in the mistreatment of animals than others, and in targeting these groups there was a recognisable transposition of human and animal characteristics (Baker 1993, 89). Hence the relative success of early movements focusing on stock and transport animals, compared to attempts by anti-vivisectionists to regulate professional men. There is also a gendered aspect to this success and failure. Middle- and upper-class women were very active in the early social movement; they were able to influence public policy regulating working-class men, but unable to regulate the conduct of the professional and capital-owning classes. While these women were politically more influential social actors than disenfranchised males, they remained subordinate to their male class peers.

This anthropocentrism, and the tradition of drawing ethical distinctions between companion animals, 'useful' animals, and pests, continues today. Taylor and Signal's (2009a) survey, using a 50-point

3 Attitudes to animals

	Animal classification		
	Companion	Commercial / utility	Pest
PPP Scale	44.6	32.0	30.5
s.d.	4.3	7.0	7.4

Table 3.7. Pet-profit-pest (PPP) scale ($n = 210$)

Strongly agree	Agree	Neutral	Disagree	Strongly disagree
24.3%	36.1%	28.3%	9.7%	1.6%

Table 3.8. Response to the statement: 'Farm animals deserve the same legal protections as companion animals'; $n = 1,041$. Humane Research Australia (2014), 14.

scale, illustrates this (see Table 3.7). Importantly, concern does not appear to increase gradually in line with perceived utility; rather, there is a rapid drop in concern as we move from animals that live in close proximity to most Australians to those that do not, whatever their perceived utility. This is illustrated in Table 3.8, in which 60 percent of the public support human-like legal protections for farm animals, but a third of the public remains unsure.

These findings are consistent with interviews I conducted with Australians engaged in animal protection, and in animal-related industries. Lyn White of the advocacy group Animals Australia highlighted the function of comparatively simple ethical heuristics in shaping behaviour and guiding legislation:

> The first and most important aspect [of] advocacy is recognising the power of conditioned thinking and that many of our choices we have actually inherited from past generations. Animals have been put into categories of 'friends' or 'food' and their legal protections divvied up accordingly. (Interview: 24 September 2014)

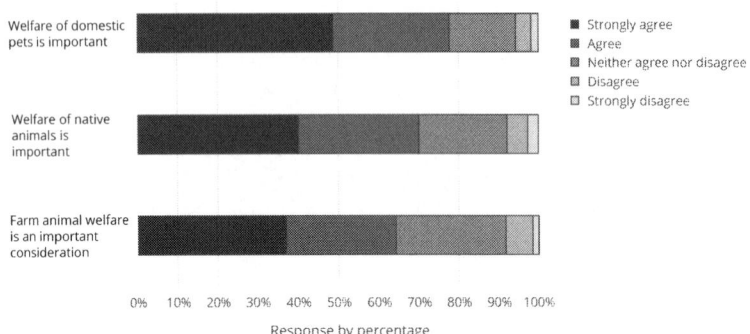

Figure 3.4. Victorians' perceptions of the importance of animal welfare, by type; $n = 1,061$. Redrawn from Coleman et al. (2005). Categories have been compressed, extracted and redrawn from the original table.

Activists working to protect specific types of animals were aware that public perceptions of 'their' animal's worthiness were a significant factor in mobilising support; they identified a vague ranking of different animals' value in the popular consciousness. For Helen Marston of Humane Research Australia, this came into focus most clearly when the interests of animals were directly compared with those of humans (interview: 23 September 2013). This is expressed in the classic 'Your child or your dog?' ethical conundrum: if your house were on fire, this hypothetical poses, would you save your dog or your child?

In the minds of Australians, then, there is a hierarchy of concern for animals. This is evidenced in successive research (Figure 3.4) showing comparative concern for different animal types, and for animals in different contexts. Companion animals, wildlife and entertainment animals are generally most valued, followed by animals used in industrial settings such as farms and laboratories. Those designated as 'pests' sit at the bottom of the ethical ladder.

This presents us with the interesting possibility that the way we define, categorise, rank and value animals reflects our sense of our ethical selves. A similar relative ethical scale has been used to define

3 Attitudes to animals

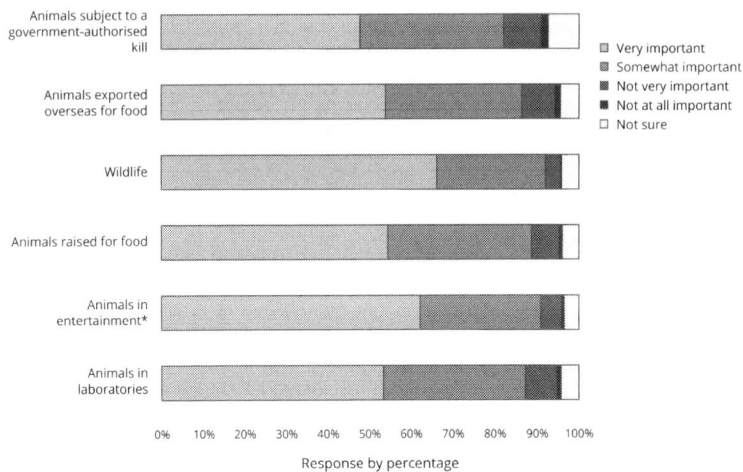

Figure 3.5 Importance of animal wellbeing, by type. *Includes zoos, aquariums, rodeos and racing.

what constitutes a good person. Ian Randles of the Pastoralists and Graziers Association of Western Australia has argued that the more central a given type of animal is to a person's life, the more likely it is that the person will judge themselves as either good or bad based on how they treat that animal (interview: 30 September 2013). As we will see later in this chapter, the inverse also appears to be true.

It would be premature to conclude that animal categorisation is clear-cut. As writers such as Malamud (2013, 35) have argued, boundaries are fuzzy and are not neatly aligned with the boundaries between species; animals' use-value and relational position to people are just as influential. Ambiguities and borderline cases abound. Franklin (2006, 226–7), for example, talks about the emotional response of many Australians to the classification of feral horses as 'pests'. Those I interviewed also observed this type of affective response. Dr Eliot Forbes of the Australian Racing Board remarked that:

> There might be people who are quite happy to eat meat, for example, however, they would feel that a horse is not a livestock animal; it's a companion animal, more akin to a dog or a cat, and so they ascribe the different set of values and expectations associated with that. Whereas other people may still continue to view horses as livestock... horses, in particular are interesting at the boundary between livestock and companion animals, and maybe how societies view that... [the] pendulum has swung more towards the companion side because we ascribed hero-type characteristics to horses such as Black Caviar, and we [in] the sport idolise our equine stars. (Interview: 9 April 2014)

This quote also demonstrates the important role of industry organisations in shaping the social meaning of animals. Black Caviar is not just a horse, but a cluster of symbolic meanings about excellence, competition, and the beauty of animal movement. Beyond her prize money, she is a brand, with her 'own' (really her owners') branded products including horse-grooming products, DVDs, posters, artwork and medallions. She featured on the cover of *Vogue Australia* in 2012 and was the subject of a bestselling biography (Whateley 2012).

We are the 99 percent

In talking about animals, animal protection and the ethical attitudes of the public, we are thus confronted with a public that has complex, quasi-coherent and highly ambiguous opinions and understandings. One of the best ways to unpack this ambiguity is by exploring the question of 'cruelty'. In legislative formulations of animal protection laws, as well as in popular parlance, cruelty is a word most commonly associated with the mistreatment of animals.[10] While the word was once applied to

---

10 The word 'cruel' appeared four times more frequently in the English lexicon in the early 1800s than in the early 2000s. Conversely 'abuse' was twice as popular in the early 21st century as in the early 19th. The term 'animal cruelty', unknown two centuries ago, was in modest use until the mid-1980s, from which point its frequency increase 45 times over the following 15 years. 'Cruelty' in reference to humans, meanwhile, fell in use over the two centuries (the phrase 'cruel man' was 45 percent as common in the later period, 'cruel husband' 48 percent, and 'cruel heart' 13 percent). Source: Google Ngram Viewer.

	Strongly agree	Agree	Disagree	Strongly disagree	No opinion/ Don't know
People who mistreat their animals should be punished in the same way as people who mistreat people	45%	39%	12%	3%	1%

Table 3.9. Attitudes towards animal cruelty offences; $n = 2,000$. Source: compiled from Franklin (2007).

humans and animals equally, mistreatment of humans now tends to be described using a range of other terms, such as 'abuse' and its various compounds (spousal abuse, child abuse, etc.). The meaning of 'cruelty' also appears to have been hollowed out, as indicated by survey data showing that 99 percent of Australians oppose cruelty to animals (the remaining 1 percent did not support cruelty, but were unable to answer the question).[11] Thus, the word has become what semioticians call an empty or 'floating' signifier: a term without agreed meaning. Floating signifiers, can, however, have political and social significance.

Whatever animal cruelty is, the public both strongly oppose it and see it as a significant social transgression. In Table 3.9 we can see that 84 percent of the public say that they support equivalent punishments for animal and human mistreatment. This seems unlikely given the weight of other evidence to date, but Taylor and Signal's (2009b) study of community attitudes towards the criminal justice system's handling of animal cruelty cases showed that the public do have an appetite for increased punishments for animal cruelty (although it is hard to determine if this is based on an accurate awareness of what punishments are currently meted out).[12]

Looking at the inverse of cruelty, animal welfare, we can see that the public's conception of what ethical behaviour might entail is neither homogeneous nor easy to define. When asked to rank a range of actions

---

11 Vegetarian/Vegan Society of Queensland (2010). This data was collected for the Society by a commercial market-research firm.
12 The general response of naive interviewees to questions about sentencing in general is to consider them too lenient (Roth 2014).

Preference	1st	2nd	3rd	4th
Preventing animal cruelty	29%	24%	13%	3%
Humane treatment of animals	21%	19%	17%	2%
Conserving native species	14%	9%	13%	6%
Caring for our pets	8%	8%	10%	7%
Minimising the suffering of animals	7%	15%	16%	4%
Balancing the needs of animals and people	7%	7%	7%	15%
Protecting the rights of animals	6%	8%	12%	11%
Promoting good food quality	5%	3%	3%	39%
Farmers using best practice	2%	6%	6%	14%

Table 3.10. 'What animal welfare means to me', ranked in order of preference; $n = 1,000$. Southwell et al. (2006).

in terms of their relevance to animal welfare (see Table 3.10), most people ranked highly amorphous actions (in particular the not-very-helpful 'not being cruel') most highly. More specific actions taken by specific categories of actors (such as pet owners or farmers) were ranked significantly less highly, as were actions that might require a trade-off of some human interests. Animal welfare in this view is often construed as simply a matter of kind vs cruel treatment. There are alternative perspectives, however. For example, Hemsworth and Coleman (2001, 130) highlight the ability of animals to engage in 'natural' behaviour as an important and more meaningful measure of their welfare, particularly in highly unnatural contexts such as industrial settings.

This ambiguity presents problems for people engaged in mediating between industrial practices and popular opinion. A frequent observation by members of animal industry organisations is that there is a lack of public awareness of production practices, and of the reasons for those practices. When particular practices are publicly targeted by activists as examples of animal cruelty, this lack of public awareness can make discourse difficult (mulesing is a commonly cited example).[13] Even within comparatively small industries, the definition of cruelty can be ambiguous. Russell Cox, executive officer of the Western

Australian Pork Producers' Association, recounted an interaction with a senior manager in a production facility:

> He said, 'Come down here, I'll show you a pig I've got in a hospital pen. It's lame.' He said, 'I want to show it to you.' He showed me the pig ... [it] had a lame left back leg. Had a bit of infection in his toe. Now, that can get worse and that can get better, but it had been treated. Now, he said, 'I'm going to euthanise that animal', and I said, 'Why?' He said, 'Because if the inspector comes up here and sees that animal, there's a possibility I'll be charged with cruelty.' I said to him, 'Well, I disagree with that.' I said ... 'You're not giving the animal [time]. It's being treated.' Although [this pig] lives a very short life, like 16 to 24 weeks for pork- and bacon-weight pigs, you've not given the animal a chance to recover to live the fullness of its life. (Interview: 2 October 2013)

Thus, even for people working within the same industry, the definition of a core concept such as cruelty is contestable. This can lead to multiple interpretations and a tendency towards regulatory risk avoidance (as in this case), or highly variable application of policy. This anecdote also illustrates an ongoing debate about the nature and significance of suffering: suffering may be deemed greater or lesser depending on the animal's capacity to recognise that its present state will be subject to change (sometimes referred to as 'informed anticipation of future states').

Ethical consumerism and animals

Given the difficulty of using public opinion as a gauge for what may be seen as acceptable practice, industrial actors such as those listed above use heuristics to gauge what the public means when it talks

---

13 Interviews: I. Randles, 30 September 2013; R. Perkins, chief executive, Pet Industry Association of Australia, 24 March 2014; S. Whan MLA, Shadow Minister for Resources and Primary Industries, Shadow Minister for Tourism, Major Events, Hospitality and Racing, and Shadow Minister for Rural Water, 19 March 2014.

about acceptable treatment of animals. This often involves looking not at opinion data but at incentivised behaviour: just where do people put their money? Justin Toohey of the Cattle Council of Australia observed:

> I mean, how do you actually measure [concern for animal welfare]? It should be measured by the number of people who actually buy based on animal welfare. Recent surveys show that five to seven percent of consumers walk through Coles' and Woollies' door buying on the basis of welfare, and that's when it comes to eggs and pigs and poultry and pork – you know, the intensive foods. (Interview: 4 July 2014)

In other words, to what extent do Australians routinely engage in ethical consumerism – the deliberate selection of products and services based on the perceived ethics of their production practices?[14]

Unfortunately, the evidence on this question is scarce in the Australian context. Ethical consumption motivated by welfare concerns has been undertaken by a majority of Australians at some point (Table 3.11), particularly since the establishment of labelling systems for meat, dairy (and presumably eggs) and cosmetics, but this data only provides insights into activities respondents have 'ever done'. It is less helpful in identifying more general or ongoing patterns of behaviour.

Table 3.12 outlines consumers' stated attitudes to a range of practices. Given the gap between consumers' stated concern in this table and what shoppers actually do in practice, many clearly overstate their objection to some practices. This reflects the fact that while it is easy to state a concern, the practicalities of making ethical purchases are not always so straightforward. Where trade-offs are necessary, ethical concerns slip, sometimes considerably. Recent market research into two of the product categories most likely to have been subject to ethical consumption by Australians provides evidence of the impact of explicit

---

14 This is a 'product-oriented' definition of ethical consumption, as opposed to 'company-oriented' definitions. This distinction can be significant in terms of the political understanding of the practice (the former focusing on encouraging or discouraging the production of a product or product category specifically, the latter focused on aspects of the behaviour of an organisation and attempting to achieve change in that organisation through a consumer boycott more generally; Harrison et al. (2005, 2–3).

Has your concern for animals ever caused you to do any of the following?	Yes	No	Do not know
Bought 'free range' or 'humane' meat or dairy products	61%	33%	6%
Bought products labelled as 'not tested on animals'	57%	34%	9%
Boycotted a particular store or brand	25%	66%	10%
Refrained from buying meat or dairy	17%	78%	5%

Table 3.11. Previous consumer action undertaken due to animal protection concerns; $n = 1,041$. Humane Research Council (2014).

trade-offs on the likelihood that consumers will engage in ethical consumption. Research ($n = 126$) conducted for the Australian egg industry demonstrates that many consumers who prefer free-range eggs will accept higher production densities if it means prices can remain within one or two dollars of cage-produced eggs (Brand Story 2012). In a more complex product category, cosmetics, research shows that female shoppers will subordinate their concerns about animal testing (which 43 percent of respondents cited as a factor in their purchasing decisions) to 'value for money' (cited by 59 percent) and product performance (such as achieving a 'natural look', cited by 50 percent) (Roy Morgan Research 2014a; $n = 6,333$).

Explaining inconsistency

The gap between reported public concern for animal wellbeing and actual public behaviour may be explainable as an artefact of survey research: survey respondents, regardless of how well constructed the survey, may give what they see as the more socially acceptable answers, rather than describing their real attitudes or behaviours. Alternative explanations are offered by Burke et al. (2014, 248), who examined ethical consumption in Australia. They looked at a range of ethical reasons, both positive and negative, for consumers' choice of products and services. They found that consumers who are motivated to choose products with ethical characteristics (who accounted for 41.5 percent

	Acceptable	Unacceptable	Don't know / no answer
Breeding animals to sell in pet shops	50%	46%	4%
Testing medicines on animals	48%	47%	5%
Making milk-producing cows pregnant every year and taking their calves from them so their milk can be used by humans	47%	47%	6%
Conducting other types of research experiments on animals	40%	52%	8%
Killing male chicks because they can't become egg-laying chickens	24%	72%	4%
Testing cosmetics on animals	17%	80%	4%
Keeping egg-laying hens in cages for their entire lives	12%	86%	2%

Table 3.12. Attitudes to ethical consumerism, as revealed by responses to the question: 'Do you personally think the following uses of animals are acceptable or unacceptable?' ($n = 1,202$) Abridged from the Vegetarian/Vegan Society of Queensland (2010). Rows may not add to 100% due to rounding.

of their sample) were most likely *not* to purchase ethical products because of a lack of availability, or because the products were only available from speciality stores. The next most common reason for not purchasing the ethical product was cost. (These factors are of course related, as obtaining ethical products from remote or specialty suppliers can entail additional costs, both in time and money.) For consumers ambivalent about ethical consumption practices (25 percent of their sample), the primary barriers were lack of information, and scepticism about the products' ethical claims. The final third of their sample lacked an interest in ethical consumption.

The issue of access or availability can be seen in the uptake of non-cage eggs in Australia over the last decade. As illustrated in Figure 3.6, the increasingly wide availability of free-range eggs (commonly promoted as having higher welfare standards) has been accompanied by higher sales, even in the face of a utility trade-off to consumers (that is,

3 Attitudes to animals

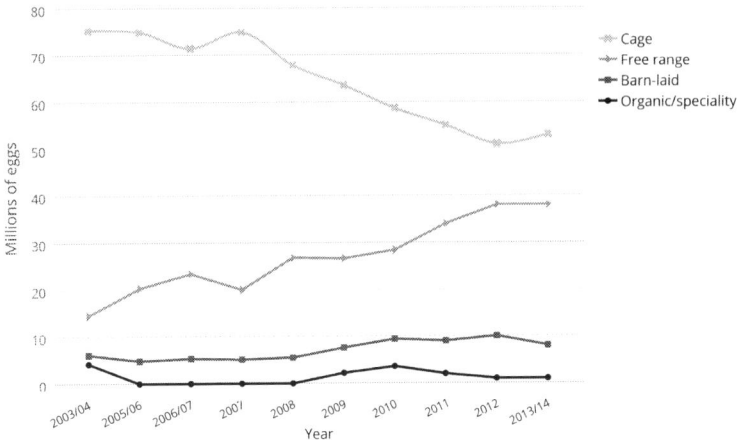

Figure 3.6. Comparative egg sales as ethical consumption, 2003/04–2013/14.
Compiled from Australian Egg Corporation Limited Annual Reports, 2004–2014.

higher prices relative to cage eggs). Research by the Australian consumer advocacy organisation CHOICE in 2014 found that most purchasers of free-range eggs based their decision on the products' presumed welfare advantages over cage eggs (68 percent purchased in part on this basis). Other reasons cited were concern for farmers (52 percent) and better taste (44 percent) (Clemons and Day 2015). As I will discuss below, while such figures may suggest an increased concern for animal welfare, they may alternatively reflect the satisfaction of a latent consumer preference.

While some of the stakeholders I interviewed did cite lack of availability as a reason for the gap between consumers' stated preferences and their actual behaviour, lack of knowledge about production practices was mentioned more frequently. Many attributed this to increased urbanisation, the smaller proportion of people employed as farmers, and the movement of production animals out of cities (interviews: W. Judd, Director, Queensland Dairyfarmers' Organisation, 19 April 2013; a member of parliament, South Australia, 25 September 2014; The Hon. Robert Brown MLC, Shooters and Fishers Party, 18 March 2014). The former NSW agriculture minister Steve Whan

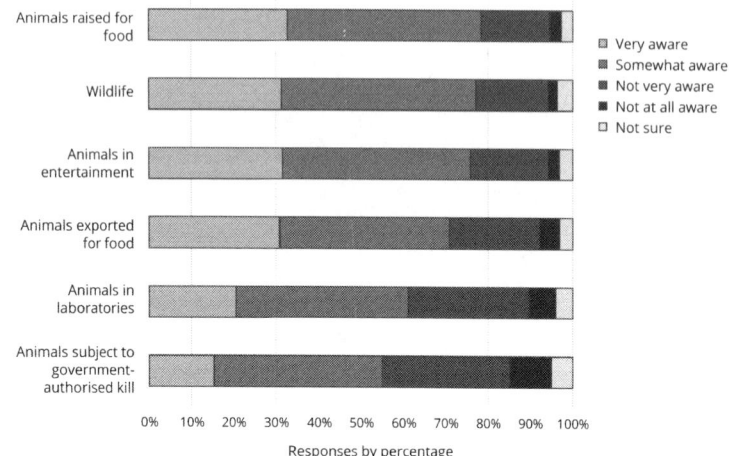

Figure 3.7. Awareness of issues affecting animal wellbeing; $n = 1,041$. Humane Research Council (2014).

observed that the decline in the domestic slaughter of chickens had 'disengaged' consumers from the reality of animal death (interview: 19 March 2014). Similarly, in reflecting on his period managing agricultural shows, Roger Perkins noted that even these opportunities for urban Australians to interact with rural life no longer include demonstrations of animal butchering or routine invasive animal husbandry practices (interview: 24 April 2014).

This question of knowledge and understanding has implications for the provision of ethical products in mainstream retail environments; demand and supply are both tied to the scale and effectiveness of activist campaigns (interview: a representative of the retail industry, 22 April 2014). Interestingly, while many respondents mentioned the low level of public knowledge about animals and animal production systems, the public tend to feel comparatively well informed about animal protection issues, particularly for those animals they most commonly have instrumental relationships with. This is illustrated in Figure 3.7.

3 Attitudes to animals

Importantly, attitudes towards animals appear to be established early, and tend to last a long time. Examining animal protection attitudes in America, Kendall et al. (2006) found that childhood background had the strongest effect on attitudes towards animal care. Those who grew up on a farm (strongest effect) or a non-urban area (strong effect) expressed the least concern about animal wellbeing. This study ($n = 4,030$) also found some evidence of an 'underdog effect', with people lower down the educational, economic and social ladder having greater concern for animal wellbeing, a finding that undermines the widely held belief that animal protection is a middle-class or elite interest. This is supported by comparative analysis of survey data by Franklin et al. (2001), who dismiss a correlation between concern for animal protection and 'post-material' values (that is, a lack of interest in material signals of social success) and education levels.

When it comes to the consumption of food, an expansive literature exists linking dietary behaviour to developmental socialisation and social norms. The acquisition of eating habits and food preferences has been extensively studied, often with sobering results for advocates of improved nutritional education (Judd et al. 2014). This research emphasises the enduring effect of a carer's food choices on the future consumption habits of the children in their care (Orrell-Valente et al. 2007), and the intergenerational continuity of these practices (Bril et al. 2001). In addition, particular ingredients are not consumed separately, but resolve into culturally and temporally specific 'cuisines', defined by the basic ingredients they commonly employ, by their flavour profiles and by modes of preparation (Rozin 1996, 236). This cultivation of expectations and taste reinforces specific types of food ingredients within what we might call a person's 'food culture'. In addition, the relationship between these social norms and matching regulation further serves to reinforce (Giddens 1986) these practices and the classification of certain animal products as necessary or essential to authentic cuisines (interview: L. White, 24 September 2014).

The influence of social norms is important in shaping the behaviour of adults over time. These clusters of normative attitudes are shared within peer groups and provide strong indicators of what behaviour is socially appropriate (Brennan et al. 2013, 28–9); they can be used to identify what constitutes 'cultural competence' in a given community (Leynse 2008, 35–7). Sutton (2010, 218) highlights the role of food and taste metaphors in key social and religious rituals that link past and present. In terms of the treatment of animals, there is strong evidence that individuals measure their own food consumption (both what they consume and how much) against their perceptions of their peers' consumption patterns (Rivis and Sheeran 2003; Lally et al. 2011). Importantly, social norms do not just determine tastes, but also define social relationships. Social positions are signalled by a range of cultural practices and relationships (Tallman et al. 1983, 35–7). This observation can be extended to how we view animals and our interactions with them. Thus, for example, the association of dog racing with working-class people (Young 2005) both reflects the activity's history and defines and sustains its current identity.

Given that developmental norms about animal use are acculturated in childhood, the work of Bastian et al. (2012) can help us to understand how Australian adults maintain conflicting ethical positions regarding animals. Focusing on what they call the 'meat paradox' – the fact that 'people's concern for animal welfare conflicts with their culinary behavior' – Bastian et al. investigated how people deal with this conflict. Based on a series of experiments, they concluded that those animals that are most commonly eaten are widely considered to have lower mental capacities than those that are not ($n = 71$). The researchers also found that, on being reminded that an animal was being raised for consumption, subjects ($n = 66$) offered a lower estimation of the animal's mental state than did those who were not subject to the same prompt. Finally, participants who were about to eat meat strongly reduced their estimation of the animal's mental capacity compared with subjects who were not ($n = 120$).

Overall, Bastian et al. argue that subjects adjusted their attitudes to align with their behaviour in order to deflect the unpleasant dissonance that would result if they were to recognise the animal's subjectiveness. Even those who abstain from animal consumption often admit to long periods of avoiding the realities of their consumption habits (interview: individuals associated with the Sydney veg*n community, 8 May 2014). This avoidance is confirmed by market research undertaken by the meat industry. As Andrew Spencer, the chief executive officer of Australian Pork Limited, observed:

> I think the vast majority of the community – and our focus group backs this up – the vast majority of the community eat meat and use products of animal agriculture in other ways such as wool and other things. They don't have a direct interest in how it comes about that they have meat on their plate or a jumper on their back. And in fact, when asking them, they understand that an animal has to die for the process of meat production, but they don't really care or know too much about that. So, that's really where the community stands.
> (Interview: 23 June 2014)

Importantly, for Spencer's focus group participants, this capacity for avoidance was predicated on a degree of trust in the meat industry. This demonstrates how the regulation of cognitive dissonance is both an internal psychological process, but also one tractable to environmental influences. Information that challenges assumptions about the source of meat, therefore, can provide a cognitive trigger to review an individual's assumptions about the production practices underlying routine food purchases and consumption. These types of informational challenges are discussed later in this volume.

Implications

The Australian public's attitudes towards animals and animal protection are complex. Public sentiment is variegated and inconsistent, with variation between and within species, over time, and between expressed views and exhibited behaviours. Both short- and long-term factors influence people's beliefs and practices. For a politician or policy-maker, therefore, the area of animal protection policy is a democratic nightmare: Australians have strong but highly abstract views about these issues, a limited understanding of production practices, and no common language in which to articulate their concerns. In the democratic responsive or 'weathervane' model of politics (Dunleavy and O'Leary 1989), this type of context is likely to lead to relative policy stasis, as policy-makers wait for popular opinion to congeal or for an agenda to be constructed by pressure groups.

While this type of unstructured opinion presents significant problems for the political class in responding to issues of sudden popular

Order of importance of the issue	1st	2nd	3rd	4th
Health	28%	23%	14%	2%
Rising prices/inflation	16%	12%	15%	3%
Family relationships	13%	9%	8%	10%
Tax reform	11%	10%	8%	7%
Education	10%	18%	18%	3%
Terrorism	7%	5%	8%	12%
The environment	5%	8%	10%	4%
Unemployment	4%	9%	11%	7%
Animal welfare	4%	3%	4%	34%
International and trade	2%	3%	5%	19%

Table 3.13. Comparative issue salience, ranked in order; $n = 1,000$. Southwell et al. (2006).

concern – as we will see in the more detailed discussion of the live-export debate – the salience of the animal welfare issues for the Australian public is not high. While competing definitions exist,[15] for our purposes 'salience' is the importance the public place on a particular issue relative to others that may be politically significant (Hutchings 2003, 143). The relationship between salience and the behaviour of policy elites is established by Epstein and Segal (2000, 66–7): elites are more likely to address issues deemed more significant by their core constituency. In Australia the comparative salience of a range of issues is illustrated in Table 3.13, with animal welfare ranked ninth in a list of ten issues of public concern.

However, keeping in mind the comparatively large sub-group in this survey that ranked animal welfare as their fourth most important concern, we can argue that the issue's overall low ranking does not reflect a complete lack of interest, but rather a potential or latent interest

---

15 For example, Mahoney (2008, 51) sees salience as synonymous with the amount of attention paid to an issue in the media, but this assumes that an issue can only have relevance to the public once it exists in popular discourse.

3 Attitudes to animals

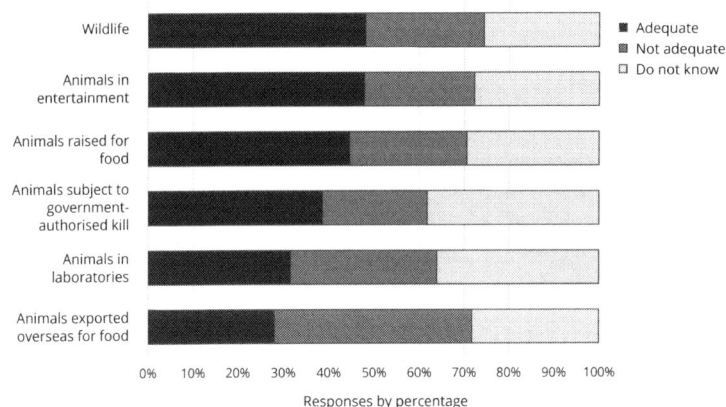

Figure 3.8 Perceived adequacy of welfare laws in Australia; $n = 1,061$. Source: Humane Research Council (2014), 18.

that could be mobilised and activated. This is attested by the public outrage over live export.

The comparatively low salience of animal welfare issues seems to be predicated on the widespread view that Australia's performance in this area is, if not good, at least 'not too bad' (78 percent of respondents; Southwell et al.; 2006; $n = 1,000$). Given the previously identified modest level of concern for animal welfare (see the discussion of the AAS score above), the level of performance overall is consistent with public perceptions of regulatory performance. Less graduated data collected more recently (Figure 3.8) shows greater variation in the public's perception of legal protections for different types of animals, as we would expect, indicating that averages may not capture the different levels of concern felt for different species and different types of animal use.

The extent to which public opinion about animal protection issues has changed over time is not possible to quantify accurately, as no genuine longitudinal data exists. Some increase in concern may be inferred by comparing the data from the last decade. The proportion of Australians who identified current animal protections as 'poor', 'very poor' (Southwell et al. 2006; $n = 1000$) or 'not adequate' (Figure 3.8) increased from about 22 percent in 2006 to about 29 percent in 2014. Differences between the two surveys in method and scale, however, make it difficult to draw more than a tentative conclusion. Certainly a dramatic shift in salience cannot be claimed from this data. As with the example of free-range eggs, changing consumption patterns may illustrate an increasing concern for animal protection (at least as it relates to one particular practice), but could just as easily be explained as a delayed response by industry to a latent consumer demand, or as a consequence of the slow diffusion of information about the product.

Overall, therefore, we can see that popular opinion about politically relevant issues can be divided into four areas of relevant knowledge:

- What is the salience of the issue (both overall and with regards to specific cases)?
- What is the public's confidence in organisations involved in animal protection?
- What is the public's knowledge of animals and industrial practices, and their understanding of the status of different animals as moral patients?
- What is the public's capacity to articulate ethical concerns in a coherent manner?

While it is possible to learn about a given issue in a structured, deliberate manner, the public does not always do so. Some changes in public opinion reflect the influence of activist groups, and this has implications for decision-makers. For example, increased salience without a corresponding increase in public knowledge may lead to calls for action that are impossible or counter-productive. Declining confidence in regulation or production may mobilise public concern even if there has otherwise been no change in the issue's salience. An increase in the public's ability to identify and coherently articulate their ethical concerns would likely see a movement towards a more conservative ethical position in opinion polling (more accurately reflecting the public's actual position), without actually reflecting a change in underlying attitudes.

Two sub-publics

In the preceding section I have attempted to paint a picture of what might be called 'mainstream' Australians' attitudes to animals and their wellbeing. The convoluted story this presents demonstrates both the complexity of our relationships with animals and the difficulty of generalising about any nation, even a comparatively small one. As Asen (2000, 424–25) observes, while terms like 'public opinion' and 'the public' may invoke a cohesive political community that learns and reasons *en masse*, the reality is that the Australian population is a complex set of nested publics, overlapping but distinct, and a range of social and political dialogues makes up popular discourse. We can map out the major currents in this ocean of opinion, but we can never satisfactorily reify the populace into a single public.

Within this complexity, however, it is useful to highlight some overlooked groups relevant to an understanding of the policy debate over animal protection. In this section we explore two. The first is farmers and other workers in animal agriculture. This economic and cultural sector is significant both for the way it contributes to the wider public's ideas about farm animal care, and as a potential site of policy intervention through the regulation of farm practice. Understanding the norms and practices of those who deliver policy, according to implementation scholars such as Lipsky (2010) and his successors, is critical to understanding the capacity to realise and implement policy change. Thus, it is important to understand how farmers think about animals and their wellbeing, as well as popular opinion about farmers and their performance in this area. The second sub-public consists of people who eschew animal products. This group's opinions and behaviour may appear to be at odds with those of the majority, but it is a sizeable and growing group. It is also significant because of its connections with activists engaged in animal protection debates.

On the farm

Farm animals may not be central to the concerns of most Australians, but in sheer numbers they account for the majority of human–animal interactions in Australia. Farming practices therefore shape the lived

	General community*			Primary-industry sector**					
				Farmers			Meat workers		
	Overall	Male	Female	Overall	Male	Female	Overall	Male	Female
AAS	67.6	63.8	69.5	61.8	64.8	58.2	58.4	60.5	56.0
s.d.	9.3	8.7	9.1	11.4	10.7	11.4	9.5	7.5	11.2
n	550	186	364			67			

Table 3.14. Animal Attitude Scale, primary-industry sector. Compiled from *Signal and Taylor (2006) and **Taylor et al. (2013), both studies employing the same instrument.

experience of most of 'our' animals. Given the significance of farmers in this ethical story, it is interesting to note what a small and shrinking group they represent. There are approximately 101,422 farmers engaged in animal agriculture in Australia, making up less than 0.5 percent of the total population.[16] This, of course, understates the significance of the sector to the Australian economy, and the corresponding number of people who work to support farmers directly or are employed 'downstream' in industries that process, move, store, value, insure, wholesale, retail, resell and dispose of the products of animal agriculture.

To get a sense of how farmers view animals, we can compare the attitudes of people in the primary-industry sector with those of the wider community. Using the AAS scale, Table 3.14 shows that this group expresses lower levels of concern about animal protection than the wider community, suggesting a more instrumental view of animals. There is variation within the primary-industry sector depending on the type of workplace interactions respondents have with the animals they produce. Meat workers, for example, have on average lower levels of concern than farmers (see Table 3.14).

It is important to remember that the notion of a linear metric for concern may be misleading. Philips and Philips' (2011) study of sheep farmers' attitudes to animal wellbeing show how differences in AAS scores may be influenced by different conceptions of what aspects of animal care are significant. In this research the authors found that sheep

---

16 Calculated from Australian Bureau of Statistics (2012).

farmers tended to conceive of animal wellbeing as the overall nutrition of their flocks, while placing less emphasis on other issues that were of concern to the general public (such as surgical mulesing without pain relief). These issues were given lower emphasis because of the cost that would be involved in addressing them (a trade-off similar to that seen in our data on ethical consumerism above). The farmers' focus clearly ran counter to general public opinion about what constitutes acceptable treatment of farm animals; in a survey of Victorians, less than 10 percent ($n = 1,061$) said they would prioritise demand for food over other issues (Coleman et al. 2005).

This difference between the general public and the 'sub-public' of agricultural workers, it can be argued, reflects very different lived relations with animals. Where the general population's experience with live animals revolves around a small number of highly individuated companion animals, farmers and related professional staff (such as rural veterinarians) have traditionally tended to focus on the meso-level, concentrating on the health of the overall population (interview: N. Ferguson, 3 October 2013). They measure animal welfare performance in ratios and against industry or regional norms (for instance, death rates may be measured in blocks of a thousand animals, and compared against sectoral averages). As one industry representative observed:

> We produce 500 million-plus chickens a year. That's a lot of chickens... even if you have a minimal mortality, [it's] still going to sound, when you multiply that, like an awful lot of chickens dying out there every year, just as an example. So, it's very easy to present things in a way that should put the industry in a bad way, whereas in reality, if you compared us to other countries, you know, it's fantastic. So, it's easy to play with figures and make someone look bad if you want to.
> (Interview: a representative of the chicken industry, 31 January 2014)

Animal protection and welfare, therefore, tend to have very different meanings in the industrial context: they are equated with overall health, as opposed to a concern for individual suffering. Wes Judd of the Queensland Dairy Farmers' Organisation expressed this view when he stated that farmers equate animal welfare with good animal-husbandry practices (interview: 19 April 2013), where 'husbandry' includes a wide range of day-to-day practices. These practices are designed to balance productivity and health, within the necessary limits of the animal's productive lifespan. Animals reared for things other than meat (such as dairy and wool) are likely to live considerably longer than meat animals; meat production has been increasingly optimised to create the fastest possible transition from birth to slaughter. Significantly, unlike animal protectionists, those working in the industry tend to see 'welfare' as relative, rather than as an absolute standard.

Thus, we are likely to see 'town and country' talking at cross purposes on the question of appropriate animal care, with the former emphasising individual treatment and the avoidance of suffering, and the latter looking at general health over the animal's whole productive lifespan. While Philips and Philips' sheep-farmer research stressed that primary producers and their families were cognisant of animal pain (to the extent that some farmers reported that other members of their families refused to participate in practices such as mulesing),[17] other research with farm workers is less conclusive that animals' pain is of ethical concern to producers. This is illustrated in Figure 3.9: fewer than 7 percent of Australian stockpeople believe that pigs or layer chickens are capable of experiencing human-like pain. This points to considerable variations between species, different production contexts and different types of farm workers. Unfortunately the evidence is scant.

Regarding farms and farming

While the Australian public may not prioritise farm animals in their ethical schema, popular attitudes towards farmers' treatment of their animals is politically relevant. To what extent does the wider public see farmers as responsible for animal protection? How does the public assess farmers' performance in this area, and their capacity to achieve the levels of care desired by the community? I have established above that popular (mis)understanding of farm practices develops by a complex and indirect process, particularly as it relates to welfare outcomes. While popular media often like to promote farming using idealised and anachronistic images of wooden barns and free-roaming

---

17 A long discussion could be had here about farming and masculinity.

3 Attitudes to animals

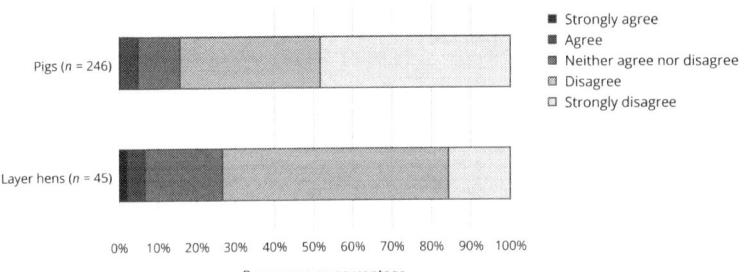

Figure 3.9. Australian stockpersons' perceptions of animals' capacity to experience pain 'like humans'. Redrawn from Coleman (2007).

livestock (see Chapter 4), critics of farm practices employ imagery of Fordist industrial production systems. This points to the public's understanding of farmers and farming as a core element in conflict over the welfare of production animals.

We can establish that the majority of Australians see industrialised and intensive farming practices as both unnatural and antithetical to animal welfare (see Table 3.15).[18] However, the use in this survey of the term 'factory farming', a term preferred by animal rights activists (and descended from Harrison's 1964 book *Animal machines*), may have skewed the responses more negatively than they otherwise would have been. Australians oppose intensive animal agriculture, but what this table does not tell us is the extent to which Australians associate current animal agriculture in this country with 'factory farming'. There is a large gap in popular knowledge of the practical realities of farms, and this highlights a major problem for both farmers and their critics: as O'Sullivan 2011 observes, not only are Australians ignorant of farm practices, they are largely unaware of their own ignorance. Moreover, although a simple majority of Australians designate industrial

---

18 This perceived trade-off of intensification and welfare need not be the case, of course. As Beggs et al. (2015) have found in Australian dairying, intensification can lead to overall welfare improvements through increasing stockpersons' skill levels or training and use of pro-welfare management systems and services that may be less affordable with smaller herds.

	Strongly agree	Agree	Disagree	Strongly disagree	No opinion / Don't know
Modern methods of 'factory farming' in the production of eggs, milk and meat are cruel	19%	33%	35%	5%	8%
Modern methods of 'factory farming' in the production of eggs, milk and meat are unnatural	15%	36%	34%	6%	10%
Meat production and processing industries can be trusted to ensure the safety of the meat product	10%	53%	25%	6%	6%

Table 3.15. Attitudes towards industrial animal agriculture; $n = 2000$. Compiled from Franklin (2007).

production as 'unnatural', over 60 percent of respondents still think these systems can deliver an acceptable product. Once again, popular opinion is neither straightforward nor easy to pin down.

What the table does demonstrate is that, unlike many farmers, the public do not necessarily link animal welfare with good animal husbandry or effective production systems. Indeed, in a spontaneous-recall question of 1,000 Victorians, Parbery and Wilkinson (2013) identified that most respondents defined a 'good farmer' as one who demonstrated: professional competence (58 percent of respondents), environmental management (43 percent), and a hard-working nature (40 percent). Caring for animal wellbeing, on the other hand, was mentioned by only 16 percent of respondents.

Enduring public affection for farmers appears to indicate that for most members of the public, modern Australian farms are not synonymous with Fordist agricultural systems. Industry representatives report that their own market research reveals strongly positive opinions of farmers among the general public. This goes beyond perceptions of competence and hard work; farming is also viewed as an honest and trustworthy profession. Justin Toohey of the Cattle Council summed up the general consensus of many farm representatives:

3 Attitudes to animals

We do have surveys around and evidence of a very high level [of] trust... [consumers rank] farmers about sixth to eighth at least in terms of trust, out of the list of 50 [occupations]... You've got the usual sort of second-hand car salesmen at the bottom. Farmers are up way, way, way up high, and that trust is kind of what we call... 'licence to operate'... and we need to retain that. And that sort of helps, I think, a lot of consumers to believe that farmers do have the welfare [of] the animals in mind, and in spite of the issues that happen in the media, we think we're holding their trust pretty well.
(Interview: 4 July 2014)

This optimism among industry representatives, however, was accompanied by concerns that the public's positive perception of farming may be under threat, and that this could undermine farmers' 'licence to operate' (interview: general manager (policy), National Farmers' Federation, 14 November 2014). As the public depend on media representations for their view of farmers (see Chapter 4), there is concern in some agricultural sectors that the public are highly susceptible to negative depictions of contemporary animal agriculture.

Certainly, when Parbery and Wilkinson (2013) asked respondents to rank farmers' treatment of animals using a ten-point scale, the average ranking was 6.8. This was lower than the average performance level respondents said they desired (8.7). If the public were more concerned about farm-animal protection, this under-performance could present a risk to farmers' good standing. However, what is significant is that the public are not sure how much capacity farmers have to influence farm practices. Thus while survey respondents say that they want farmers to have a high level of influence on farm practices (4.2 on a 5-point scale), they see farmers' actual level of influence as far more limited (3.5). The implication is that, even though the public may not be entirely happy with farmers' treatment of animals, farmers are not held fully responsible for this shortfall. Organisations further along the supply chain are seen to be more responsible for influencing farm practices, including supermarkets (with an influence score of 4, compared with a preferred level of 2.1) and chemical and biological technology companies (3.5, with a preferred level of 2.1). Importantly, consumers assess *themselves* as having a low capacity to influence farm practices (2.7, with a preferred level of 3.6).

Overall, Australians have a high regard for a type of farming that is rapidly disappearing from our shores: the family-based small-business farmer using traditional methods that he or she determines and implements autonomously. Australians are more sceptical of intensive, conglomerate farming practices, which they see as unnatural and providing poor welfare outcomes for animals. Farmers, interestingly, are not seen as key determinants of welfare outcomes, suggesting that public opinion is oddly bifurcated in its concerns for farmers and for non-human animals.

The abstainers

Another important sub-public (or sub-publics) comprises what might be called *non*-consumers: those who regularly avoid the consumption and/or use of animals and animal products. While abstention might be considered just another type of the ethical consumption discussed above, we can distinguish these individuals as a distinct sub-public by their systematic or enduring commitment to avoiding or minimising animal use. While this distinction is one of degrees, delineating this group is important due to its size, and to its relationship with political activism.

These types of communities are sometimes poorly conceptualised by the literature on ethical and political consumerism. Theoretical literature tends to treat ethical and political consumerism as 'lower-order' social-change actions than electoral participation or formal membership of a political organisation. These practices have been characterised, for example, as 'less organized, less structured, and more transient than traditional political participation' (Stolle et al. 2005, 252). This view, however, is unlikely to resonate with those Australians for whom political consumerism is a holistic lifestyle, and who give a formal label to their consumption choices. In fact, formal participation in organisational politics (for instance in political parties, interest groups and social movements) is increasingly influenced by political consumerism, rather than vice-versa (Gauja 2012, 170). Formal political organisations are increasingly adopting product boycotts and corporate campaigns as major parts of their political strategies (Karpf, 2012).

3 Attitudes to animals

Category	Description
Pescetarian	Avoids meat, with the exception of sea-life
Pollotarian	Avoids meat, with the exception of bird-life
Pollo-pescetarian	Avoids meat, with the exception of sea- and bird-life
Vegan	Avoids meat, animal products and animal labour
Freegan	Vegan, but will consume meat and/or animal products that have been recovered from the waste system (so-called dumpster diving), on reductionist/anti-capitalist grounds
Fruitarian	Generally follows a vegan diet and primarily consumes fruits, nuts and seeds
Lacto-ovo vegetarian	Avoids meat and animal products, with the exception of milk and eggs
Lacto vegetarian	Avoids meat and animal products, including eggs, but consumes milk
Ovo vegetarian	Avoids meat and animal products, including milk, but consumes eggs
Flexitarian	Generally follows one of the vegetarian diets, but will occasionally consume animal products

Table 3.16. Typology of Australian abstainers.

In examining the proportion of the public who routinely or systematically avoid consuming animals, we find an array of practices that can be divided into a range of subclassifications and sub-subclassifications. As a reference for the discussion to come, Table 3.16 maps the major categories, although I will focus largely on vegetarian and vegan diets.[19]

It should be recognised that such tables can be misleading. In this case, the potential deception takes two forms. First, jokes about the 'vegan police' aside (that is, the idea that vegans are humourless self-appointed moral arbiters of dietary compliance; see Greenebaum

---

19 An alternative classification schema used in the literature is that of vegetarians and semi-vegetarians, however the slightly more fine-grained classification presented below is preferred. The two approaches are not comparable, as the system articulated in Table 3.16 does not resolve neatly into the alternative schema.

2012), an individual's identification with a specific designation may not be absolute. Is a self-identified vegan no longer a 'real' vegan if they undertake a cancer treatment originally tested on animals? Does the accidental but inevitable death of animals in agricultural farming invalidate all categories bar the flexitarian? Interviewees from this community recognised that some people who self-identify with such categories can exhibit a tendency to become 'gung-ho', or, in the other direction, to be more pragmatic (interview: individuals associated with the Sydney veg*n community, 8 May 2014). Second, reliance on such labels fails the scientific test of true typology: the categories are neither comprehensive nor completely exclusive.

To get a clearer sense of what actually occurs within this wider group, it is possible to map out the types of choices made by people who abstain from animals or animal products using three sorting questions: (1) What type of animal products are not consumed? (2) How is this consumption constrained? (3) When, or under what conditions, do exemptions from this abstention arise? An inclusive mapping of the choices made by abstainers reveals an array of practices, some of which fall clearly into recognised categories, and some of which exist within or between these groups.

How big is the abstainer subset of the Australian population? In this area some evidence exists, thanks to market research that has examined both self-identification and actual behavioural practices. This data, from 2010 and 2013, is presented in Table 3.17. The underlying research shows that, while 6 percent of the public identified as vegetarian or vegan (veg*n) in 2010, when questioned about personal consumption practices, the number of Australians who reported consuming no animal products at all was 2 percent. The four percentage-point difference can be explained by the existence of ovo- and lacto-vegetarians, flexitarians, pescetarians, pollotarians and freegans. A study of South Australians in 2003 produced similar results: from a sample of 603, 1.5 percent identified as vegetarian and a further 7.2 percent as semi-vegetarian (Lea and Worsley 2003, 407).

On the other hand, the 2013 data is somewhat ambiguous. In a 2013 survey the market-research firm Roy Morgan reported that 10 percent of Australians self-identified as vegetarians. If we employ the ratio of vegans to vegetarians from the 2010 results,[20] as well as the that of self-

		Vegetarian	Vegan	Total veg*ns
2010*	Self-reported	5%	1%	6%
	Behavioural (assumed)	2%	n/a (0.33)	2.33%
2013**	Self-reported (assumed) (i)	10%	n/a (1.66)	11.66%
	Imputed behavioural (ii)	3.33%	0.55%	3.88%
Imputed number	Lower estimate (ii)	770,000	128,487	898,487
	Upper estimate (i)	2,310,000	385,500	2,695,500

Table 3.17. Reported and imputed veg*ns in Australia, 2010–2013. Compiled and imputed from *Vegetarian/Vegan Society of Queensland (2010; $n = 1,202$) and **Roy Morgan Research (2013; $n = 20,267$).

classification to actual behaviour,[21] we can argue that as at 2013, 3.33 percent of the Australian public meet the generally agreed definition of vegetarian, and 0.55 percent the generally agreed definition of vegan, together accounting for approximately 4 percent of the population. Thus, the total number of abstainers is somewhere between 900,000 and 2.7 million people, who range from strict abstainers to semi-vegetarians. Overall, this represents a considerable sub-public and points to an uptake in abstention in recent years, at a rate of between 0.43 and 1.66 percent of the total population per annum.

Why do these people abstain? The motivations of this large subgroup in the community sit within a range of ethical traditions. Referring back to Appendix B, the work of Adams and Donovan, Warren,

---

20   A ratio of 1:5 (16.6 percent of all veg*ns). An alternative way of estimating might be to look at references to each in published books, and using this indirect measure as a means of estimating comparative 'market share'. As of 2000, using the British English corpus, 'vegan' is referred to at a ratio of 1:10 (9.1 percent). While this data is quite old, using this ratio would make the imputed range of vegans between 70,090 and 210,272, and the total number of veg*ns between 840,090 and 2,520,272.
21   It should be noted that Roy Morgan Research, writing in 2015, did not consider the reliance on self-reporting an inaccurate approach to data collection. However, I believe that behavioural evidence, combined with inherent ambiguities in the subcategories of abstainers, make variation highly likely. This reflects categorical inspecificity and is not an 'error' per se.

Singer, Regan and Francione may be relevant in describing the various practices and motivations of this sub-public. However, it is not possible simply to equate consumption decisions with ethical concern for animals: consumption habits are commonly based on a combination of explicit and implicit factors that can be difficult to unpack. Moreover, not all abstainers are motivated only or primarily by animal welfare concerns. Several of the participants in the focused discussion of veg*nism highlighted the perceived environmental advantages of the diet as their primary motivation for abstaining from animal products (interview: 8 May 2014; M. Collier, 17 April 2013). Personal health and social trends can also be influential determinants for some individuals. Certainly, in comparisons between self-reported vegetarians and the wider public, Roy Morgan Research (2013; $n = 20{,}267$) found that abstainers were more likely to report that they:

- favour natural medicines and health products (50 percent more likely)
- follow a low-fat diet (47 percent more)
- enjoy health food (30 percent more)
- enjoy doing 'as many sports as possible' (23 percent)
- undertake exercise (7 percent).

Market research also supports the importance of age, showing that people under 35 are far more likely to identify as abstainers. Population health research also highlights the greater tendency of vegetarians and semi-vegetarians to reside in urban settings (12 percent higher than non-vegetarians; Baines et al. 2007, 439).

In a final demographic observation, it is important to note a gender bias: most Australian vegetarians are women. The higher participation by women in abstention is noted by an array of authors (Neale et al. 1993, 24; Janda and Trocchia 2001, 1227; Ruby 2012, 142; Parks and Evans 2014, 15), and we will see in Chapter 6 that women who engage in animal protection politics score higher than male activists on the Attitudes to Animals Scale. The source of this variance is unclear. Essentialist or developmentalist theories that women have greater empathy with, or concern for, animals (Paxton 1994) are undermined by the AAS scores presented in Table 3.4 and by other studies that looked at peoples' stated motivations for adopting vegetarian diets (Lea and Worsley 2003). Lupton argues that the relationship between gender and vegetarianism is a social construct, reflecting a tendency in Australian society to masculinise meat consumption (1996, 105): many will recall the Australian Meat and Livestock Corporation's advertising campaign of the 1980s featured the slogan 'Feed the man meat'. Lupton also suggests that female vegetarianism may be a response to women's relative lack of power in society (16, 57), in that control over the bodily consumption of food is a site of power for women in a patriarchal environment – particularly for younger women. Vegetarianism and other types of abstention represent an assertion of power or control, with women exercising their capacity to regulate both the type and quantity of their food intake.

There also appear to be some deeper differences between abstainers and the omnivorous majority. Using functional Magnetic Resonance Imaging (fMRI) machines, Filippi et al. (2010) examined the automatic responses of omnivores, vegetarians and vegans to a series of images, some neutral and some featuring negative images of humans and animals ($n = 60$) – these images showed mutilations, murdered people, humans and animals under threat, torture, wounds, and the like (e10847). Using mapping produced by the fMRI, the researchers were able to compare the brain activity of these three groups. They observed that veg*ns displayed a greater tendency to generalising empathic responses to other species than omnivores (e10847).[22] This may scale up into the political positions individuals adopt. Allen et al. (2000), from a study of New Zealanders ($n = 348$), identify that vegetarians have different underlying social values. They are more likely to reject social norms that lead to hierarchical domination and authoritarianism (they score low on the psychological measure of social dominance),[23] and to prefer norms associated with equality, peace and social justice; they also place more significance on emotional states and awareness.

---

22 Interestingly, and relevant to the discussion of the validity of typologies outlined in Table 3.16, Filippi et al. also observed fMRI differences between vegetarians and vegans in the activation of different parts of the brain in response to negative images of animals (e10847–8).

23 'the extent to which one desires that one's in-group dominate and be superior to out-groups' (Pratto et al. 1994, 742).

The authors endorse the argument that systematic avoidance of meat is associated with rejection of conventionally constructed masculinity as both dominating and emotionally distant.

While these findings support a view that aligns abstention with the left of the political spectrum, the stated reasons that the omnivorous majority do *not* abstain, in whole or in part, appear far more prosaic. Using our compounded market research data again (Table 3.18) to examine the attitudes of average consumers, we can see that egocentric factors dominate the decision whether or not to reduce meat consumption: first, does the meal taste good, and second, is it perceived to be healthy?[24] If a meat-free meal meets these criteria, omnivores are more likely to choose it, but they are unlikely to adopt a holistic shift to an alternative diet. Veg*nism is not considered a viable alternative by many Australians due to the importance traditionally placed on meat and dairy, an importance reinforced by official nutritional guidelines, as discussed in Chapter 1. These views are enduring. In their 2014 survey, the Humane Research Council (2014) found that almost 70 percent of Australians agreed that 'using animals for food is necessary for human survival' (21.9 percent strongly agreed), with only 9.2 percent disagreeing with the proposition, a figure in line with the current proportion of abstainers in the community, as previously estimated (encouraging further confidence in the estimates derived).

What Table 3.18 does show, however, is that contrary to some popular misconceptions, veg*ns do not appear to be considered significantly outside of the social norm. Only 14 percent of respondents in 2013 reported eschewing vegetarian dining due to a perception that it was only 'for alternative people'. Inversely, in 2010, only 17 percent of the public said that a greater number of vegans in the community would be necessary for them to be motivated to adopt a vegan diet – a proxy we can use as a measure of the perceived threat of social

---

24 The South Australian study of Lea and Worsley (2003; $n = 601$) presents very similar findings as those presented in Table 3.18 with a different set of barriers and enablers, but places concern for animal welfare/rights higher, at 36 percent. The difference between 'avoiding meat' and 'welfare/rights' is significant in the construction of the enabler: positive in the older study, versus negative in the 2013 dataset.

	2013* – periodic abstention			2010** – holistic abstention	
%	Reasons cited for not abstaining	%	Reasons cited for abstaining	%	Reasons cited for becoming vegan
75	Nutrition	76	Vegetarian food tastes good	36	Animal welfare
64	Would miss the taste of meat	71	Health	35	Health
34	Vegetarian food is not filling	45	Weight loss	31	Environment
31	Lack of vegetarian recipes	33	Cost	25	More vegan dining choices
26	Vegetarian food tastes bad	31	Environment	20	Cost
14	Vegetarianism is only for alternative people	26	Desire to avoid meat	17	More vegans in the community
9	Preparing vegetarian meals is time consuming	13	Religious reasons		

Table 3.18. Motivations for and against abstention. Compiled from *Roy Morgan Research (2013; $n = 20{,}267$) and **Vegetarian/Vegan Society of Queensland (2010; $n = 1{,}202$).

alienation associated with veganism (Bruno et al. 2009). This reflects both the work of activists in selling these dietary alternatives, and considerable social change.

The notion that veg*nism is now widely accepted by the community is contestable, however. Considering vegetarianism in the late 19th and early 20th century, Crook (2008, 154–6) argues that some of the historical hostility to this diet in Australia came from its association with ethnic minorities (particularly the Chinese) during a period of political ferment, when these alien influences were being excluded from the body of the new state. Before this discursive reframing, political leaders such as Deakin were able to enjoy non-standard diets, but Australian public culture may never have returned to this pre-federation openness to alternative diets. As recently as the mid-2000s, a contender for the role of premier of NSW, Carl Scully, was criticised in the media for his veg*nism (but possibly more vociferously for being a cyclist) (Devine 2009).

Conclusion

We have considered Australian attitudes towards animals and animal protection from a number of perspectives, including that of the 'average' or general public and those of a number of small but significant sub-publics directly involved in animal protection debates. While the changing character and intensity of some of these attitudes is hard to measure, there does appear to be a shift, both in the wider community and within various sub-groups, towards increased concern for the welfare of animals, albeit at a low level relative to other political and ethical issues. In Chapter 4 we turn to the origins of these attitudes and the possible sources of change by examining how animals and their wellbeing are represented in a range of media.

4
In the media

Chapter 3 examined one facet of the relationship between the 'public(s)' and their attitudes towards animals: what people think, as well as what they do. In this chapter we expand our analysis to examine what might be called the 'discursive context' in which animals and welfare-related issues are considered: Habermas' (1989) concept of the public sphere. The public sphere is an idealised view of society as an open and participative arena of popular dialogue in which ideas are shared and issues debated. It exists in conversations between individuals and in groups, as well as in the opinion pages and in electronic media. In Habermas' usage, the public sphere is more than just a 'talking space'; it is an important part of the political and social fabric. Through dialogue, debate and disagreement, the public sphere facilitates the formation and articulation of the popular will: that general consensus of the public that provides direction for political elites, and the political legitimacy for them to enact public policy.

In today's public sphere, the media are critical both as spaces for public discourse and as institutional participants in their own right. This is particularly so when it comes to the representation of animals and animal issues, given their remoteness from the majority of Australians' day-to-day lives. Aside from the very specific subcategory of animals with which Australians live, most Australians have only very infrequent interaction with animals and industrial animal use (sea-life being the only animals consumed as meat that are commonly served whole or in a recognisable form). As Baker (1993, 3, 11–14) argues, this distancing has diminished our view of animals and has reduced their wider social meaning: where once animals featured in the public sphere in metaphor, star signs and heraldry, they have been reduced to being either pets or parts. Farms are geographically distant, remote in our consciousness, and obscured by hyper-real representation.

This distance increases the power of media to shape our understanding of animals and animal industry, to influence popular opinion about animal protection, and to set the agenda for animal-related policy debates. As Soroka (2002, 86–90) has observed, the media's effect on public opinion is strongest when the issue in question cannot be directly or systematically observed by the public, as there is no alternative source of evidence. In the absence of competing information, the media's representations of the issue – particularly if these representations are homogeneous and consistent[1] – can come to dominate public understanding.

In this chapter we explore two general areas of media representation. The first involves a policy-orientated analysis of how animal welfare is reported in Australian newspapers. The second, following Tyler and Rossini's (2009, 45–6) argument about the importance of mediated images of animals and animal industry in shaping cultural norms and standards, looks at how animals and farming are represented in popular culture, examining representations of animals and their welfare in a cultural context, rather than a political or public-policy one. Both approaches are important in understanding how public opinion about animal welfare policy is formed. Policy is a formalistic and specific discourse, but it is also predicated on cultural norms, rituals and assumptions.

---

1   In two senses: that the issue is newsworthy enough for it to be reported, and that the audience either engage, or fail to actively disengage with, coverage. The latter notion – active disengagement – is related to the concept of cognitive dissonance (Festinger 1957), where audiences actively avoid media content because it is objectionable in some way.

4 In the media

Animal policy in print

We will first consider the representation of animal protection issues in Australian media between 2005 and 2014 (inclusive). While the print media's circulation has been declining since the growth of the internet (Tiffen and Gittins 2009, 181), print remains a significant source of policy and political information. This is due to its continued consumption by social, political and economic elites, as well as the tendency for print publications to set the news agendas of more popular media such as television and radio (a phenomenon known as 'inter-media agenda setting') (Young 2011, 45–6, 147). I have chosen to analyse a decade of news articles because this span of time allows us to see policy debates and reportage across a number of changes of both federal and state governments and to delineate between significant trends and minor 'blips' of coverage. This aligns with a general consensus (Capano 2012, 455–6) that a decade is often the most analytically useful window: long enough to observe change, while short enough to comment on in a way that practitioners may find valuable.

What coverage looks like

In the broadest terms, examining this decade of coverage allows us to delineate between two specific periods in print reporting of animal welfare issues. Prior to 2011, print reporting on animal protection can best be described as idiosyncratic. Unlike other policy areas that are either systematically reported by all major newspapers (politics, crime, economic issues) or are 'owned' by specific mastheads (such as the *Australian*'s coverage of the higher education sector), animal protection is neither systematically reported nor owned by particular mainstream publications. Animal protection, unlike topics such as international affairs, crime and the environment, is not a specific 'beat', with journalists specialising in the area and developing a detailed understanding of the topic (Becker and Vlad 2009, 64–7).

This lack of focus has implications. The first is erratic news coverage. The quantum of coverage of animal welfare issues within each of the major Australian newspapers changed considerably from year to year during the decade. The second is the nature of the coverage.

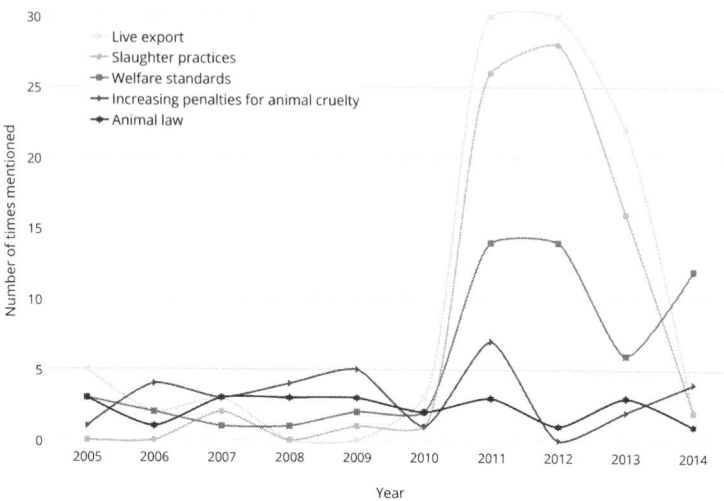

Figure 4.1. Number of issues mentioned in newspapers, 2005–2014. Issues mentioned fewer than five times per year have been ommitted for clarity. The full dataset may be viewed at hdl.handle.net/2123/15349.

Without a dedicated beat, journalists writing in the area are unlikely to develop technical expertise or a deep understanding of the relevant policy and industry actors (their motivations, interests and reliability as sources), or to become sensitive to changes in the policy landscape. The third is the source of coverage. Prior to 2011, coverage spikes tended to be driven by the effectiveness of animal protection organisations in promoting specific issues and causes within their jurisdiction. This explains, for example, the high level of reporting during this period in the comparatively small jurisdiction of Tasmania (see Chapter 6).[2] Overall, before 2011 news coverage tended to be erratic and highly

---

2 Tasmanian-specific issues, for example, receive more than three times the level of coverage of Western Australian-specific issues in the time period. Per capita, Queensland is also significantly over-reported.

4 In the media

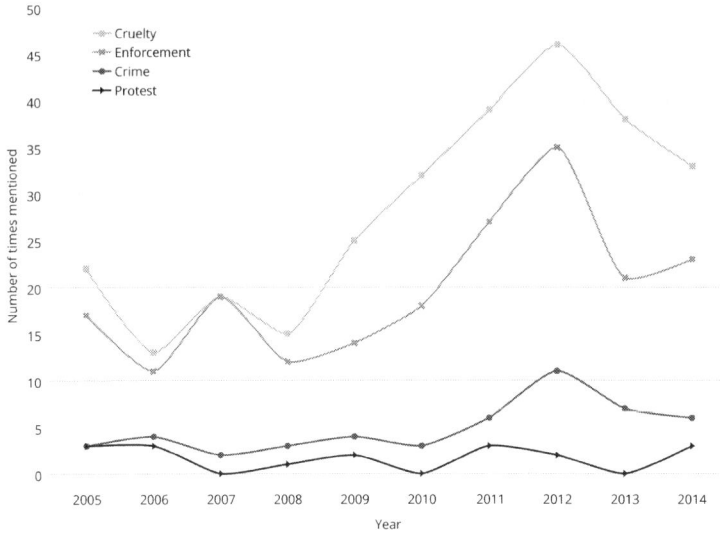

Figure 4.2. Number of events mentioned in newspapers, 2005–2014. Events mentioned fewer than ten times in the recording period have been omitted for clarity. The full dataset may be viewed at hdl.handle.net/2123/15349.

variable, written by generalist staff writers, and focused on particular events rather than long-term trends or topics.

Since 2011 the proportion of coverage among the major outlets has become more structured: reporting on animal protection-related issues has become more systematic and consistent across the news industry. The cause of this drastic reshaping is the same event that motivated the writing of this book: as we can see in Figure 4.1, the issue of live exports of cattle to Indonesia is directly responsible for this change in Australian reporting. This event led to a considerable spike in the total news coverage of protection issues during 2011–2013. This increase remained highly focused on coverage of Indonesia and was directly tied to the popular, political and industrial reaction to the 2011 *Four Corners* special on Indonesian abattoir practices.

Regardless of this very narrow focus post-2011, the shift in the news agenda does represent a large increase in reporting on animal protection issues in Australian print media. This change did not, however, displace existing patterns of reporting. Prior to 2011, coverage of animal protection was mostly comprised of local crime reporting of cruelty offences. As we can see in Figure 4.2 (the reporting of specific events), acts of cruelty tend to be strongly associated with law enforcement in the Australian media, and the increased focus on live exports correlated with higher levels of cruelty reporting overall. Given the term's lack of clear meaning in the community, as identified in previous chapters, the focus on animal cruelty cases is interesting. While animal protection organisations tend to focus on highlighting cruelty in farming and industrial contexts (see Chapter 6), the press tend to focus on acts of individual cruelty, especially those perpetrated against companion animal species[3] in or near residential areas.[4] Prior to 2011, dogs and cats were the focus of most reporting; from 2011 onwards they were later joined by the two major live-export species (cattle and sheep).

The Indonesian issue was such an unusual media event, the spikes it produced in the data set can make it difficult to see the other activist-led shocks from the same period. There were, however, two other major news-making events. PETA (USA)'s campaigns against the use of Australian wool by major fashion labels (in 2004 and 2011) are visible only as minor increases in reporting about sheep in 2004–2007 (see Chapter 6). Meanwhile Russia's suspension of kangaroo-meat imports (2008, 2009–2012) because of concerns about food safety and handling is hard to identify amid the background noise of periodic cruelty cases involving kangaroos, although a small peak can be found in the 2009–2010 data. A further suspension of exports to Russia in May 2014 went virtually unreported (Tapp 2014).

---

3 The reporting of cruelty offences against dogs tends to be related to an owner or carer, while cat cases tend to be associated with seemingly random attacks against ranging animals. It is difficult to determine if reported attacks against cats focus more on domestic or stray animals.
4 Rural and regional areas see a greater level of reporting (though still a low level overall) of cruelty acts against native animals. Often these are associated with illegal or botched hunting (for example, the discovery of live animals with arrows in them).

Apart from these distinct spikes, most reporting of animal welfare issues in Australia during this decade consisted of crime stories. These stories tend to be police procedural in nature, prompted either by a court case and the result of a news organisation's court beat,[5] or by press releases about mistreated animals, often with appeals for information, put out by welfare organisations such as the RSPCA. In structure, these stories tend to take the form either of a 'spot' (where a case is presented and resolved, usually through a prosecution, in the course of a single story) or a 'continuing' story (in which the perpetrators remain at large or the court case is ongoing). Both types of stories emphasise events and facts over depth or a broader perspective (Tuchman 1978). Only the most 'newsworthy' spawn follow-up reports (bestiality prosecutions, for example, although exceedingly rare, are more likely to generate additional prurient coverage).

Exception and norm: 'A bloody business'

One exception to this trend is worthy of detailed discussion. On 30 May 2011, the Australian national broadcaster aired its now-infamous episode on slaughter practices in Indonesia. Prepared in collaboration with the animal advocacy organisation Animals Australia and the RSPCA Australia, the episode included graphic footage of the slaughter of cattle exported from Australia. The premise of the episode was that, regardless of claims made by the live-export industry that considerable work had been done to ensure that slaughter practices in Indonesia were humane, actual practices remained rudimentary, with some animals experiencing a slow death at the hands of inexperienced meat workers. Animals Australia's Lyn White had gained considerable access to places of slaughter and provided the ABC's flagship current-affairs show, *Four Corners*, with video footage. It depicted the realities of

---

5   This may be a long-established reporting convention in Australia. Newspaper reports from the 19th century similarly resulted from policing actions. Interestingly, a number of these reports focus on prosecutions made for veterinary procedures police deemed inappropriate (see, for example, *Age*, 20 November 1864, and *Sydney Morning Herald*, 14 November 1865).

animal processing in a developing nation in a way that is rarely, if ever, seen on prime-time television.

Not for the first time in the program's half-century of production, a high-profile episode set the political agenda for an extended period. Every major newspaper reported extensively on the show's claims and the subsequent fallout: the public reaction and popular mobilisation; the government's decision to suspend the live-export trade with Indonesia; the industry's reaction and counter-mobilisation. Parliamentarians reported an increase in direct calls to their electorate offices (interview: K. Thomson MP, Member for Wills, 26 June 2014; ABC 2011). The issue also had longevity, and was still among the top 30 policy concerns in the lead-up to the 2013 federal election (Roslyn 2013).

In his analysis of the issue, Coghlan (2014) highlights the emotional impact of the show and its focus on the suffering on individualised animals that are normally lost in herds. However, there is some debate as to the extent to which this impact was felt in rural constituencies.[6] As the live-export industry was previously largely unknown among the general public, there was much scope for the story to 'run', with follow-up articles tracking policy debates and industry responses, background features into the industry and the long history of activist complaints about live export going back 30 years, and discussions of the lived experience of Indonesians, Australian production and distribution systems, access to refrigeration overseas, and a raft of related topics that gave the issue 'oxygen'.

In managing the sudden influx of media demands, the industry was hampered by the comparatively small size of the export sector and divisions within it. This led to a slow and uncoordinated response to media inquiries. Justin Toohey of the Cattle Council observed:

> When the crisis hit, again, it comes down to territorialism: 'Oh, that's live exporters, they need to deal with this issue, they need to be in the media, they need to fix this, they need to say why this happened and where we're going with it.' So, we rest, wrongly, on

---

[6] Kelvin Thomson argues that the issue mobilised both urban and rural constituencies, whereas Steve Whan MLC (interview, 19 June 2014) argues that this was not the case and that concern remained contained to urban areas.

live export and their experts in that area. So, what happened ... the chairman at the time of Live Corp, and the representative council, [were] so inundated with media reaction, that they couldn't cope with the workload. They kind of almost went underground, and then in stepped the Cattle Council. (Interview: 4 July 2014)

Without a media strategy, the industry rapidly lost the capacity to control media coverage of the issue.

Thus, the coverage of Indonesian live exports was a unique media event in the decade in question. From an agenda-setting perspective, the case was the first animal protection issue to attract consistent and sustained media coverage at a national level. It appeared to attract considerable initial public interest, which was sustained and increased by ongoing reporting by journalists who developed expertise in the area. It was also distinctive in terms of content. The scope of the story tended to expand over time to include more actors (both political and industrial), and the coverage articulated the complexity of the industrial production process, as well as of the competing interests at play. Specific policy instruments developed to respond to the problem, such as the Exporter Supply Chain Assurance System (ESCAS), also received media attention. ESCAS was discussed in the media in unusual detail: in the content analysis discussed previously, it was the single most frequently mentioned act or regulatory instrument discussed in print in 2012, the year of its introduction. This coincided with a general increase in discussion of policy options in the print media in Australia. Specific policy instruments, such as the use of CCTV in meat processing and other animal-industry settings, are rarely directly examined in reporting of animal protection debates, but now began to receive more attention.[7] While the live-export issue had largely subsided by 2013–2014, alterations to ESCAS were covered by the media, demonstrating an ongoing interest in the issue and its resolution. Some of these stories were clearly the result of monitoring of implementation by animal protection organisation. The press also reported changes to

---

7   A good example of another instrument that received some attention during the decade was the establishment of a register of cruelty convictions, created with the objective of monitoring individuals with major anti-social tendencies.

import quotas by the Indonesian government in 2015, and the signing of live-export market agreements with China the same year.

It could be argued that, although the issue of live exports received intense and sustained media attention for about four years, the coverage remained within the established patterns of animal protection reporting in Australia. Attention was paid to a specific type of animal seen as valuable within a specific context; while the coverage gave readers an insight into a part of the animal agricultural sector seldom seen in Australia, the reporting of the issue remained within a relatively narrow news agenda. This can be seen as an example of rapid agenda closure: once the possibility of a full ban on live exports was discarded in favour of the ESCAS, the option of total abolition disappeared from the popular debate and the industry resumed its trajectory towards growth. For the casual reader, the policy debate revolved around the extent to which ESCAS was being effectively implemented, and the cost–benefit of this model of welfare assurance.

This reflects a distinct contrast between the wide range of theoretical and ethical positions discussed in Chapter 2, and media discussions of animal protection. As Pendergrast (2015) argues, based on his analysis of media coverage of the live-export debate in the immediate aftermath of the *Four Corners* broadcast, while the issue was constructed by the media as an industry scandal, it was largely reported within a conventional framework that extended Australian industrial production norms overseas: the central question of much reporting was to what extent Australian cows received the same deaths in Indonesia as Australia. Seen simply as a 'welfare' scandal, the issue never escaped the perspective of 'new welfarism', as discussed in Chapter 2. While the issue's longevity meant there was opportunity for journalists to branch into wider debates and employ narratives from different ethical traditions, this did not occur. Pendergrast found that more radical arguments, such as those of abolitionist thinkers and organisations, were excluded from media coverage, while more conventional 'welfarist' animal advocates were privileged.

Live exports, like individual cases of animal cruelty, tended to be reported through an episodic rather than thematic frame. Thematic framing places a specific event or issue into a broader context, highlighting the ongoing nature and underlying causes of an issue.

Episodic framing, in contrast, tends to emphasise the particular event, focusing on proximate causes in an ahistorical fashion (Iyengar 1991). This leads to an understanding of the immediate event but limits deeper learning. Episodic accounts tend to focus on individualistic attributions of blame or responsibility, rather than on systematic or societal causes. In addition, as Gross (2008) argues, while episodic reports tend to evoke a greater emotional response in media consumers (as seen in the public response to the *Four Corners* episode), they are often less persuasive instigators of policy change. Without a connection to wider systematic or causal narratives, the individualised focus can be engaging but not necessarily productive.

What gets covered, how, and why?

The lack of an established media beat for animal welfare presents a problem for all parts of the animal welfare debate. Pendergrast's complaints, outlined above, come from a critical animal studies perspective, with an emphasis on animal liberation (ICAS 2015). From the perspective of established and emerging organisations that promote enhanced welfare standards within current legal paradigms, however, the view was quite different. One senior animal-welfare advocate reported that it was relatively easy to get media coverage for his organisation, observing that 'the media absolutely loves reporting on animal cruelty matters' (interview: 5 September 2014). Similarly favourable coverage was reported by a number of RSPCA representatives (interviews: M. Mercurio, CEO, RSPCA Victoria, 4 June 2013). As Michael Beatty, the head of media and community relations for the RSPCA Queensland, noted, such access enabled these organisations to get their preferred visuals communicated, maximising the impact of their media coverage:

> If I get [a] large article in the paper or on the TV news, inevitably [a peer in another industry] either texts or rings me up and says, 'You bastard, I'm working with lumps of coal and you've got little animals.' Yeah, so it's a lot easier. (Interview: 16 April 2013)

Importantly, however, using particular cruelty cases and images of individual photogenic animals to 'sell' stories may perpetuate the use of episodic framing, and so limit the range of narratives employed by the media.

While welfare organisations are able to generate considerable 'free media', industry tends to speak through paid advertising. Outside of rural media, industry representatives can see journalistic interest as problematic; they complain that the media are prone to generalise about whole sectors based on the conduct of atypical 'bad eggs' (interview: A. Spencer, 23 June 2014). Rural media have been critical of mainstream coverage of issues such as live export for this reason, arguing that the activists' footage was unrepresentative of industry practices overall (Nason 2015). The scale of animal agriculture, its wide geographic distribution, and a lack of sustained reporting in major mainstream media work against the type of thematic framing that might put 'bad eggs' into a broader context. This is particularly true of reporting about foreign nations, where language barriers and the decline of local bureaux hamper reporting.

Media coverage of live exports, and the dominant role of activists' footage in initiating public debate, infuriated many in animal industry, including those outside of the sheep and cattle sectors; some saw it as the ill-treatment of fellow farmers by an ill-informed press (interview: N. Ferguson, 3 September 2013). Some conservative politicians were suspicious of the national broadcaster's motivations in reporting on animal protection issues. This took place against the backdrop of a wider public controversy about the ABC's editorial position, a debate that has flared up over the last decade (Boucher and Sharpe 2008, 82). One South Australian MP observed:

> [The ABC] mainly run [the story] in one direction, and they run it really hard, and they make it easy for the activists to get a run. You don't see that happening with the commercial media... There wouldn't be any DNA on it, but I think there are people in high places within the ABC that are probably fairly closely associated with the animal activists, and prepared to give them a fairly good run. That's my observation... it's really interesting because [on] the other side of the debate, the ABC has *Country Hour*, they have *Landline*,

4 In the media

and they traditionally [have] been fairly focused on agriculture and rural people, but on this [story] they do [so] much damage [to farmers] because it's been blown out of all proportions. (Interview: 25 September 2014)

As discussed above, others in the animal industry have expressed concerns about the industry's own media management. The extent to which the MP's view of the media is shared within the industry appears to vary. Such views do reflect a sense of existential threat within some communities, generated by some of the recent media coverage.

Interviewees also identified the technical and scientific knowledge of journalists reporting on animal protection issues as a significant factor in the quality and fairness of reporting. The level of scientific literacy among journalists reporting on technical policy has been raised as a problem more generally (Dunwoody 1999, 76). In the area of animal protection, the media's relationship with scientific organisations can be tenuous at times. The director of the Victorian Bureau of Animal Welfare expressed some exasperation in dealing with journalists:

The most difficult group I have to deal with are the media. They can be quite vindictive. I can provide them with what I think is balanced information and they'll write pretty awful articles. So, we tend to steer away from them. (Interview: 21 August 2013)

However, avoiding the media can be counter-productive in the long run. If, following negative experiences with journalists, the technical experts in such organisations tend to send media requests 'upstairs' to the minister's office, they may miss an opportunity to steer public discussion towards a more technical, and therefore thematic, understanding of issues and events. This ensures reporting remains in the 'political' space.

An alternative explanation for the intensity and longevity of the Indonesian live-export issue credits the power of national identity. This argument links the atypical coverage of this specific story with wider cultural concerns and currents in Australian society. In Fozdar and Spittles' 2014 analysis of the coverage of the live-export issue, they highlight the significance of the continual identification of the cattle in question – both in the original *Four Corners* broadcast and subsequent reporting – as 'Australian' or, more informally, as 'our cows'. It seems not all cows are equal in the eyes of Australians: cattle raised in this country are given more and different moral concern than cattle raised overseas. Interestingly, in a nation created by a shared xenophobic urge and presently in the throes of a decades-long political debate about the recognition of refugees' rights (Jupp 2007), it is surprising how quickly metaphorical passports were made available to the bovine.

This outpouring of concern, Fozdar and Spittles argue, was a response to persistent negative characterisations of Australians in the international and domestic media. The Australian public were criticised by one British journalist for having 'tiny hearts',[8] and the United Nations High Commissioner for Refugees has consistently been critical of the detention of asylum seekers.[9] Thus, the outpouring of concern for cows at slaughter provided a counter to other examples of our profound lack of humanitarianism. In addition, Fozdar and Spittles argue, the story played on Orientalist traditions of seeing Western behaviours as civilised and Eastern practices as barbaric.

Additional evidence of this tendency can be found in the response to domestic animal-welfare issues. When similarly confronting footage emerged of live animals being used as training bait in greyhound racing in 2015, the public and media response was more muted, with only modest coverage of the initial report, subsequent investigations and government response. This difference is notable, given the greyhound story involved clear breeches of anti-cruelty laws as well as attempts by owners and trainers to gain unfair advantage in competition. Similarly, the media and the public paid comparatively little attention to international bans due to sheep mulesing and kangaroo-meat processing. In all three cases, the chief difference was that the concerning practices took place within Australia, and were largely conducted by Australians. This explanation accords with Baker's (1993, 67–71) analysis of media representations of 'Britishness' in the UK, and of the perception that

---

8 Katie Hopkins, writing in the UK tabloid newspaper the *Sun*, in response to migrant deaths in the Mediterranean in April 2015.
9 This was highlighted at the Geneva Roundtable in May 2011 by UNHCR and the Office of the High Commissioner for Human Rights.

affection for animals and concern for their welfare is a British national characteristic. According to Baker, this perception is articulated via popular media reports that emphasise the ordinary Britisher's revulsion at the practices of other nations (he cites a famous case of British tourists 'duped' into eating dolphin sausage; *News of the World*, 22 July 1990), or at the behaviour of immigrants.

In Australia, we can identify a similar association between 'Australianness' and concern for animal welfare in the mobilisation or confection of public concern about halal food production practices. This issue has been taken up by parts of the Australian political right (for example, through the Senate inquiry into third-party certification of food, established in May 2015, largely at the insistence of South Australian Liberal Senator Cory Bernardi) and by far-right groups (Gartrell 2015). The final committee report, released in 2015, largely dismissed these concerns (Economics References Committee, 2015). Image 12 shows animal rights messages displayed by the Party for Freedom outside a halal expo in the western suburbs of Sydney in 2015. The Party for Freedom was established circa 2013, and takes inspiration from the Dutch party of the same name (*Partij voor de Vrijheid*) set up by Geert Wilders (Flemming 2013). The group is an offshoot of the Australian Protectionist Party and its main policy focus is anti-immigration, especially concerning Asian and Muslim migrants. Under its current name the group has undertaken small demonstrations outside supermarkets that have celebrated the end of Ramadan (2014), run anti-refugee counter-protests (2015), and participated in the Reclaim Australia protests (2015). It is unlikely that animal protection is the group's primary concern; it does not even mention the issue in its policy documents.[10] Halal slaughter and a professed interest in animal

---

10 https://www.partyforfreedom.org.au/policies/. Folkes (2015) did, however, highlight animal welfare issues in an email sent to supporters to promote the event. There is an established connection between far-right groups and animal welfare. It is often noted that the National Socialist government of Germany (1933–1945) had some of the most extensive animal protection laws of its time. As Bruns (2014, 40) observes, these laws were also used to demonstrate the moral superiority of Germans to 'Jewish-materialistic' medical practices such as the increasingly popular use of vivisection by scientists. In Australia today the far-right appears on both 'sides' of this issue. In 2015 the neo-Nazi United Patriots

protection are used to exaggerate the differences between 'Australians' and the small Australian Muslim and Jewish communities who are granted variations to conventional slaughter practices.

While it is significant that the majority of Indonesians are Muslim, this does not explain the unusual interest in live exports to this particular destination. Fozdar and Spittles are likely right not to attribute this to simple cultural chauvinism. (Reports about live exports to nations in the Middle East have not prompted the same response.) Why, then, did the public take such an interest in the Indonesian story? Ongoing characterisations in the Australian media of Indonesian society and its government provide some clues. Of all the nations in the region, Indonesia has received the most media attention in Australia in recent decades, particularly in extensive and often sensationalist reporting of Indonesia's treatment of 'our people' (Noszlopy et al. 2006). Since 2005 the Australian media have been obsessed with the treatment of Schapelle Corby, a young white woman arrested for importing a commercial quantity of cannabis into Indonesia. Concurrent with the live-export coverage was intensive scrutiny of the trials and executions of the 'Bali Nine' heroin importers Andrew Chan and Myuran Sukumaran; much Australian coverage was critical of the application of the death sentence (described as 'barbaric' by public officials, academics and in media editorials; Lines 2015; Maguire 2015; Goodsir 2015) and of the Indonesian political and judicial machinery (McNair 2015; ABC 2015). Indonesia thus serves a kind of cultural double duty in the Australian imagination: Indonesia's treatment of animals shows the true humanitarianism of Australians, while its systems of governance treat Australians as little more than animals.

Which animal protection issues attract media attention, and how they are reported, thus appear subject to a range of factors. Domestic issues are reported sparingly or idiosyncratically, with little continuity over time. Issues that cross the threshold into major public debates are few and far between, and determined by a range of highly unpredictable variables and cultural insecurities.

Front found themselves in opposition to animal liberationists over the latter's plan to protest against a circus (Belot and Inman 2015).

4 In the media

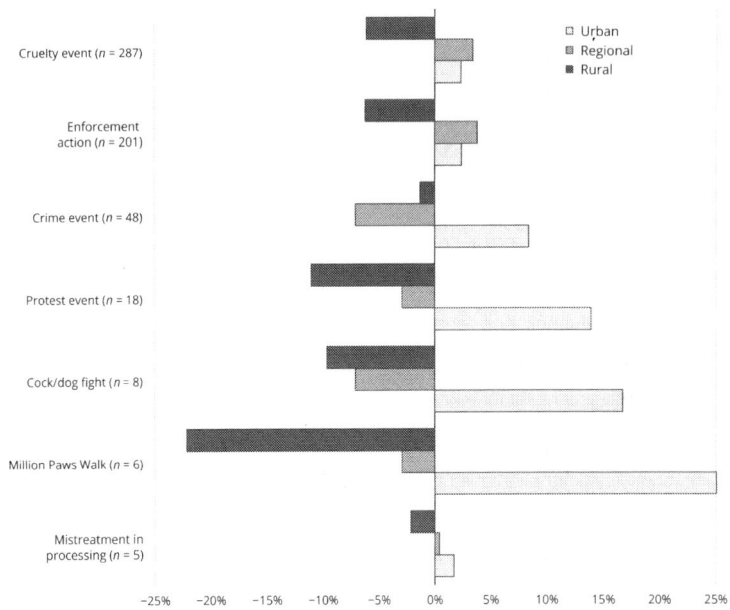

Figure 4.3. Regional variations in event reporting from the national average (percent), 2005–2014.

Variations across the nation

Notwithstanding the generalisations outlined above, there is considerable regional variation in the Australian print media. Looking at the newspaper data set, we can sort coverage by the primary location of the reporting newspaper and its audience ('urban' or capital-city newspapers, 'regional' or non-capital municipalities, and 'rural' areas) and compare different regions to the national average. (These categories are, of course, to some degree misleading. Many 'capital city' newspapers are effectively state or national papers and are read widely in regional and rural areas, both in print and online.)

This analysis shows that there are considerable differences between metropolitan and rural media coverage (where 'metropolitan' includes both capital and regional cities). As we can see in Figure 4.3, specific animal-cruelty events receive greater coverage in metropolitan newspapers than in rural papers. Events run by welfare and activist organisations (such as protests and the RSPCA's annual mass 'dog walk') also tend to receive more coverage in capital-city newspapers. This can be explained in part because such events are more likely to occur in larger population centres. But it also appears to be in line with the attitudinal orientations identified in the comparative Animal Attitudes Scale data presented earlier in the book. The greater coverage of animal cruelty issues in metropolitan papers aligns with the higher levels of concern for individualised animals' wellbeing identified among metropolitan people.

Looking at the reporting of animal protection issues between regions, Figure 4.3 demonstrates a logical divergence in the level of reporting. Issues strongly associated with rural industry are more frequently reported in rural newspapers. This includes situationally specific issues (such as live exports), as well as ongoing issues affecting rural production (such as stock transport, the development of new welfare standards, and the use of CCTV in production settings). Reflecting the findings in Figure 4.2, meanwhile, the policy implications of animal cruelty events are more often discussed in urban newspapers (such stories include calls to increase penalties for animal cruelty, changes to animal law, adoption of surplus animals, and methods of mitigating cruelty in society). Chicken-cage issues are an interesting outlier, perhaps reflecting the tendency for chicken production to take place closer to population centres than other kinds of animal agriculture; chicken-cage issues are disproportionately discussed in regional newsprint.

Print media does tend to behave in a predictable manner with regards to the editorial choices of mastheads in different geographical markets. Newspapers cover the stories they anticipate their target audience will be interested in. In doing so, the print media tend to create regionally specific content that serves the interests of local readers even if that means concealing some information (Pariser 2011). For all the talk of 'national conversations' about policy issues, the public sphere is fragmented into different communities, distinguished from one another by both interest and geography. In addition, some of the concerns of industry about the lack of depth and context in media coverage of farm production are confirmed by this comparison: more detailed discussions of animal production policy tend not to leak into the popular print media of the major population centres. Importantly, this underlines the comparatively superficial level of concern identified in Chapter 3.

Animals on screen

It is also useful, in attempting to understand popular attitudes to animals and their welfare, to examine the representation of animals in popular culture. The value of looking at culture (Raymond Williams' 'one of the two or three most complicated words in the English language'; 1976) was touched on in Chapter 3's discussion of the power and origins of our social norms concerning the treatment and use of animals. While technical and rational debates about policy issues may be the ideal of democratic liberal theorists such as Habbermas, culture provides an important anchor to policy-making. Policies that uphold accepted norms are seen to reflect 'common sense'. Those that run counter to folk logic run the risk of being dismissed as belonging to *das Wolkenkuckucksheim* – 'cloud cuckoo land'. In her philosophy of decision-making, Hannah Arendt (1953, 387) identifies the intimate relationship between politics and social norms: the ability of elites to demonstrate awareness of, and be simpatico with, popular 'common sense' is the most important political skill in modern times. For Arendt, political common sense is not an innate characteristic of 'the great', but the product of a politician's engagement in the wider cultural context (what she calls *Weltsinn*, a 'sense of the world'), including an understanding of their constituents' cultural history and traditional practices (Borren 2013).

Mass or mainstream culture (Davis 2014, 28) shapes policy-making by creating a policy terrain in which it is politically safer to tread the well-worn paths of social norms than to scale the heights of innovation. Culture provides the metaphorical language with which complex policy can be explained, as well as everyday examples and justifications for decisions (Stone 2002). Popular media's selective and distorted representation of animals habituates a particular view of animals, and constrains the public's understanding of the realities of the lives of animals and the people who work with them. As we have seen in the public reaction to the *Four Corners* episode about live export, when viewers' limited awareness is challenged, the shock can be profound.

Television's power lies in its capacity to cultivate viewers' attitudes over time through the repetition of social norms and stereotypes (Gerbner and Gross 1976). Television has been, until very recently, the most significant communication channel in the media life of most Australians. Effective television presents complete vignettes or synecdoches of life to the viewer, creating linear narratives about the role of animals and people in society. But visual media is also richly symbolic. As Tait (2013, 183–4) states, this can have a powerful effect on how animal meanings are constructed and sustained:

> animals are engaged by humans in the process of embodying and hence performing human emotions through the *mis-en-scène* and the constructed framing in television and cinema. Humans unthinkingly transact and communicate their emotions with and through other animals . . .

In doing so, our cultural unconscious, and the meanings we give to particular animals, are exposed. Drawing upon a content analysis of each of the five major free-to-air television stations during prime-time viewing, we can get an understanding of how animals are most commonly depicted on Australian screens. We will then turn to an example of how less mainstream attitudes are depicted in popular culture: the representations of atypical diets on television.

Any analysis of Australian television must also include advertising. Advertising can be a highly important indicator of popular culture for a variety of reasons. First, it indexes against the popular. That is, more popular products and services generally receive more advertising, by nature of the political economy of media (Herman and Chomsky 2002). Second, because of the increasingly compact way advertising is communicated in all media, it is often informationally dense and uses sophisticated interpretations of popular culture to create its messages. Animals in advertising are often used as symbolically rich metonymies of broader contexts (Berger 2011, 62). From a content analysis of

4 In the media

Australian free-to-air television, therefore, we can get a sense of which animals appear on Australian television screens, how they are depicted, and in what contexts.

Given the diversity of animals in nature, only a very narrow band of animals appears frequently on television.[11] Reflecting and reinforcing the anthropocentric attitudes identified in Chapter 3, the animals most often seen on television are those used as food, followed by companion animals: cows, dogs, chickens, fish and other birds. What is also interesting is the comparative absence from our screens of pest animals (collapsed into the 'other' category given their scarcity in the dataset), and of native animal species, which appeared almost exclusively in tourism and travel advertising. The latter is not an artefact of the inclusion of non-Australian content; television advertising in Australia is almost completely produced domestically.

The dominance of food and industrial animals (including animals used for service, transport and entertainment) in the sample is partially explained by examining which types of programming are most likely to feature animals on Australian prime-time television: most animal appearances are in advertisements. This is consistent with the idea already articulated that advertisements are likely to use animals as signifiers to maximise their bandwidth (Pieters et al. 2010). The preponderance of animals as products (and in products) goes some way to explaining their frequent appearance in television commercials. One example is typical. In an advertisement for a national supermarket chain, the viewer follows a protagonist through a series of vignettes depicting food consumption and preparation, all of which feature animal products as a key ingredient. The journey leads the viewer back to an idealised farm and farmer. In this advertisement, the number of different elements and scenes, and the overarching narrative (namely that quality products are supplied to happy customers as a result of

---

11 For the purposes of this study, an 'appearance' was defined as the distinct representation of an animal, in whole or in part, in a television program or advertisement. There was no attempt to measure the length of time on air (the random sample, however, included no cases where animals were protagonists). Animals included were live, dead, and animated representations, but animals as stylised logos were excluded.

a partnership between retail and production), could be said to be as complex as the surrounding programs. In addition to the simple representation of animals as products to be consumed, the dataset also included examples of animals being used as more complex signifiers. Advertisements use visual cues to signal meanings and values to the audience without having to make these connections explicit (Lloyd and Woodside 2013, 14). Companion animals often play this role in advertisements. Where they are not advertising products specifically for companion animals (such as pet food), these animals may be employed to signify the security of home and family. In familial settings, often alongside children, dogs are commonly used to represent the happy, clean and modern home. Threats to the home may be signified by unhappy or at-risk pests (as seen in a series of insurance advertisements featuring claymation dogs and cats).[12]

Outside of advertising, the second most common category of television content to feature animals is cooking and lifestyle shows.[13] In these shows most animals appear as ingredients (Figure 4.4), rather than as live animals. Meat tends to feature as the dominant or most valued ingredient in these programs, with vegetables secondary in significance. Demonstrating the influence of 'foodie' movements on popular culture, the quality of the animal ingredient is sometimes highlighted (either directly, through appeals to the audience to use quality ingredients, or by describing the meat using adjectives that convey quality). When companion animals appear in these shows, they tend to provide background scenery (happy homes again); occasionally they take a more central role, for example as the subjects of veterinary

---

12   This may be the result of broadcasters' codes that limit their use of messages that generate fear. The 2015 Free TV Australia Commercial Television Industry Code of Practice states that General Classification content should ensure that 'Where music, special effects and camera work are used to create an atmosphere of tension or fear, care must be taken to minimise distress to children'. Thus in the insurance advertisement, rather than depict a human at risk from a storm, a cat is blown away by the strong winds. This demonstrates that pets are considered family members, but with a lower status than human family members, as identified in Chapter 3.
13   The former being more common in the sample than the latter, but each sharing many similar thematic and visual elements.

4 In the media

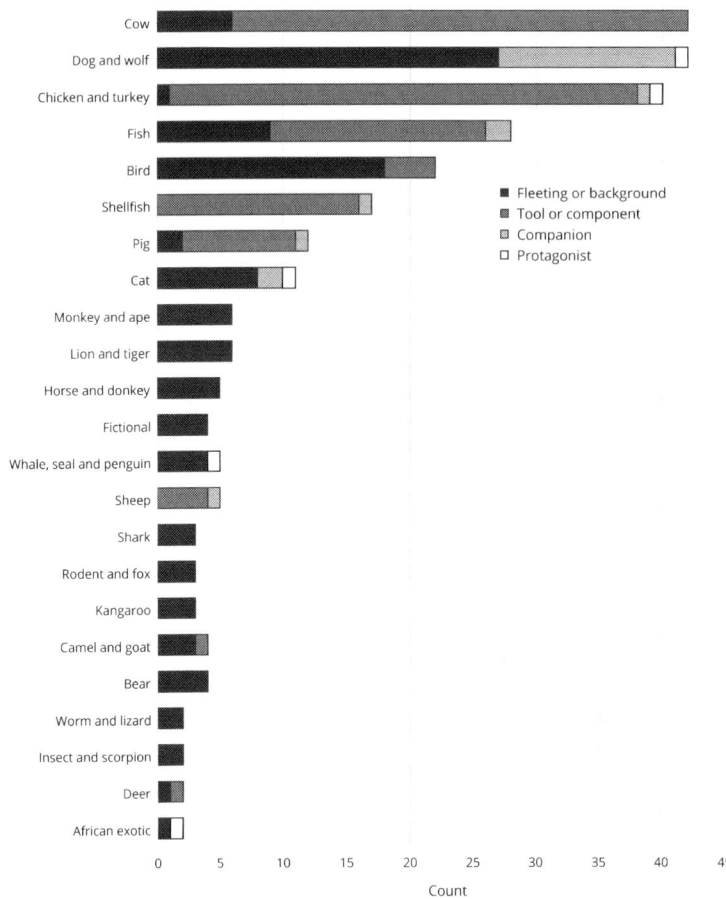

Figure 4.4. Animals on Australian free-to air television, billing or characterisation.

treatment (one lifestyle program in the sample included an extended segment about pet psychology and fear management). Overall, however, as we can see in Figure 4.4, animals are nearly never depicted as demonstrating significant agency relative to people; they are very rarely protagonists or antagonists.

Turning from average representations, let us now examine how popular culture presents atypical diets to the general community, by drawing on separate case material selected for this purpose. Using a selection of episodes of the long-running cooking programs *MasterChef Australia* (FremantleMedia Australia 2009–2011; Shine 2012–) and *My Kitchen Rules* (*MKR*; Seven Network 2010–), we can examine the representation of veg*n meals. *MasterChef* and *MKR* are useful examples for a number of reasons. First, although it has spawned a range of imitators and competitors, *MasterChef* set the standard for competitive prime-time cooking shows. Both shows have rated extremely highly in their timeslots for many years. And, both programs' content is directly influenced by commercial tie-ins with advertisers and in-show promotions. They are thus calibrated strongly towards a mainstream audience. Finally, *MasterChef* and *MKR* have tended to set the agenda for other media: their content, contests, and personalities have been closely reported and discussed in the wider media.

In season two of *MasterChef* (2010), contestants were faced with an 'invention test': as a special challenge, they were to prepare a vegetarian meal (episode 42). Demonstrating that gendered perceptions of meat consumption continue to hold sway in Australia, the challenge was judged by 'six of the most meat-loving men in Australia' (a cattle farmer, two builders, two truck drivers and a firefighter). The episode reiterated the conventional association between meat, muscle and labour, with one of the guest judges observing that he considered it 'hard to work eight or nine hours on the tools with a stomach full of broccoli'. Here the distinction between the guest judges – working class and uniformly white – and the show's contestants – mostly urban professionals of both genders, including some visible minorities; of the 24 finalists, only three worked in a trade – was put into sharp relief. Five years later, a similar challenge on *MKR* did not appear to need the same conceit: three pairs of contestants made vegetarian meals and were assessed by the regular judges, in a format no different from most of the show's challenges (season six, 2015, episode 40). In this episode, the major challenge was the use of specific ingredients, rather than the absence of meat.

The gendering of meat consumption and vegetarianism was still visible in *MKR*, however. In season four (2013), teams were set the challenge of cooking for the public in a series of themed street-food vans, one of which was vegetarian (episode 39). Teams had to compete for customers with their respective offerings. After failing to entice a group of male customers away from the vegetarian van with the promise of meat, one competitor, a young woman, exclaimed, 'Boring! There are grown men wanting a veggie burger over a steak.' Interestingly, the episode uncovered a high demand for the vegetarian option among customers in the Sydney CBD, a phenomenon mentioned several times by the contestants. The contestants, uniformly omnivorous, recognised the increasing prevalence of abstainer diets, an increase consistent with the findings in Chapter 3. This gap between the public and the competitors is to some extent a structural feature of these programs: because they require contestants to cook omnivorous meals if they are to compete effectively, the shows rarely feature contestants with non-mainstream diets. (Season six of *MasterChef*, in 2014, did include an advocate of veg*n cooking, Renae Smith, who remained in the running until the last month of broadcasting; although she cooked meat during the competition, she was vocal in her support of veg*n food. The show has also featured several 'former vegetarians' as contestants, who have discussed this as part of their show persona.)

Demonstrating this tendency to sequester veg*n meals, in season three (2011; episode 46) of *MasterChef*, contestants were required, in pairs, to cook for people with special dietary requirements. Two of the pairs were set the challenge of cooking a vegan meal; they were in competition against others cooking for people on low-salt, low-fat, low-sugar and low-gluten diets. Veganism was presented as one of a number of dietary restrictions that chefs may encounter in their normal work. The show's producers did not feel the need to explain veganism to the audience, suggesting that they felt confident viewers would be familiar with the term; veganism's connection to animal rights was not discussed. Interestingly, the teams set other challenges (such as restrictions of salt and fat) were portrayed as struggling more than those assigned vegan meals.

While these programs certainly present veg*n cooking as outside the mainstream of Australian cultural life, the reception of the contestants' veg*n meals by the public via the use of in-show competitions and challenges and by the judges was largely positive, and involved a wider range of dishes than simply those that might be described as simulacra of meat-based meals.[14] This appears to demonstrate the popular attitudes towards vegetarian food identified in Chapter 3: the diet may be widely considered non-mainstream and, in Australia, considered not masculine, but it is not generally seen as deviant and its market share is not trivial.

Animals online

During the last decade the uptake of broadband and mobile internet services has dramatically reshaped the Australian media landscape, with rapid increases in the amount of time Australians are spending online (Chen 2013, 8). Thus, in considering the representation of animals in popular media and how the public use media to access information about animals, the online habits of Australians are relevant: are they similar or different to other media consumption habits?

To examine this question we can map what Australians explicitly look for on the internet by using Google search data from the same period as covered by our newspaper content analysis. Search data is useful and telling because, unlike the comparatively passive connection between television content and consumer interests, search provides specific and quantifiable evidence of what the public are actively interested in. In this case Google is a good indicator of general trends in search behaviour in Australia, as the site has had an extremely high market share (over 90 percent of all searches) for a considerable period of time in this country (Cowling 2010; Cowling 2012; AFP and Bloomberg 2015). This data provides a picture of animal searches over the period 2005–2014 (inclusive), and reveals that the same two 'privileged' groups of animals are the most frequently searched for: companion animals and food animals. Thus, the most frequently searched-for animal aggregated terms for the decade were (in descending order): dog/puppy, chicken/bird, fish, pig/pork/bacon, horse, cat/kitten, beef/cow/cattle, and lamb/sheep/mutton.

---

14 *MasterChef* (season two, episode 42) featured one dish described as 'vegetarian shepherd's pie' and *MKR* (season six, episode 40) a veggie burger, but the majority of meals were not simply veg*nised versions of conventional meat-based recipes.

4 In the media

Remarkably, the list of the most commonly searched-for animals is almost identical to the list of animals most commonly represented on television. Of the top eight searches for animals (which comprise the majority of all searches for animals), seven also appear in the equivalent list for television. Digging further into this data, we can see that the search context (the broader interest or motivation for the search, if it can be ascertained) often has similarities with how animals are displayed on popular television. For example, we can see that searches for dogs tend to focus on pet-related information, while searches for food animals tend to focus on recipes (a list of related search terms is provided in Appendix G). This confirms the idea, already established above, that animals are given chiefly instrumental and anthropocentric meanings in popular media.

Examination of the search data does reveal some differences with television content. The first is the comparatively high level of searches for horses, usually in the context of recreational activities (whether riding or racing). Horses are the fifth most popular animal in the search data, but only the 11th most commonly depicted animal on television. The second is the frequency of Google searches for 'wild' and 'pest' animals, which tend to be largely invisible on Australian television. Searches for sharks, for example, tend to spike in the context of recent attacks or sightings in populated areas. (The appearance of spiders in the data, meanwhile, seems to be an artefact, reflecting interest in the popular superhero rather than the animal.)

Animals and farmers 'in real life'

While the media is an important source of imagery and information about animals and animal production, Australia's highly urban population also encounter non-companion animals directly, through recreation and tourism (undertaking over 30 million day or overnight visits per annum; Moyle et al., 2015). Physical exposure to production animals, on the other hand, is most commonly seen in highly stylised urban contexts: in supermarkets, and in agricultural shows, by which the 'country comes to the town'.[15]

A stroll down the aisle

Of Australia's 14 million shoppers, 12 million visit a supermarket at least once per week (Langley and Hogan 2015), with the top two chains controlling 72.5 percent of market share (Roy Morgan Research 2014b). As Elliott (2012, 302) observes, supermarkets are where most food choices occur. Product packaging is therefore another important and pervasive source of information about animal products and production processes. Often, packaging uses symbolism to convey information or impressions about the product and its origins (Maher 2012, 502–3). Using a content analysis of the packaging seen on supermarket shelves,[16] we can identify the most common representations of animals and, importantly, of farming. Given the scarcity of depictions of farmers and farming in electronic media, the latter is particularly interesting.

Looking first at how animals[17] are represented on product packaging in supermarkets, Figure 4.5 shows some continuity with the anthropocentric selection of animals seen in television and in Google searches (that is, there is a focus on companion animals and food animals). But there are important differences. Pest animals (particularly insects and rodents) finally make a significant appearance, as do birds other than chickens (often playing a role as brand identifiers, or on bird-food packaging). Only two product categories regularly feature animals or farming-related images on their packaging: household traps and poisons, and pet food and pet accessories (Table 4.1). Interestingly, and in line with previous evidence about how Australians engage in cognitive avoidance of animals as we get closer to their consumption (Chapter 3), animals whom we intend to eat or kill (either as food or as pests) are more

---

15 For a broader and deeper discussion of animals in the contemporary human environment, see O'Sullivan (2011).
16 Drawing on Moskowitz et al.'s (2009, 54) characterisation of the content analysis of packaging, this is an explicitly external product analysis aimed at assessing the range of content as seen in situ, as opposed to a complete, detailed analysis of single product items.
17 In this study, as opposed to that of the analysis of television content, animal parts were excluded from classification, in order to look at the connection between animals as products and animal representations in the context where purchasing occurs.

4 In the media

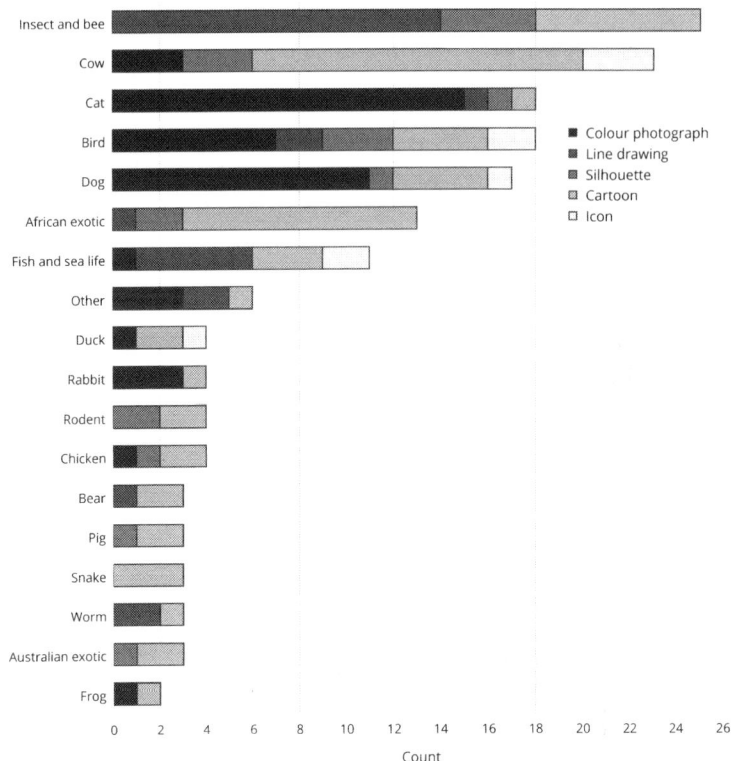

Figure 4.5. Representations of animals on Australian supermarket shelves. Compound categories use the same more common/least common convention.

likely to be depicted in abstract representational forms on product packaging than in a realistic manner. Thus, in Figure 4.5 we can see not only the type of animals represented on supermarket shelves, but their progression away from lifelike images, moving along a scale of abstraction from photographs (least abstract) to icons (most abstract).

Interestingly, animals are almost completely absent from the packaging of meat products, with the exception of fish. (Fish products for both human and animal consumption commonly feature illu-

Product category	Percentage including animals on packaging
Poison or household cleaner	21.5
Pet food or pet product	21.5
Dairy or eggs	12.8
Meat (fresh or canned)	9.2
Sweets and biscuits	9.2
Beverages (including tea and coffee)	4.6
Fruit and vegetables (packaged)	4.1
Body or beauty	3.5
Cooking oils	3.0
Cereals and breakfast foods	2.5
Misc. ingredients	2.5
Pre-packaged complete meals	2.0
Baby or infant products	1.5
Other	1.5

Table 4.1. Categories of supermarket products employing animal or farm imagery on their packaging.

strations or photographs of fish. As previously noted, fish purchased from fishmongers is one of the few meat products purchased whole and served in recognisable form.) Apart from fish, most meat sold in supermarkets has little in the way of imagery on its packaging, with producers electing for clear film instead. Only a very small subset of meat included images of any kind. The most common animal imagery on meat packaging were the animal silhouettes featured on RSPCA-approved meat products; the second most common were pastoral scenes. In the latter category, photographs of pasture were devoid of the animals contained in the product: they featured empty landscapes, referring only implicitly to the animal contained therein.

Turning to representations of farmers and farming on food packaging, Figure 4.6 provides a breakdown. We can see that representations of farms are dominated by pastoral scenes, with farms commonly signified by barns or old-fashioned windmills. These representations

4 In the media

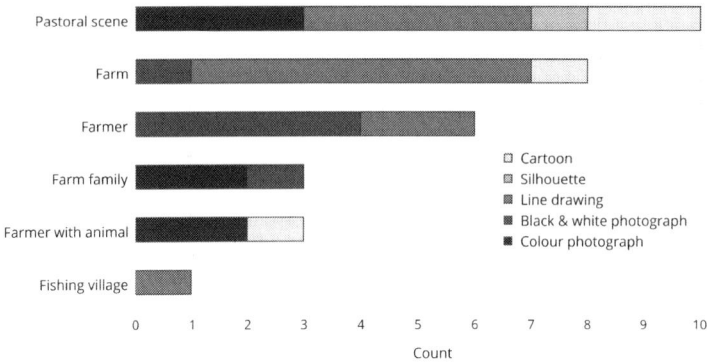

Figure 4.6. Representations of farmers and farming on Australian supermarket shelves.

are less stylised than the depictions of animals in Figure 4.5, and are more likely to be photographic. Yet most images of farms are still hardly lifelike: they tend to take the form of idealised or archaic portrayals, rather than realistic representations of modern production facilities. This carries over, to some extent, into images of farmers themselves: this is the only category where large numbers of black and white photographs are used. Farmers are depicted as individuals (predominantly men) or as part of 'farm families', avoiding the reality that farms in Australia today comprise large agribusiness enterprises as well as family owned and operated properties. Interestingly, farmers are rarely shown with farm animals. Overall, in the symbolic language of the Australian supermarket, farmers and farms are depicted as clean, largely free of animals, and somewhat quaint.

Farmers and farming on display

These abstract and unreal representations can have a spiralling effect, further reproducing accepted social norms and expectations (Noelle-Neumann 1984). For some involved in animal industry, this is part of a virtual 'fight to the death' over the ideological and cultural image of animal agriculture. The Hon. Robert Brown MLC, a member of the NSW upper house for the Shooters and Fishers Party, observed the 'cleansing' of agricultural shows:

> This is how bad it is. Must be probably about 20 years ago now, the Royal Agricultural Society decided because of community pressure that they would not any longer exhibit carcasses. You know how they used to hang carcasses and grade the carcasses... They don't do that anymore; you only see live animals. So, you march your bull around the ring, and the bull gets the [ribbon], but the meat industry no longer gets to hang carcasses and have [a] first-place carcass. (Interview: 18 March 2014)

For Brown, this continues a process whereby the expectations of an increasingly sheltered urban community encourage the further sanitation of representations of farming practices. Popular understanding of the realities of animal agriculture become increasingly distorted over time. Animal advocates, however, cite these agricultural shows as an example of the deliberate concealment of agricultural practices by the industry itself, which is aware that its practices are no longer popularly accepted (Ellis 2013, 361–2).

While the exact process that drives this self-representation by agricultural industries and individuals can be debated, it is certainly true that the urban agricultural shows have become far more sanitised than they were in the past. Taking the example of the 2015 Brisbane agricultural show ('the Ekka') it is clear that, while agricultural and other animal demonstrations (including pet shows) still occupy most of the physical space allocated to participants,[18] there has been a Disneyfication of representations of animal use at these events (Bryman 2004, 2). While some animal production practices are still on display, they are limited to 'harvesting' activities (such as shearing and milking). Food animals such as cattle and goats are displayed, but with little or no reference to meat production, while juveniles (including chicks,

---

18 Including the Community Arena (chiefly used for the display of large animals such as horses and cattle), the display and housing of animals occupied approximately 60 percent of the space in 2015.

calves and piglets) are provided for handling and patting (Images 2, 3). Throughout, there is a heightened emphasis on animals' cuteness, both in the imagery on display and in the ways participants are encouraged to interact with animals. At the 2015 show, education about animal slaughter was limited to a small display in the Beef Pavilion, including a 'Carcase to Cuts' diagram of the various meat cuts (Image 1). Discussions of animal welfare at agricultural shows tend to focus on the 'good husbandry is good welfare' model discussed in previous chapters. For example, at the same 2015 Brisbane show, the presenter of a milking display emphasised the need for dairy cattle to be free of stress in order to produce milk effectively. Another display in the Beef Pavilion provided brief information about the welfare and environmental aspects of cattle farming, apparently aimed at children.

This sanitised and hyper-real version of farming is also identified by O'Sullivan (2011) in her discussion of the Sydney Royal Easter Show. Importantly, linking back to the Habermasian ideal of spaces that provide opportunities for policy-related debate, her interpretation of the show space highlights the absence of the most contested animal-use practices from public display. From a democratic-idealist perspective, this undermines dialogue about those practices: it removes an opportunity for defenders of the status quo to argue for its necessity, or for opponents of contemporary farm practice to challenge them.

Counter-narratives

So far we have examined popular and mainstream representations of animals, farming and abstention. These depictions provide the cultural context in which policy-making generally occurs. Just as political activism challenges legal norms, however, this mainstream vocabulary of animal use does not go unchallenged by abstainers. Abstainers who are motivated by ethical reasons do not seek only to reduce the quantity of animals used and consumed by humans; they also present a challenge to the cultural and linguistic status quo. Where the general public have an anthropocentric and egocentric attitude to animals, through the *propagande par le fait* (the 'propaganda of the deed'), this group demonstrates a willingness and capacity to live as non-conformists.

Members of the veg*n community are not just a notable sub-public; some can also be said to form a 'counter-public'.

The term 'counter-public' was first proposed by Fraser (1990), with particular emphasis on repressed or oppressed groups within the body politic. These groups differ from other sub-publics in the way they threaten and/or challenge dominant cultural and political norms. Counter-publics form and sustain their own distinctive discursive communities, developing group awareness and affinity, and producing and distributing discourses about themselves and their relationship with the wider community and its norms. By naming the unnamed and presenting alternative social and political theories, they can present a competing view of reality and so undermine dominant norms. In presenting alternatives to the everyday social order, counter-publics can develop and propagate what Warner (2010, 119) calls a 'special idiom for social reality': a language for social critique and for the reformulation of social power relations.

This can be overstated, of course. There are often debates within these communities as to the extent that membership entails a moral imperative to proselytise and to uphold the political values of the wider group (often expressed as the notion of 'being a good veg*n'; interview: individuals associated with the Sydney veg*n community, 8 May 2014), and the extent to which members actively promote their alternative viewpoint varies within and between groups. From an ethnographic study of Australian freegans, for example, Edwards and Mercer (2013, 184) found that this subset of the veg*n community tends not to promote their waste-minimisation practices in the same way as their US counterparts do. They might practise the same dietary lifestyle, but reflect different local political characteristics. Australian vegetarians and vegans, on the other hand, have a long history of actively proselytising, in both the first (19th century) and second (1970s onwards) waves of these movements (the Anti-Vivisection Union of Australia was actively engaged in the promotion of ethical veganism as early as 1978; AVUA 1978, 5). Such dietary alternatives have a longer history in Australia than is often recognised.

4 In the media

Alternatives to the mainstream

This production of counter-hegemonic messages takes a variety of forms, including criticism of conventional practices and the promotion of alternative representations of them (for example, using the term 'factory farms' rather than 'agribusiness', or the phrase 'happy meat' to mock claims of improved animal welfare standards by meat producers). To some extent, these groups are increasingly adopting a transnational identity and language. However, while they do often promote internationally sourced content, the Australian veg*n counter-public also has a long history of producing its own material. This includes:

- information about community events, products and services
- educational or outreach material, encouraging the adoption of, and adherence to, veg*n diets (including recipes, dietary and health advice)
- information about the veg*n community itself (as seen in the market research commissioned by the Vegetarian/Vegan Society of Queensland, research employed extensively in Chapter 3)
- adaptations of international material for local purposes; and
- uniquely Australian content about local issues and concerns.

This variety of material speaks to an increasingly wide range of audiences. One interesting recent example is Marston's (2014) *Leo escapes from the lab*, an illustrated children's book that describes the experience of a cat used for invasive scientific research, his eventual adoption, his ongoing post-traumatic fears, and his hope for a world without animal experimentation. Produced by an anti-experimentation advocacy organisation, this volume is interesting for its willingness to directly engage with children. The publication of popular political fiction by activists has strong parallels with the first era of vegetarianism in Australia, such as Hudson's 1914 novella *The red road: a story by a roan bullock on the wrongs suffered by animals at the hand of man*.

While established veg*n organisations still actively sell domestically produced books that are unlikely to be stocked by commercial bookstores (although cookbooks may have the potential to cross over into the popular marketplace), the internet has seen a significant shift towards online communication and a fall in demand for print publications (interview: M. Collier, 17 April 2013). Thus, for example, while the VVSQ still maintains a DVD-lending library, newer organisations have tended to focus on the online space. Vegetarian Victoria (vegvic.org.au) is an early example of an organisation with an extensive online presence, distributing dietary and shopping information on its website since its formation in 1998. The site today includes social media and extensive curated video content ('VegTube'). The more recently established Vegan Australia (veganaustralia.org.au, founded in 2012) has similarly focused on a web-only communication strategy, providing a national list of events in addition to its advocacy work (interview: Greg McFarlane, Chair, Vegan Australia/Vegan Society of NSW, 17 May 2013). Each organisation combines outreach and service activities.

Some parts of the veg*n community retain their 'outsider' status through the active use of alternative and subversive media. *Freedom of species*, an animal advocacy radio program and podcast, is produced in Melbourne at the community radio station 3CR (www.freedomofspecies.org); it combines activist discussion and academic interviews. Another animal studies podcast, *Knowing animals*, is produced by Dr Siobhan O'Sullivan of the University of New South Wales (knowinganimals.libsyn.com). Veg*n graffiti, meanwhile, puts the message directly in front of the wider community and is used both to promote veg*n dietary practices or to publicise related media. That this type of guerrilla marketing challenges social norms is evidenced by the frequent presence of counter-messaging on these graffiti (in Image 7 and 8, 'Fuck up' and 'Stop forcing your opinion on everyone else you vegan fuck wits!').

Bonding and sustaining

'Vegan fuck wits' may thus not feel as accepted by the broader community as the evidence presented in Chapter 3 might suggest (Table 3.18). This can also be seen in the discursive practices commonly employed by and within the veg*n community, which can be both inclusive and defensive. This demonstrates the other important aspect of Fraser's notion of counter-publics. In addition to challenging social norms, they can serve as 'spaces of withdrawal and regroupment' where the community can develop its capacity to resist rhetorical assault from the mainstream. An Australian example of this is Waddell's (2004) book *But* *you kill ants: answers to 100 objections to vegetarianism and veganism*. A not-for-profit publication, the book provides a set of clear, canned responses to common concerns and objections that veg*ns may encounter. Similar combinations of the informative and the defensive are common in outreach and educational literature. These publications tend to synthesise a wide range of materials, from medical information (such as questions about protein and calcium deficiency) to summations of animal rights philosophy. This reflects Louw's (2010, 131–5) argument that successful popularisation of alternative worldviews involves a 'two-tiered intelligentsia system': an interaction between a scholarly or intellectual group that generates the theoretical elements of the worldview, and popular communicators who translate these conceptual arguments for a wider audience. Vegan Australia, for example, clearly identifies its mission as one of popularisation: it aims to be a 'focused, media-aware organisation dedicated to getting the vegan message out there for the sake of animals, people and our planet' (Vegan Australia n.d.). Individuals such as the Fairfax columnist Sam de Brito (2014), who was a vegan, may use their public profiles to talk about their own dietary choices and about animal welfare issues. Given the conventional associations between meat eating and manhood discussed above, de Brito is particularly interesting, as he was also strongly associated with writing about – and personifying – contemporary Australian masculinity.[19]

Communities based on alternative diets are not united only by defensiveness. The service work of veg*n organisations also creates social cohesion. Veg*n community organisations run social events (frequently meals, which account for 32 percent of national events in a given year), activist events (including talks, outreach activities, political activism and organisational meetings; 31 percent), and instructional activities (such as cooking classes and expos or fairs; 31 percent). Some of these activities are aimed at internal 'bonding' within the community; others focus on 'bridging': building links to the wider community. To use the language of social capital, such social networks generate trust and reciprocity (Field 2003, 5). As Bandura (1997) has observed, communal investment in building internal social capital and cohesion can improve the group's ability to take effective collective action.

---

19   de Brito (1969–2015) died during the writing of this volume.

Conclusion

In this chapter we have examined representations of animals, farming and non-mainstream diets in the Australian mainstream media. This provides the cultural context in which policy-making occurs; it reflects the social norms of a society that is dominated by people who routinely consume and use animals. In reviewing media representations of animals, farming and alternative dietary choices, we can see the origins of popular attitudes towards animals discussed in Chapter 3. While the media landscape has expanded in recent years, it is still strikingly narrow where depictions of animals are concerned. The media act as a kind of feedback loop: animals of interest to humans as prey or as pets dominate the media landscape, but they do so largely as shades: they appear as fleeting background images, or as stylised representations of the real. Farms and farmers fare little better; caught in a permanent nostalgia, they appear in black and white or in theme-park-like fantasies. Such depictions reinforce the moral status quo, but can only do so thanks to popular ignorance about the realities of animal use and farm life. In the media's distorted mirror of the world, consumers see what they want to see. When challenges to this sanitised view pop that bubble, the public may be shocked and angry – but without a strong base of knowledge, this anger tends to remain unfocused and can be quickly sated.

For policy-makers, this presents a complex challenge: if public interest is shallow and can easily be driven by media campaigns, animal protection issues run the risk of breaking out like bushfires. Public outrage is unpredictable, fast moving, but also quickly extinguished. With low levels of consistent community concern, political elites may feel they lack a popular mandate to address even widely known welfare problems in the face of organisational interests who may be resistant to change, or who may themselves lack the capacity to control their own stakeholders. This suggests a policy domain, therefore, that is not structured around the interests and concerns of policy-makers to ensure orderly policy development. This may result from a failure to engage in the work of agenda building, or from the fact that policy-makers are seldom the central actors in the policy domain. In Chapter 5, therefore, we will map out the animal protection policy domain in Australia.

5
Mapping the policy domain

Keeping with this section's focus on a broad view of animal protection politics, this chapter presents an overview of the policy domain in which animal welfare issues are discussed and addressed. The policy domain is a 'meso-level' unit of analysis: it exists above the micro-level of individual actors (which I will consider in Part 3), but below the macro-level of national and societal institutions, which we have examined in the preceding two chapters. An analysis of such meso-levels can help us to understand the complex patterns of interactions between individuals and organisations.

By focusing on the interactions between political actors involved in making and implementing policy, we can begin to map the policy-making space. This map can then be used to examine the enduring pattern of recurrent relationships between actors involved in policy debates and policy development. To do so, in this chapter I will draw on the concept of resource exchange, and on the dependence model of policy networks. We will see that in the field of animal welfare, the policy network is structured around a small network of animal protection and welfare organisations. It can be described as a loosely coupled system of governance, in which power is distributed widely and originates from sources other than traditional state authority. This has implications for how policy is made, as well as for power relations within the policy domain.

The domain orientation

A policy domain is defined as 'a component of the political system that is organized around substantive issues' (Burstein 1991, 328). That is, the main focus of analysis is not on institutions or structures (such as federalism or the parliamentary system), but on how a shared interest in a particular policy area binds actors together, irrespective of where they sit in the structural map. Policy networks are notoriously hard to define, but for the purposes of this book I will use Knoke's notion of a network of 'public and private actors linked by communication ties for *exchanging* information, expertise, trust and other political resources' (italics added) (Knoke 2011, 211). The point about exchange is a critical one, and we will expand its application in the next chapters. In complex policy areas, policy-making is no longer the preserve of unitary actors with complete authority. Through design, luck or activism, policy development and implementation are now disaggregated across a range of participants, each with their own scope of influence, expertise and capacity to act. Policy-making via networks, therefore, conceives of the policy process as a negotiated series of exchanges.

Focusing on the policy domain and the networks within it involves looking at regular and comprehensible patterns of substantive policy-making. This follows a post-war political science tradition of disaggregating polities into more manageable, functional, intermediate-level units for analysis and comparison (Jordan and Maloney 1997). Browne (1999) points out that this approach has the advantage of emphasising relationships and the interconnected nature of policy formation in complex polities, without sacrificing depth. This approach also recognises the importance of thinking about a broader range of non-state actors. Such actors are increasingly engaged in policy development and/or administration. While there is a tendency to assume that this is a recent phenomenon (the participation of non-state actors in the policy domain is often associated with the 1980s and the era of New Public Management; Wallis and Gregory 2009, 257), the history of animal welfare policy in fact shows that the involvement of non-state actors in the policy landscape was pioneered in this field much earlier, with societies for the protection of animals and animal welfare leagues playing a significant role ever since Richard Martin's private prosecution of offenders under the *Cruel Treatment of Cattle Act* of 1822.

The animal welfare and protection domain

Animal welfare and protection debates, even in a small polity like Australia, are expansive and attract large numbers of participants. While an exact estimate is difficult – if not impossible – to determine, the plurality of stakeholders is clear. As we will see in Part 3, as many as several hundred organised interests may in theory be active in the policy space at any given time, thanks in part to the dramatic proliferation of animal welfare and abolitionist organisations in Australia since 1980 (between 200 and 300 organisations) and to a similarly high number of relevant industry organisations. Animals valued for their status as human companions are 'represented' by a raft of generalist and breed-specific organisations and appreciation societies (this 'representation' may be direct, as in organisations directly concerned with the animals' welfare, or indirect, in organisations that represent the interests of the animals' owners). Similarly, animals employed industrially and for recreational pursuits are represented by both specialist and generalist organisations, as are the human actors involved in every stage of these activities.

In the high number of participants, the animal protection domain is similar to agriculture more generally. Different farming systems and environments are represented by both specialist and generalist organisations (Moore and Rockloff 2006). In addition, the historical emphasis on agriculture's role in Australia's economic development means that state governments have retained considerable control over policy development in this area, despite the prevailing tendency towards centralisation post-federation: in many cases, this multiplies the number of active organisations nine-fold, with separate organisations for each of the six states and two major self-governing territories, as well as national and peak bodies. Given this array of actors, understanding the policy network is essential if one is to make sense of the processes and relationships in the policy domain.

In this world of network and exchange, it is generally considered that highly dense relationships in a policy network indicate efficient policy subsystems and the efficient exchange of resources, whether by consensus or necessity. Networks with dense ties can also be attributed to high levels of trust, and/or to the work of policy entrepreneurs – actors who resolve collective-action problems by identifying opportunities and mobilising resources (Mintrom and Vergari 1996) in order to build relationships (Henry et al. 2011, 422). Where a network contains subclusters, particular actors may act as gatekeepers, chokepoints or bridges between the various sub-nets.

In Image 16 – a simplified map of the policy domain – we can see that the graph is quite attenuated in places, with clusters focused on specific industry segments, animal types or political groupings. A graph of the complete network,[1] including all actors captured in the data collection ($n = 396$), shows that this extends to the whole network, which has a high 'modularity'(0.661): it is comprised largely of subgroups with high levels of inward links, but limited linkages between clusters (what we will later discuss as 'siloisation'). The overall diameter of the network is 14 (wide), with an average path length between any two actors in the network of 4.58 (the 'degrees of separation'). This indicates that the flow of information across the network is likely to be comparatively slow. That the network does not reflect the 'small world' phenomenon is evident in its extremely low density of ties (0.008) and low average network clustering co-efficient (0.236; low transitivity).

Factors structuring the domain

The forces behind this structure are threefold. First, some clustering within the policy network is associated with the federal nature of animal welfare policy. This is axiomatic: compared with their national counterparts, state and territory ministers for agriculture and related areas have more frequent and significant relationships with bureaucrats, local animal welfare service providers, non-government enforcement bodies, members of parliament, and internal party interest groups. Farm and

---

[1] A simplified network is shown in Image 15; the complete network is available online at hdl.handle.net/2123/15349.

5 Mapping the policy domain

animal industry bodies tend towards clear delineation of engagement along federal lines, having evolved to reflect Australia's federal distribution of powers and responsibilities. That these structures continue today reflects the significance of departments of agriculture in the production of animal protection policy at the state level, but also the influence of history and path dependency, which stabilise institutions over time (Pierson 2000).

Similarly, even though some animal protection organisations have adopted a federal structure, they still demonstrate a tendency to clearly delineate spheres of operation between local branches (interview: executive officer of an animal welfare organisation, 9 October 2014). This is also evident in the noticeable absence of major clustering around the Commonwealth government. This is due largely to constitutional constrains and to the Commonwealth government's comparatively small area of responsibility in regards to animal welfare (which is largely limited to co-ordinating the production of national standards, and to narrowly focused areas of policy such as the regulation of live exports). Additionally, following the abolition of the Commonwealth-funded Australian Animal Welfare Strategy Advisory Committee in 2013 (as part of a general policy of abolishing Commonwealth boards and committees following the change in government in late 2013; Vidot 2013a), another cross-jurisdictional and cross-cluster bridge was dismantled (interview: D. Kelly, 25 August 2014).

Second, some clusters are associated with specific industry segments or animal protectionist groupings. While state-based activist and welfare organisations tend to engage with other network actors at the state level, the relatively low level of access of many of these organisations (some of which are quite small) to government actors means their strongest ties are often within the animal protection community itself. Even some notionally national organisations, if their resources are limited, may exhibit mainly local relationships purely due to proximity and limited capacity (interview: S. Watson, 25 June 2014). By the same token, smaller activist groups do not always restrict their activities to their state jurisdictions (interviews: L. Drew, 23 July 2013; D. Tranter, 22 September 2014), but may respond to tactical opportunities and seek out new arenas for action. This points to the tactical flexibility (Larson 2013) of some activist organisations.

Centrally placed bridging organisations such as Animals Australia (originally formed as a peak body) and Voiceless tend, therefore, to act as information hubs between smaller groups, as gateways and gatekeepers between them, and as decision-makers in interactions with industry and government.

Third, the network incorporates and expands upon pre-existing market and supply-chain relationships. The increasing uptake and adherence to non-government standards and quality assurance systems by producers, processors and transporters means that the policy network often mirrors the power structures of industrial supply chains. Rahbek Pedersen (2009, 111) has observed that consumer expectations about corporate social responsibility standards can produce a blurring of the boundaries between organisations within the same supply chain. Policies about sourcing, for example, can become quite prescriptive. The implications of these policies often extend upstream to ensure the availability of products perceived to be ethically produced.

Where this leads to premium pricing, it can produce principal–agent problems, if purchasers are not aware whether or not suppliers are meeting their contractual obligations, particularly for 'intangibles' such as ethical production; this can necessitate action to ensure that standards are met or risks managed. Where principals have power, this can entail intrusive and directive intervention in upstream providers' production practices (Wiese and Toporowski 2013): a form of non-state industrial regulation. This is clear in animal industry, where retailers actively monitor standards for ethically produced products using quality-assurance systems (interviews: a representative of the chicken industry, 31 January 2014; a representative of the grocery industry, 9 April 2014; a representative of the retail industry, 22 April 2014).

In summary, the policy network for animal welfare and protection appears complex, comprised of very diverse actors whose relationships are structured by a variety of pre-existing legal, economic and political opportunity structures that shape the strategic and tactical choices of political actors through the provision of access and/or resources. Compared with other comparatively cohesive closed 'policy communities' that are dominated by small numbers of 'insider' groups, such as those seen in defence policy (Grant 2001, 337), the animal protection domain can be described as an 'issue network', in which barriers to entry are

5 Mapping the policy domain

limited and participation is highly pluralistic. This is in line with findings regarding changes in food-policy networks in the United Kingdom, where food standards were 're-politicised' following successive salmonella and bovine spongiform encephalopathy ('mad cow') crises (Smith 1991).[1] However, despite the consensus-breaking impact of these events on the national policy domain (in opening the network to new entrants after the demonstrated failure of previous policies), the animal protection domain as a whole is a network with a contested centre. In Australia, the key network participants tend to be major animal protectionist advocacy organisations (such as Animals Australia and Voiceless), long-standing animal welfare NGOs (such as the various RSPCAs and Animal Welfare Leagues), and key industry groups. Therefore, rather than network structures reflecting tradition or continuity, the emphasis away from state regulation in Australia means that entrepreneurialism dominates over hierarchical power, leading the network to be more dynamic and changeable than other areas of policy-making.

This non-state centrism is different from the type of policy networks discussed by Rhodes (1996) in his formative work on the exchange model of network governance. While his model of quasi-autonomous networks recognised the growing role of non-government actors in the development of a policy context in which the state's role consists of 'steering not rowing', in this type of network 'insiders' are those with resources such as money, expertise and implementation capacity. In policy subsystems such as the animal protection domain, however, groups conventionally seen as political 'outsiders' are able to become brokers of interest. This is not a general or theoretical criticism of Rhodes' model (and in fact, Rhodes [2007] has observed that network scholars tend to over-emphasise the role of state institutions in structuring networks), but rather appears to be case-specific. In this case, the lack of a single authoritative actor has given service providers and activists greater significance, making this policy network quite atypical.

---

1 Australian animal protectionists have, at times, attempted to systematically monitor for health risks in industries that have been the focus of their campaigns, such as salmonella testing in eggs (correspondence: J. Roberts, Animal Liberation Victoria, 13 November 1995).

Understanding the relationships

Given the complexity of the animal policy domain, the number of actors involved and the many distinct clusters of participants, relationships within it cannot be characterised in a single way, but consist of an array of connections, both stable and transient. To understand the network, it is necessary to examine the types of relationships that exist both between and within important clusters. These exchanges provide insight into where the centres of power (or dominant actors) lie, what the sources of this power are, and why the network tends to exhibit stability over time.

Exchange relationships, power and stability

The concept of the policy network implies that network actors come together to exchange resources with the objective of achieving long-term policy goals. This reflects the complexity of the contemporary policy environment: solitary actors are unable to achieve policy objectives alone, but are mutually dependent on one another. While some exchange relationships may be temporary or one-off, enduring relationships are significant in the long-term process of policy development and implementation. This underlines the observation that policy change can only be meaningfully understood over a longer time period (Sabatier 1997, 278), as the implementation process (including innovation and refinement) means policy is realised on the ground. This longer view also allows for an agenda-setting process that includes strategic action as well as simple proximate causes (as illustrated in the long 'prehistory' of live-export activism, dating back to the 1970s and 1980s).

Organisations engaged in enduring relationships tend to be those that are captured by the issue (often involuntarily, by regulation), have a commitment to it, and have resources that they are willing to trade (as opposed to possessing a monopoly on resources, which could encourage others to develop alternatives). Table 5.1 lists a range of resources generally accepted by policy scholars, along with the type of actors most likely to possess them.

5 Mapping the policy domain

Controlled by	Resource
Public actors alone	- Policy amendments - Formal instruments - Power to grant access to policy-making fora - Power to construct for and to compel participation - Bureaucratic action and implementation - Electoral legitimacy
Public and private actors	- Veto power over decisions - Information - Co-operation with implementation - Recourse to the courts - Money and/or capacity (i.e. human resources) - Political support through public opinion (legitimacy) - Patronage by elites
Private actors alone	- Private invest-/divestment - Fluid funds

Table 5.1. Main tradeable resources of members of the policy network. Adapted from Compston (2009).

Resources are exchanged in a range of ways to produce stability. These include:

- Memoranda of understanding: Animal welfare inspection and prosecution activities undertaken by NGOs are commonly governed by formal agreements with government departments, law-enforcement agencies and public prosecutors. These documents serve both to delineate spheres of activity, and to establish processes of investigation and prosecution (for example, in states where commercial animals are not subject to RSPCA inspections, memoranda of understanding set out the process for complaints) (interviews: M. Beatty, 16 April 2013; M. Mercurio, 4 June 2013).
- Fee-for-service: Welfare training for commercial and research organisations working with industrial animals is undertaken on a cost-recovery basis by animal welfare agencies (interview: director of a bureau of animal welfare, 21 August 2013). Where organisations are formally or legally required to use qualified staff (for example in animal research), these costs are compulsory.

- Formalised information exchange: A range of standing policy committees, such as ministerial advisory groups and policy advisory committees for animal welfare, serve as 'institutionalised venues' for information exchange (Leifeld and Schneider 2012). These lower the cost of information exchange and bring together a wider range of participants than would otherwise occur (see the discussion of homophily below). The capacity to form and abolish these venues is a power of political elites.
- Standards-making bodies: Standards regimes involving NGO 'branding' (such as RSPCA-approved meats and eggs) also involve ongoing interaction. Fee-for-service quality assurance and brand licensing provide financial resources to the NGO involved, while necessitating the exchange of information with producers (interview: M. Mercurio, 4 June 2013). This occurs primarily at the level of peak bodies (interview: a representative of the chicken industry, 31 January 2014), but also on the 'shop floor' when inspectors interact with producers and their staff.
- Homophilic ties: The animal policy network demonstrates Leifeld and Schneider's (2012) finding that shared preferences encourage information exchange. Groups seen to be 'shooting in the same direction' are more likely to exchange information, both technical and strategic. While this produces mutual exchange, there does appear to be a tendency for information to flow towards those actors perceived as more influential, both in general (interview: C. Neal, 16 April 2013) and in order specifically to provide a 'heads up' about opportunities to organisations seen as having the greatest capacity to act (interview: an animal welfare advocate, 5 September 2014). Other exchanges take the form of capacity aggregation: that is, where activists participate in one another's campaigns based on proximity and shared interests (interviews: L. Levy, 30 August 2013; D. Tranter, 22 September 2014). In some cases, staff move between organisations working in the same sector (interview: M. Beatty, 16 April 2013).

In addition to these ongoing, stabilising ties, some relationships are impermanent. A good example of this is seen in project funding in the activist community. One emerging type of exchange has been the provision of specific project funding by generalist organisations, such as Voiceless (interview: D. Campbell, 30 January 2014), to specialist activist organisations, commonly to develop informational campaigns. By offering such grants, the larger organisation can diversify its reach without needing to increase its internal capacity. Additionally, these exchanges secure greater authority for Voiceless, both through the distribution of resources to smaller organisations and through the formal application and reporting process, which 'disciplines' the smaller organisations (which must meet minimum organisational criteria and must structure their programs according to the strategic objectives of the funding organisation). In the process, the funding organisation becomes a network hub, through which more information flows (interview: D. Tranter, 22 September 2014).

Power in supply chains

The role of commercial interests is unremarkable in the study of interest-group-based politics. These organisations demonstrate both the attractive and repulsive tendency noted in homophilic clusters above: they are drawn together by common interests, but may be driven apart by commercial competition. Attraction stems from shared interests in the wider agricultural policy space (for example, a desire to attract government support for industry, for the consideration of agriculture in free-trade negotiations, and to minimise regulatory requirements), cultural affiliation among primary producers, and cohesion in the face of opposition from other social movements (Polletta and Jasper 2001, 297; interview: general manager [policy], National Farmers' Federation, 14 November 2014). Repulsion stems from internal market rivalries, as well as dissent from individual producers, who may be resistant to the voluntary adoption of industry standards (interview: R. Cox, 2 October 2013).

In the animal policy domain, power relationships inscribed in supply chains are also a significant variable in explaining the relative position and influence of different actors. The best illustration of the significance of these power structures is the way activists have focused on real and perceived supply bottlenecks, treating them as what social scientists call political opportunity structures – potential opportunities for political success – and adjusting their tactics in response to these opportunities over time (Goldner 2001, 71–2). Major restaurant chains (such as KFC and McDonald's) and retailers (such as Coles and Woolworths) have been subject to activist pressure to alter their purchasing policies, with the expectation that their marketplace power will achieve the policy outcomes that have proven extremely difficult to secure through legislative strategies (interview: M. Pearson, 5 June 2013). The tendency towards consolidation in some agricultural supply chains gives certain actors considerable power in dealing with their upstream suppliers (interview: J. Toohey, 4 July 2014). A good example is the highly concentrated egg industry in Australia, which is dominated by a small number of very large processors. While these producers have maintained their capacity to resist the adoption of higher welfare standards, pressure from retailers has had a greater impact than that from legislators in seeing the adoption of higher standards.[2] Legislation, in this case, has tended to follow the adoption of industry or NGO standards, reifying these new norms.

The use of supply-chain power to shape welfare outcomes can be seen in an array of voluntary standards adopted for eggs, chicken meat, pig meat and – temporarily at least – sheep mulesing. However, the significance of this supply-chain power tends to be limited to industries that display a combination of characteristics:

- Their products are undifferentiated in nature – that is, there is little discernible difference between the products of different brands or producers, either because:
  - the product is seen by consumers as a 'natural' commodity
  - there are few niche markets for the product
  - there is low consumer understanding of the product, or
  - the product has been 're-branded' under a generic label in some way (for example, Australian wool).
- Alternative downstream buyers for the product are few, either because:
  - the supply chain displays increasing concentration closer to the end consumer

---

2   In addition, it appears that small producers have used welfare as a means of competing against the dominant producers. An example of this would be early adoption of online cameras by smaller operators (see, for example: http://manningvalleyeggs.com.au/free-range-cam/).

- the product undergoes reprocessing or finishing involving expensive equipment, and/or
- the capacity to switch to alternative purchasers is limited by a reduced ability to export, or by long-term binding contracts.
* Internal industry processes are standardised.
* Geographical factors are not significant (that is, production practices do not change dramatically across Australia).

If egg production demonstrates what happens when the factors above are present, beef production in Australia shows what happens when they are not. The product is highly differentiated, with large numbers of primary producers and processors and a more competitive retail sector that includes both large retailers and small independent butchers (interview: I. Randles, 30 September 2013). Production systems differ across the industry (for example, between feed-lot and pasture farms), and vary geographically in both type and scale, owing to Australia's diverse ecologies. Beef is exported in a variety of forms (live, processed simply and processed complexly) to a wide range of regional and international markets, many of which are seen as growth areas (interview: J. Toohey, 4 July 2014). The presence or absence of these factors allows us to predict the extent to which supply-chain factors will or will not be significant in the propagation of welfare standards.

Change in the network

Given the overall low transitivity of the policy domain – that is, the relative slowness and inefficiency of exchanges across the network – relationships within clusters are considerably more coherent than relationships between them, and it can be relatively easy for new actors to enter this loose network. The establishment of Voiceless in 2004, for example, demonstrates the openness of the network to new organisations that position themselves as cluster cores and bridges. While Voiceless is an advocacy organisation, its focus on animal law recognised a specific area of advocacy where Australian organisations were comparatively under-represented and ill-equipped. In a tight policy community this would only have been achievable through the expenditure of considerable resources – that is, the new organisation would have had to force its way into the network – or through an external reconfiguration of the operational environmental. The relative openness of the animal welfare domain, however, meant that a new organisation willing to expend some resources could join the network relatively easily. This openness appears to be more common within the activist community, which is in line with the observations of Stern (1999), who has argued that political interest groups and social movement organisations can be seen to engage in a form of 'competition' to successfully create and occupy ecosystem niches due to the often intangible nature of their concerns when compared with producer groups.

Additionally, the diverse ideological mix of the various activist groups is idiosyncratic, and does not represent a neat spectrum. Among the loosely affiliated Animal Liberation organisations, abolitionism has been taken up by those in Victoria, the ACT and Queensland, but not by the NSW organisation, the largest group. Although it is the largest single Australian jurisdiction, NSW lacks a significant abolitionist organisation. This points to a determining driver of organisational choice. An abolitionist organisation in NSW *would* be an attractive niche if ideological differentiation was a significant factor to (actual or potential) organisational publics (both members and other stakeholders). The emergence of an abolitionist public in NSW would serve to motivate the formation of an activist organisation in that area, as this public would provide resources for that organisation. This highlights the usefulness of applying resources competition more generally to understand intra-cluster competition over time.

The emergence of new commercial interests, by contrast, tends to be associated with the generation of new markets. While Stern focuses on membership numbers and policy victories as measures of success (following the resource-mobilisation tradition of social-movement research from which her work stems), a focus on resource exchange highlights the importance of considering a wider range of resources that may be subject to intra-group competition. This may be particularly important where policy victories are unlikely, but alternative markers of success may be used to measure the health of the policy network. My interviews with members of animal protection organisations reveal that they sometimes have difficulty determining how effectively to measure their own performance. Internally, protection organisations tend to measure success in strategic and tactical victories in policy change (interview: L. Drew, 23 July 2013; M. Pearson, 5 June 2013), which may in turn liberate other politically useful resources (access, information, prestige, etc.).

Two other potential sources of change or instability in the policy network are worth noting. The first comes from within the network itself. By altering consumer preferences, activists can reshape the commercial operating environment. This can lead to the emergence of new market segments and the creation of new industry bodies. The second cause of change is external. The use of non-government processes and bodies to set and enforce welfare standards reflects a more general tendency in public policy towards market-based instruments, and an environment subject to more rapid change as policy can be developed and implemented incrementally through the conversion of private organisations' internal policy on a piecemeal basis (interview: H. Marston, 23 September 2013). This facilitates change within the network, as the existence of competing voluntary standards systems permits producers to switch relatively easily and cheaply between regulatory regimes. This competition also means, however, that the exchange relationships involved in non-governmental standards regimes are fragile: in order to limit defection, NGOs may have to provide concessions, at the same time as pushing for welfare improvements in order to ensure their reputation.

Conclusion

In identifying the animal-welfare policy domain as one of network governance, we can understand why policy-making in this area tends to be disaggregated. This has implications for how policy is made, both in terms of the diversity of policy instruments employed as well as the actual policy settings. The loose nature of the domain does mitigate against a consistent and cohesive national policy. In this way, the policy domain reflects the incoherence of popular opinion established in Chapter 3. This could be interpreted as a causal claim – that policy-making is indexed against popular opinion in the Habermasian sense – but it is not. Given the role of industrial and activist organisations in shaping public opinion (established in the previous chapter), the chaotic nature of the domain could just as easily be seen to drive the confusion in popular opinion through the generation of competing messages regarding human–animal relations.

In the next part of the book, we turn from the meso to the micro level, looking at specific political actors and the strategies and tactics they employ to achieve their policy objectives, before examining more closely the role of state policy elites.

When the country comes to town

Agricultural shows have traditionally brought farming life to the city, but how realistic is the image they present? Here, the 2015 Brisbane Agricultural Show (aka the Ekka) educates consumers about cuts of meat, and gives city-dwellers a chance to 'pat a pig' and meet a goat in its idyllic 'mountain' setting.

Image 1. Cuts of meat at the Ekka. Photogaph by the author.

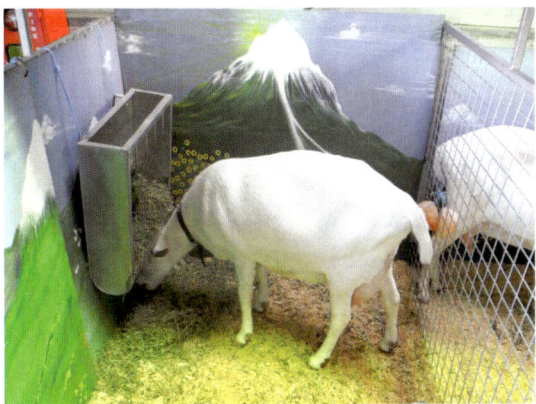

Image 2. Goats in a 'mountain' habitat at the Ekka. Photograph by the author.

Image 3. 'Pat-a-Pig' at the Ekka. Photograph by the author.

Advertising: from 'Feed the man meat' to 'The flavour of freedom'

Advertisers continue to link meat-eating with masculinity and Australian identity, although they also increasingly target women ('1 in 3 women doesn't get enough iron. Don't be one of them'). Meanwhile, advertisements for animal products such as free-range chicken claim that 'happier' animals produce tastier meals (a marketing strategy mocked as 'happy meat' by some animal-welfare activists).

Image 4. 'You're better on beef' Australian advertising campaign. Photograph by the author.

Image 5. 'The flavour of freedom' is a selling-point for a Sydney pizza chain. Photograph by the author.

Messaging and counter-messaging: Australian veg*n graffiti

Image 6. Sticker on a Sydney street sign. Photograph by the author.

Image 7. Veg*n stencil in Melbourne. Photograph by the author.

Image 8. Vegan poster in Canberra. The addition in pen reads: 'Stop forcing your opinion on everyone else you vegan Fuck wits!' Photograph by the author.

Image 9. Polite graffiti in Sydney. Photograph by the author.

Animal protection and Australian political parties

Both left and right have included animal welfare issues in their platforms in recent years.

Image 10. ALP campaign material from the 2013 federal election.

Image 11. Greens NSW stall at the 2015 Cruelty-free Festival in Sydney. Photograph by the author.

Image 12. Far-right Party of Freedom protestors picket the Sydney Halal Expo in 2016. Richard Milnes / Alamy Stock Photo.

Taking to the streets

Animal protection activism in Australia has been described as 'grassfire' activism: constantly burning but springing up in new locations unpredictably. More widespread public outrage can break out quickly and unexpectedly – but is also quickly extinguished. Media coverage of live-export practices in 2011 prompted such outbreaks on both sides of the debate.

Image 13. Vegan protesters in Sydney. Photograph by the author.

Image 14. Pro-live-export protestor, Western Australia, 2013. Central Station (centralstation.net.au).

Image 15. Anti-live-export rally in Sydney, 2015. Photograph by the author.

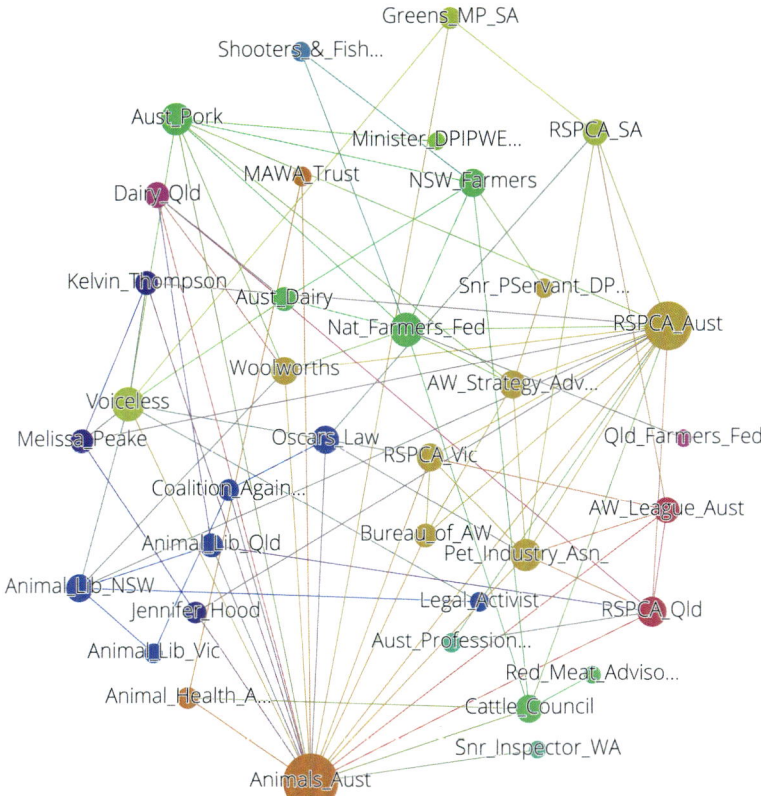

Image 16. A simplified map of the policy network. The higher the number of connections, the larger the node. The different colours represent distinctive clusters or communities within the policy domain. The complete network may be viewed at hdl.handle.net/2123/15349.

Part 3

6
Animal protectionism

As discussed in Chapter 5, policy actors in the animal welfare domain tend to be clustered into three broad types: political activists and welfare organisations, industry organisations and related actors, and political and policy elites. These general classifications draw on the 'interest group' model of political analysis, which classifies politically active organisations distinct from the state using various competing typologies. As we will see, this follows a tradition in political science of making stronger distinctions between civil-society actors and the state than may be warranted in practice. In this approach, non-government actors are generally conceptualised as either:

- *public interest groups*, promoting issues seen to be of general public concern
- *ideological groups*, at the vanguard of more radical causes
- *business groups*, promoting or protecting economic interests, or
- *professional groups*, representing specific professions (Rinfret and Pautz 2014, 109).[1]

---

1 The US-centrism of this typology is evident in the absence of organised labour groups, but this absence is not problematic for this study, as will be discussed below in the identification of the marginal involvement of union organisations in this policy domain.

In this chapter I examine the work of animal protection organisations (APOs), which generally fall into either the first or second of these categories. In Chapter 7 I will consider industrial organisations and other groups involved in the use of animals for economic gain, from primary producers to retailers (groups 3 and 4 in the list above). In Chapter 8, I will look at the role played by the state through its policy processes, legislation, regulation and enforcement.

As we will come to see, this is an imperfect method of classification: policy processes in animal protection debates are extremely diverse and fragmented, subject to siloisation as we have noted, and resistant to homogenisation. For the purposes of effective generalisation, this structure has been adopted as the least-worst way of talking about a complex domain. The tendency to divide organisations into strict 'camps', however, will be resisted as much as possible, and the limits of this analysis are highlighted where appropriate; animal protection politics in Australia vary in interesting ways from the 'textbook' models of political action.

With these caveats in mind, I will begin this chapter by looking at Australia's APOs. By way of practical definition, APOs are defined as non-government organisations that work in whole or significant part to promote the wellbeing of animals, either individually or collectively.[2] We begin by asking: Who is who? How many groups can be called APOs, and what do they look like as a collective? This leads to a consideration of the structure of the organisations discussed. Following this exploration is a more detailed examination of the strategies and tactics of these groups, considering examples of both continuity and

---

2   This definition is a construct generated for this book, and is contestable on three grounds. First, including this array of groups in a single category may not be accepted by the organisations themselves: groups with very different philosophical positions may not recognise one another as fellow-travellers. Second, it can be challenged from without. Some groups that do not work predominantly on protection issues – such as some breed-specific animal appreciation groups – may see their welfare education and promotion roles as significant enough to merit inclusion. Finally, the regulatory functions of some RSPCAs, Animal Welfare Leagues and state departments are quite similar. Overall, however, the categorisation is analytically useful, as it provides meaningful distinctions between types of actors in the policy domain.

6 Animal protectionism

change. The chapter concludes with a discussion of the effectiveness of these groups in advancing their causes.

Organisations

Australia is home to a large number of APOs. It is likely that the average citizen would be startled to know the number of organisations that commit significant time and effort to the care of animals. Based on a thorough search and an analysis of state-based association registration data, it can be estimated that there were over 200 APOs operating in Australia in 2015, or about one per 100,000 citizens. APOs range from the nationally recognised federated RSPCAs, with annual budgets in the tens of millions of dollars each, to tiny and purely online organisations with no formal income or expenditure. Survey data from these organisations shows that, based on annual organisational income, they include a very small number of large and medium-sized organisations; the vast majority (over 90 percent) are small organisations that measure their annual budgets in the thousands of dollars. This seems in line with wider trends in the charities and not-for-profit sector, where larger charities have had greater success in dominating donor income (Backus and Clifford 2013). Overall, however, animal protectionism in Australia is not a well-financed area of activity, and relies on resources with low fungibility: volunteers and expertise.

As foreshadowed, generalisations about these organisations risk concealing important differences between them. They can, however, usefully be classified by asking three questions: (1) What is the primary activity of the organisation? Is it an organisation that provides welfare services directly to animals, or political advocacy or campaigning on behalf of animals? (2) What is the ideological or philosophical position of the organisation regarding human–animal relations? and (3) Where is the organisation active, and/or where does it focus its activity in the Australian geographical and political landscape?

The classification of organisations along these lines is unpacked in Tables 6.1, 6.2 and 6.3 below ($n = 50$). Summarising these tables, APOs are diverse:

Primary activity	Proportion of all groups	Jurisdictional activity		
		Local	Inter-state	National
Welfare services	42.9%	53.3%	6.7%	40%
Advocacy	45.2%	93.75%	0%	6.25%
Equal mix	11.9%	50%	25%	25%

Table 6.1. Primary activity and jurisdiction of APOs. Local refers to operation within a single state, inter-state refers to operation in more than one state, and national refers to operation in all the Australian states.

Ideological orientation	Proportion of total groups	Jurisdictional activity		
		Local	Inter-state	National
Welfarist or weak rights	69.8%	63.6%	9.1%	27.3%
Liberationist or strong rights	14%	83.3%	0%	16.7%
Abolitionist	16.2%	87.5%	0%	12.5%

Table 6.2. Ideological orientation and jurisdiction of APOs.

- They tend to focus on either service provision (to animals and/or their owners) or public or political advocacy, with few APOs committing equal time to both tasks.
- The majority of them are – consistent with the discussion in Chapter 2 – philosophically welfarist organisations, taking a weak animal-rights perspective.
- They tend to focus their activities primarily on the local level (either state or sub-state).

These variations necessitate a number of observations and explanations. The first observation is that, while the largest and best-funded APOs in Australia remain the registered charity organisations born of the first wave of animal protection politics discussed in Chapter 1, the ongoing dominance of a welfarist approach does not fit neatly into the two-wave history presented in that chapter (as well as by

Ideological orientation	Primary activity		
	Welfare services	Advocacy	Equal mix
Welfarist or weak rights	55.5%	26%	18.5%
Liberationist or strong rights	0%	100%	0%
Abolitionist	0%	100%	0%

Table 6.3. Ideological orientation and primary activity of APOs.

other authors; see, for example, Garner 1993). The established history of animal protectionism might lead us to expect that organisations founded after the publication of Singer's *Animal liberation* (1975) and other major new animal ethics texts by thinker-activists such as Regan and Francione would reflect the new intellectual direction, with a focus on liberation, a strong animal-rights agenda, and abolitionism respectively (for brevity's sake, I will refer to this more radical agenda as LSRA: liberation, strong rights, abolition). Contrary to this, however, a weak-rights or welfarist approach continues to drive the establishment of new APOs in Australia even today. Importantly, as illustrated in the table above, LSRA organisations tend to focus predominantly on advocacy, rather than on directly improving animal welfare (although there are some welfare providers in Australia with an LSRA ethos, as indicated in the table).[3]

Thus, although some industry observers and others express concern about the radicalism of animal welfare organisations (see later in this chapter, and Chapter 7), the majority of Australian APOs, and all of the largest organisations, take an incrementalist position and either accept, or are pragmatically tolerant of, the continued dominion of humans over animals. Most engage in a combination of direct welfare services and advocacy for incremental change (interview: M. Beatty,

---

3 This is an artefact of the small sample size. Organisations such as Edgar's Mission Farm Sanctuary in Victoria provide a mixture of individual welfare for farmed animals and education as advocacy. While it is not explicitly an abolitionist organisation, many of the staff have an underlying abolitionist philosophy (Behrend 2015).

16 April 2013). In the language of our interest-group typology, only a minority are 'ideological interest groups' seeking a radical departure from the status quo.

Given the variety of activities undertaken by APOs in Australia, however, it is clear that conceiving of them all simply as 'interest groups' – organisations co-operatively promoting a particular cause or concern in the political sphere (Yoho 1998) – is potentially misleading. Although the interest group model recognises that groups may undertake activities other than political activism, it privileges the latter (Loomis and Cigler 2015). The tables above indicate that fewer than half of Australian APOs are interest groups in this classical sense. The rest more closely resemble charitable organisations, in that they (1) have a strong primary mission of providing welfare and protection to animals as individuals, rather than at the ecosystem of species level, (2) expend the majority of their financial resources in providing services or treatment to specific animals, (3) undertake public education and awareness campaigns in the service of the first two activities, and (4) engage with the state as only a small proportion of their overall activities, and then often with a focus on attracting greater public resources or co-ordination, rather than of effecting wider political change. O'Sullivan (2011, 2) attributes this to the fact that many of the older welfare organisations have their origins in the great benevolent traditions of the 19th century.

A second observation is that there has been a rapid expansion in APOs during the last two decades (see Appendix C). A search of state-based incorporated associations data, in combination with survey evidence, shows that the most active APOs in Australia today were formed since 1990, and the majority after 2001.[4] While this in part reflects the changing public attitudes to animals discussed in Chapter 3, the phenomenon is not confined to the animal welfare domain. Berry (1997), among other writers, has described the advocacy 'explosion' that accompanied post-war political liberalism, when a proliferation of public and ideological groups (as opposed to established groups representing private interests) emerged as a result of increased education, individualism, optimism about the political system as a site for social

---

4 There is a tendency for survivor bias here, which searches of associations' data attempt to moderate.

change, and a 'more is better' view that coalition politics are superior to single-interest negotiations (Skocpol 1999). Recently, the internet has made it easier to form groups and to take collective action (Chen 2013). Thus, industry representatives are correct when they report an increase in animal advocacy, but they are not alone in this: private interests of all kinds have faced an expansion in activities by organised public interests and a loss of dominance over their respective policy domains.

The third observation of note is that the scholarship of animal ethics appears to be largely disconnected from animal protection practice. From interviews, it is clear that many organisational leaders do not identify strongly with formal ethical texts, either in explaining their original interest in animal protection or as practical references from which to draw theories of social change.[5] (There are exceptions. Both the NSW and Victorian Animal Liberation organisations resulted, separately, from readings of Singer's book; Munro 2001a, 59; Townend 1981; interview: P. Mark, 3 June 2013). More radical ideas about human–animal relations tend to enter the activist arena through popularisations (activist documentary films, for example, appear to play an important role currently; previously, generalist books and speaking events played a similar role in popularising scholarly ideas).[6] These popular 'translations' of academic concepts often break them down into numbered lists or focus on their practical application.

This makes individuals, as populariyers and promoters of ideas, significant in a way that a focus on interest groups fails to recognise (Louw 2010, 135–6). My discussions with members of APOs demonstrate this: organisational leaders were more likely to cite their interactions with individuals as influences than to refer to specific reference works. Peter Singer, for example, was active in personally promoting his ideas

---

5   This phenomenon can also be found in examining the biographies of Munro (2001a) and Divine (2011).
6   Mark Pearson MLC, for example, was first introduced to Singer's arguments about animal liberation through the popular volume *Save the animals! 101 easy things you can do* (Singer et al. 1991) (interview: 5 June 2013). This volume, like *So you kill ants?*, is comprised of a large number of short chapters, with simple responses to anticipated questions and practical advice. Patty Mark's move to veganism and abolitionism was the result of reading brief summaries and through personal interactions with activist vegans (interview: 3 June 2013).

in Australia during the 1980s and 1990s, and was important not just in inspiring the formation of groups such as Animal Liberation and Animals Australia, but through his influence on individuals, including his students, at the time (interview: S. Watson, 25 June 2014). For other activists, personal interactions with philosophers were significant in shaping their early interests (O'Sullivan 2015a).

More recently, individual activists such as Andrew Knight have been important in revitalising the movement – in Knight's case, with his critique, from within the scientific paradigm, of the use of animals in veterinary education and medical science and his attacks on the efficacy of animals as models of human systems. The significant role of such individuals in addressing weaknesses within the scientific community has been acknowledged by activist groups (interview: H. Marston, 23 September 2013). As discussed in Chapter 4, dietary abstention is a particularly active locus for entrepreneurial individuals (interview: G. McFarlane, 17 May 2013), from those promoting cooking skills and selling the 'diet' to a range of other professional specialists such as communicators, business development consultants, nutritionists and psychologists.

The fourth observation, the tendency for APOs to focus their activities on their local area, is more easily explained. The small size of the majority of APOs makes localism a practical necessity, and many serve specific localities, ecosystems or species. Even for the largest organisations, localism still dominates, despite the federal structure of the RSPCA and AWLs. This is explained by organisational path-dependency: having been established as state or colony-based organisations, they have retained these local identities; although they have since come together to form federal organisations, this has not resulted in complete national integration in practice.[7] Further, the strong relationship between these two organisations and the local government sector – through interactions with local politicians, project funding, co-ordination with local law officers, and in the provision of animal pound

---

7   The RSPCA is technically a single, national organisation, but retains a highly federal operational and decision-making structure based on consensus to ensure the organisation maintains support from each of the state and territory organisations (interview: CEO, RSPCA Australia, 24 June 2014).

6 Animal protectionism

services – further reinforces connections at the local level for what, on paper, are 'national' organisations.[8]

For advocacy organisations, localism can also be partly attributed to the structure of the Australian political system. Constitutional arrangements will have a stronger influence on the position of political actors than more transient phenomena (Tarrow 1994). With government policy concerning animals still made mostly by state governments (see Chapter 8), this encourages organisations to focus on the state level when advocating for change or seeking resources. With the rise of more national issues (including standards-making, live export, and the establishment of national and international commercial organisations with regulatory power), there has been an increase in the number of organisations with a national focus. However, this has also meant a shift in the distribution of power towards those national organisations already in existence. This process is indicative of the dual nature of social and political organisations; as Giddens (1986) observed with his theory of 'structuration', social and political life are influenced both by underlying structures and by individual actors exercising political agency. The shape and distribution of APOs are thus influenced by systemic factors, but also by human agency.

Illustrating the latter, the formation of first state and the then national representative structures was encouraged by federal politicians, who offered APOs access to policy-makers if the APOs could organise themselves into a few representative peak structures. The achievement of this (first at the state level, with animal-welfare consultative bodies, and later at the national level, with the Senate Select Committee of Inquiry into Animal Welfare in Australia, which concluded in 1985) saw the emergence and stabilisation of what would become the RSPCA Australia and Animals Australia (Oogjes 2005, 2; interview: P. Mark, Founder, Animal Liberation Victoria, 3 June 2013; O'Sullivan 2015b). This is an example of how external agents can reshape political structures by means of a formalised exchange. Since the 1980s, APOs have increasingly established peak bodies to represent

---

8 The AWL's federation remains relatively recent, however, so it is unclear how this will develop over time and if the League will mirror the development of the RSPCA, now 35 years into its national integration.

them at the national level; today, only the LSRA organisations do not have such a body. The formation of Animals Australia in 1980 also saw the emergence of a national membership-based organisation comprising both individual and organisational members.[9]

This practice to some extent reflects a wider trend towards corporatism among the political elite in Australia during the 1980s and 1990s. Corporatism is a model of government–group interaction that envisages the state not as autonomous from, or subservient to, interest group action, but as able to 'pick winners' and to discipline groups into representative structures that regularise the process of government–group negotiation (Hampson 1997). While this model is clear in the peaking strategy of APOs at the time, its failure to deliver significantly beyond the senate inquiry and subsequent national codes of practice (see Chapter 8) limited nationalisation as these processes provided few opportunities to achieve change. This can be seen in the relative growth of the number of local APOs since the 1980s, and in the smaller expansion of Animals Australia during this period (it was established in 1980 with 24 members, and had 37 in 2015). Overall, this reflects Giddens' view about how structures may be influenced by the will of actors, but how resilient they are over time without concerted attempts to remodel them.

The past two decades have been a particularly fruitful time for new APOs in Australia, and they have filled ecological niches in the opportunity structure. During the same period, there has also been a rise in species-specific organisations, some of them campaign-oriented, such as those aimed at horse racing, duck hunting and the puppy-breeding industry (interview: D. Tranter, 22 September 2014). Other new organisations have focused on areas otherwise neglected by

---

9   However, given the governance structure of Animals Australia only represents organisational members, there is a niche for a directly representative body to emerge, or for Animals Australia to see the type of internal conflict over organisational governance similar to that experienced by RSPCAs after the Second World War. Animals Australia's move to a dual organisational and individual membership structure has been useful in securing greater direct income for the organisation (Clark 2013), giving it its own revenue stream that does not tax member organisations directly (but does indirectly lead the organisation to be in soft competition with its member organisations for donations).

mainstream APOs. The Medical Advances Without Animals (MAWA) Trust (2000), for example, subsidises research and scholarship aimed at producing technologies that will reduce the use of animal models in research (interview: S. Watson, 25 June 2014),[10] while Voiceless supports developments in domestic legal theory and practice in animal welfare law.

As these niches become occupied, the rate of new group formation is likely to plateau. The comparatively rapid expansion of organisations may now be slowing, particularly when it comes to formal organisations with physical offices and paid staff.

Movement of ideas

The last example mentioned above, Voiceless, is an interesting case and worth expanding on because of its rapid rise in importance as a key node in the policy network. Founded in 2004, Voiceless was established self-consciously as an organisation aimed at a gap in the existing range of APOs. It has explicitly chosen not to expand beyond its self-imposed remit into wider activism, and has thereby avoided 'competing' with existing organisations directly. Voiceless' establishment also illustrates the transnational nature of the animal activist community (interview: D. Campbell, 30 January 2014). Participation in these types of organisations by high-profile legal practitioners and scholars (former High Court Justice Michael Kirby, for example, is a patron; Dwyer 2011) is also important in increasing the profile and credibility of animal protectionism overall (interview: T. Geysen, Brisbane Lawyers Educating and Advocating for Tougher Sentences, 19 April 2013).

The potential of these organisations to act as vehicles of transmission is seen not just in the movement of ideas between jurisdictions, but also in the direct transfer of staff between them (including the CEO of Voiceless, Dana Campbell, who came from the United States with experience in animal law in APOs in that country). Similarly, recent Animals Australia staff have both professional and

---

10 Following the '3Rs' of animal ethics in research MAWA focuses on providing proven technologies for replacement.

voluntary experience in the USA with APOs such as PETA (USA). This also reveals a change in the nature of career progression in these organisations, as the larger APOs have become more professionalised and bureaucratised. Where once they were staffed by foundational members or by staff with a long-term commitment to the particular organisation, increasingly careers in the animal protection sector are the result of deliberate CV-building activities over time.

This type of vertical transfer of staff and political strategy is mirrored by the horizontal transfer of organisational models between social movements. This can be seen in the 2013 establishment of the Animal Defenders Office in the ACT: a non-profit legal centre specialising in animal law that is modelled on the structure of well-established and successful examples from the environmental movement (Marshall 2010). Members of existing APOs, in particular Animal Liberation ACT, adopted organisational and strategic concepts from other movements in order to address a niche or deficit in the existing network of APOs.

New organisational forms can come about in a number of ways. They may emerge spontaneously within a jurisdiction and without connection to existing APOs, as was the case with Lawyers for Animals (Melbourne) and BLEATS (Brisbane Lawyers Educating and Advocating for Tougher Sentences), both organisations that fulfil a similar function to the Animal Defenders Office, but through network and legal-clinic models (interviews: T. Geysen, 19 April 2013; M. Beatty, 16 April 2013). They may spread between jurisdictions, as in the various animal-law groups within the state-based law societies, which continue the long-established tradition of pro-bono legal work (interview: a lawyer involved in animal law, 13 May 2014; Glasgow 2008). In federal systems, knowledge and ideas are often transferred across borders; the combination of constitutional similarity and local variation promotes both comparison and experimentation, more so than in unitary political systems (what Spahn calls 'laboratory federalism'; Spahn 2006, 196).

6 Animal protectionism

Neither fish nor fowl

Any analysis of APO typology raises questions about the nature of APOs: do they reflect the dominance of a politics of organised interests, or do they collectively comprise a more amorphous social movement? This distinction is not simply abstruseness; it is closely connected to the relationship between APOs and the wider community. Conventionally, the interest-group model of politics expresses a modernist conception of social organisation, in which specialisation rules. In this view, formal groups tend to supplant wide-scale political participation: citizens may be mobilised, but where their interests or concerns are being addressed effectively, they are happy to concede the political ground to 'the experts' (Van Biezen et al. 2012, 39–40). The political sociology of social movements, on the other hand, sees interest groups or 'social movement organisations' (SMOs) as semi-formalised concentrations of activity within in a wider group of active, mobilised citizens. The aim of social movement organisations is to advance the goals of the wider movement (Staggenborg 2016, 8). Compared with interest groups, movements see individual action as more common and significant in the process of attempting change because of the emphasis on collectivity and networked activity.

Animal protectionism is often included in a wide set of 'progressive' policy areas (including the environment, LGBTI rights and global justice) that represent a second wave of 'new social movement' (NSM) politics (Guither 1998; Stallwood 2012).[11] This 'new' type of social movement is distinguished from older ones (such as labour movements) by authors such as Diani who emphasise the role of culture and personal identity in binding together participants over older, Marxist-inspired explanations of class conflict (2000, 155). The former tend to see identity as a more fluid concept, while the latter see it as predetermined by one's family origins and comparatively fixed. NSMs are characterised by the participation of large numbers of networked individuals through self-identification with the cause, the location of movement knowledge (both motivational and practical) in relations between individuals, rather than just in institutional reservoirs, and

---

11 For a more detailed discussion, see Munro (2012).

the construction of ideological opponents as 'enemies' to be overcome. Within such movements, social-movement organisations serve as points of co-ordination and resource pooling, formal interfaces with authoritative elites and state institutions, and potential future 'insider' groups following the bureaucratisation of the movement's concerns into the formal political agenda (Gamson, 1990).

Given the observations made above about the organisational elements of animal protectionism, it is clear that this simple classification of animal protection concerns with movement politics, at least in Australia, is an over-simplification. Despite the limits of movement analysis, however, it can aid our understanding of the collective of individuals and organisations that is the focus of this chapter.

Size of the animal protection 'movement'

The first technical characteristic of a social movement is that its organisations are embedded in a networked, collective group of individuals who perceive themselves as part of a struggle for, or aligned with others active in, social change. This identity comes from within (self-identification) and through association with social movement organisations. The latter is most testable: do APOs have large 'catchments' of people who feel the organisation reflects their concern for social and/or political change, regulate the groups' conduct (formally or informally), and – significantly – are active? These catchments are more than simply counts of formal organisational members, but include individuals with variable degrees of interaction with organisations and their activities. Interest groups are likely to have comparatively passive supporters when compared with social movement organisations.

For the purposes of this analysis, three types of relationship between individuals and APOs are discussed below: members, supporters and contacts. They are defined as:

- *members*: including paid individual members and/or those members with a right to participate in organisational decision-making (e.g. by voting)
- *supporters*: including those individual who participate in organisational activities on a regular basis (members may be counted as supporters if they are active participants)

	Members	Supporters	Contacts	Organisational members*
Mean	343.5	2,887.2	13,658.3	107.1
Median	98	76	895	8
Standard deviation	612.3	8,752.5	58,515.5	223.8
Total reported	12,308	65,015	373,172	5,199
Imputed national total (sans duplication)†	63,117	370,315	1,761,696	31,509
n	39	30	34	33

Table 6.4. Average numbers of participants in APOs. *'Organisational members' refers to members or those making another significant ongoing contribution (such as sponsors and donors) of other organisations, companies or businesses.
†Members are removed from the total figure for supporters and supporters for the total figure for contacts for this calculation.

- *contacts*: those individuals included in regular communications (such as mailing lists). Contacts may include both members and supporters.

Drawing on our survey data (Table 6.4) we can get a sense of the catchment we are considering. This table in informative in a number of ways. First, the mean, median and standard deviation figures for each of the three categories of individuals and the organisational base of APOs in Australia indicate that the distribution of members, supporters and contacts is considerably negatively (or 'right') skewed. Most organisations have small catchments, with a very small number having large catchments in the public. Second, attrition 'up' the ladder of participation applies to APOs. That is, as the intensity of commitment to an organisation increases (from passive/occasional support to active support, to commitment via participative/formal membership), rates of participation decline (Chen 2015). Overall, it appears that each 'step' up the commitment curve sheds over 80 percent of individuals. Finally, among the estimated 200 or so APOs in Australia, we can see the size of the national public base of support across the three types.

These final figures are quite large, and need validation and explanation. By way of validation a number of sources can be employed. The first is Franklin's (Table 6.5) estimate that 2 percent of the Australian adult population are 'members' of the RSPCA (supporters in the parlance of my analysis),[12] equivalent to 375,000 people.[13] This helps to inform the estimate of formal members or active supporters of APOs in Table 6.4. However, as we move away from more formal participation to an estimation of the total number of less-active 'contacts', we must accept that these figures are likely to be far less accurate, with a high probability that some individuals will be counted twice, given the numbers come largely from mailing lists and online interactions such as Facebook likes. As a point of reference, the combined number of online supporters (likes) for all of Australia's RSPCAs and Animal Welfare Leagues on Facebook was approximately 722,508 as of October 2015, making an estimate of one million contacts a reasonable upper limit (in comparison, automobile associations claim seven million members).[14]

There are considerable differences in patterns of membership, support and contact between organisations predominately focused on the provision of welfare services and those engaged in more overt political work advocacy. Only half of the total number of the most active members of the public are engaged in advocacy-focused APOs, and these organisations have contact with less than 8 percent of total contacts. This means that those organisations most focused on political and policy advocacy have a relatively small catchment into the wider community (circa 80,000 individuals nationally), membership being 40 percent of their total catchment. Welfarist/charitable organisations, meanwhile, have the largest share of popular support in the Australian

---

12 As this figure massively overstates formal memberships and represents an instrument error (i.e. conflation with 'supporters').
13 Estimated from the total population of Australia aged over 15 years (81.1 percent of the total population).
14 Source: Australian Automobile Association (n.d.). This also demonstrates, to some degree, the power of interest groups in offering 'private goods' (services) exclusively to members (such as roadside assistance), as it is unlikely these the majority of these 7 million members join primarily to support their political objectives.

Organisation	Member	'Admirer'*	Opponent	No view
RSPCA	2%	91%	1%	6%
PETA	0%	31%	2%	67%
Canine Defence League	0%	16%	1%	83%
Greenpeace	2%	57%	7%	34%
Wilderness Society	1%	64%	1%	33%
World Wildlife Fund	1%	63%	1%	35%

Table 6.5. Comparative participation, animal protection and environmental organisations, 2007; $n = 2,000$. Source: Franklin (2007). *In the original, Franklin uses the term 'supporter' rather than 'admirer'. I have changed this to reflect a difference in research nomenclature, with apologies to Franklin.

community, membership being 3 percent of their wider catchment. However, supporters and members of advocacy organisations are more motivated and active in general, something which distinguishes social movements from interest groups.

Relations with the public

With an average of 343 members each, APOs are lean structures, regardless of their focus on activism or welfare services. While it is difficult to compare these figures effectively to organisations in other policy domains, the last national survey of 'interest group' membership[15] undertaken by the Australian Bureau of Statistics was in the late 1990s, and reported an average membership of 3,292 (1997, 7). During the intervening two decades, the national rate of participation in volunteering, measured both per capita and in total hours given, has increased (DFHCSIA 2007; this is particularly relevant given half of these organisations are conceived as 'charity-like'), while McAllister (2011, 63) identifies a comparatively static level of political interest over the same period. Thus, this figure appears to remain a robust

---

15 'Associations, clubs or organisations for the promotion of community interests [not elsewhere classified]. It also includes units of political parties'.

Members	Supporters	Contacts	Organisational members	Budget 2012–2013
-0.84	-0.75	-0.57	-0.04	-0.77

Table 6.6: Organisational performance indicators, correlated to year of establishment; $n = 39$.

comparator, making APO memberships about 10 percent that of the average interest group in Australia.

The smallness of many APOs appears to be due in part to the relative newness of many of them. Looking at survey data we can see that groups formed in the last 15 years tend to have the fewest members and supporters, and organisational age is positively correlated with catchment and budget, as illustrated in Table 6.6. This may be attributable to the natural advantage of established organisations in acquiring and retaining members.[16]

The comparatively low membership rates of APOs also appears to reflect a deliberate decision by organisations to prioritise other types of participation (such as donation and mobilisation) over traditional mass-membership. The survey data suggests that the recruitment of members remains a very low priority for these organisations, regardless of whether they are focused on service provision or political work. The large catchment of those interested in the former points towards their status as professional interest groups: the recruitment of non-member supporters whose donations support the employment of professionals with technical expertise in service delivery. For the larger welfare organisations, staff include a mix of technical professionals engaged in direct welfare work, as well as an administrative structure to support fundraising and its related activities, and the administration of skilled volunteers (such as veterinary students, for example) (interviews: M. Beatty, 16 June 2013; CEO, RSPCA Australia, 24 June 2014).

---

16   One structural determinant may be for newer groups to be national in orientation, as there is a positive correlation between the geographic scope of operations and its number of organisational members (0.69).

6 Animal protectionism

'For the animals'

Social movements, as networks of individuals, groups and organisations, rely on 'soft' cultural regulators (such as social pressure and group norms) and a sense of shared identity to ensure cohesion and effective collective action (as opposed to interest groups, which tend towards more formal regulation of membership benefits through stricter governance; Leach 2005). This shared identity or self-image includes an awareness of the group's behavioural and other cultural norms, as well as an understanding of the boundaries between the in-group and the out-group (Stryker et al. 2000, 21–4). When identity is conceived as not just a marker, but also a means to understanding the dynamics of social movements, it can be akin to what political scientists call 'bonding' social capital: when members feel they have a shared identity and/or a shared identification with the movement's cause, they are more likely to co-ordinate their activities and share resources (Tindall et al. 2011, 149–50).

Can such a shared identity be found in the diverse collection of Australian animal protectionists? Drawing on data collected using the Animal Attitude Scale (AAS) introduced in Chapter 3, we can see that individuals who identify as animal protectionists tend to have – as would be expected – a higher than average AAS: their participation is motivated by a greater than average concern for animal welfare.[17] This is illustrated in Table 6.7. If we consider that about two-thirds (68.26 percent) of animal protectionists fall within one standard deviation of the mean, we see there is a small crossover between the majority of animal protectionists and the general public: most animal protectionists sit outside the anticipated spread of popular opinion. Where they are aware of this, we might expect to see the emergence of a group identity among animal protectionists, as distinct from the wider community.

---

17 The extent to which an individual's AAS score changes if they participate in organisational or movement activities, however, is unclear. It is likely that membership and participation will enhance their commitment to the group and to the cause through learning and enculturation. In tracking work undertaken by Munson (2008), he found that only about half of entrants into a NSM tended to follow the 'logical' belief-to-membership path, while others entered through a range of paths (such as personal invitations to events) and developed issue commitment post membership.

	Animal protectionists	General community
AAS Score	84.7	67.6
s.d.	10.5	9.3
n	396	550

Table 6.7. Animal Attitude Scale: animal protectionists compared with the wider public; n = 946. Extracted from Signal and Taylor (2006).

The distinction between the general public and animal protections is not straightforward, however, and protectionists do not necessarily represent a single social movement bound by a shared identity. Using a breakdown of animal protectionists by their ideological orientation in regards to human–animal relations (see Table 6.8) we can see that animal protectionists who have a welfarist or weak animal rights perspective are far more closely aligned with the general population and have a higher level of crossover when considering the mean and standard deviation. On the other hand, those individuals who report a strong animal rights orientation have higher AAS scores (unsurprisingly), and have a very low level of overlap with those with a welfarist or weak rights orientation (assuming the normal distribution).[18] The upshot is that welfarists or weak animal rights protectionists have more in common attitudinally with the wider public than with protectionists who hold an LSRA perspective.

This points to a sharp division between these two positions, one which may work against a sense of shared identity.

A range of components can contribute to a sense of shared identity. Cultural signifiers (Flesher Fominaya 2010, 396) that are taken to be representative of an individual's attitudes may be used to signify membership of the group. These might include:

---

18 While these data were not collected using the same ethical distinctions used in this volume, this cohort includes both strong rights and abolitionist views, as per Chapter 2.

6 Animal protectionism

	Ideological orientation		Radicalism of tactics	
	Welfarist (weak rights)	Strong animal rights	Low	High
AAS Score	72.5	89.9	79.1	89.9
s.d.	12.2	7.3	11.2	7.4
n	62	241	113	168

Table 6.8. Animal Attitude Scale, animal protections compared; $n = 946$. Adapted from Signal and Taylor (2006). This table changes the nomenclature employed in the original to align with the terminology used in this volume. Apologies to the original authors.

- The use of different organisational memberships as a means of expressing one's political identity (self-identification with named political groups)
- Fashion, including clothing styles (but also, in the context of abstainer groups, specific materials) and tattooing. Tattoos of animals and as signifiers of veg*nism are frequently seen among strong rights and abolitionist communities (interview: individuals associated with the Sydney veg*n community, 8 May 2014), and their prominence and permanence are important indicators of status and commitment (Haenfler, 2004).[19]
- Direct involvement with animals; for instance, companion animals are present in some APO workplaces (personal observation; see also Clark 2013), and some activists are careful to choose venues that permit companion animals when organising events (Oceania Collective ICAS 2015).

---

19   There is potential for a major study of tattoos in the animal protection community in Australia. The importance of tattooing in social movements has been discussed in detail by Atkinson (2003) in reference to the Canadian Straight Edge community (which overlaps with vegan subcultures because of its links to abstention). In the Australian context, St John (1997) discusses the acquisition of tattooing and other body modification as marking a personal transition into a new subcultural identity.

- Diet, which is sometimes seen to signify an individual's position in the wider network. In the Australian context, veganism, for example, is often associated with an abolitionist perspective, and several interview subjects used this designator (whether they identified as vegan, or specifically as *not* vegan)[20] to signal their position in the wider community (Munro 2001a, 100).[21]

An individual's perception of their own position along the 'spectrum' of animal ethical positions (which may involve a well-developed and explicit identification with a particular ethical tradition, or be more vaguely expressed), their level of commitment to the issue, and their beliefs about what strategic and tactical actions are appropriate to promote the cause also play a role in their sense of group identity.

This final point reflects two aspects of how individuals perceive the political context. The first is that, in developing an ethical position regarding the nature of animals (in particular towards their capacity and their moral worth), human–animal relations, the relative importance of human and animal interests, and the subsequent source of social problems, individuals develop a political identity that incorporates a conceptual schema – a schema with which they can evaluate political actors and institutions and which provides the actor with a personal theory of how to achieve political and social change. The second aspect is captured in the last two columns of Table 6.8: identity also shapes the individual's willingness to engage in different types of political action in the pursuit of change (Jasper 1997). An individual's approval and disapproval of various political tactics can be both a measure of their personal commitment to the issues, and a reflection of their assessment of the capacity of existing political structures to

---

20 For example, of the RSPCA's attempts to delineate itself from more radical APOs in forming a relationship with a new government in Queensland, Michael Beatty: 'So, for the last year we've been trying to sort of build up the relationship with the new government. So, they understand what we are and we're obviously sort of strongly about animal welfare, but we're not totally a vegan society' (interview: 16 April 2013).
21 The assumption that activists are vegans was a common rhetorical tool used by speakers at the 2015 Animal Activists Forum, aligning the event with the more radical end of the protectionist community.

produce the desired change. Again we see a distinction between individuals who take a welfarist or weak animal rights position and those with a strong rights perspective, with the former more willing to employ conventional strategies and the latter more willing to pursue more radical change by tactics such as direct action.

Identity does not only divide participants in the policy domain, however; it can also unite them, by bonding members together over shared aspects of identity and concealing differences. In her study of the views and practices of personnel and volunteers in animal sanctuaries, Taylor (2004) identifies the importance of perceived shared motivations in uniting these individuals. Shared motivation and group identity can be seen in the oft-cited claim by active animal protectionists that they are 'in it for the animals' (333; and interview: individuals of the Sydney veg*n community, 8 May 2014). In Taylor's observation of the conduct of protectionists, this somewhat elusive term was also identified as a personal motivator, a bonding agent, a guide for decision-making, and a means of assessing members of the public's orientation to the work of the sanctuary. In the latter case, potential animal adopters were assessed by volunteers against their standards of appropriate concern and commitment to the animals they sought to adopt.

This type of language is also employed to minimise ideological differences within groups. The most obvious example of this is in the public self-representation of Animals Australia. As a peak body for APOs, representing member organisations with a range of positions on the appropriateness of animal use by humans (Munro 2001a, 78; Clark 2013), Animals Australia explicitly positions itself as a more moderate organisation than its political adversaries often claim. Thus, it strongly rejects association with veganism and abolitionism, even though some member organisations are motivated by abolitionist objectives and see welfare tactics as only worthwhile if they are the first steps towards abolitionism (interview: C. Neal, 16 April 2013).[22] In dismissing claims that it has a radical 'hidden agenda',[23] Animals Australia employs the

---

22 'I mean we'll use welfare examples to highlight that cruelty, say in factory farming situations. But we won't invest a large amount of our resources lobbying for a slightly bigger battery cage, or something like that. Or encouraging people to buy free-range eggs instead of cage eggs, because as far as we're concerned people

basic 'for the animals' formulation identified by Taylor: the organisation does not promote particular groups or ideologies, but states that 'Animals Australia exists first and foremost to represent animals.' Such rhetoric can also be used to assert the political legitimacy of animal welfare organisations, particularly those that lack a representative membership structure or a large membership base. A representative structure is often seen as essential to political legitimacy in human-centric social movements; non-anthropocentric organisations may lack such a structure, and so must find other ways to demonstrate their political legitimacy (Tilly 1999, 270).

Overall, APOs in Australia lack a common overarching political and cultural identity, although attempts are made to conceal this for pragmatic reasons. The existence of readily identifiable subcultures marks out adherents of more radical activists from the weak rights or welfarist majority. These are cultural expressions of fundamentally different worldviews, including views about the relative ethical position of humans to animals, but also about the nature of social change and what types of strategies and tactics are appropriate to achieve it. While some are apt to see the welfarist and abolitionist subgroups as sharply distinct, this is not the case. In fact, these different organisational and cultural identities are intertwined. This occurs through crossovers in organisational memberships, where group publics are not strictly differentiated due to a lack of ideological clarity in the public, as well as among active participants in the movement. It is also seen in relations between different groups in the policy network, who may co-operate in tactical actions when it suits their wider, if unaligned, strategic aims. Finally, it is visible within the emerging federated bodies of once-autonomous state- or issue-based organisations, where significant differences in worldview are suppressed through the promotion of a unified protectionist identity.

---

shouldn't be choosing either. But we will use those examples to show how bad it is to get people thinking about those sort of things.'
23 Some industry representatives are suspicious that Animals Australia is a crypto-vegan organisation (interview: A. Spencer, 23 June 2014).

6 Animal protectionism

A transposition of two movements

Between social movement and interest group politics there exists a third category, a hybrid that results from what can be called the 'lifecycle' model of political challenge and incorporation: the tendency for some successful social movements to transition into stable institutions once they have won popular or elite support for either all or parts of their critique (della Porta and Diani 2006).

In making this transition, social movement organisations become increasingly bureaucratised through their cultural interactions with, and the need to provide services to, state institutions. In effect, they become interest groups representing stakeholders, stakeholders with whom their relationship becomes attenuated as their primary ties shift increasingly to organisations outside the movement. This process, of course, is neither immediate nor automatic. Some social movement organisations may not desire institutionalisation (Fitzgerald and Rodgers 2000), either because of the focus of their advocacy, because of the trade-offs institutionalisation would require, or because cultural characteristics would make institutionalisation unacceptable to their membership (for instance, in movements based on an anti-system critique or on anarchism; such groups are 'ideological outsiders' and unlikely to accept institutionalisation; Maloney et al. 1994). These social movements may continue with their established strategies and tactics, running parallel to, or in friction with, social movements that have transitioned into interest groups. In some cases, the formalisation of a movement into an interest group marks the extinguishment of radicalism within the organisation.

This is true of many animal protection organisations. The majority of APOs engaged in policy debates and advocacy are the bureaucratised and professionalised successors of a radical movement of the late 19th century. For many founders of such organisations, the RPSCAs provided a successful template for organisational practice, even though newer organisations may be in tension with these pre-existing ones (as rivals, or because they began as dissenting defectors from the RSPCAs). For others, institutionalisation comes from an acceptance of the politics of accommodation and negotiation, but also reflects the success of the first wave of welfare-focused organisations in establishing some of their core values as public norms. As such, the base of support in the community for these types of APOs is heterogeneous and large, but as professional organisations, their active core is considerably smaller than their wider public catchment.

In transforming from radical challengers into partners of government and industry, these organisations have achieved a measure of insider status in the policy process. Their political legitimacy depends on their presenting themselves as the 'sensible centre' of popular opinion. This is also important to their financial survival. As the national CEO of the RSPCA observed:

> In terms of the RSPCA reflecting middle Australia, we know middle Australia supports us doing this; where we get our money from, we get it in the main through small amounts of money rather than large amounts of money, with the exception of bequests, which go particularly to the older, more established societies. (Interview: 24 June 2014)

The transition from social movement to interest group also tends to alter the ideology and tactics of an organisation. As Munro (2005a) argues, in the early 20th century the RSPCAs moved from being presented (and presenting themselves) as 'moralising reformers' to 'societies of pet lovers'. Popular acceptance can tie the hands of the newly institutionalised, as they become cautious not to be seen to move beyond their popular remit. It also changes their support base in the community and is often at the root of organisational fragmentation and multiplication. The transition can make them adopt a pragmatic approach to change, and to focus on developing long-term relations with other stakeholder organisations, with whom they have increasingly synergistic relationships.

We can observe this bureaucratisation in the way these organisations have been able to access state resources to undertake welfare services. Their expanding service role involves higher running costs and requires a larger asset base and more staff; this in turn necessitates a focus on stability and steady growth. Partnerships with government and other major institutions further encourage professionalisation. Senior organisational managers are increasingly selected for their professional competencies rather than (as in the early 20th

6 Animal protectionism

century) their group affiliation (interviews: M. Mercurio, 4 June 2013; CEO, RSPCA Australia, 24 June 2014).

A cluster of LSRA groups is still politically radical relative to mainstream opinion and retains classic social movement characteristics. The behaviour of individuals is important in understanding the conduct of groups, and the relationships between organisations cannot be understood without some insight into the interpersonal histories of key organisational members. Because these organisations operate primarily in a social context, rather than in official policy networks, interpersonal 'cliques' remain significant within them and are important to an understanding of (the lack of) co-operation between them (interviews: T. Geysen, 19 April 2013; E. Hill, president, University of Melbourne Animal Protection Society, 20 August 2013; a lawyer involved in animal law, 13 May 2014; L. Drew, 23 June 2013). Some of these relationships are short, while some reach back into the dawn of the second wave of the animal protection movement (interview: L. Levy, 30 August 2013).

The proliferation of social movement organisations is the result of the work of individual 'entrepreneurs' (Munro 2001a, 59) and of the fragmentation of existing social movements into new bodies and subgroups. Some jurisdictions contain a large number of loosely clustered specialised campaigning groups, many of which emerged from larger 'catch-all' organisations (interview: D. Tranter, 22 September 2014), while other jurisdictions are more homogenous in nature. Fragmentation and multiplication are common in social movements owing to low barriers to exit, and divisions can be due as much to interpersonal conflict as to differences of opinion about strategy. The outcome of fragmentation can lead to balkanisation, particularly where personal animus exists, but specialised campaigning groups have the ability to form productive coalitions in a dynamic way when necessary if this fragmentation is overcome (interviews: P. Mark, 3 June 2013; D. Tranter, 22 September 2014; L. Levy, 30 August 2013). Commitment can be more important than technical competence in determining a person's level of participation in an organisation (interview: M. Pearson, 5 June 2013), a tendency exacerbated by dependence on small numbers of volunteers, many of whom are members (either formally or informally) of multiple groups.

Ideological differences within the LSRA community are important, but tend to be concealed by homogenising language. New entrants into the arena may form an association with a local organisation before they fully understand its ideology and the implications of their choice of group. Further, social movement organisations are not as static in the strong-rights or abolitionist community as they might be in other social movements. A number of Animal Liberation organisations have been moving from the position advocated by Singer (liberationism) towards a strong rights or abolitionist perspective, making the nomenclature within the community confusing to outsiders (interviews: P. Mark, 3 June 2013; C. Neil, 16 April 2013; L. Drew, 23 June 2013).

Gendered politics?

As has been observed in previous chapters, animal protection politics has historically been, and remains, dominated by women. Surveys of participants, as well as my own observations of events connected with animal protectionism, confirm the dominance of women. In October 2014, 61.2 percent of RSPCA board members were women ($n = 60$). By way of comparison, the average number of women on the boards of Australian charities is 39.9 percent ($n = 600$; Dale and Waterhouse 2015), and 16.2 percent for private companies (Australian Institute of Company Directors 2015).

This sometimes leads to a view that women's prominence in protectionism can be explained by some essential female characteristic. This notion is seen in arguments linking concern for animal rights to a feminist ethics of care (see Chapter 2), in observations about the crossover between animal protectionism and ecofeminism, and in more negative associations between protectionism and excessive emotion or sentimentalism. However, attitudinal data (Table 6.9) shows that the attitudes of men and women, while different on average, overlap considerably (recall Table 3.4). This confirms Munro's (2001a) observation that the attitudes of female and male animal protectionists on a variety of issues within protectionism do not significantly differ.

The gendered nature of animal protectionism has remained fairly static over the medium and long term. As discussed in Chapter 1, middle- and upper-class urban women were particularly important in

	Animal protectionists		
	Overall	**Male**	**Female**
AAS Score	84.7	78.4	85.9
s.d.	10.5	14.8	9.0
n	396	65	331

Table 6.9. Animal Attitude Scale: animal protectionists compared with the wider public; n = 946. Extracted from Signal and Taylor (2006).

the formation of APOs in the 19th century, and remain important in the movement today. The support base for Animals Australia, for example, has not significantly changed over the past 15 years: the average participant at a live-export protest organised by the group in 2015 was female (72 percent), older (with a mean age of 52) and professional. This is consistent with a circa 2000 survey of individual Animals Australia members: 74 percent were women and the mean age was 51; Munro 2001b). The same profile is reflected in the leadership of APOs, but not necessarily in their core active membership, who, while still overwhelmingly female, tend to be much younger. This was clear in observations of the Animal Activists Forum 2015, where speakers were generally older and audiences younger.

Without relying on essentialism, there are three explanations for this enduring trend. First, history is important in this story. Organisations with strong female participation when they were established maintain structures of recruitment and management that are more resistant to 'patriarchal closure' (the usurpation of an organisation by men following its growth or success) than are traditionally male-dominated organisations, even if the latter have been desegregated. Thus, just as we see enduring under-representation of women in traditionally male-dominated sectors, we see enduring openness in APOs. Second, following Luke's (2007) analysis of Western culture's construction of masculinity as predatory, and Dunayer's (1995) analysis of the connection between speciesism and sexist language, there are enduring cultural deterrents to male participation in animal protectionism. The lasting connection between maleness, muscles and meat is only the most obvious expression of a wider cultural norm that tells men that animal protectionism is 'a bit soft'. This has implications for advocacy. Munro (2001b) observed that the early dominance of APOs by women led to them being painted as 'emotional' rather than rational actors. Finally, and possibly more provocatively, APOs remain dominated by women because they are marginal. Those APOs with larger budgets and greater influence are more likely to have male management and senior staff. Women have at times been marginalised in these larger organisations. The periodic creation and abandonment of women's committees and auxiliaries in Australian RSPCAs reflects this (Budd 1988, 201–4). While this last point may be controversial, it is in fact the unsurprising corollary of the first.

Relations across the network

As we saw in Chapter 5, there are patterns of interaction within the network, both between individual APOs and within clusters of groups with historical ties and ideological similarities. Given their ideological differences, we might expect collaboration between welfarist and more radical members of the network to be characterised by conflict. Conflict is present, but there is also an underlying pragmatism in the Australian animal protection community, perhaps more so than in some other countries (Munro 2001a, 76–7). To illustrate this, let us explore these various connections in more detail.

Co-operation, co-ordination and adjustment

For organisations focused on the provision of services, other similar organisations may represent the competition. In some cases organisations may take a zero-sum view and see any success by other groups (especially in fundraising) as a direct loss to themselves. In other cases, such competition is avoided, either through direct negotiation or simply by a unilateral decision not to compete in particular areas. When the RSPCA Queensland lost access to the council land on which it had run an animal shelter in the Gold Coast, for example, it decided not to re-establish the facility elsewhere, as the local Animal Welfare League was deemed to provide a sufficient alternative service (interview: M. Beatty, 16 April 2013). In yet other areas competition serves to highlight policy differences, as in the spread of no-kill animal shelters (such as the Save-a-Dog Scheme in Victoria, founded in 1985), created as rivals to established welfare organisations that euthanise unwanted companion animals (as distinct from mercy killings for medical reasons).

Organisations with different ideological orientations may collaborate at the tactical level, even if they have different longer-term strategic objectives, different worldviews and/or different conceptions of how social change occurs (interview: L. Drew, 23 July 2013). This reflects Australian political culture, but also the size of the community: with a small catchment of activist members, there is more overlap between interest groups and social movements than in other policy domains. The need to mobilise resources often creates a bond between small APOs, and can be a motivation for larger actors to co-ordinate activities across the sector. For example, the Queensland 1300 ANIMAL hotline, which allows people to report injured animals, co-ordinates calls to participating individuals and groups in areas where the RPSCA Queensland lacks reach. Establishing this service took persuasion, as some smaller groups were cautious about being absorbed into the RSPCA (interview: M. Beatty, 16 April 2013).

The largest organisations sometimes come together for tactical collaborations, operating more like interest groups. A recent example is the 2014–2015 undercover investigation of greyhound training and racing practices, particularly the use of live animals as bait. This investigation involved the Australian Broadcasting Corporation (a *Four Corners* episode, 'Making a killing', was broadcast in February 2015), Animal Liberation, Animals Australia, and state-based RSPCAs. Combining resources was one reason for forming this coalition, but the aforementioned resource exchange model also helps to explain how these collaborations overcome organisational boundaries, historical suspicions and ideological differences. Local APOs maintained connections to activists who were willing to undertake direct action and able to obtain access to the facilities of greyhound trainers (Guppy 2015). Animals Australia had considerable expertise in running public media campaigns focusing on consumer boycotts, while the RSPCAs had mainstream legitimacy and, if necessary, the ability to prosecute.

The integration of investigation with prosecution is particularly important since the proliferation of anti-activist and 'ag-gag' legislation prohibiting the unauthorised filming or broadcasting of footage from commercial farms. In the 'post-ag-gag' environment, activist investigations have been criticised for undermining prosecutions (see Chapter 7 for a further discussion of legal restraints on activism).

The greyhound investigation built on previous successes that had helped to overcome scepticism about such collaborations. As the CEO of the RSPCA Victoria observed of the live exports campaign of 2011:

> We joined with the activists, if you like – [with] Animals Australia. We had the footage; they had the evidence that was put before the public community as well as the government. That was a really, really important campaign. And by the RSPCA stepping into that space with that, it just lifted the power of that campaign enormously. And I would say it's one of the most successful campaigns the RSPCA has ever run in its 142-year history ... In fact, to some extent, we've gained more in terms of supporters, in terms of donor support, or supporters, if you like, in the last little while from being, or being seen as, more on the activist side. (Interview: M. Mercurio, 4 June 2013)

Such collaborations, therefore, continue as long as mutual benefits can be identified in advance, and as long as the outcomes are beneficial to participants. This also reflects the networked nature of these organisations: they maintain enduring and regular relations to the extent that campaigns can be developed and implemented in useful timeframes to achieve their tactical objectives and without the risk of the targets of campaigns becoming aware of them (either through poor implementation, or through the types of leaks experienced by government regulators; see Chapter 8).

Conflict, risk and creative tension

Collaborations are not without risk, and the management of this risk is part of the careful 'boundary maintenance' conducted by institutionalised and bureaucratised APOs. This has shaped relations between the RSCPAs and other organisations since at least the late 1940s.

Tensions between the RSPCAs and other organisations occasionally flare into open conflict, such as the rift between Animals Australia and the RSPCA NSW over animal experiments undertaken at RSPCA facilities in the early 1980s (Townend 1981). In 2004 activists from Animal Liberation Victoria threw red paint at the president of the Victorian RSPCA to protest against the RSPCA's relative conservatism (Butler 2005); Animal Liberation Victoria also maintains the 'RSPCA Watch Dog' website, which is critical of both the national and state branches of the organisation.[24] Of such conflicts, the CEO of the RSPCA Victoria observed: 'We don't spend a lot of time worrying about that. We have to pay attention to it because sometimes it's a little barometer as to what's going on in the broader community' (interview: M. Mercurio, 4 June 2013). These types of conflict were significant in the RSPCAs' decision not to join the Australian Federation of Animal Societies in the 1980s, and in the departure of some organisations from Animals Australia.

Even where conflict is not open, a low level of tension exists. In the case of the RSPCA and Animal Liberation ACT, the latter observed:

> I try not to . . . put too much negative energy into the campaigns because I would rather put my focus into the way we conduct campaigns, rather than getting online and bad-mouthing them. But rather, I personally don't want to put my energy into that. But I am exceptionally uncomfortable with RSPCA, as are other people in the organisation, having things like Bacon Week [an annual pork promotion run by Australian Pork Limited. The RSPCA has used the week to promote its welfare standards for pork production], and we do make a point of it by sometimes writing to them, writing things on Facebook, or writing to [CEO] Michael Linke, who runs the RSPCA in Canberra, and telling them of the problems of their campaigns. (Interview: L. Drew, 23 June 2013)

While Animals Australia and the RSPCAs work together in some of their larger campaigns, they both also go out of their way to ensure that

---

24 http://www.rspcawatchdog.org. It is not clear if this site has been significantly updated since 2012.

they are still seen as distinct. When lobbying politicians, for example, they do not undertake joint meetings, even on issues where they largely share the same view (interview: M. Parke MP, 4 September 2014). Some political elites see this as simply indicative of underlying tensions that must be bridged, while others see it as an opportunity to play the groups off against each other. For the RSPCA, the rationale for such measures is to maintain its brand as mainstream, and to avoid being perceived as too close to an organisation that is seen to harbour more radical objectives. This reflects the internal politics of the RSPCA, some branches of which are more conservative than others. As a spokesperson for the RSPCA Victoria put it, 'There are other RSPCAs who are much more conservative... who were worried very much about the live-export campaign, [and] who were almost panicky about the relationship with Animals Australia' (interview: M. Mercurio, 4 June 2013). Some branches also have a history of conflict with Animals Australia itself, and/or with some of its current and former member organisations. The RSPCA's efforts to maintain some distance from Animals Australia and other groups is to some extent a response to these internal sensitivities. Animals Australia must also manage its boundaries with the RSPCA: the RSPCA's involvement in recent activist campaigns means it has crossed over into Animal Australia's core area of competence.

Smaller collaborators in joint campaigns also share this perceived risk, and try to ensure that their contribution to high-profile events is not subsumed into the work of national bodies. Chay Neal of Animal Liberation Queensland observed that Animals Australia is becoming an 'organisation of its own' and less a purely peak body. Thus Animal Australia's objectives and those of its member organisations need careful management as 'an ongoing – not issue, but something that you're always aware of... when we collaborate [it's] sort of important to be clear on what the end result is, and we've got to [get] credit for it' (interview: 16 April 2013). The resulting level of media coverage highlighting Animal Liberation Queensland's role in the greyhound investigation shows that the organisation continues to maintain this boundary; it still managed to ensure it was recognised for its contribution to the wider campaign (Guppy 2015).

6 Animal protectionism

Such tensions over the boundaries between organisations continue to develop and change. Recently the formation of the various state-based Animal Welfare League organisations under a single umbrella means that the RSPCA has a nationalised competitor that works directly in its areas of key competency and public focus: the provision of welfare services and, in some states, law enforcement involving companion animals. A degree of convergence among the largest organisations in Australia also explains the rise of Voiceless in recent years (combined with its large private financial base). As the three largest APOs in Australia, the RSPCA, Animals Australia and Voiceless increasingly share common interests and tactics, and engage in active co-operation.

The existence of more radical and conservative APOs can serve to calibrate mainstream organisations in an era of shifting public opinion. Radical organisations play an important role in introducing new campaign techniques and identifying new causes. Once an issue attracts more mainstream interest, their efforts may then be colonised by more established organisations. Sheep exports, for example, was the foundational issue of Animal Liberation NSW; since the 1980s, the live-export debate has moved from the periphery to the centre.

In extremis, risk avoidance is associated with stagnation. In the mid-20th century, the comparative absence of this type of horizontal calibration was reflected in decades of organisational conservatism, as identified by authors such as Smith and Townend. Using the Victorian RSPCA as an example, Smith (2007) argues that the organisation became overly cautious in its activities through a combination of alignment with political elites, reaction to the perceived radicalism of other smaller welfare organisations, and disconnection with activities in other jurisdictions. Smith also argues that, in line with the spirit of the time, the organisation's status as a royal society contributed to a conservative tendency to defer to social and political elites. Townend (1981), meanwhile, posits that internal disputes in the RSPCA NSW from the 1950s through the 1970s meant that the organisation's energies were focused on perceptions of poor governance and the associated mismanagement of the organisation's facilities, rather than on law reform (although the society did manage to get coursing banned in 1947).

In both cases, a push for reform from within served to highlight gaps in the organisations' performance as well as governance problems.[25] These disputes led to the creation or expansion of other welfare organisations in Victoria, NSW and SA, and to belated reforms to the original societies over time (interview: M. Mercurio, 4 June 2013).[26] If we compare the RSPCAs of the mid-20th century with the APOs of today, we can clearly see a reduction in outright conflict and the emergence of a more competitive and organic process of change at the start of the 21st century.

The older tendencies, however, still exist to some degree. Animal Liberation NSW attempted to gain RSPCA board positions in the 1990s in response to similar moves by farmers' groups, with short-term success (some board members achieved election and then expulsion; interview: M. Pearson, 5 June 2013). More recently, internal conflict within the RSPCAs in the ACT, Tasmania and WA have involved concerns about management of the organisation and/or interpersonal conflicts (interview: B. Green MP, 22 September 14; Raggatt et al. 2013) that are reminiscent of the disputes of the mid-20th century. While the involvement of the national body in an attempt to resolve conflict is new (Rosemary 2012), and to some extent demonstrates the changing power relations, other aspects of the conflict are familiar: the intervention of the state government as the RSPCA's significant funder and source of statutory power (Dawtrey 2012); criticisms from activists from social movement organisations, conflict over the use of 'entryism'

---

25 Examples of internal demands for reform include the intense legal conflict between the RSPCA Victoria and Constance May Bienvenu and her RSPCA Reform Committee, and the defection of W.R. Lawrence MLA from the NSW board in the late 1950s. Such divisions highlighted in particular an increasing gap between Victoria and NSW in the area of legislative reform. There appears to have been a higher degree of isomorphism among Australian RSPCAs in the early part of the 20th century, but this may be due to indexing of these comparatively new organisations with their UK counterparts, a closeness refleted in the constant references to the UK in RSPCA organisational histories-cum-promotional books produced in the early 20th century (see, for example, White's *Lesser lives,* 1937).
26 In the case of the RSPCA Victoria, circa the 1970s. The delay appears to be partially organisational in nature (a result of the inherent slowness of change in conservative organisations), but also due to the highly personalised nature of the legal conflict between individuals fighting for control of the organisation.

(a tactic whereby members of one organisation infiltrate another to access its resources, to hobble it, or to change its positions); and a strengthening of critics of, and alternatives to, the RSPCA. As we shall see below, conflict within the RSCPfA enabled competing organisations to gain considerable visibility as spokespersons on animal protection issues in Tasmania.

Informality and endurance

Nearly all APOs, even those in the process of becoming bureaucratised, retain the more informal structures usually associated with social movements. They share members and volunteers, and deliberately use their social networks to exchange ideas. An example can be seen in the annual Animal Activists Forum, held since 2009 in a different capital city each year. The forum provides a space for the exchange of information about issues, strategies and tactics, and opportunities for social networking. It attracted about 220 participants to Melbourne in 2015; the two-day meeting included local and international speakers and representatives from a range of organisations. The event is presently supported by, but not run by, Animals Australia, illustrating how even this more formalised body remains something of a hybrid between social movement and interest group. This type of hybrid informal structure is discussed by Haug (2013) as a significant part of social movements; it reifies network ties, produces movements of information and cultural material, and permits more formal co-ordination than results spontaneously from shared interests and culture.

Some LSRA activists, meanwhile, have tactics and beliefs in common with the first wave of animal protectionists. There has been a resurgence of anti-vivisectionism over the last two decades in Australia, prompted partly by a 'rediscovery' of the issue, but also by the work of small, enduring organisations that remained active, albeit on a small scale, throughout the 20th century. These groups would largely fit Taylor's (1989, 765–70) concept of social movement 'abeyance structures': enduring organisations that remain active during periods of limited political opportunity, sustaining the ideas and culture of a social movement. We can see direct connections between the two waves of animal protectionism, both between welfarists and strong-rights/

abolitionists, and between the more radical new social movement and abeyance structures descended from late 19th-century abolitionism. For example, the Australian branch of the World League for the Protection of Animals (WLPAA; whereas the RSPCAs are descended from British organisations, the WLPA originated in Germany and traditionally took a stronger interest in anti-vivisectionism) existed for a long time as a small rump organisation, then saw a dramatic rise in membership in the mid-1970s (Townend 1981). The Anti-Vivisection Union of South Australia, founded in the early 20th century, has more recently supported a new generation of activists, while organisations such as Humane Research Australia and Choose Cruelty Free (Victoria) have emerged as new organisations in the second wave.

(Dis-)continuities across policy domains

In addition to the links between APOs, connections between organisations and activists operating in other policy arenas are also important. Although conventional thinking holds that social movements commonly attempt to expand their popular support by broadening the 'frame' or narrative of their interests (Beamish and Luebbers 2009), in this case, APOs appear to operate relatively independently of other, possibly relevant, social movements and policy domains.

Environmentalism

The limited interaction between animal protectionists and environmentalists in Australia is interesting. Activists and members of APOs often report an interest in conservation or the environment (interviews: M. Collier, 17 April 2013; G. McFarlane, 17 May 2013; M. Beatty, 16 April 2013; individuals associated with the Sydney veg*n community, 8 May 2014; S. Watson, 25 June 2014; L. Levy, 30 August 2013),[27] and a strong environmental theme runs throughout the members of the APO

---

27 A counter-example would be the president of Animal Liberation Queensland, who has overlapping memberships in the Wilderness Society (interview: C. Neal, 16 April 2013).

community more strongly associated with social movement practices, with core movement concerns often expressed in environmental terms. Further, the transfer of organisational structures between environmental and animal protection movements reflects an enduring closeness that dates back to the first and early second wave: Animal Liberation NSW's first meetings, for example, were facilitated by the Total Environment Centre (Sydney), and Townend reports that her interest in liberation stemmed from her environmentalism (Townend 1981). So, exchanges and collaborations do occur – but the domains are clearly delineated, and this separation appears to be enduring.

This delineation can be explained in part by differences in the fundamental worldviews of the two groups. At the surface level, animal protectionists and environmentalists share certain political values, including a lower tolerance for authoritarianism/social dominance and an interest in the preservation of animals. This might lead us to expect a greater intersection between the memberships and values of the two movements than research has found (Jackson et al. 2013). However, as Perry and Perry's (2008) case analyses have pointed out, animal protectionists and conservationists often have difficulties collaborating over basic differences in their focus of care: the maximisation of the wellbeing of individual animals on the one hand, and an emphasis on larger populations and habitats on the other. These tensions persist despite a recognition that both groups have areas of shared interest, a capacity to collaborate effectively, and similar cultural norms. The weak links between the two movements can also be partly explained as another example of boundary maintenance. (My discussion here has been informed by the evidence of informants from APOs, for whom collaborations with environmental organisations and interest groups was rarely considered a tactical option. A number of environmental organisations declined my interview requests, either because they felt issues of animal protection were outside of their remit, or because the questions could be more comprehensively addressed by APOs.)

Where there has been crossover between environmental and animal protection organisations in recent years, it has tended to involve one of three things. The first involves shared tactics. One of the most high-profile environmental organisations to receive considerable support from animal protectionists in Australia is the Sea Shepherd

Conservation Society (SSCS). The organisation, an offshoot group from Greenpeace and inheritor of its more radical tactics from the 1970s and 1980s, has become the most well-known direct-action organisation in Australia because of its annual campaign to physically disrupt the taking of whales from the Southern Ocean by Japanese hunters operating under the guise of scientific whaling, and to direct sustained popular attention to this issue (Morell 2014). Animal protectionists have supported and participated in the SSCS's activities, and SSCS Australia has participated in animal protectionist events and conferences; the movements share information about their tactics, particularly direct action and the use of media attention to affect popular opinion. The association of SSCS with veganism (Shapiro 2010; all crew on Sea Shepard vessels follow a vegan diet while aboard, and the organisation puts out calls for donations of vegan food when Sea Shepard vessels are at port) also creates a sense of solidarity between the two movements, while reinforcing the sacrifices that SSCS crew make in taking their high-risk direct actions.[28] This shared commitment creates a further source of solidarity between SSCS volunteers and members of the LSRA activist community.

The second type of crossover involves an interest in what Thiriet (2010, 163–5) calls 'unpopular species': animal species with a long history of being antagonised or denigrated in human culture (either in Australia or more generally). In recent years, flying foxes have been subject to considerable attention (interview: C. Neal, 16 April 2013), particularly around attempts by state and local governments to deal with large colonies in inner-city areas. In the ACT, the culling of kangaroos has energised APOs in that jurisdiction. Proposed and/or implemented measures against sharks in WA and NSW have been subject to considerable popular mobilisation, with protesters focusing particularly on the perceived cruelty of the use of baited drum-lines to catch and kill the animals. This has seen joint action by environmental groups and APOs (some environmentalists, however, prefer this approach because of its reduced tendency to harm other sea-life, compared with netting; Shiffman 2014). Outside of the live-exports issue, shark culling has

---

28 As evidenced by the sinking in 2010 of the SSCS' MY *Ady Gil* following a collision with the MV *Shōnan Maru 2*.

provided the animal protection movement with some of the largest public protest events in recent years, particularly in Western Australia, which traditionally has had a smaller number of APOs.[29]

The involvement of animal protectionists in these environmental issues is perhaps not surprising. Animal protectionists are less likely to accept the negative social construction of 'unpopular species' than the wider public. The examples above also tend to be of greater interest to urban-dwellers, involving as they do the management of wild animals either in cities themselves or off the beaches near them. On issues largely affecting rural and remote areas, such as dingo conservation and protection, activists have had less success in rallying public support (Probyn-Rapsey 2015). When mainstream APOs move into debates about environmental protection, their emphasis tends to be on wildlife protection, a focus sometimes described as 'light green' conservationism. This can be seen in the types of animals treated by Australian RSPCAs over the last decade. Using a comparison of animals received and processed by RSPCAs between two periods, 2004–2005 to 2008–2009 and 2009–2010 to 2013–2014, we can see in Table 6.10 that there has been a considerable increase in the number of animals classed as wildlife handled by the organisation. This reflects both 'push' and 'pull' factors (e.g. the decision by the associations to define themselves as more than groups of 'pet lovers', and increased public reporting of, and action on, injured wildlife).

The final area of crossover is discussed in greater detail in Chapter 8, but must be noted here: the relationship between animal protectionists and the Australian Greens. As we will see, there is an unresolved uncertainty for the Greens as to whether they want to be seen primarily as a party of social justice or one of environmentalism. The tension between these two priorities reflects the ongoing tension between the two movements more generally.

There are several barriers to greater collaboration between the two movements. As foreshadowed above, there may be a conflict between

---

29 The extent to which the defence of sharks is seen as radical was evidenced in the inclusion of a photograph of the Cottesloe anti-shark-cull rally in the Commonwealth Government's 2015 schools kit *Preventing violent extremism and radicalisation in Australia* (it was later removed).

Animal type	% change	Annual average
Horses	89.31	198
Wildlife	38.75	13,541
Other	33.42	6,344
Livestock	30.54	3,047
Cats	-7.89	58,621
Dogs	-14.06	62,100
Total animals	*-4.79*	*143,851*

Table 6.10. Change in the number of animals processed by Australian RSPCAs between the periods 2004/05–2008/09 and 2009/10–2013/14. RSPCA Australia.

concerns for the welfare of individual animals and environmental arguments for culling, where a basic difference in ethical worldviews inhibits collaboration (interview: S. Rattenbury MLA, 23 July 2013). Perry and Perry (2008, 31–2) argue, however, that these tensions can be resolved by reframing the issue around a consensus position that maximises animal welfare. Certainly in Australia some such bridging work is being undertaken within the animal protectionist movement. A good example is Crossman's 2011 book *The animal code: giving animals respect and rights*. In this slim and accessible volume, Crossman clearly links environmentalism and animal welfare, arguing that human civilisation and technology have developed in such a way that they subordinate animals and degrade the environment. In this view, environmental conservation and the protection of non-human animals are both aspects of a strong rights position.

A second barrier to collaboration is the emergence of new strategic alliances among environmentalists that are antithetical to many animal protectionists. An example is the rise of the 'Lock the gate' movement in response to coal-seam gas exploitation. This movement has created new relationships between conservationists, farm communities and agricultural producers. These relationships have been productive for the environmental movement in winning support in rural areas of Australia, but have been pursued by those parts of the environmental movement that are most ideologically distant from animal protectionists (as well as from those parts of the environmental movement that have historically clashed with farmers over issues such as the clearing of native vegetation). In addition, in supporting farmers against intrusion from mining companies and the state, this movement has, perhaps inadvertently, reinforced the privacy and sovereignty arguments often used by farmers in calls for anti-activist legislation.

Unions

A second limited link between animal protectionists and other policy domains involves organised labour. As with the environmental movement, we can find examples of partial and contingent collaborations (unions and animal protectionists worked together on the live-export campaign, for example), as well as some fragile connections with the ALP, which I will discuss in Chapter 8.

The 'unholy alliance' (Gulbin 2015) between meat workers and animal protectionists is completely understandable from both a pragmatic and a weak-rights perspective: sending meat processing offshore significantly undermines local employment, as well as the capacity of animal protectionists to influence the regulation of welfare standards. Co-operation between animal protectionists and meat workers is not new; in the early to mid-20th century, for example, farmers worked with the protection movement to promote 'rural slaughter'. This served the interests of reformers concerned about the cruelty of stock transport (Budd 1988), while saving producers the cost of moving animals to regional towns or cities for butchering. Rural politicians from both Labor and the conservative parties supported these reforms.

However, these relationships are fragile and tend to pull apart. Historically, 19th-century reformers saw slaughter and stock-transport workers as just the type of working-class men whom they considered central to the problem of animal cruelty because of their perceived ignorance; some of these underlying attitudes and suspicions persist today (O'Sullivan 2015c). In addition, contemporary investigations into animal mistreatment tend not to delineate between the acts of individual production workers (especially those captured in undercover or whistle-blower footage)[30] and the larger systems that foster animal abuse. This suits employers, who tend to shift responsibility for mistreatment back to individual employees. This presents a strategic and tactical problem for parts of the animal protectionist community who have become focused on an underlying analysis of animal abuse through the lens of a critique of capitalism and/or 'intersectionality'. In diversifying the study of social categorisation and power to include non-human animals and the greater complexities of privilege and oppression (Twine 2010, 9–11), they attempt to focus popular concerns on systems, but the use of media imagery and the generation of 'crisis' events like live-export tend to be framed in episodic and individualised terms.

The potential for future collaboration in this area has been demonstrated in some recent successful tactical campaigns, and in significant moves in the United States to identify an overlap between the interests and welfare of workers and animals (Pachirat 2013). This has led to a consideration of the welfare of agricultural producers themselves; some APOs have attributed poor animal welfare not to owner-operators, but to the supply-chain systems of major meat wholesalers. This type of bridging work, however, is yet to be seen in the Australian context.

Strategic direction and organisational tactics

In their day-to-day work, APOs in Australia are guided by a long-term strategic view. In this context, strategy refers to long-term planning and decision-making processes that incorporate a particular theory of social change[31] and an analysis of the policy environment to identify potential opportunities, resources, allies, barriers and foes (Rubin and Rubin 2008). Strategies include the use of specific tactics or actions that are aligned with the larger goals of the group. While some APOs

---

30 Although Animal Liberation NSW reports receiving complaints from whistle-blowers in one part of the supply chain about the practices of other actors in the chain (interview: M. Pearson, 5 June 2013).
31 Theories are constructed from beliefs about causality (if x, then y), whereas heuristics as simplified and often routinised decision-making practices or rules that may be unrelated to, or significantly separated from, theory.

undertake extensive strategic planning processes akin to corporate or public-sector practice, others tend to take a less formalised approach, or to opportunistically follow actions generally aligned to the realisation of larger movement objectives (interviews: a lawyer involved in animal law, 13 May 2014; M. Pearson, 5 June 2013).

In describing their organisational decision-making processes, interviewees revealed a wide range of strategic approaches, including: regularised, formalised strategic planning and evaluation processes designed to satisfy a range of internal and external stakeholders (interview: CEO, RSPCA Australia, 24 June 2014; M. Mercurio, 4 June 2013); utilitarian calculations to select campaigns and allocate resources (interview: L. White, 24 September 2014); referring to the organisational founders' interests as their major guide to action (in this case in the context of a newer organisation; interview: D. Campbell, 30 January 2014); and short-term planning matching volunteers' capacity and interest to undertake tactical campaigns, where these can be found to align with issues that might gain support and legitimacy from the wider community (interview: C. Neal, 16 April 2013; L. Drew, 23 June 2013). This model assumes a small working-party type structure, with strategic alignment ensured by the shared cultural and ethical norms of the active members.

Importantly, while APOs employ a range of strategic planning processes, these organisations tend to have less developed performance-assessment processes. Those organisations focused on providing welfare services are the most performance-oriented, both when it comes to generating resources (particularly money and volunteers), and to providing services (interview: M. Mercurio, 4 June 2013). The abstract nature of many organisational goals (such as 'ending cruelty') presents a considerable difficulty for all APOs, and so those smaller and medium-sized organisations that produce performance measures have a tendency to use proxies (the use of social media data to measure the effectiveness of a campaign, for example; interview: L. Drew, 2 June 2013), and/or to rely on opinion data produced by market-research organisations (interview: L. White, 24 September 2014).

Given the largest and best-funded organisations tend to have the more formalised and comprehensive strategic planning processes, it may be tempting to attribute quality strategic practices directly to organisational capacity. However, there is more than simply a 'capacity'

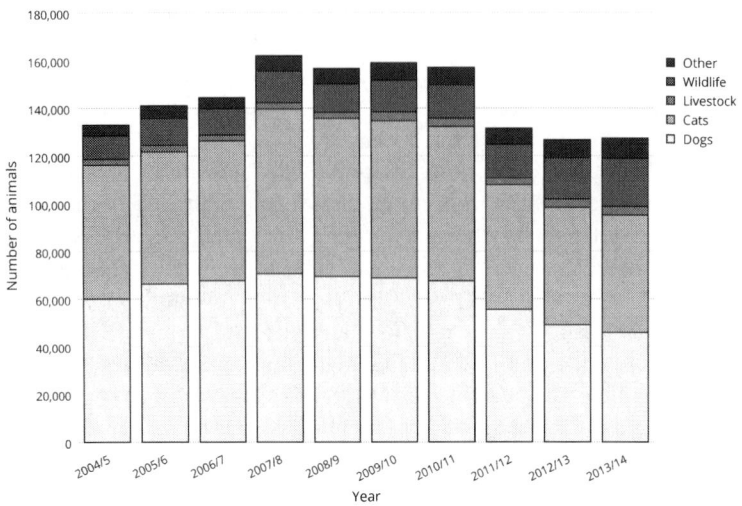

Figure 6.1. Animals processed by Australian RSPCAs, 2004/5–2013/4. RSPCA Australia.

connection between an organisation's resources and its commitment to strategic management. Yaziji and Doh (2013, 771–2) identify how the relatively homogeneous supporter base of smaller and more radical organisations allows for greater flexibility and capacity for innovation, where established and more mainstream organisations have reduced flexibility as a result of needing to serve a heterogeneous stakeholder base.

In examining the strategic and tactical behaviour of APOs in Australia, four broad trends can be identified. I will now consider each strategic trend and its component tactical practices in turn.

A focus beyond the state

That the emphasis of most APOs in Australia is on social change beyond the state is evident in the number of organisations that focus on providing charity-like welfare services rather than advocacy, and in

6 Animal protectionism

the dominance of these groups in securing public resources. In this area of volunteering, these professional staff and volunteers provide the majority of animal protection services in Australia today. This primarily involves processing animals (including receiving them, treating and/ or euthanasing them, and sheltering and rehoming them), with the RSPCA alone processing 133,495 animals in the 2014–2015 financial year (RSPCA Australia 2015). As we saw in Table 6.10, there has recently been a shift in this intake towards a greater diversity of species, especially wildlife. As illustrated in Figure 6.1, however, the total demand for direct services has declined in the last four years. This reflects a longer-term trend of increased care for domestic pets by Australians, as measured using a number of key criteria (Headey 2006). However, the presence of a 'hump' circa 2007 demonstrates that companion animals are still susceptible to significant downturns in the Australian economy (Munro 2008). This type of graph, therefore, illustrates some of the difficulties in using 'headline' figures to measure performance in this area, given broader social and economic factors determine many of the demands on these organisations' services.

Possibly a better measure of the success of APOs in promoting greater public interest in the wellbeing of animals is illustrated in the other 'service' role of a small number of APOs with prosecutorial powers. In Table 6.11 we can see that complaints to Australian RSPCAs have increased 156 percent over the decade from 2005–2006 to 2014–2015. This is a dramatic increase and there is ambiguity as to whether it reflects an increase in animal abuse, or greater popular sensitivity to it (Tiplady 2013, 14).[32] Given the tendencies identified in Chapter 3, the latter seems more likely. However, the trend is very significant and the societies have only partially managed to deal with the increased volume of complaints, with only a much smaller increase in prosecutions.[33] This increase in complaints is a significant indicator of an increase in general public concern; it also reflects a greater awareness of the suffering of animals in situations such as domestic violence (where animals can be significant both as co-victims, and

---

32   A similar trend is seen in the UK.
33   The delay in undertaking prosecutions can make the direct comparison of complaints to prosecutions within a single year misleading.

Year	Complaints	Prosecutions	Ratio
2005/06	38,913	377	0.97
2006/07	41,915	352	0.84
2007/08	49,494	266	0.54
2008/09	50,765	259	0.51
2009/10	53,544	247	0.46
Five-year average (2005/06–2009/10)	**46,926**	**300**	**0.64**
2010/11	54,398	275	0.51
2011/12	45,717	206	0.45
2012/13	49,861	358	0.72
2013/14	58,591	236	0.40
2014/15	60,809	274	0.45
Five-year average (2010/11–2014/15)	**53,875**	**270**	**0.50**

Table 6.11. Cruelty complaints and prosecutions by RSPCAs, 2005/06 to 2014/15. RSPCA Australia.

as barriers to victims leaving abusive relationships; Stark et al. 2006; Tiplady et al. 2013, 93–96).

It is interesting to consider, however, whether the number of prosecutions will increase to match this increase in reporting. The development of legal expertise through the teaching of animal law, and the growth of a cache of legal experts interested in prosecutions and willing to work with APOs that have relevant statutory powers, points to an up-tick in prosecutions, and also possibly to an improved rate of success in these cases. The pro bono work of the legal sector is not simply an extremely valuable resource; it also serves to 'professionalise prosecutions' when they occur (interview: M. Beatty, 16 April 2013), increasing the likelihood of success and of more severe punishment by the courts (interview: T. Geysen, 19 April 2013). The latter can help to motivate APOs, who have traditionally been under-motivated by the possibility of undertaking costly and time-consuming prosecutions likely to attract only comparatively token punishments (Markham

2009, 194–7; Taylor and Signal 2009b, 35–6). An increase in the severity of punishments is seen as a means of broadcasting the moral harm of animal abuse.

On the other hand, the chance of a significant increase in prosecutions is constrained by a variety of factors, including:

- *Culture*: The small number of prosecutions documented in Table 6.11 is demonstrative of a long-standing tendency to avoid 'the whip' where possible in favour of education and 'reproof' (Budd 1988, 19).
- *Cost*: Even with free legal expertise, prosecutions still cost money and evidence must be collected. In many cases the latter is not forthcoming, especially when perpetrators cannot be found.
- *Constraint*: APOs are aware that they may risk losing powers if they exercise them too energetically, and that as technically private organisations with police-like functions, they are encouraged to act very conservatively in the use of their coercive powers (interview: a lawyer involved in animal law, 13 May 2014). Animal Liberation NSW had members appointed as special constables in the 1990s and began a strategy of prosecuting the state government over the treatment of animals in zoos and environmental culling (interview: M. Pearson, 5 June 2013). This short-lived provocation saw their status revoked. Irrespective of the legal merit of their actions, this served as an object lesson to other organisations that aggressive prosecution is a risky strategy that may lead to the loss of enforcement powers by APOs.

The changing number and mixture of pets entering the care of APOs also reflect another feature of these organisations: the cultivation of consumers through direct advocacy and education. APOs have long worked directly with the owners and overseers of animals to increase the level of care the latter provide, and have more recently expanded this activity to focus on the increasingly consolidated Australian pet industry to use its marketing channels to promote 'responsible' (or high-welfare) pet ownership (Zambrano 2013). This type of work has expanded to include involvement in policy debates about the presence of pets in rental and strata accommodation, with the aim of expanding access to accommodation for pet owners but also encouraging tenancy managers to consider the welfare of pets in rented accommodation.[34]

As discussed in Chapter 5, partnerships between APOs, producers and retailers have been used to create high-welfare branded foods, involving APOs both as regulators and in actively building a base of concerned consumers to ensure that uptake matches supply. This work on supply chains also reflects a simple tactical logic. As the CEO of the RSPCA Australia observed: 'Talking to two retailers is a hell of a lot easier than talking to eight governments or however many cattle producers or pig producers' (interview: M. Mercurio, 24 June 2014). In the governance environment of private supply chains, this can lead to a shift to an 'insider' strategy. Having criticised production practices from outside, a shift to the enforcement of RSPCA-branded welfare standards allows the organisation to shift its campaigning energy to other issues. Thus, in the case of pigs, the combination of a high-welfare standard (RSPCA-approved pork) and the voluntary phase-out of sow stalls has led the RSPCA to cease public criticism of the industry. (The degree to which this reduces conflict, however, is considered in Chapter 7.) This is not a one-sided relationship, but an exchange that creates a degree of mutual capture. The RSPCA has recognised that, in adopting a concrete set of standards for animal production, their brand is on the line: 'We lend people our most valuable asset, which is our logo and our name' (interview: CEO, RSPCA Australia, 24 June 2014). The APO's industrial partners, in turn, take on additional compliance and oversight responsibilities. This sort of relationship can create problems, particularly if enforcement capacity is limited. At the turn of the millennium Animal Liberation Victoria endorsed a production facility for eggs that was subject to criticism from other high-welfare producers over the presence of de-beaked animals (correspondence: D. Moore, 18 December 2001). Attempts to influence other areas of private governance – such as attacking claims made through the Advertising Standards Bureau on the basis of misleading communication or offence – have been far less successful (Law 2014).

As much as they might appear to exist in a Randian world of private governance, however, industrial supply chains are not completely outside the sphere of state action. In creating and advertising

---

34 The Animal Welfare League has run a competition to find 'Australia's most pet-friendly landlord' (2015) as part of this wider policy debate.

these private welfare standards, APOs have been able (both deliberately and incidentally) to draw into animal protection debates areas of law that have greater sophistication and a higher capacity for enforcement, in particular as regards consumer protection. A good example is the pursuit of producers in recent years by the national consumer protection and competition regulator, the Australian Competition and Consumer Commission (ACCC). The ACCC has tended to focus on misleading conduct about welfare claims made by particular companies (Pepe's Ducks 2012; Luv-a-Duck 2013; Baiada Poultry 2013) and peak bodies (the Australian Chicken Meat Federation). The enforcement of these standards and claims under generic commercial law principles is also significant because it allows APOs to draw on an area of legal practice with more experienced practitioners than are currently involved in animal law in Australia (interview: a lawyer involved in animal law, 13 May 2014). These actions have been helped by the emergence of a more coherent national framework for consumer law (Bruce 2012b), a tactical and strategic decision to overcome the limited opportunities presented by Australian animal law, and a lack of skilled practitioners in the emerging field.

This approach to consumer protection law has also facilitated new connections. These include co-operation between APOs and general consumer protection NGOs. CHOICE, for example, has become very active in consumer protection around the marketing of free-range eggs,[35] while Animals Australia and free-range egg producers have worked together to attempt to formalise free-range standards at the high-welfare end of the spectrum (Clark 2013). Significantly, when dealing with comparatively disengaged legislators and political elites, APOs can point to litigation by the ACCC as an argument for the state becoming more involved in the issue. Ultimately, the success of this type of work, observes Kurland and McCaffrey (2014), is strategically useful in the process of delivering change over time through the mobilisation of 'bystanders' (such as the ACCC and CHOICE), but also in legitimising the APO, particularly to established elites and economic actors.

---

35 Established to increase consumer information and informed purchase decisions (McLeod 2008), the organisation has expanded to include periodic campaigning.

This process can create tensions between the interest group and social movement ends of the APO community. As discussed, the conceptualisation of a social movement as 'first' or 'second' generation can be significant in determining whether organisational actors perceive their model of social change as incremental or revolutionary. Interest-group APOs tend to be more comfortable cultivating an expansive set of weak ties between themselves and the wider public they are attempting to influence. Through these ties, they may encourage members of the public to make small adjustments to their personal behaviour. Social movement organisations, meanwhile, see themselves as networks of individuals who have acquired politically acceptable self-identities, and this points to a practice of social change that can be driven by 'conversion': through the popularisation of the movement's ideas, but also through the promotion of those identities that automatically incorporate individuals into the cause.

Ultimately, the strategic decision to focus on state, quasi-state or non-state activities is determined by a number of factors. History and continuity play a role. The establishment of the RSPCAs and some AWLs as auxiliaries to the police on matters of animal welfare, supported by incomplete state funding, became a standard model for these organisations across Australia during the first part of the 20th century. This model of governance provides benefits to the state (the provision of public goods at low cost via 'voluntary taxation') and to the APOs (autonomy from the state; freedom of action), which provided the model with longevity. While other approaches involving delegated legislative enforcement exist, this model has only been challenged by the state's takeover of the enforcement of welfare standards in production settings, largely at the behest of industry. Enforcement for non-production animals and the provision of general welfare services remain costs that the state is unwilling to bear. However, the risk of losing enforcement powers and state funding is something that hangs over these organisations as a threat to their social position.

Past success or failure in achieving political access can also contribute to an organisation's decisions about where to focus its efforts. Many advocacy-oriented APOs began with a strong emphasis on lobbying for legislative change and administrative action, but over time have focused increasingly on community engagement and non-state

6 Animal protectionism

activity. One explanation for this is that it reflects a relative failure to access the state to achieve social change. Following the rational political opportunity model of group behaviour, engaging in activities where success seems more assured represents a logical choice. As 'outsider' interest groups, advocacy APOs are forced to choose from a smaller range of options (Maloney et al. 1994).

But this explanation is only partial, as it overstates failure and underplays success. The political reality of policy change is that successes are fleeting moments between long interstitial periods during which it may appear that nothing is happening. A good example of this is the movement to ban duck hunting across Australia. This campaign has classic APO characteristics: formed through the work of a core issue entrepreneur, a focused campaign group (Coalition Against Duck Shooting, or CADS) emerged out of a generalist APO (Animal Liberation Victoria). While maintaining ongoing ties to that group and its catchment, CADS developed a specific and distinctive set of tactics (the rescue and recovery of birds during shooting season, an action that maximises media-friendly drama) and expanded interstate, where similar policy issues existed. That this campaign began in Victoria is unsurprising, given the size and visibility of the hunt in that state (interview: L. Levy; 30 August 2013). There is therefore some irony in the fact that subsidiary campaigns in WA, NSW and Queensland have demonstrated greater and faster success in achieving outright bans on duck hunting, while in 30 years CADS has won only incremental improvements in its home state. The quick wins are significant and disrupt the simple analysis that 'outsider' interest groups are limited in their effectiveness in legislative change.

Time is significant in measuring success. Quick victories are preferable to protracted campaigns when measuring policy impact. An incremental policy process is of mixed benefit for campaigners: it may provide reportable wins and sustain participation in the movement over time, but also permits time for counter-mobilisation, and for industry or others to ameliorate the most serious protection issues involved, which are often the most powerful in terms of campaigning. In Victoria, for example, the introduction of recognition training for hunters, designed to reduce the inadvertent shooting of protected species, has undermined one of the core 'rituals' of the early campaign, in which activists highlighted the environmental impact of hunt bycatch. Such loss of momentum can be problematic, not only because it provides an opportunity for oppositional forces to counter-mobilise, but also because it may move the campaign towards the 'insider' politics of negotiation and adjustment, where APOs often lack relationships, influence, or even a seat at the table.

Mediatisation

The second broad strategic trend among APOs is mediatisation. In our use of this term, mediatisation refers not simply to an intensification of the quantum or pervasiveness of media, but an institutional process whereby – in response to this increase and to the correspondingly greater impact on public opinion of media attention – organisations of all kinds adapt their structures and goals with a view to producing and being responsive to media coverage. Mediatisation is not unique to this policy area; like the neoliberalism discussed in Chapter 8, it is a metaprocess of change that affects the whole of society (Lundby 2009).

Looking at the first aspect of mediatisation – uptake and intensification – we see the increasing significance of mainstream media, particularly news reporting, for APOs. All interviewees observed that formal reporting is important to APOs. Regardless of what their 'core business' may be, APOs tended to see media engagement as an essential channel for their message:

> Getting out what we want to do to the public – they're the ones that are going to drive the change in terms of who gets elected and what products get produced, and so on and so forth, and the way we do that is through the media. We have very good relationships with the media, between the media and our communications department. So, we spend a lot of time either writing or submitting articles for publication, op-eds, or soliciting them from some of our higher profile people. (Interview: D. Campbell, 30 January 2014)

Several interviewees also highlighted the capacity for a good media campaign to break through a longstanding deadlock. In discussing the issue of mulesing, the CEO of the RSPCA Victoria observed that the

6 Animal protectionism

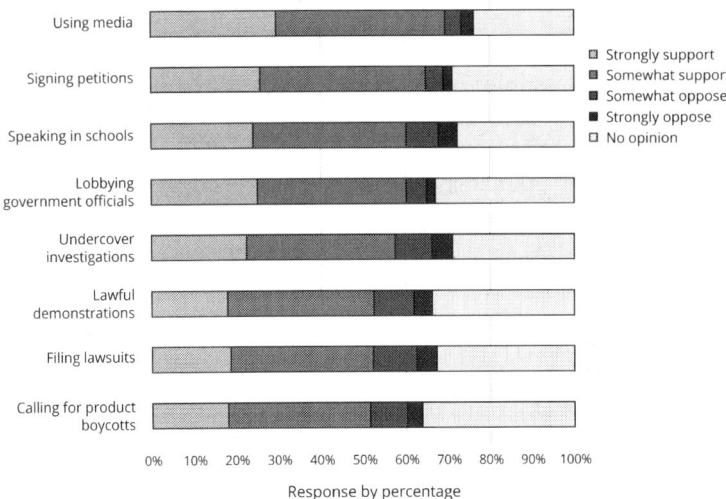

Figure 6.2. Public support for different activist tactics; $n = 1,061$. Humane Research Council (2014), 16.

PETA campaign on the topic put the issue back onto the public agenda, where for decades the RSPCA had made limited progress (interview: M. Mercurio, 4 June 2013). Overall, the view that media coverage is essential to any successful campaign has become a heuristic in major APOs (G. Oogjes in Munro 2005b, 79; interview: L. White, 24 September 2014), a view shared and reinforced by the journalists they work with (interview with Sarah Ferguson of ABC Television in Tiplady 2013).

The accuracy of this heuristic is difficult to determine, but data about which activist tactics the public will accept, and which are most likely to attract media attention, can shed some light. The degree to which the public sees various activist tactics as legitimate is illustrated in Figure 6.2. According to these figures, using the media is the most positively viewed protectionist tactic, and communicative strategies in general are favoured over tactics seen as 'disruptive'.

If the media are the communicative bridge between activists and the public, it is telling to consider the amount of media coverage received by APOs involved in animal policy issues in Australia. Analysis of media coverage demonstrates that established APOs tend to receive the lion's share of print media reporting. This stems from their popular legitimacy, high public awareness of their brand, and their larger professional media staff. It also reflects the tendency for established and known NGOs be provided automatic comment on public issues by journalists. Those smaller organisations that have invested heavily in developing their media profile also have a strong presence here, but largely around 'breakthrough' campaigns (for example Animals Australia in 2011–2012). That PETA (both its Australian and US branches) attracts strong media coverage reflects the group's willingness to engage in creative media tactics to gain attention, as well as the high-profile work of the American parent organisation. Interestingly, the problems associated with the RSPCA in Tasmania (which was more commonly in the media for the 'wrong' reasons during this period of study due to internal conflict over management of the organisation) provided an opportunity for a very small APO (Animals Tasmania, operating as Against Animal Cruelty Tasmania, to be listed in the top 15 APOs most commonly included in media coverage of animal welfare issues nationally during that decade. Animals Tasmania was able to use the internal conflict within the local RSPCA as an opportunity to speak authoritatively to the media on animal welfare issues. Thus, while creative media tactics can help smaller APOs to get media coverage, the major organisations appear still to have an advantage thanks to greater perceived legitimacy, presence and capacity.

The prevalence of animal advocacy appears to have had an impact, not just on news agendas, but on shaping what Australians talk about. In 2014, the Humane Research Council's survey reported three-quarters of the population had discussed, or heard discussion of (Table 6.12), animal advocacy in the preceding three-month period. While only one person in ten discussed the topic on a regular basis, the reported rate of discussion appears quite high for an issue of low salience to most people.

The opponents and interlocutors of APOs are also very aware of the critical role of media in activist campaigns. Thus, APOs need not run a media campaign on every occasion; simply demonstrating that

Frequency	Percentage
Frequently (daily or almost daily)	11.3%
Occasionally (weekly or monthly)	34.8%
Rarely (once or twice)	27.7%
Not at all	26.2%

Table 6.12. How often did you talk about or hear discussion of animal advocacy in the last three months? ($n = 1,041$). Humane Research Council (2014), 13.

they have the capacity to do so has an impact. Mark Pearson recounts a meeting with a major retailer:

> I said, 'Look, before we get to the next topic, I've just got this 35-second video that I want to play you'... We took a Woolworths trolley with 'The Fresh Food People' [slogan] on it to a battery-hen farm, because the aisle where the battery cages are is very similar to the aisle of a supermarket – the same width. And we got the trolley... and we had Woolworths home-brand [egg] cartons in there, which were empty, and a woman dressed up as if she was going shopping. And we filmed her going down the aisle with the Woolworths trolley and she'd take the eggs from the battery cage and put it into the carton with 'The Fresh Food People' [on it]. All these birds squashed in the cages, and one of [the cages] had a dead corpse in it with an egg in it. Because that's what the birds do... And so, we just played this... and when it stopped, there was this dead silence. (Interview: 5 June 2013)[36]

This attention to media strategy shows a number of things. First, the importance of comparatively simple, easily communicated ideas,[37]

---

36 This campaign is an interesting example of the process of ideational exchange through the network of APOs. Animal Liberation NSW initially envisaged a campaign using a branded trolley as a battery cage, but this was combined with Animal Liberation Victoria's tactics of audacious entry into production facilities to create the final message (internal Animal Liberation NSW document: *Woolies egg campaign update*, c1995).

often making animal protectionists think 'like advertisers' (see below). Second, some tactics can have long shelf-lives, but others need to be reviewed creatively more frequently to continue to attract media attention (interviews: P. Mark, 3 June 2013). Third, the way the media (or the threat of media attention) can be used is significant in overcoming the outsider status of some APOs. They may make demands and claims by talking to political elites 'through the media' (interview: L. Levy, 30 August 2013). This can be a means of gaining more direct access for lobbying. Before publishing and promoting a series of reports on welfare standards in production facilities, Voiceless warned producers in advance, and so generated meetings with pork and egg producers. Although the meetings did not produce an agreement to change production practices, they provided a point of interaction that could be built on in the future (interview: D. Campbell, 30 January 2014).

Looking at the second element of mediatisation – the way the adoption of, and focus on, media practice reshape organisations – there is also considerable evidence. First, using the survey of APOs, we can see that these organisations are significantly up-to-date in their use of media to communicate with their key stakeholders. Low-cost internet communication dominates their interactions with members, supporters and contacts, reflecting the comparative youthfulness of many volunteers and the relative newness of some organisations, but even established APOs have been prioritising new media in recent years (interviews: M. Beatty, 16 April 2013; executive officer of an animal welfare organisation, 9 October 2014). As Heckscher and McCarthy (2014) note, the usefulness of social media lies in drawing in those extended members of a movement who have weak ties with core social movement organisations.

A second indicator of mediatisation is the treatment of media interest as an important measure of performance. Particularly early in the life of an organisation, a campaign or a new tactic, media interest can be critical in shaping the tactical practices of the organisation (interviews: L. Levy, 30 August 2013; M. Pearson, 5 June 2013). Animal

---

37 Laurie Levy, for example, talks about the power of duck rescue as the simple inversion of the hunting/killing paradigm (interview: L. Levy, 30 August 2013).

Liberation Victoria, for example, has long engaged in 'open rescue', in part because of its power to get media attention, especially when the organisation was young (interview: P. Mark, 3 June 2013). Open rescue involves the seizure, treatment and re-homing of animals from industrial production facilities without permission, in a manner that makes participants available to public scrutiny (as opposed to more clandestine rescue methods) (Milligan 2013, 117–21). The power of media coverage has been evident to the organisation since Animal Liberation Victoria's beginnings, when Patty Mark's first call to hold a meeting was reported in the *Herald-Sun*. More recently, the initial media response when Debra Tranter, founder of the APO Oscar's Law, tentatively began promoting her organisation's concerns about puppy breeders encouraged her to believe that the issue would attract public and media interest (interview: 22 September 2014). Oscar's Law has also been remarkable in its ability to attract celebrity endorsements, given its comparatively small size.

Mediatised APOs think carefully about events that can mobilise participation and gain media attention. For some, like CADS, the annual hunting season provides a regular window for media coverage, with some journalists covering the hunt and protests each year (interview: L. Levy, 30 August 2013). Other organisations create annual events as showcases, designed to maximise media interest: What will appeal to the media? What story 'hooks' should be provided? Does the event provide opportunities for good imagery? Will it allow participants to create their own social media content? Significantly, the process of mediatisation can see the repurposing of established movement tactics. Physical protests are a good example of this. While protest marches are still a mainstay of activist APOs, the RSPCA has repurposed the political march into its national Million Paws Walk ('Walk to fight animal cruelty!'), which mobilises up to 10,000 individuals annually and generates much social media activity, chiefly involving photographs of dogs and their owners at the event. Many of these participants would likely not see the walk as a political activity.

The institutional aspect of mediatisation also points to the impact of media thinking on how organisations are configured and envisaged. As a spokesperson for CADS explained:

I see the Coalition Against Duck Shooting as being an advertising agency or a public relations company, as well as a fighting force. So, if you're running an advertising agency, your clients will go to you and say, we need to get publicity to sell our products, whether it be a car company or soap product or whatever. And that's what we really do, for [the birds] can't speak for themselves: they can't lobby the governments, they can't campaign, and they can't talk to the media. So we just really act as their spokespeople. And what we're selling to the public is native water birds. Native water birds used to be down the bottom of the ladder; they were on the bottom rank. They didn't have any value. The only value they had was they were living targets for duck shooters. So, when you're getting media coverage, you've got the public sitting there watching the television news, saying, 'That's bloody terrible, what's happening to them?' (Interview: L. Levy, 30 August 2013)

This strategy is sound. In her detailed analysis of animal visibility and enforceable regulation in NSW, O'Sullivan (2011, 45–51) establishes a clear correlation between higher levels of animal welfare protection and the visibility of the animal in the jurisdiction. For O'Sullivan, out of sight *is* out of mind.

This has led to the widespread acceptance among APOs of a model of social change predicated on the concept of 'sousveillance': observation of the powerful from below as a means to moderate their conduct and detect the misuse of power (in this case, power over animals) (Mann et al. 2003). The push to open industrial production to public observation is based on a belief that the average member of the public is inherently concerned with the wellbeing of animals, and would be distressed to see the reality of production systems (M. Pearson in Sacre 2013). This view is reinforced when the 'enemy' (i.e. animal agriculture) is seen to prevent transparency, such as by using laws to limit the filming of farm practices. However, the extent to which 'glass walls' would solve welfare problems may be overstated. As we saw in Chapter 3, Australians have a complex relationship with animal welfare, involving complex psychological techniques that allow us to combine high levels of empathy with wilful ignorance.

6 Animal protectionism

Some animal protectionists attempt to force transparency through direct action. Direct action is a contested term, but generally entails legal disruption, civil disobedience, and/or criminal activities to force change within the existing political, economic and legal framework of a society. By nature it is a controversial strategy, particularly where it prompts debates about non-violent direct action, violence against property and violence against persons (Carter 2012). One particularly high-profile case of direct action took place on the evening of 13 March 2013. An activist known as 'The Blackbird' broke into the Parkwood egg farm in the ACT. The facility, then the only caged-egg production farm in the ACT, had been subject to protests and vigils by Animal Liberation ACT in preceding years (Animal Liberation ACT 2012). It exemplified the type of intensive production that animal protectionists had been attempting to shut down for years amid debates about the capacity of a territory to regulate trade that may cross borders. On gaining entry, he, she or they proceeded to film inside the facility[38] before damaging conveyor belts, egg processing equipment, forklifts and office equipment. This raid was significant in that considerable property damage was inflicted and stopped production for a time. Management described the incident as 'one of the worst examples of industrial sabotage in Australia' (Knaus 2013). In September the same year, Woolworths in the ACT announced it would not stock cage-produced eggs. In the following year, the ACT government paid Parkwood's parent company $7 million to transition to cage-free production as the territory introduced legislation outlawing cage-egg production (Raggatt 2015).

As we will discuss in the next chapter, this example is often cited to promote concern about an increasingly radical animal activism associated with threats and violence against property (ABC News 2013a). But how significant is this type of criminality in the Australian context? This is somewhat difficult to quantify, given many crimes go unreported, and political motivations for crime are unevenly captured in the police and justice systems. However, indicative and comparative figures can be gleaned using self-reported incidents of illegal direct

---

38 The accuracy of the film's content, uploaded to YouTube (www.youtube.com/watch?v=bEwhPUlM3AA) was disputed by the facility's management.

action reported to *Bite Back* (www.directaction.info), an online magazine that catalogues and encourages the type of illegal direct action that inspired The Blackbird.[39] Using an analysis of its annual list of reported direct-action events, we can see in Table 6.13 that over a ten-year period, Australia is the 19th highest-ranked nation for self-reported direct action events in the world. That might sound impressive; however, the number of direct actions involved was small, and there was a stark difference between the top five nations listed and Australia. In the ten-year period illustrated in Table 6.13, Australia's reported number of direct actions was 4.4 percent that of the United Kingdom, the jurisdiction most commonly associated with the image of ski-mask-wearing Animal Liberation Front (ALF) activist/terrorists, an image associated with violence against people as well as property. Using Flükiger's (2008) distinction, the actions of individuals like The Blackbird are more isolated 'lone wolf' attacks than representative of a culture of leaderless resistance, the hallmark of the ALF – although the distinction is hard to determine. Australia's experience of illegal direct action is overwhelmingly associated with illegal entry into farming facilities for the purposes of filming and evidence gathering (the so-called caring sleuth model; Munro 2005b), and/or open rescue.[40] These practices may involve property damage to gain access, but they differ significantly in scale from the sabotage and destruction of property seen in some parts of Europe and North America. The Blackbird's type of radicalism appears extremely rare and outside of the cultural norm of most Australian animal protectionists.[41]

---

39 The magazine does not provide a specific definition of direct action, but uses a basic classification system to flag actions it deems worthy of reporting: arson, liberation (i.e. animal rescue), prisoner (i.e. an action resulting in arrest), sabotage and vandalism.

40 In this decade-long sample of the radical end of Australian animal protectionists' direct action, 22 percent of actions entailed graffiti, 29.3 percent property damage and 48.8 percent animal rescue/theft. There were no reports of violence against humans in this sample.

41 Interpersonal violence does occur, but this is normally the result of isolated incidents. A number of more significant incidents should be noted. Most significantly, an RSPCA inspector was murdered in 1989 (Bezzina and Collins 2011, 192–200), and another shot in the face in an attempted murder in 1999 (the accused died while awaiting prosecution). There have been other cases of minor

6 Animal protectionism

	Country	n
1	United Kingdom	857
2	Sweden	469
3	United States	436
4	Italy	392
5	Spain	319
6	Mexico	310
7	Germany	284
8	France	184
9	Netherlands	104
10	Ireland	95
19	Australia	39

Table 6.13. Countries with the highest levels of self-reported animal-related direct action, 2004–2013.

This is partially explained by the small size of the more radical LSRA animal protection community in Australia. Going back to the ideological distinctions between the welfarist or weak-rights animal protectionists and the strong-rights or abolitionist perspective, we can see that the higher AAS scores of the latter (column b in Table 6.8) correlated to a greater willingness to engage in radical or direct action. However, this may be overstated. The association of more radical parts of the animal protection movement with illegal or legally dubious

---

and serious assaults on inspectors (Taylor and Osborne 2015). After decades of actions involving protesters moving through the hunting area, one rescuer was shot in the face by a 14-year-old hunter in 2011, requiring surgery (AAP 2011b). Reflecting on this incident, Laurie Levy noted, 'I thought about giving it up ... a rescuer was shot in the face, and a shotgun can blow your head off. And when I first heard that it happened ... I immediately thought the worst ... And I really thought a lot after that about giving up, because the police have always said to us, "You've been out there for a long time. The law of averages is, it's going to happen eventually." But the first thing, the rescuers wanted to continue out there ...' (interview: 30 August 2013). CADS invested in ballistic eye protection following this incident.

practices is not necessarily accurate. In her detailed ethnographic study of animal shelters and re-homing services in the UK, for example, Taylor (2004, 326) talks about the theft of companion animals from 'bad' homes by welfare personnel from mainstream charity-like organisations. The difference here is one of focus (companion animals from private homes, as opposed to production animals in industrial settings), and emphasis (the latter incidents go unreported to groups like *Bite Back*).

Direct action does, however, play an important tactical role for animal protectionists in Australia. During the last decades, direct action has become one of the most effective ways that animal protectionists have achieved media coverage of their concerns (Park 2006). Much of this is focused on the obtaining of covert footage, and the polarising open rescue method developed largely by Animal Liberation Victoria.

The symbolism and meanings of direct action in Australia having been de-radicalised, over time it has become integral to the media strategies of some APOs. While direct action in the UK has been employed to attack the commercial viability of animal agriculture (Donovan and Coupe 2013), access to animal production facilities and laboratories in Australia is primarily for the purposes of producing media content for the movement. This is illustrated in the use of the crossed bolt cutter and camera in materials produced by Animal Liberation NSW.

A good example of this direct action–media nexus is the 2013 *60 Minutes* story on the production of free-range chicken meat. *60 Minutes* is a popular mainstream news program, a sort of commercial equivalent to *Four Corners*. While the episode provided a comparison of the ethics and costs of four chicken-meat production systems (conventional intensive, RSPCA-provided, small-flock free-range, and backyard), most of the episode focused on an open rescue by members of Animal Liberation NSW. In openly breaking the law, the activists showed their commitment to the issue, while highlighting their narrative that treatment standards reflect a failure of state regulation. This type of drama makes for good television, and the close working relationship between the APO and journalists saw an exchange of frame, with the reporter picking up the activists' language to describe production systems as 'factory farms' (Sacre 2013). The use of the point-of-view camera shots from inside the facility made the journalist and audience appear to be 'embedded' with the rescue team.

Direct action's symbolic importance also has significance at the social movement end of the protectionist community. This has four elements. First, the 'muscular activism' of direct action, even in its less violent form in Australia, has been seen as attractive to parts of the Australian community, as demonstrated in the rapid rise in popular support for the Sea Shepherd Conservation Society, which has combined aggressive confrontations with whalers from a nation that is both ethnically 'alien' and historically an opponent, with the preservation of species held in high regard by Australians (Jabour and Iliff 2009). Second, following a long period of negotiation, the shift towards direct action has been useful in demonstrating action and activity by protectionists and APOs – it can be proof that 'something is happening'. Third, closer association with direct action has been useful for some groups in delineating themselves in an increasingly crowded and competitive space; it can be used to 'brand' APOs relative to others, and as a fundraising vehicle. Finally, knowledge of, or participation in, direct action is a mark of 'insider' standing and personal commitment. The small size of the animal protection social movement means that direct actionists are often open secrets among core actors in the social movement.

For all the talk of 'open rescue' and 'caring sleuthing', direct action does, however, create real concern and fear. One group with a heightened sense of risk is animal researchers. From the 2014 survey of university animal-welfare officers, we can see that perceptions of physical risk to staff and property at their universities is quite high, particularly among university management and researchers working with animals (Table 6.14). While animal researchers were directly subject to intimidating campaigns in the 1980s and early 1990s, the development of research ethics processes during this period (see Chapter 7) significantly reduced these campaigns. Welfare officers, however, continue to report high levels of risk perception (interview: M. France, 19 May 2014), which is likely in part residual, but also a result of the international nature of the research community and the high degree of attention paid to violent direct action in the USA and the UK (Posłuszna 2015). Nevertheless, fear is fear.

Reported perceived risk to	Average	Median	s.d.
University management	4.61	4.5	2.35
Researchers working with animal models	4.5	5	2.04
Researchers who do not work with animal models, but work in cognate areas	3.22	3	1.22
The general public	3.35	3	1.66
Yourself (Animal Welfare Officer)	4.03	3	2.24

Table 6.14. Perceived risk of physical damage to staff or property on a scale of 1 to 9, where 1 = negligible, 5 = moderate, and 9 = extremely serious, as reported by animal welfare officers; $n = 18$.

Collaboration and creative tensions

A third strategic tendency is towards collaboration between organisations and individuals. Major campaigns in recent years have all involved collaborations at their core, often with groups not traditionally allied. While both the interest group/network governance model (resource exchange and dependency) and the social movement (resource mobilisation) models anticipate this, the sharp up-tick in these collaborations in recent years forms part of a wider strategic orientation that recognises the political landscape in 'ecosystem' terms.

The PETA (USA) campaign against mulesing (2004–2010) is a useful example. The core of this campaign focused on PETA (USA) attacking the use of Australian merino wool in the United States and Europe through advertisements targeting the product as unethical and cruel (Wells et al. 2011). This campaign was undertaken at the suggestion of, and with local input from, Animal Liberation groups in Australia (interview: M. Pearson, 5 June 2013). Domestically, the rationale for this shift to an international campaign was the failure of Australian organisations to make headway on mulesing over several decades, and the strong, closed policy-making relationship between producers and a marketing-focused industry body (Australian Wool Innovation). For PETA (USA) this campaign also permitted the development of a greater level of visibility in Australia, which led to the establishment of PETA (Australia) in 2009. Attacking the brand value of the product at the end of the supply chain is a useful example of strategic 'arena-switching' (Holyoke et al. 2012), shifting the debate into a different jurisdiction (the USA) and using a tactical model (a media-driven campaign) best suited to APOs. Significantly, it caught the industry off-guard, which delayed their response to the new challenger (Bowmar 2009). This delay allowed the campaign to grow, with more retailers opting out of merino products.

What is interesting in the PETA (USA) campaign is how the RSPCA benefited from a campaign by an organisation very different, ideologically, from itself, and from a type of media campaign that it could not or would not run itself (because of its use of images of women's bottoms, and because of its confrontational tone against commercial interests with whom the RSPCA had, or hoped to have, long-term relationships). The CEO of the RSPCA Victoria recognised this, observing:

> We need all of these groups to be appealing to different groups... we are quite traditional and quite conservative and relatively risk averse, those [are] things that we can't do or wouldn't do. (Interview: M. Mercurio, 4 June 2013)

Confrontation, however, is rejected by those animal protectionists who see it as either counter-productive, or against the general ethic of care:

> When people within the animal protection movement demonise animal researchers, I have a real discomfort with that. And I think that really sets us back, sets everybody's goals back when that happens because certainly working as a psychologist for many, many years... I understand the complexity of people's motivations and their level of commitment, and the fact that people draw a line differently on the continuum. (Interview: S. Watson, 25 June 2014)

Mark Pearson, then with Animal Liberation NSW, recognises that the end-stage of the campaign led to a process of negotiation and compromise that was beyond his organisation's capacity. Following the maxim of Martin Luther King Jr[42] (and showing the ongoing influence of Singer's liberation message of the 1960s), he observed: 'I'm more

Animal welfare in Australia

interested in creating embarrassments and international crises, which force the government to instigate a change' (interview: 5 June 2013).

But this crisis model is not without problems, particularly as it leads to incremental reforms that – as discussed above – may blunt the campaign. This was clearly the case with mulesing. Following litigation (see Chapter 7) and a negotiated agreement to phase out the practice by 2010, the industry has declared it cannot and will not meet the timeframe, and the progress of replacement has slowed. Even when working (whether formally or opportunistically) in concert, APOs have a limited capacity to advance their concerns significantly once campaigns have become more incremental processes of negotiated reform. In addition, once incrementalism begins, this often limits the ability of APOs to successfully reactivate more forceful campaigns: industry and elites are able to respond to the issue and talk about developments in welfare to the public, and APOs significantly lose the initiative to control the agenda once industry actors are primed that they are active on the topic. This was evident in PETA's 2011 campaign against mulesing, and in the issue of live exports after the suspension.

In addition, cross-organisational collaborations are limited by differences in ideology and outlook. As Lara Drew of Animal Liberation ACT, an abolitionist organisation that works with non-abolitionist organisations, observes, she feels highly ambivalent about working across the network. This reflects incompatibilities at the strategic level, where collaborating groups may ascribe to different models of social change:

> It's difficult because how the world and the system works is through incremental change, so it is difficult to kind of counter that ... system and that way of change. For example, I guess with [a local egg producer], when we got the news that they're converting [their] barn-line system, a lot of people – some people – a few people were happy

---

42 Of the tactics being employed in the civil rights movement, King wrote: 'Nonviolentdirect action seeks to create such a crisis and foster such a tension that a community which has constantly refused to negotiate is forced to confront the issue. It seeks so to dramatize the issue that it can no longer be ignored.' ('Letter from a Birmingham jail', 16 April 1963)

about that, but we kind of put the message out there that, hold on, it's still a barn-line system and thousands of hens will be crammed in the barn. (Interview: 23 June 2013)

But it can also reflect a clash at the tactical level:

> Now, a lot of our campaigns are entrenched in this capitalistic way of pushing vegan commodities onto people, and 'Just buy this vegan commodity and the world will be a better place', sort of thing, and I'm very uncomfortable with that because, yes, I want people to adapt to a vegan diet, but I realise that while those capitalistic approaches to campaigns still are entrenched, I think these industries are still going to exist; we won't abolish these industries at all. (Interview: 23 June 2013)

This reflects both an underlying concern about the strategic direction of some organisations and campaigns, but also the power of mediatisation. The radical anti-consumerist ideas that exist in the LSRA community (Munro 2005b) are awkwardly placed in a movement that is increasingly focused on cultivating alternative consumption practices using marketing techniques and rhetoric reminiscent of commercial advertising (Mann 2015).

Capacity building

The final strategic tendency among APOs is an increasingly active focus on capacity building across the community. This can be seen in the goals of 'growing the movement' by expanding the range and spread of APOs. Additionally, it is visible in moves to increase the resources and technical base of organisations.

The former pertains to the ecosystem model presented above, in which some organisations identify issue or tactical gaps and, rather than expanding their own operations to address them, seed others operating in or around that space. This specialisation is useful given the fragmented political structure in which animal welfare policy-making takes place: despite the corporatist drive of the 1980s, catch-all APOs run the risk of being spread too thinly. Voiceless grants have been mentioned elsewhere, and are a significant example of how these conditions increase the number and professionalism of small APOs in Australia, while strategically building the prestige of the organisation offering the grants. Seed funding also comes out of identified abeyance structures, like the Anti-Vivisection Union of South Australia, which financially supports and encourages 'successor' organisations (interview: H. Marston, 23 September 2013).

The second aspect of capacity building, resourcing, can be seen in the expansion and professionalisation of simple and long-established recruitment and fundraising activities. For instance, the continued use of campaigning tactics that have limited direct effect, but which allow the creation of extensive databases of supporters and contacts who can be tapped for donations or mobilised into action (interview: CEO, RSPCA Australia, 24 June 2014). Capacity building can also be seen in the way some APOs are attempting to become integrated with, or auxiliary to, established public institutions. This can include an exchange of 'hard' resources (i.e. money), but also builds the legitimacy that comes from cultivating such long-term relationships. The Medical Advances Without Animals (MAWA) Trust, for example, has been working for a decade to develop a more formal institutional home for work on alternative methods and tools for animal research. This has focused on negotiations with universities for the establishment of an institute-type structure located within a major university (interview: S. Watson, 25 June 2014). This type of integration is significant because it allows access to resources such as federal research funding (via the Australian Research Council), and a legitimate place within institutions that use large numbers of animals in invasive research.

Similarly, Voiceless has the long-term objective of significantly increasing the teaching of animal law in Australian universities (interview: D. Campbell, 30 January 2014), as a means of creating a new generation of interested and effective practitioners. In addition, law students are more likely than other groups, on average, to go on to become political and economic elites (O'Sullivan 2015d). In this case the APO's objective fits with the strategic objective of the university sector, which may look to increase student recruitment by introducing new and appealing specialties (White 2012), just as the growth of human rights teaching in universities expanded dramatically during the past three decades, breaking out of a narrowly specific discipline to inform other areas of instruction (Castles and Farrell 1983).

While changes to educational practice have external drivers, this is also being responded to from within the academy. The distinction between formal ethical scholarship on human–animal relations and animal protection practice in Australia was established at the outset of this chapter. This has been changing in recent years, with greater engagement with practitioners by academics and other scholars. From within the conventional university structure, the University of Queensland established the Centre for Animal Welfare and Ethics in 2005, the University of Sydney established the Human-Animal Research Network in 2011 and the University of Melbourne established the Human Rights and Animal Ethics Research Network in 2013. These networks connect academics from a range of disciplines working on various aspects of animal protection. More directly embedded academics-as-activists have also established organisations in Australia, such as the Oceania Collective branch of the Institute for Critical Animal Studies (ICAS). An explicitly liberationist organisation, ICAS Oceania was established circa 2012 and holds annual conferences that explicitly mix the arts, activism and scholarship.

Conclusion

APOs are made up of a variety of individuals, interest groups, social movement organisations, hybrid organisations and abeyance structures. Using the analysis in this chapter, an example of the diversity of APOs is provided in Appendix C. A large number of actors and organisations makes this a complex community that has greater diversity than is often acknowledged (either externally or internally). The overlapping 'waves' of the protection movement have produced two distinct types of organisations – those focused on welfare-service provision and those on policy advocacy – but within these two categories exist a range of philosophical positions on human–animal relations. Differences between these groups do not prevent effective collaboration, even if the network of organisations is attenuated. Using an exhausted metaphor, this community is like an iceberg: considerable attention is paid to a highly visible cap of organisations and campaigns that rest above the waterline, while concealed below is much more activity dominated by charitable services for animals but also including an array of localised campaigns.

Because of this, popular awareness of APOs is quite low, beyond a few 'category-killer' brands. This makes understanding the diversity of actors and their motivations difficult for those not actively engaged in the issues. While the last decade has led to some talk of 'breakthrough' campaigns that have changed the power dynamic between actors in the policy domain, change is relatively slow, with the same topics subject to APO campaigns over many decades. The majority of these groups are policy outsiders. But outsider status has not prevented them from having some successes, particularly in shifting popular opinion and in the world of private governance. Their outsider status is, however, a factor of the power of industry and professional groups to maintain close relationships, the topic we turn to in Chapter 7.

7
Animal-using industry

In this chapter we examine the relationship between animal welfare and protection policy and organisations that use animals – directly or indirectly – largely for commercial purposes. Unlike the animal protection organisations (APOs) discussed in Chapter 6, these organisations fit clearly into the interest-group model introduced at the start of that chapter. They are predominantly formally constituted organisations, largely designed to represent the interests of business and professionals externally, with the primary objective of producing an environment favourable to the production of 'private goods'. Because of this, animal-using industry organisations (AIOs) may be seen as more homogeneous than APOs. However, this is not necessarily the case. While their profit-making objective is straightforward, this group of organisations is complex compared with other sectors of the economy. Partially, this is an artefact of the convergence of two policy concerns – animal welfare and economic protection – but it also relates to the extremely long history of some AIOs and variations in the industries that they represent.

This chapter begins by discussing the structure of AIOs as a collective group, before examining how animal welfare policy is made. It argues that policy-making is predominantly undertaken within the comparatively closed and close policy networks of animal-using industries in a regularised set of relationships with government organisations. Importantly, while animal welfare has increased in significance for AIOs over the last 40 years, the issue remains a comparatively minor – if increasing – problem from the perspective of AIO executives. They face a 'grassfire war' in which slow, consistent policy processes tend to be disrupted by APOs in a recurrent but unpredictable manner. Because of this, the later part of the chapter discusses how AIOs have, individually and collectively, responded to the challenge of APOs, and the pressures that this demonstrates within this community.

Who are they?

In looking at animal welfare, in Chapter 3 we identified the wide range of contexts in which humans have instrumental and commercial relations with animals. Thus, in describing AIOs, our net is wide, incorporating industries and quasi-industries[1] that use animals as commodities; transform animals into other products such as food and clothing; transport and retail animals and animal products; and employ animals as labour and as research and teaching tools. As noted, there are about 500 organisations theoretically involved in the animal protection and welfare domain in Australia. Of this, about half are the APOs and related organisations discussed in Chapter 6. The remaining 250 or so are organisations involved in the use of animals for instrumental purposes.

This necessitates the observation that, as with Australian APOs, the large number is potentially misleading. It may give rise to the image of an army of lobbyists and organisations active in the policy space at any one time, but this is not the case: as with APOs, while some organisations are purely advocacy groups, many others have little or no role in direct political advocacy (Halpin 2005a). Instead, they may be focused on the provision of services within their membership group or

---

1 Activities that have commercial elements, but are not operated strictly for profit. In the context of animal protection and welfare, these can include hobby farming and recreational activities associated with clubs, where commercial opportunities cluster around largely voluntary activities.

7 Animal-using industry

sector, or engaged in some other type of activity, such as marketing. Some are 'potential' actors – that is, groups that are rarely called upon for policy expertise, but that may take action when called upon or in response to a threat or challenge; Schudson 1998, 310–1). Others play a policy role that is outside the remit of the state, such as in the regulation of pure-breed standards, or are only marginally 'industrial'.

With this in mind, it is possible to divide Australian AIOs into eight general types:

- *Farmers' organisations*: Australia's agricultural history produced a range of organisations representing farmers and farming. Some of these developed as generalist bodies, others from specific sectors within agriculture. Over time these have tended to coalesce into a set of organisations in each state and territory. State Farming Organisations (SFOs) generally have direct, individual membership[2] and long-term, very stable relations with political elites and public servants (Zhou 2013, 56–7). From the late 1970s, these organisations were joined by a national body, the National Farmers' Federation (NFF) of which most but not all SFOs are organisational members.

- *Commodity councils or groups*: In addition to organisations representing farmers, the historical pattern of agricultural assistance led to the development of commodity councils. Commodity councils represent the interests of particular agricultural sectors, such as the beef, chicken meat, eggs, goat, pork and dairy primary production sectors, but also some secondary industries such as meat processing and lot feeding. Because of the history of localised industry support, some commodity councils in established sectors are federated (dairying, for example, has a national body as well as state-based representative groups), whereas newer or more marginal sectors may have only a few or one commodity council representing them. Commodity councils have varying relationships with the NFF and SFOs, with some 'integrated' into farming organisations and others independent.

---

2 The Queensland Farmers' Federation and Primary Producers South Australia, for example, are peak bodies of commodity councils, and therefore mirror the NFF's membership structure.

- *Service organisations*: Agriculture's specific policy history in Australia has also produced a range of service organisations (sometimes called marketing organisations, operational organisations, or rural research and development corporations). While some of these organisations rely on volunteers, most are supported by compulsory industry levies to fund services such as research.[3] Similarly, most are owned collectively by their industry and have enabling legislation that spells out their objectives and gives them levy revenue.[4] These organisations tend to focus on service provision, but their research role can be significant in considerations of welfare and they have a strong relationship with the more advocacy-focused commodity councils they support. This does not, however, mean that they are 'creatures' of specific commodity councils.[5] The role of legislation in creating and prescribing their activities is a constraint on their freedom of action, and some have service relationships with multiple commodity councils (Meat and Livestock Australia, for example, services the goat, cattle, sheep and feed lot commodity councils), which can constrain their activities where there is a potential for conflict between commodity councils.[6]

---

3 As Halpin (2004) observes, the strictly voluntaristic nature of SFOs has seen their memberships declining. Levies, therefore, represent a realistic way to ensure financing for industry support without recourse to the use of general taxation (a transfer) or SFO funds (which may encourage free-riding).
4 AIO rural research and development corporations (RRDC) owned by industry include the Australian Egg Corporation Limited (enabled by the *Egg Industry Service Provision Act 2002*), Australian Livestock Export Corporation Limited (LiveCorp) (*Australian Meat and Live-Stock Industry Act 1997*), Australian Meat Processor Corporation (*Australian Meat and Live-Stock Industry Act 1997*), Australian Pork Limited (*Pig Industry Act 2001*), Australian Wool Innovation Limited (*Wool Services Privatisation Act 2000*), Dairy Australia Limited (*Dairy Produce Act 1986*), and Meat and Livestock Australia (*Australian Meat and Live-Stock Industry Act 1997*). The sole government-owned RRDC is the Fisheries Research and Development Corporation (*Primary Industries Research and Development Act 1989*).
5 Australian Pork Limited, however, combines the activities of a commodity council and a service organisation, reflecting the size of the industry.
6 A good example would be the promotion of 'grass-fed' meat by producers as being of better quality. The MLA is forced to avoid these issues, as it services both pasture and lot feeders (interview: J. Toohey, 4 July 2014).

7 Animal-using industry

- *Industry sector organisations*: Outside of primary production, any industry with significant enough revenue is also represented by one or more industry organisations. These trade organisations have a range of structures, from federated national peak bodies to membership-based associations. They also range from broad sectoral organisations (e.g. the Pet Industry Association of Australia) to bodies representing specific parts of an industry supply chain. While commodity councils are essentially industry sector organisations, in that other areas of primary production are 'arbitrarily' excluded from one category and put into another (e.g. the Australian Association of Dog Breeders), there is a real cultural difference between commodity councils and other organisations, a difference that can be attributed to Australia's history of farming practice, the valorisation of some forms of animal rearing over others, and the more formal legislative integration of commodity councils into the state.
- *Individual actors*: While many industry actors choose to rely on their representative organisations, some are large enough, or consider their interests unique enough, to engage directly as policy actors. Previously cited examples included major international fast-food companies and domestic grocery chains, but others may include major agribusiness corporations (e.g. Elders).
- *Industry governing bodies*: Another set of organisations comprises those that oversee the conduct of their industry as governing bodies. Of these, many have a statutory basis, making them official regulators with legislative backing. The most significant examples of these are the national and state-based horse and dog racing bodies. Established from the 1990s onwards, these organisations were split from horse racing clubs so as to separate administration from regulation. Acting under their enabling legislation, they maintain and police the Australian Rules of Racing (by agreement) and their local rules (by law), which focus on the integrity of the gambling system, human safety and animal welfare. A similar organisation – that is, one that regulates its own competition, with rules that include animal protection standards – is the Australian Professional Rodeo Association (APRA). Unlike the racing organisations, however, APRA has not achieved a statutory basis (which it would prefer

to have, in order to rationalise the rodeo industry; interview: S. Bradshaw, 5 May 2014).
- *Breed societies*: A more eclectic group of organisations consists of the various breed societies and regulating bodies. Focused either on specific species or subspecies (such as pure-breed animals) these organisations include fancier groups, breed standards and stud registering bodies, animal showing and competition groups, and others. Of all the organisational types, this group is most ambiguous with regards to its 'industrial' status, and commercial activities included in this area may be minor or secondary to the generation of individual utility. They can, however, play a significant role in animal protection issues through their breed certification requirements.[7]
- *Professional associations*: The final set of organisations comprises those bodies that represent professionals who work with animals. The largest and most significant of these is the Australian Veterinarians Association, which includes state and local branches and an internal set of interest groups, but a range of groups exists in this category. These organisations have split interests: they aim to promote their profession, regulate entry and professional standards, and police and promote their members' duty of care or professional ethics in a way that makes professional associations different from unions.

This organisational breakdown, while lacking the sharpness of true typology, provides a good overview of the diversity of relevant actors who are, have been, or could be engaged with the domain. As with APOs, these organisations are diverse and, as with the Animal Welfare Leagues (AWLs) and RSPCAs, some have enabling legislation that governs some of their functions and provides a direct interface with the public sector. Where they differ is in their considerable financial and

---

[7] Two examples are significant. The first is the selective breeding of animals likely to produce or reproduce known genetic defects (a negative outcome for animals) in order to meet the definition of purebred. Breeding standards can be important in exacerbating these problems. The second is required physical modifications to animals. For example, some cattle-breed associations require hot-iron branding of animals, and are given exemptions from anti-cruelty legislation.

human resources, their presence throughout Australia, and their long-standing relationships with policy-makers. This means that the state (whether regularly or occasionally) has an interest in engaging with these groups to advance its policy objectives. A map of the AIOs and their relationship with state policy-makers is provided in Appendix D.

Industrial relationships surrounding protection and welfare

The diverse range of organisations across the domain mitigates against a coherent and consistent set of organisational responses to issues. Significant institutional actors in the policy network are commodity councils and industry sector organisations dealing with specific issues seen as unique to their sector. The main interlocutors of these organisations are state governments and major APOs. There is limited horizontal interaction across industry. What horizontal interaction exists tends to focus on those organisations most similar in structural, cultural and historical terms. This results in a de facto fire-breaking, for example, of agricultural organisations from those engaged in companion-animal policy debates.

The significance of state agencies as primary sites of policy development and consultation is an important part of this story, reducing the role of national peak representative bodies like the NFF as potential co-ordinating bridges, but also defining the policy paradigm in which organisational participation is interpreted and anticipated. Further, while this is exacerbated by the abolition of bridging structures like the Australian Animal Welfare Strategy (AAWS) (Chapter 8), even these structures tended to include selective industry representation within their specific code development processes, 'siloing' policy-making to a large extent. Because of this, commodity councils tended to see the AAWS process as comparatively clear, while cross-sectoral industry representatives reported the process as opaque.

Within some communities of AIOs, there has been discussion of less disaggregated ways to engage in industry advocacy. In 2015, the NFF and some SFOs engaged in a national strategic conversation about the structure of agricultural advocacy in Australia overall.[8] This included calls to further consolidate the relationship between farmers as individuals, commodity councils and national representative structures. The argument underpinning this proposal was that, while individual organisations may be effective, the somewhat ad hoc development of the representative system undermined efficiency and effectiveness (Bettles 2014). This is a broader political project, which would involve a significant reduction in organisational overlap but also the resolution of explicit and underlying tensions between competing organisations and views about agricultural policy.[9] Thus the scale of this proposed change cannot be underestimated.

Specific attempts have been made to develop formal structures to address cross-sector animal protection activism. Many of these have not been successful, or have not been sustained. For example, the NFF established the short-lived Livestock Industry Group in 1983 to provide a determinant, holistic, cross-sector working group on animal welfare activism (Graham 1983). At the state and commodity council level, the value of a co-ordinating role for animal protection issues is recognised by smaller AIOs. Peak organisations can be referred issues that cross either jurisdictional or sectoral boundaries. In this view, issues can be identified locally, then 'filtered up' to peak structures (interview: CEO, Queensland Farmers' Federation, 16 April 2013). This can only occur, however, where industry segments maintain a strategic and longer-term 'horizon view of things' (interview: general manager [policy], NFF, 14 November 2014).

This has not always occurred. Even when issues have been identified well in advance, some commodity councils are loath to intrude on others' remit. This can be to their own detriment. In the 2011 management of live exports, excessive deference to other commodity councils' sphere of control led the Cattle Council of Australia (CCA) to:

> deal with that in a reactive way, unfortunately, and make such a mess with things we'd really have to get boots and all involved very

---

8 'Project Streamline and Strengthen', following the recommendations of the Newgate Report, commissioned by the NFF.
9 Queensland, for example, has two SFOs: the Queensland Farmers' Federation (not an NFF member) and AgForce (an NFF member) that have had mixed relationships over the last decade (conflict, co-existence, collaboration, cross-membership). AgForce represents a merger of commodity councils (cattle and cane growing).

quickly... Now, the live exporters have their own big council, Australian Live Export Council. And in a normal set of circumstances you left them to drive those sorts of issue. It's their bailiwick. That's where we've got these nice little boxes – but this really genuinely is a crossover issue, [it] crosses over to the producers and the live exporters. So, through [peak red-meat commodity council] the Red Meat Advisory Council, a lot of debate [went] on, and it seemed that the Cattle Council's constituents' interest [was] to get this sorted because it affects our members that rely on live-export trade for income. Some areas, there's no other choice. (Interview: J. Toohey, 4 July 2014)

Thus, effective co-ordination of animal welfare and protection policy appears to have eluded the sector. The NFF in 2013 admitted to failing in its attempts to address animal protection issues in a unified way, conceding 'a history of sectoral response to animal welfare issues' (Sefton & Associates 2013, 43).

Why the sectoral response?

In addition to structural siloisation, a number of factors contribute to this lack of co-ordination between industry actors.

The first barrier to effective collaboration is the disparate state of environmental awareness amongst the public, especially regarding animal protection issues. Commodity councils from the chicken and pork sectors, for example, report occasional use of systematic surveying (interview: a representative of the chicken industry, 31 January 2014) and focus groups (interview: A. Spencer, 23 June 2014) on this topic.[10] Others have less structured environmental scanning practices (interview: E. Forbes, 9 April 2014). This may be problematic, as public opinion can be fast-moving. But it also stems from the difficulty of establishing a truly informative set of measures in an area where industry considers public opinion to be unstructured and volatile (interview: J. Toohey, 4 July 2014; E. Forbes, 9 April 2014). Where high-

---

10   The dominant market research focuses in general terms on product characteristics and demand.

welfare products exist, retailers (interview: a representative of the retail industry, 22 April 2014) and highly integrated industries (particularly eggs) are best placed to measure the conversion rate of concern into high-welfare product options, but the movement of this type of information across the sector can be limited by the desire of retailers to ensure they have better intelligence than their suppliers.

Second, relationships can be very pragmatic and groups may not support related enterprises where both welfare standards and the economic value of the practice are low. A good example of this is jumps (hurdle and steeple) racing in South Australia. With low levels of participation (O'Sullivan 2015a) and a comparatively high injury rate to horses (Ruse et al. 2015),[11] the South Australian Jockey Club has pushed for the sport to be wound up by the state government (ABC News 2015). While this may be thought to reflect the susceptibility of marginal enterprises with 'poor' welfare records to legislative bans, this is not strictly the case.[12] In this example the opportunity cost of using racing facilities for jumps compares unfavourably to thoroughbred racing, making this a pragmatic decision by the jockey club to push out the last of the jumps competitors (in comparison, a temporary suspension in Victoria in 2010 was lifted by Racing Victoria; McManus et al. 2012). This argument about industry size and susceptibility to regulation is born out in a counter example: the comparative unwillingness of political elites to entertain blanket prohibitions on exotic circuses (Browne 2012). In the latter case, neither opportunity cost nor direct competition with zoos exists.

Third, breakages between different economic sectors produce barriers to industrial collaboration. Some of these are simply related to the social and/or other distance between industries that might otherwise have strong grounds for collaboration. Wool producers and laboratory researchers, for example, face similar campaigns (international secondary boycotts), by similar APOs (PETA [USA]), over

---

11   Although in recent years Ruse has observed an improvement in the safety of jumps racing in Australia, steeple racing remains the most dangerous to horses.
12   Sponsors and third-party users of racing venues were targeted by activists opposed to jumps in South Australia, which did have an impact on the profits of venues associated with the practice (interview: T. Franks MLC, 26 September 2014).

similar issues (inherent practices in their use of animals). Other breakages are related to conflicting stakeholder interests. This can produce conflict between industrial actors over what appear to be symbolic slights but are in fact more significant in nature.

An example of this is the 2013 Coles–Animals Australia 'Make it possible' campaign. In this in-store promotion, Coles sold Animals Australia-branded shopping bags, in line with the positioning of Coles as a supplier of certified high-welfare products (free-range, RSPCA-approved and grass-fed). The promotion, similar in structure to the retailer's cross-promotion with Landcare Australia, was not received well by the agricultural sector. Farmers threatened to boycott Coles and its parent company, and to refuse to supply them. In this case Coles significantly misjudged the sensitivity of farming communities towards Animals Australia (Clark 2013), and the role of downstream industries in pushing for increased animal welfare standards that primary producers see as antithetical to their profitability. But this shows how these two groups have very different sets of stakeholder relationships that drive their commercial concerns. Importantly, while the NFF was successful in getting Coles to withdraw from the promotion,[13] the channelling of displeasure through the federation (FarmOnline 2013) illustrates the weakness of suppliers relative to retailers. Using their representative body to engage with Coles presented fewer long-term risks in confronting one of the two major grocery retailers in Australia, one with massive market power over individual suppliers.

Finally, as this demonstrates, mediating structures or organisations are rarely able to broker agreements between APOs and AIOs. The ongoing dominance of issue management by individual commodity councils means that organisations with a history of dealing with cross-cutting and social issues are not seen as natural solutions to welfare issues. This has been observed nationally, but also among SFOs:

---

13 Technically Animals Australia asked Coles to stop selling the bags, but this was widely interpreted as a decision by Animals Australia that allowed Coles to 'save face' (ABC News 2013b) while ensuring the APO maintained a positive relationship with the retailer.

I think that's one of the challenges for the policy environment, and my observation of industry bodies and how they'll react to it, is there isn't any real proactive discussion going on with... those people who believe that animal welfare standards are too low... [The policy domain] still has very strong camps and polarised debates... and therefore that's a very difficult environment for someone like our organisation to sort of try and put our hand up and say, 'We'd like to broker a better relationship here,' as we would do in environmental issues. (Interview: CEO, QFF, 16 April 2013)

Here the disconnect between APOs and the environmental movement is significant: the integration of environmental pressure groups into negotiated processes in other areas of policy-making has not been mirrored in the animal domain.

Animal welfare: significance and meaning

The comparatively scattered response to animal welfare and protection policy reflects a comparatively low salience of the issue to AIOs in Australia over many years. This, however, has been changing. Respondents report that the importance of these issues for AIOs has been increasing steadily in recent years, across a range of organisations (interview: general manager [policy], NFF, 14 November 2014). For the dairy industry, animal welfare has become a far more salient issue in the last decade and is now a 'top five' issue (interview: W. Judd, 19 April 2013), up from a mid-level issue just five years ago (Queensland Dairyfarmers' Organisation 2009). This shift has coincided with Voiceless focusing on dairy welfare as a neglected ecological niche among APOs. Similar, if less dramatic, changes in significance were reported by the other commodity councils and industry organisations interviewed for this volume.

Responses to this shift have also included the institutionalisation of new structures designed specifically to embed welfare policy development in organisational activity. Racing includes regular board items on welfare (interview: E. Forbes, 9 April 2014). The Cattle Council of Australia, in establishing a subcommittee system in recent

7 Animal-using industry

years, formed an Animal Health subcommittee with explicit remit to work on animal protection issues. The NFF has set up a taskforce to consider welfare issues.[14] In 2010 the Australian Professional Rodeo Association appointed an animal welfare representative to drive policy development and training. For many respondents, this reflected a desire to become 'proactive' on the issue:

> My attitude has always been that . . . if we see our own issues in association or as a federation, we need to be addressing them. Because we say, 'We love the animals, and we look after animals', if there's anything that we see because we're the experts, we should be addressing it ourselves and not waiting for someone else to address it for us. It must be proactive and primarily for the benefit of the animals. (Interview: S. Bradshaw, 5 May 2014)

Proactivity here includes an acceptance that APOs have been driving welfare debates during the last decade.

Thus, we need to ask the question: if AIOs see animal welfare as increasingly important – internally and externally – how do they perceive the issue? That is, following on from our discussion of what cruelty means for the Australian public in Chapter 3, what does welfare mean for those involved in animal industry?

The first meaning was introduced in our previous consideration of 'husbandry' and animal-rearing. When interviewed, many industry representatives suggested that there is a direct relationship between effective industry practice and good welfare. Whether it involves primary production or entertainment, this argument can be summarised as: it is in our industrial or commercial interest to maintain the highest standards, because otherwise productivity (however it is measured) will decline. This notion that 'good husbandry equals good welfare' allows their industrial or commercial productivity to act as a measure of good animal protection practices.

---

14 There does not appear to be any significance in the name; 'taskforce' normally refers to a special organisation with a limited scope of operations and a limited timeframe (interview: general manager [policy], NFF, 14 November 2014).

As we will see below, in this model the ideal level of welfare is reached just before the point at which productivity begins to decline. In this formulation, animal welfare depends on an economic trade-off between competing interests and their 'utility'. These interests include:

- the value to the producer (measured in productivity or profit) in working their animals as 'hard' as possible
- the wellbeing of the animals involved (their welfare, however measured, but excluding any intrinsic value to the animals themselves)
- the 'public good' of having an animal industry that is 'not cruel'.

This view of welfare considers it as a series of economic trade-offs.

McInerney (2004) argues that, contrary to the 'good husbandry' argument, welfare improvement in commercial settings is non-linear. As we can see in Figure 7.1, human intervention produces a more positive relationship than that which animals might experience 'in the wild' (point A, at which there is no human intervention in the animal's health), rising to a point of maximal welfare (B, at which there is a positive intervention). However, for further productivity to be gained from animals beyond this point, society must accept declining levels of animal welfare (negative utility for the animal, with the possibility of negative externality to society if they 'care'). In extremis, productivity can reach a point of negative value (point E), where both productivity and welfare rapidly decline (for example, working an animal past exhaustion; this point is indicated in the figure by the dotted arrow). In this type of economic analysis, welfare debates exist in the shaded area of zone C, where productivity and welfare are economic trade-offs necessitating a political rather than technical debate. The debate is political in nature because it is about the authoritative allocation of utility to different groups due to the increased costs of production.

As an abstraction this model overplays similarities between sectors. There is no simple 'unit of welfare' comparable to monetary costs and profits, and so welfare is measured in different ways for different types of animals and in different contexts. The value of this model lies in its demonstration of two factors. First, and most simply, the model shows how economic value is privileged in the shaping of welfare policies. Thus, in a discussion of hot-iron cattle branding – an activity largely abandoned in most of Australia because it can be

7 Animal-using industry

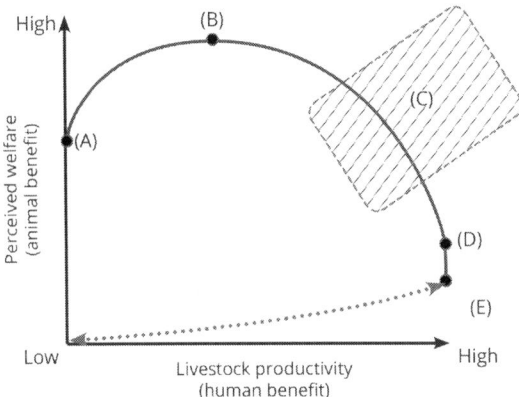

Figure 7.1. McInerney's 'conflicts between animal welfare and productivity' model (adapted). (A) 'natural' welfare/non-intervention, (B) 'maximal welfare', (C) 'desired/appropriate' welfare range, (D) 'minimal welfare' and (E) system collapse. Simplified and annotated from McInerney (2004, 18).

replaced with other, less painful stock management and identification systems – the welfare calculus follows this exact formulation:

> You go to any property, particularly the big ones up north where they've got hundreds of thousands head of cattle – whatever we bring in, they need to maintain viability... They have welfare in mind... it's in their interest to look after the welfare of the animals or else they'll not make as much money as they would otherwise. But at the moment, particularly with the drought and bits and pieces, they are really doing it tough and so it's a balancing act for them. (Interview: J. Toohey, 4 July 2014)

Second, it shows that signals about value can be complex. Wells et al. (2010; 2011) researched wool producers' decisions about abandoning mulesing following the PETA (USA) campaign, during the period in which the industry had committed to phase out the practice by 2010. In their research, they found that decision-making included:

- a recognition by producers that they could ignore the voluntary commitment (non-compulsion)
- an assessment of the costs and practicality of alternative practices (generally high)
- an assessment of the comparative welfare impacts of mulesing versus breech (fly) strike in probabilistic terms (unfavourable to change)
- an assessment of the probability that consumer interest would translate into a demand for alternative products (low, given low levels of public understanding and therefore low willingness to pay for alternatives).[15]

In addition, Wells et al. identify that interaction with farmers who had already voluntarily phased out mulesing was significant in shaping the decisions of others to adopt above-minima welfare practices. The willingness of some producers to abandon the practice voluntarily demonstrates that decision-making using strict cost–benefit analysis is moderated by a range of factors associated with local norms and expectations, as well as the practical capacity for improved welfare.[16] Additionally, the value of this model becomes less informative as we move away from strictly economically rational sectors.[17]

---

15 Which, as of 2015, is mixed. Brokers report interest from European buyers and sellers in the EU market in non-mulesed wools, but limited interest in domestic Chinese production (Locke 2015). This would indicate that mixed switching in the industry, and investment in longer-term solutions (such as genetic breeding to reduce the risk of fly strike), have been effective in adjusting supply to demand.
16 Some of this clearly has an economic basis. Thus, for example, the use of electrical immobilisers in remote areas – a technique that permits surgery on large animals by forcing muscular contraction, but does not provide pain relief – is often justified with reference to a 'lack of veterinarians' (interview: director of a bureau of animal welfare, 21 August 2013). This lack, however, could be factored into the model as a welfare cost that would significantly change the economics of cattle production in remote areas. This shows the problem of the economic model: it trades tangibles (money) against intangibles (units of welfare, externalities) that are highly and subjectively discountable.
17 For AIOs operating on a less strictly economically rational basis, this model is moderated by a range of other drivers that relate to cultural norms and expectations about what constitutes appropriate standards of care and treatment. This can lead to what might be described in a strictly economically rational model as 'over-investment' in care. Such distinctions can be seen in industries where there is a

Overall, animal welfare policy and protection campaigns have become significant for industry, but are largely only seen through an economic lens. In addition, while producers in theory might be expected to have no preference about where they sit on the animal welfare curve provided any lost productivity can be recouped from their buyers, this does not appear to be the case. AIO constituents do not perceive a willingness by the public to accept higher retail costs in exchange for welfare gains. The NFF has reported that many primary producers see animal protection primarily as a threat to their major concern: profitability. Where activist campaigns move other AIOs to adopt standards that are enforced upstream, their limited market power relative to retailers does not always provide producers the opportunity to add value (Sefton & Associates 2013, 53).[18] Utility, in this model, can be generated at a different point of the value chain, with cost being shifted to producers.

For some, activist campaigns represent more than simply a risk of increased production costs. These organisations are cognisant of the risk of reaching a 'tipping point'. While the general community may have little interest in animal welfare, this lack of interest is sustained by a general sense of trust in industry. As the CEO of Australian Pork

---

mix of high-end, economically successful participants and a large number of quasi-hobby or marginal actors. A good example of this is in equestrian industries, where there is an 'over-investment' in animal care over strict productivity calculations (interviews: D. Dekker, 17 April 2013; E. Forbes, 9 April 2014).

18   This emphasis on the power of primary production relative to downstream actors in the supply chain has the impact of drawing international debates and issues into the domestic policy conversation. International campaigns may directly affect domestic production if transnational APOs target Australian producers. More indirectly, the use of global supplier standards by transnational corporations often embeds responses to welfare issues fought in other jurisdictions. In some cases these issues are more or less directly transferable to the Australian setting (such as chicken-density stocking levels; interview: a representative of the chicken industry, 31 January 2014). In other cases, such as moves by retailers away from feed-lot beef to 'pasture-fed' meat, the driving concerns are less relevant to Australia (interview: J. Toohey, 4 July 2014). In the latter case, feed-lot production is a major animal protection issue in the USA, in part due to issues of agricultural economic distortions associated with farm subsidies that do not exist in the Australian context (Marcus 2005, 188–9).

Limited observed, his consumers would switch from pork to another meat should they lose confidence in the industry's ability to provide appropriate welfare:

> They are not fickle about that switch, but they are definite about it... if they see a systemic problem with our industry, over time they will make that shift... They don't change their mind quickly. But if they get piece[s] of evidence one after the other, they will make the shift. (Interview: A. Spencer, 23 June 2014)

This points to an additional concern in some sectors: that their members are not as motivated about animal protection – as a risk – as are sector leaders, making mobilisation and response less effective.

The Victorian Farmers' Federation, for example, lists animal welfare as a primary threat to farming in its promotional materials (Victorian Farmers' Federation 2014), and SFOs have referred to the need to counter activist campaigns when raising funds for industry advocacy. However, in 2014, the agricultural sector overall saw more basic economic issues as far more important than activist campaigns (see Table 7.1), although industries more recently targeted by activist campaigns reported higher levels of concern. This has implications for attempts to mobilise these constituents against activists, and reveals a perceived disconnect between profits (A), supply-chain power (B), and activist campaigns (C).

The inside track: welfare as a policy routine

Having a largely passive membership on these issues, AIOs have been forced to pursue insider strategies to negotiate and manage policies involving the treatment of animals. Thus all major, and most minor, AIOs retain regular and enduring relationships with policy-makers and regulators, such as key public servants, enforcement personnel, and (depending on the stature of the industry) politicians. These relationships are exchange-based: industry organisations tend to offer information and program implementation capacity (they are large 'delivery agencies' of industry programs, directly or through their service

Issue	Percentage
Profitability (A)	45
Costs / supermarket duopoly (B)	33
Production costs	29
Regulation	22
Drought	11
Minority groups and activities (C)	10
Labour shortages	9

Table 7.1. Primary issues affecting farmers (respondents could select more than one); $n = 1,002$; annotated. Guthrie and Akindoyeni (2014).

organisations), in exchange for favoured access to key decision-makers. They may not always achieve their policy objectives, but AIOs always anticipate getting a 'hearing'. As discussed above, these interactions are partitioned into various industry-segment silos, with these silos commonly reproduced in each jurisdiction where the industry has a significant basis of operations. Where policy is pushed up to the national level, SFOs, the NFF, and only the largest commodity councils tend to have enduring and regularised relationships with policy-makers.

To some extent this suits a close, closed policy-making style that tends to keep policy development out of the public eye, and, as Halpin (2005b, 145) has observed, often out of the gaze of parliaments, by keeping policy in the administrative space where possible. This is the source of a common belief that AIOs have 'captured' the public sector.

Capture or captives?

A popular explanation by many APOs for the perceived gap between public expectations about animal production in industrial contexts (Chapter 3) and industrial or regulatory practice is regulatory capture. Regulatory capture is one of a range of principal–agent problems in democratic practice where the complexity of the state, and the disproportionate power of some interests (commonly economic), subvert regulation, either to negate its effect (by declawing the regulator) or to provide advantages (for instance, by preventing market entry with high regulatory barriers in order to create a mono- or oligopoly; Croley 2008). This view is promoted by animal protectionists, as well as by scholars (Goodfellow 2012). A number of hypotheses are promoted:

- Following a political-economy analysis, economic interests are seen to receive favoured access to policy-makers, giving them greater influence to shape policy and/or to prevent issues from coming onto the political agenda.
- The operational closeness of regulators and industry creates shared cultural norms and distorts regulation.
- The inherent design of regulation, largely focused on state departmental inspector models, results in regulatory capture owing to the orientation of government departments towards 'pro-growth' economic objectives rather than public interest or animal welfare (this can be described as the 'conflict of interest' argument).

The latter is at the heart of calls for independent animal-welfare regulatory offices (see Chapter 8).

The question of capture is a complex one. Agricultural interests, in particular, have a strong historical and structural position relative to their state interlocutors for a variety of reasons. These include history and path dependency. The significance of the agricultural sector to the Australian economy previously provided the sector with direct political influence through rural constituencies. This was entrenched in a series of closed policy networks – 'iron triangles' – focused on specific production segments in the form of the various marketing bodies that focused on ensuring minimum prices for commodities before the 1970s. While the relative significance of agriculture to the overall economy declined after the Second World War, the sector's interface with government – through state and Commonwealth agriculture departments – provides the sector with an enduring key ministry with whom it is engaged. Second, while rural population decline and urbanisation have increased the overall number of non-rural seats in parliament, rural seats have a tendency towards smaller population sizes. This leads rural interests to have higher numbers of MPs than a strict one-vote-one-value model would produce (Robinson 2003). Third, the sector

7 Animal-using industry

has developed stable and enduring peak political structures, providing greater capacity for relationship building and maintenance with bureaucrats and political elites.

On the other hand, the past 50 years have seen the dramatic dismantling of the type of policy networks that were the most prone to capture: the marketing boards. What remains is a closeness between peak bodies and agricultural policy-makers, but not the interleaved relationships that once existed in each commodity area. This residual closeness can be mistaken for capture (Botterill 2005). In considering relationships with agricultural policy-makers, Marsh and Pannell (2000) identify how the adoption of neo-liberal economic policy has shifted the role of government agencies from service provision to client-driven approaches that are based on stricter cost-recovery models. Greater accounting for the bottom line requires a willingness of producer groups to pay for government services, and for state service providers to pay greater attention to the public interest in co-investment in services.

Further, the micro-economic reform agenda since the 1980s forces policy-makers to consider interests from across the economy. This gives the representatives of other economic interests, such as importers, wholesalers and retailers, a metaphorical 'seat at the table'. Policy-makers may need to consider the wider implications of any support for industry through the lens of public interests and public goods, and/or to consider free-trade arguments. This is one reason why governments have yet to substantially respond to producers' concerns about concentration at the retail end.

The wider implication is that agricultural interests have, through the disciplining effect of free markets and neo-liberalism, a significantly smaller array of policy options to draw upon, while at the same time having their policy representations channelled towards agriculture departments and rural political representatives. This is evidence of a declining structural power-base in policy networks, if not at the level of regularised interactions with bureaucrats. These enduring relationships are strongest at the state and territory level, where regionalised programs and activities are commonly generated and co-managed, but their influence has declined over the last decade. The non-prioritisation of 'producers' (including primary industries and manufacturing) in post-Keynesian economic thought has given transporters, wholesalers and retailers greater influence, particularly when it comes to competition policy at the national level. Overall, argue Cockfield and Botterill (2013), the policy-making process relevant to rural and regional industry tends to be one of long periods of incrementalism based on an overarching policy model (first protectionism, then adjustment, now global free markets). Within this framework, agricultural interests have a favoured seat at the policy-making table, but only to the extent to which this input fits into the dominant policy model of the day.

The implication for policy-making around animal welfare and protection issues is clear. The bias towards incrementalism is a strong one and provides stability for producers in dealing with regulatory change. Agricultural interests will retain a strong capacity to influence the design and implementation of regulation given their close relationships with policy-makers in this area. However, this tight control is limited to a very focused subset of the policy-making landscape, and is subject to external shocks. As Cockfield and Botterill (2013) argue, this incrementalism has been subject to considerable and radical punctuations to which the whole of Australian agriculture has tended to eventually succumb, albeit with a willingness by the state to help with adjustment to the new state of affairs. We have seen this model in the ACT, where cage-free production was not simply regulated out of existence; instead, the territory government paid adjustment payments to producers. The industry did not 'win' this conflict, but its losses were moderated and paid out.

New relationships: legitimisation?

Halpin's observation that the policy role played by AIOs is often sub-parliamentary may reflect a waning capacity or desire to win 'big fights' in the public arena. As Ian Randles observed:

> We're prisoners here of our own rhetoric, in some respects. We often say, 'This is an industry that Australia can't do without. This is an industry that the whole pastoral economy revolves around. The Kimberley will fall over for instance, or northern Queensland, if we

don't have this industry.' Maybe it will, maybe it won't. I don't know. Once you start that, then you're suggesting you've got more capacity than you really have. (Interview: 30 September 2013)

By 'digging in' to retain relevance and influence, in Halpin's words, and by their reluctance to fight policy debates in public, AIOs have lost much of their political legitimacy and thereby their political capacity. This is reflected in the suspicion evident in some APO criticisms of industry – insider politics can be seen as illegitimate because it is shielded from popular participation (Tham 2010, 251).

This has led a variety of organisations to experiment with the formation of new types of relationship to address the issue of legitimacy and the allegations of capture. The most tentative has been at the level of ad hoc meetings between key AIOs and APOs. In some cases, this produces positive interactions that are marked by genuine information exchange (interview: R. Cox, 2 October 2013); in others, outcomes are less positive. The latter often results from the proximity of interactions to activist campaigns; meetings that take place during or close to the start of a campaign provide little perceived value to AIOs (interview: A. Spencer, 23 June 2014). One industry representative described hosting a visit with an APO that produced few enduring results and little trust, 'just so they can say they've been on a chicken farm' (interview: a representative of the chicken industry, 31 January 2014).

Better initial meetings may lead to enduring and regular if unstructured interactions between organisations (interview: W. Judd, 19 April 2013). These may produce useful levels of trust that result in information exchange and the resolution of concerns in informal ways that, in more hostile contexts, might 'blow up' (interview: CEO, QFF, 16 April 2013). For some organisations, this may lead to 'backchannels' of communication that reduce conflict, or are necessary where organisational stakeholders would be intolerant of meetings with 'enemy' organisations (some AIOs will not meet with organisations they perceive as an existential threat, but some will). Trust between organisations of this type, however, takes time to build, and negative interactions may limit potential relationships for long periods of time (interview: an animal welfare advocate, 5 September 2014). In some cases, this allows AIOs to 'shop' for preferred APOs with whom to form partnerships, demonstrating the value of mutual exchange in cross-validating organisational legitimacy.

Some of these exchanges are formalised. The most significant and amenable APOs willing to do this are the RSPCAs. The RSPCAs' relationships with industry are complex, and include purely informal information exchange, representation in organisational policy-making, shared committee memberships, and formal commercial or cost-recovery relationships. Of the latter, RSPCA-branded standards processes have been discussed in detail, but the society's formal relationships with AIOs also include programs like the PIAA's 'Dogs Lifetime Guarantee Policy on Traceability and Rehoming'. This program sees dogs purchased from PIAA members provided a guarantee of rehoming should they become abandoned or unwanted at any time. This is an interesting program because – on paper – it extends a *lifelong* duty of care over companion animals by the industry body. More significantly, it does not really seem necessary: PIAA members sell around 65,000 dogs a year nationally. Given the number of rehomed dogs to date remains small, the organisation's membership would appear to have ample capacity to place these animals themselves. But the PIAA has utilised the agreement with the RSPCA for other internal and external reasons. Internally, the decision to outsource re-homing reflects an unwillingness by industry members to accept the cost and responsibility of the program (what if an animal cannot be homed?). Thus the industry body has socialised the cost of the program across its members.[19] Externally, the program gives the comparatively unknown industry association stronger legitimacy through association with the strong welfare brand. This was on display in 2015, when the organisation used the program in making a case to retain industrial-scale pet breeding and retail sales in NSW, even in the face of opposition to these practices from the RSPCA itself (Joint Select Committee on Companion Animal Breeding Practices in NSW 2015).

---

19 Which may be a problematic policy design from an animal welfare perspective. If the need to rehome animals increases due to poor retail practices (such as a failure to assess or prepare potential owners), socialising the costs of rehoming will not incentivise individual retailers to improve their sales practices.

7 Animal-using industry

Constantly conflicted? Veterinarians and welfare officers

Within AIOs, a special category of industrial workers exists: veterinarians (and their associated support staff) and laboratory animal officers. Both are professional groups of workers, in that they have a duty to their clients, the wider public, and their profession. This category of animal workers has ethical codes of conduct regulated by legislation, organisational governance systems and convention. Strong adherence to these codes is necessary to protect the welfare of the animals with whom they work, but these workers are usually employed or paid by animal owners (although some are employed by APOs or by the state). Unlike many other professional groups (Cribb and Gewirtz 2015), veterinarians and animal-welfare officers have two clients, whose interests may not coincide – or, from a strong rights or abolitionist perspective, may be fundamentally at odds. This tension is recognised within the professions.

As Williams, observes, this often leads to veterinarians playing a mediating role between the interests of animal owners and wider community standards in the course of their working day:

> We live in countries with agriculturally based economies, where human use of animals is accepted by the majority of the population – including, quite obviously, the veterinary profession. So, in accepting such use, and given the competitive and global nature of the agricultural business of today, it's inevitable that farmers' aims are constantly to improve efficiency of production so as to be able to keep costs as low as possible. However, the line between increasing productivity and animal welfare cost is a fine one. A combination of a greater understanding of the effects of stress on animals as well as increasing scrutiny from society in general means that there is a continuing shift – that may be incremental but is also persistent – as to where that line is drawn. (2002, 2)

The formal policy of the Australian Veterinary Association (AVA) is to encourage its members to get involved with local animal welfare societies (Australian Veterinary Association 1997).

Some have suggested that negotiating this conflict places considerable moral stress on people in these professions. Fawcett (2013,

213–4) has argued that the considerably higher than average rate of suicide among vets results from pressures associated with their unavoidable involvement in activities that disproportionately prioritise non-animal interests. She cites the example of the practice of euthanasing animals purely for reasons of convenience (such as when the owners of a pet move house). This may be the case, and certainly it appears that proximity to regular euthanasia lowers inhibitions around suicide. However, in a recent analysis of data from 2002–2012 in Australia, Milner et al. (2015) argue that a variety of factors are at play in the profession's suicide rates, including moral stress unique to the profession, but also issues that affect other professionals (such as high self-expectations and workload) and other rural workers (isolation), and having access to an easy means of death.[20]

Depression and burnout appear to be spread across the spectrum of veterinary practice, although small-animal practice (i.e. those treating companion animals) seems to involve additional stress. As Hatch et al. (2011, 465) argue, this is likely caused by the higher intensity of relationships between clients and their animals in non-industrial settings, combined with unrealistic expectations of veterinary intervention, but it may also be associated with the fact that individuals from rural backgrounds are more likely to work in large-animal practice (such as industrial veterinarians). As we saw in Chapter 3, those with rural backgrounds score lower on the Animal Attitude Scale, and so may suffer reduced moral stress.

Certainly tensions are evident between the reasons why people enter the profession and the practical realities of their work. In a survey of university veterinary students in Queensland, Verrinder and Phillips (2014) identified the motivations of young people coming into the profession. In their analysis, students are primarily and overwhelmingly motivated by care for animals over an interest in animal industry or personal rewards (Table 7.2). Over time, a clearer understanding of the realities of the profession are associated with stress and some

---

20 The majority of cases (80 percent) in the analysis employed pentobarbitone as the method of death. This barbiturate is a sedative that is also employed as a euthanasia drug in Australian veterinary practice (Australian Research Review Panel 2014).

Reason for studying veterinary science	Primary motivator	In the top three
Enjoyment in working with animals	57	117
Helping sick and injured animals	50	101
Improving how animals are treated	10	55
Interest in science	7	49
Using practical, hands-on skills	5	48
Becoming part of a valued profession	3	21
Wanting a physical, outdoor job	3	18
Farming background	2	9
Developing a profitable animal industry	2	3
Good job security	2	5
One of the hardest programs to get into	1	4
Other	2	7
Family or friends work with animals	0	5
Financially rewarding job	0	3

Table 7.2: Primary reason for studying veterinary science ($n = 144$). Verrinder and Phillips (2014).

disenchantment, which, as noted, is more common among those without prior exposure to animal industry (Heath 2002).

But this ethical tension is also important in shifting the internal regulatory norms of professional organisations like the AVA. The significant role played by students in highlighting ethical challenges to the status quo is seen in their advocacy for enhanced welfare standards on campuses across Australia (O'Sullivan 2015a). As Verrinder and Phillips (2014) have found:

> The majority of students were concerned about animal ethics issues and had experienced moral distress in relation to the treatment of animals. Most believed that veterinarians should address the wider social issues of animal protection and that veterinary medicine should require a commitment to animals' interests over owners'/caregivers' interests.

Key figures in the animal welfare movement such as Dr Andrew Knight, for example, emerged from this very type of ethical conflict in the teaching of veterinary practices, and the issues that motivated his move from practice to advocacy still exist in veterinary teaching institutions. These issues include the refusal of some universities to provide a mechanism for conscientious objection to performing some types of medical practices on live animals, the use of 'waste' animals from racing (both live and dead) (O'Brien 2014), the use and handling of animals in education (interview: E. Hill, 20 August 2013) and the underperformance of universities in adopting the 'three Rs' of animal use in teaching and research (interview: S. Watson, 25 June 2014):

- replacement of methods that use animals
- reduction of the number of animals used
- refinement of practices to increase welfare.

Some trends run against the overarching assumption that this type of regulatory environment will reduce animal use. The development of genetically modified animals (a form of refinement and replacement) that provide better 'models' for particularly human diseases, for example, is one area where increased sophistication will increase the quantum of animals used in research. Similarly, there are concerns that structural issues that drive unnecessary use (such as funding cultures that privilege programs with animal models over non-animal methodologies; H. Marston, 23 September 2013) are actively ignored by university management because animal facilities provide higher research-funding yields.

This type of institutional gap is demonstrated in survey data from animal-welfare officers (AWOs) at Australian universities. In Table 7.3 we see that welfare personnel remain in tension with managers and those they regulate in advancing the three Rs. Thus, even in these sites of increased friction, the establishment of professional oversight of animal use has not produced a 'regulatory revolution' since the 1980s.

Universities have, however, been particularly significant places for activism due to their comparatively open governance structures and the diversity of members on ethics committees. Activists have been able to see the impact of their work in changes to teaching practices, particularly around the sourcing of animals for veterinary training and

Supporting actor	Average	Median	s.d.
University management	4.61	4.5	2.35
Researchers working with animal models	4.5	5	2.04
Animal ethics committee members	3.22	3	1.22

Table 7.3. Animal welfare officers in Australian universities: reported support received on a scale of 1 to 10, where 1 = extreme hostility to the role, 5 = neutral (neither support nor hostility), and 10 = maximum support for the role ($n = 18$).

the use of highly invasive and/or destructive teaching practices (interview: M. France, 19 May 2014). Because of the presence of scientists, veterinarians, welfare organisations and laypersons on these committees, they also serve as a communicative bridge between different ethical and technical perspectives (Scott and Carter 1996), within a framework that still privileges human interests. More recently there has been a move towards the institutionalisation of interest groups pushing for changes in veterinary standards based on arguments about enhanced welfare more familiar to mainstream APOs than to industry. Sentient, aka the Veterinary Institute for Animal Ethics, emerged from this type of campus activism in the mid-2000s as an interest group within veterinary medicine. This group forms another bridge between APOs and the animal-using industry, thanks to the presence of veterinary professionals working both for animal welfare organisations and in animal industry.

Both veterinarians and animal-welfare research staff have interactions with a wider set of stakeholders through various formal structures intended to ensure professional ethical integrity and calibration to social norms. The formalisation of these relationships, however, is variable. As the largest recognised professional group in animal welfare, veterinarians – both individually and through the AVA – have an automatic place in consultative and decision-making structures of government pertaining to animal welfare, as well as in other institutions and as a direct member of many AIOs (for example, the NFF and the Australian Companion Animal Council), while laboratory and teaching animal professionals have both institutionally based (the Australian and New Zealand Council for the Care of Animals in Research and Teaching, or ANZCCART, and individually based (the Australian and New Zealand Laboratory Animal Association, or ANZLAA) organisations that provide a locus for the consideration of animal welfare practices in lab and teaching contexts. These organisations have reacted, in different ways, to challenges from activists (ANZCCART through organisational inclusion, ANZLAA via dialogue).

While much of this exists in the insider world of local policy and administration, the nexus between science and public visibility is significant in considering the treatment of animals in public laboratories, as well as in zoos and circuses. We can consider these three animal-use industries on a continuum from 'pure'[21] science (public labs), to a mixture of education and entertainment (zoos), to pure entertainment (circuses). Significantly in these three settings, concerns about animal welfare have focused disproportionately on particular classes of animals, predominantly companion-animal species (particularly in veterinary education), primates (in labs and zoos), and exotic animals (zoos and circuses).

Circuses have been subject to considerable pressure to abandon the use of animals as entertainers, but the most effective campaigns have centred on their use of particular exotic animals, as opposed to animal use in general (Tait and Farrell 2010). Public laboratories have seen a decrease in activism around their use of animals in general, and an increase in campaigns targeting primates in particular. This has followed the introduction of improved welfare standards. Zoos, on the other hand, are subject both to the norms of 'welfare-focused conservationism' (Kazarov 2008) and to an intense public gaze. It is clearly easier to justify the use of animals for science and education than it is for entertainment. Nevertheless Australian zoos have had to invest significantly in the creation of high-welfare environments and treatment programs for a range of animals (particularly apes and elephants) to ensure that keeping these animals in captivity remains socially acceptable (Tribe 2009).

---

21 Universities and research programs are increasingly co-funded or supported by commercial interests.

7 Animal-using industry

Responding to external challenge

AIOs are increasingly proactive in addressing the increased interest in welfare among consumers and the wider public, as well as some of the campaigns of APOs that aggressively target industry practice. On one level this is reflected in the quantity of policy development in animal welfare undertaken in the closed and private policy world of the inside track, where multiple stakeholders are engaged in negotiating acceptable practices incrementally. This can often take the appearance of 'running dead' on an issue: resisting change or making minimal adjustments based on a view that external pressure is inconstant and may abate. Often, this is a very effective strategy, as seen in the case of mulesing, where the cost of changes to welfare standards was spread out over a longer timeframe than activists demanded, with individual organisations leading change based on their own sense of the market.

This, however, provides an overly saccharine view of adjustment that misremembers the sense of 'ambush' experienced by industry actors, and underplays the frustration felt by more established APOs when their long-running campaigns and warnings were not heeded. The ongoing salience gap between individual industry actors and their more attentive representative AIOs raises a question: can industry effectively and proactively manage animal protection advocacy in the long term? While some issues remain largely consistent over time, in that APOs have maintained a core set of concerns over a long period, some industry actors are concerned that other industry members can be obtuse in recognising repeated warnings about welfare issues that present a significant risk (interview: I. Randles, 30 September 2013). Following the 2003 controversy over live-export deaths at sea, the chief executive of the peak live-export organisation compared the incident to an aircraft crash for the airline industry (AAP 2004): that is, an unfortunate but predictable event that necessitated a review of procedures, would have a negative effect on popular opinion, but would soon pass out of the public's memory. Such complacency significantly contributed to the conditions that led to crisis in 2011.

In addition, the 'hit and run' nature of some recent campaigns (Bang 2004), as well as switching activist tactics, present challenges for industries that have adopted a static position on welfare issues.

Some AIOs describe a 'grassfire' of activism: constantly burning but springing up in new locations unpredictably (interview: CEO, QFF, 16 April 2013). Owing in part to this, the response to external pressure often swings between adoption of new welfare paradigms and active resistance to change. These types of responses tend to occur in the more public political space, either because they happen in the context of well-publicised campaigns, or because the decision to change requires political legitimacy that can only be won in the public domain. In the following final section I will examine the range of responses to external pressures, from collaboration to conflict.

Getting on board: retail standards

Major retailers are sensitive to consumer mobilisation by advocacy organisations. Data about spikes in customer inquiries filters up from individual stores to head offices (J. Healing, Coles, in Clark 2013). This has led to the adoption of third-party standards or to retailers developing their own standards where none exist, or where they prefer (usually for cost reasons) to devise their own. However, the connection between consumer advocacy and changes in the supply chain is neither linear nor straightforward. A number of factors are at play.

The first is that consumer mobilisation has the capacity to signal initial shifts in consumer sentiment (by early adopters) in advance of more wide-spread changes. Active monitoring of these by retailers can be a first step towards adapting supply chains to provide higher-welfare products. This can be a medium-term process, where welfare concerns require considerable investment in new plants and equipment. On the other hand, if consumer mobilisation produces only quick 'spikes' that subside once APO public campaigns end, they may reinforce retailers' belief that consumer commitment levels are weak and unlikely to translate into a long-term willingness to pay higher prices. Further, where demand cannot be met easily and quickly, retailers and producers may adopt changes that have more to do with branding than with any significant modification of their systems and infrastructure. If this effectively allays consumer concerns, the welfare shift may be largely symbolic, although retailers are aware that this can run the

7 Animal-using industry

risk of being seen as 'welfare-washing', which can itself prompt activist mobilisation and affect the retailer's brand.

A second factor is that consumer mobilisation is strongly moderated by analysis from retailers' own information-management systems. While APOs that mobilise consumer activism online are able to determine the success of their campaigns more actively than ever (for example, by using online petitioning systems or analysing data from their own websites), retailers employ aggregated sales data. An APO, therefore, may see a campaign as successful if it results in a high level of mobilisation (interview: L. White, 24 September 2014), whereas retailers are looking at changes in sales volume and conversion rates on a more granular level (A. Dubs, Australian Chicken Meat Federation, in Clark 2013). The exception to this, of course, is the RSPCA, which captures sales data through its RSPCA-approved product system.

Finally, behaviour can be a prisoner of expectation. Major Australian retailers are international in their orientation, following global trends closely through their environmental scanning processes, employing transnational advertising and marketing firms (which both generate new ideas and resell them into different markets), and with an international movement of management personnel. Thus one interesting explanation for the responsiveness of major Australian retailers to consumer mobilisation is that they were forewarned by the experiences of retailers overseas. Australian welfare standards, and retailers' capitalisation of welfare to promote brand loyalty and product differentiation (particularly in the face of new, low-cost international providers such as the German retailer Aldi), has been identified as lagging behind comparative markets overseas (interview: a representative of the retail industry, 22 April 2014). Thus when Australian APOs became more active in consumer mobilisation, major retailers recognised that this was in line with the experience of their international peers, and had already prepared responses.

Overall, the ability and willingness of retailers and producers to adopt higher welfare standards depends on a number of factors:

- Is there measurable consumer demand?
- Is there expectation of future demand?

- Does this provide value to the retailer and if so what type (overall 'brand value', demand value for a specific product, or a reduction in the risk of future consumer campaigns)?
- Can a downstream actor control or coerce compliance upstream?
- Is an authoritative or legitimate standard or standard-making body available?
- Could a less expensive standard be used to achieve the same result? For example, both Coles and Woolworths introduced pasture-fed certifications into their beef supply programs in 2014. Woolworths adopted the CCA's Pasture-Fed Certified Assurance System (CPAS) with annual inspection, while Coles adopted an in-house standard with random inspection (McKillop 2014a, 2014b). It is likely Coles thereby negated any competitive advantage of Woolworths' adoption of CPAS, but at a lower cost.

Based on this we can compare retail – the most frequent adopter of third-party standards – with other segments of the animal industry to explain the level of pressure to respond, and the capacity and likelihood of industry to do so (Table 7.4).

Marketing and counter-framing

This emphasis on community perception, trust and branding highlights another key area of AIOs' response to welfare issues and protectionism campaigns: strategic communication. In this area the media landscape has significantly changed over the last two decades. As we have seen in Chapter 4, in recent years APOs have been able to achieve increasingly regular 'breakthrough' campaigns with high levels of media attention. These have tended to shift media coverage of animal protection issues away from police procedurals involving offences against companion animals towards greater reporting of systematic issues about animals in production systems. This follows a deliberate strategy of lobbying with a view to changing popular opinion about the significance of animals, their treatment, and the responsibility of producers and retailers for improving welfare standards.

This success may seem surprising given the seemingly natural advantages of industry when it comes to media access and agenda setting. Industry has vastly greater financial resources for promotion.

7 Animal-using industry

Industry	Consumer demand for voluntary standards	Future demand	Do voluntary standards add value?	Can the industry coerce or control actors further up the supply chain?	Is there a voluntary standard available?
Grocery retail	Medium	Increasing	Yes (brand equivalence or competition)	Yes	Yes
Companion animals	High	Static	Yes (trust)	No	Potentially
Dog racing	Low	Uncertain	Uncertain	Yes	Potentially
Horse racing	Medium	Increasing	Risk of death of some 'stars'	Yes	Potentially
Research animals, pest species	Low	Low	Uncertain, risk*	Yes	Yes
Research animals, privileged species	Medium	Static	Uncertain, risk*	Yes	Yes
Display animals, general	Low	Static	Uncertain, risk if negative event	No	Potentially
Display animals, privileged species	Medium	Static	Yes (animal 'stars' can be marketed)	No	Potentially

Table 7.4. Animal-using industries' relationship with voluntary standards. *The majority of Australian welfare officers (66 percent) do not think implementation of the three Rs leads to improved research outcomes (using publishing as the 'standard' measure of research value presently dominating university performance metrics), while some perceive it as a risk because of the higher costs it would entail.

Less obviously but importantly, key animal-using industries also enjoy significant cultural privilege. As we saw in Chapter 4, these two elements – cash and culture – are connected. As Botterill (2006) argues, Australian agriculture has benefited from a deep fondness for rural life and rural people in the Australia psyche: farming is a noble profession, farmers are practical and straightforward people, rural life is healthy and wholesome, and rural communities are strong and resilient. These ideas are reproduced in the marketing language of producers and retailers. This demonstrates how farming, wrapped up as it is in history, nationalism, mythology and a politics of nostalgia, has not fully negotiated the transformation, begun in the 1970s, from privileged sector to a business just like any other.

Botterill observes that rural communities often perceive ignorance and anti-farming bias in the dominant city-based media. She argues, however, that while the accusation of ignorance is correct, that of bias is not. Farming and farmers generally receive extremely positive coverage in the Australian media, which often reproduce a nostalgic pastoral idyll. This has provided political advantages for the sector, as well as concealing some issues from wider debate. For the rural sector, however, this reliance on a reservoir of good will is problematic, based as it is on Baudrillard's (1994) simulacrum: a self-referential media image rather than an accurate portrayal of the world. While this has obvious advantages for farming, it also presents challenges. The distance between the real and the representational heightens the risk that if reality fails to match expectations, a cognitive shock can occur. As seen with the impact of activists' footage, this heightens the emotional response of viewers and affects trust.

The power of this myth is clear when we consider how practices that are in effect 'farming' are not cognitively included in this category. The clearest example is the supply of animals for laboratories and as companion animals (so-called puppy farms). These commercial breeders do not have an established commodity council, nor the symbolic respect of being 'real farmers'. This lack of cultural deference has made it easier for these sectors to be brought into regulatory dialogues and to be subject to state intervention. In Victoria and NSW, governments have openly entertained regulations that would scale down the size of production facilities, something that would be unthinkable in 'real farming'.[22]

Attempts by farming organisations to acquaint citizens with conventional farm practices have struggled. Partially this is because the message is not controlled by farming organisations, but produced as commercial advertising by secondary processors and retailers. Advertising's power lies in the reactivation of latent or pre-existing attitudes (Bullo 2014). Thus, while farmers may want to update how they are perceived to reflect modern agricultural realities, they are effectively counter-messaged and outspent by retailers and producers who are invested in more sentimental tropes.

In addition, reframing can be complex because animal welfare is complex. In work done for the chicken industry in 2012, market researchers found that communicating stocking densities as a ratio per square metre elicited a more favourable consumer response than per hectare (because of the smaller absolute numbers involved), but that attempting to create euphemisms for beak clipping ('beak treatment') only elicited negative responses from focus groups, presumably because it alerted consumers to practices they prefer not to consider (Brand Story 2012). The complexities of educating consumers are beyond the capacity of many AIOs, and some fear that engagement with the topic will raise the salience of the issue while not actually improving community knowledge.

This assumes that industry would win a pure 'war of ideas' if only consumers had the full picture, an assumption that is contestable. Since the 1980s, some industry groups have pushed for animal protection and welfare in closed, technical review processes as a means to combat the emergence of the second wave of protectionists. This was based on a belief that industry had the superior knowledge of animal welfare. The Livestock and Grain Producers' Association of NSW,[23] for example, published a report in 1980 calling for the formation of an inter-jurisdictional mechanism to review and resolve welfare concerns (Brown 1980). In describing the politics of animal welfare as '*objectivity* versus *emotionalism*' (5, emphasis in original), the report clearly put industry in the first category, and dismissed APOs as having little more than lay expertise:

---

22 In Victoria during the November 2014 state election campaign, when issues presented by Oscar's Law attracted a high degree of public attention, and in NSW through the mid-2015 parliamentary inquiry process.
23 1978–1987, a rival SFO to the NSW Farmers' Association.

The diagnosis of animal health/welfare problems – mental or physical – by untrained or unqualified personnel is no more valid than the opinion of a person in the street on human medical issues. (23)

Industry has since invested money in third-party animal welfare research. In Queensland, for example, AgForce (as the Cattlemen's Union) played a role in establishing a chair in animal welfare at the University of Queensland in the 1990s, from which the Centre for Animal Welfare and Ethics later emerged. This is not without problems, however, particularly where research outcomes clash with established practices. In these cases, the reliance on pure evidence-based policy-making is often moderated in such a way as to undermine the basis of industry's claim to dominate knowledge. As a Western Australian SFO officer observed:

> Typically the refrain you will hear is, 'We want animal welfare decisions based on science, evidence-based' (brackets: 'but only if they suit us') ... A classic example is teeth grinding for sheep ... So, what [farmers] do is grind [sheep's] teeth so they don't fall out so they can continue to graze properly and they have a longer productive life. However ... they use an angle grinder. They put a gag in the sheep's mouth. If you've ever seen it, it's pretty confronting. And it's commonly done because it's considered to be prolonging the productive life of the animal ... In Victoria, they did a substantial survey a number of years ago, I believe on 30,000 sheep with their control group, and there are no nutritional benefits for the sheep [in] grinding their teeth.[24] So, these [results] are fact, science, evidence-based, okay? So, teeth grinding in the new standards would have been illegal. However, we still had people in WA saying, 'I've got to grind those sheep's teeth, otherwise they won't be able to put on condition, I'll have to send them to abattoir.' But the science has been there for a number of years, so: what do you do there? A very difficult situation. And the way we did it was, we said, 'Why don't you just let us grind the teeth on the sheep we think need it – not all of them? Make it illegal on a flock basis.' Because people used to do it on age

---

24 Williams (n.d.).

basis, and we said, 'Let's not do that. Let's satisfy these guys who still believe [it has] some practical basis.' (Interview: I. Randles, 30 September 2013)

In some areas this has led industries to back away from supporting welfare research that may challenge current practices (interview: a former animal welfare officer, 1 August 2014).

Because of the overwhelming focus on production efficiency, much of the established research on production systems has failed to provide industry with useful data on welfare outcomes (interview: R. Cox, 2 October 2013). Thus, calls for the use of evidence-based policy can be less effective in smaller industry segments where research investment around welfare has not been a priority. Further, the connection between science and implementation can be problematic in those industries with large variations in operator size (interview: CEO, QFF, 16 April 2013). Thus we can see a difference between, for example, cattle on the one hand, and chicken production on the other, and connect the latter's tighter industry integration and generally higher scale of operations to the greater capacity to develop an evidence base from that industry.

While many APOs may have been largely or completely dominated by laypeople in the 1980s, their capacity has changed considerably. The RSPCAs have always taken pride in advocating for evidence-based policy (interview: M. Mercurio, 4 June 2013). But this varies across species, locations and contexts. To some extent this is consciously managed by the RSPCAs' willingness to engage in some issues more deeply than others. As their national CEO observed:

> So, companion animals get obviously much more expertise in state and territory societies than there is on some of the nuances of farm animals or transport or wild animals. It's not always the case but . . . [most societies] feel very confident talking about companion animals. (Interview: 24 June 2014)

Different industry organisations have different levels of regard for APOs, but in general are more likely to challenge the capacity and accuracy of smaller and more radical organisations than the larger brands. This reflects the comparative capacity of different organisations to some degree, but also the level of public acceptance that different organisations have when they claim to speak for animals. When interviewed, some industry representatives recognised that their disagreements with APOs tended to concern ethics, worldview and the interpretation of observations about production systems, rather than facts. A representative of a chicken commodity council observed:

> How can you be critical [of APOs]? You can only be critical of something that is factually incorrect. I know you may not have heard that view before, and I'm sure our [member] companies [would think] it was the most ridiculous thing they've ever heard coming out of my mouth, but it's true. I mean, we did go through the process at the time, [following the release of a critical report about the industry], of saying [to our members], 'Okay, tell us what they've said that's *wrong*, that's *factually* incorrect.' (Interview, emphasis added: 31 January 2014)

Similarly, a state-based commodity council representative observed:

> I must say the Voiceless people are pretty well across production. They do their homework. I've got a lot of respect for them. We agree to disagree but you can have a very pragmatic discussion with them. (Interview: R. Cox, 2 October 2013)

This inability to dominate arguments about facts has become institutionalised as APOs have increased their representation in formal policy-making contexts.

Australian agricultural producers have, however, begun to take very seriously their representation in a mediatised environment where few Australians have even passing experiences with rural production systems.[25] During the past decade producers have increasingly developed communications strategies designed to enhance their image

---

25 However, the extent to which this is truly new is debateable. The Farm Writers' Association of NSW and the Rural Press Club of Victoria, for example, were founded in the 1960s. Similar initiatives followed in South Australia and Queensland. The aim of these organisations was to promote rural and farm

7 Animal-using industry

and popular standing and to increase public understanding of the lived experience of primary producers (Botterill 2006, 23). This 'agvocacy' movement has tended to promote rural industry and country life in general, as opposed to specific issues or sectors. To some extent this was motivated by the successful media campaigns of organisations such as PETA (USA), whose campaign around mulesing was seen as presenting farmers as ignorant, barbaric and cruel. But the need for primary producers to be proactive has been reiterated by those within the sector (interview: W. Judd, 19 April 2013; Guthrie and Akindoyeni 2014), the Farm Institute (Potard and Keogh 2014) and politicians (interview: South Australian MP, 25 September 2014).

For the NFF, this takes the form of promoting agriculture as 'a good industry' to work in (interview: general manager [policy], NFF, 14 November 2014), which appears to reflect a desire to address welfare alongside a number of other issues, including concerns about profitability and the perception during the 2000s that rural Australia was chronically in drought. The unwillingness to tackle welfare issues head-on makes it difficult for industry to counter messages from activists effectively, and reflects the low priority placed on this issue relative to others and a reluctance to acknowledge the impact of APO campaigns.

One area where animal-using industries have increasingly taken a more assertive approach to protection issues and APO campaigns has been in the use of social media. Industry clearly recognises that the rise in social media campaigns by animal protectionists is a significant political threat (Thorne 2012), and one where industry's financial advantages are negated by the ability of APOs to mobilise a large catchment of supporters, as discussed in the preceding chapter.

Many in industry also see social media as better suited to emotional messages and resistant to counter-messaging, although others consider this an inherent problem when dealing with urban stakeholders. The director of the Bureau of Animal Welfare reflected on the way the realities of farming practice may be at fundamental odds with the sensibilities of Australia's urbanised community, illustrating

---

writing, but also to form a communicative bridge between rural and urban media organisations and professionals.

how codes of practice and industry 'norms' are alienated from public understandings and sensibilities:

> If you look through the codes of practice on farms, the destruction of premature calves can be quite effective. They've got very soft heads – one blow with a heavy mallet would kill them – and the farmers don't like carrying rifles around in cars, it's dangerous... So, you have to have an alternative. You have to accept some things. So, that's an example where you say, 'Well, the outcome must be the animal is knocked unconscious and then it's killed.' That could be another ten blows. If that was seen on TV, the community would be in outrage.
> (Interview: 21 August 2013)

Structurally, the failure to mobilise a large number of farmers and associated workers via social media appears to be caused by the lack of co-ordinating structures. Guthrie and Akindoyeni's 2014 survey of farmers found that 89 percent[26] supported the creation of a 'GetUp'-like body for the sector – that is, a virtual campaigning organisation with campaign expertise and contact lists, which could organise members into campaign activities (Vromen 2015). Based on agricultural workers' reported willingness to engage in campaigns directly (about 56 percent of survey respondents), the sector has a pool of potential participants in such mobilisation of about 25,000 people (not to mention a catchment of pro-farming supporters in the wider community).

This remains a possibility. To date, most pro-agriculture campaigns remain localised or associated with commodity councils, and tend to be in response to particular events. From the content analysis of media reporting introduced in Chapter 4, organised media coverage of welfare issues and protection campaigns is driven by crises, not proactive messaging, and between different organisations there is competition for ownership of issues rather than a clear delineation of responsibility. Some proactive campaigns also run counter to the wider desire to change the public image of farm workers as old-fashioned yeomen. For example, dairy farmers have been featured in advertising designed to

---

26 With 33 percent strongly supportive, 56 percent quite supportive, 3 percent opposed and 8 percent neither/don't know ($n = 1,002$).

highlight the 'family' nature of their industry as a direct counter to the notion of 'factory farming'. Farmers are portrayed as 'good people' unfairly targeted by activists (A. Spencer in Clark 2013).

More recently, AIOs have sought to co-opt activists' messages in the way that activists co-opted welfare expertise. This may involve emphasising the care and attention paid to animals by industrial workers and farming families, depicting them as caring and responsible 'custodians' of the animals and of the land. Recent supermarket pricing wars between the two major suppliers have focused on a small range of products (including milk and bread). In focusing on the lowest price, these campaigns have tended towards presenting the products as genericised, rather than following product differentiation strategies commonly associated with revitalising 'commodity' products. In response, dairy wholesaler and collectives advertising campaigns have begun to focus on producers rather than on attributes of the product itself (MacDonald 2012). Other messaging more assertively addresses activists' claim to moral superiority. Following the 2015 Melbourne Cup, the industry website racingbase.com responded to anti-racing activism with messaging that highlighted the way industry members are themselves 'for the animals':

> You know who really care? You know who is really hurting when these animals are injured? The ones that spend up to 16 hours a day by their side. That rise at 3am six days a week to help feed, groom and nurture these beautiful animals. The ones who have dedicated their lives to horse racing. They are the ones who are truly hurt when a tragedy happens on a racetrack. They also understand how much these animals love racing. They understand that accidents happen...[27]

Other counter-messaging aims to presenting activist organisations as elitist groups reflecting a narrow middle-class sensibility. Speaking for the Live Exporter's Council in 2010, Alison Penfold said of APOs: 'I think they like to see a world where everybody goes to farmers' markets and takes their wicker baskets and shops in that form' (in Clark 2013).

---

27 Extract from a longer post by racingbase.com, reportedly written by a user of the organisation's private forums before being reposted on the public page.

Overall, this demonstrates the complexity of industry getting 'on the front foot' on welfare issues and industry characterisations in the wider community. The need for a coherent messaging strategy appears to be emerging in response to wider trends and a recognition of the impact of a mediatised society on generating unexpected risks. To date, however, reactivity and a failure of co-ordination have led to the continued propagation of overly sentimental views of agricultural production and, in response to crisis events, aggressive push-back.

Legal restraint on aggressive activism

One approach to managing negative publicity has been to limit the effectiveness of open rescue and other APO strategies by starving them of content. Some parts of the sector have actively lobbied for this approach, and their efforts paid off in August 2015 when the NSW state government introduced the *Biosecurity Act 2015*. Biosecurity is broadly defined as the 'the protection of the economy, environment and public health from negative impacts associated with pests, diseases and weeds' (NSW Department of Primary Industries 2008). In creating a general biosecurity obligation for all people in NSW, the 2015 Act requires that:

> Any person who deals with biosecurity matter or a carrier [of biosecurity matter] and who knows, or ought reasonably to know, the biosecurity risk posed or likely to be posed by the biosecurity matter, carrier or dealing has a biosecurity duty to ensure that, so far as is reasonably practicable, the biosecurity risk is prevented, eliminated or minimised. (s. 22)

The 2015 Act also requires that any breach of this obligation must be reported (s. 38), and introduces new powers for the inspection and prosecution of such breaches (part 8). Maximum penalties under the act are $1,100,000 and/or imprisonment for three years.

While similar legislation was introduced in 2014 in Queensland,[28] for animal activists the NSW legislation represented the first successful introduction of what they call 'ag-gag' laws. Previously seen in the United States, such legislation is designed to limit the effectiveness of animal activism through a combination of:

- increased criminalisation of trespass onto agricultural property
- prohibitions on photographing or filming animal agricultural practice (blanket prohibitions)
- requirements that evidence of animal mistreatment is provided to authorities within a short timeframe after collection (thus reducing the capacity for ongoing investigations) (Potter 2011; Mackinger 2009).[29]

The characterisation of the 2015 Act as ag-gag is based on its broad reach, which criminalises not only activities that directly affect plant or animal health, but also those that may have negative economic impacts (which is precisely what some activist campaigns aim to achieve) (s. 13). The act aims to capture incitement, reduce the effectiveness of covert investigations, and prohibit support and conspiracy (and so may criminalise APO campaigns) (s. 307).

While neither the minister for agriculture nor his predecessor (who originated the bill prior to the 2015 NSW state election) stated that the legislation was aimed at animal activists in their second reading speeches (a significant reference point for future juridical interpretation), elements of the 2015 Act clearly respond to long-standing AIO concerns about the impact of covert filming, both on their industries and on individual workers (Gotsis and Roth 2015). In a

---

28 The *Biosecurity Act 2014* (Qld), commencing mid-2016. Significantly, while this act also creates a general biosecurity obligation (s. 23), if focuses on failures by individuals to undertake action to minimise known (or ought-to-be-known) biosecurity risks. For this reason, the Queensland legislation has not been as controversial as the NSW legislation. Failure to act can incur a penalty of $3,000 or three years' imprisonment (s. 24).
29 Though, as we saw in Chapter 6, the first significant case of aggressive anti-activist litigation was the declaration of the RSPCA Victoria critic Constance May Bienvenu a vexatious litigant in an attempt to prevent her push for organisational reform.

speech to farmers, the minister with initial responsibility for the legislation stated in 2013:

> It seems every week now... you've got animal activists breaking into intensive farms. In one of the cases a number of piglets died through the disturbance. We simply have to win. I've spoken very strongly to other government ministers in relation to this and the NSW government is now looking at what we can do in this space as well. We have to keep putting it up to city people that don't, may not necessarily understand our farming practices and how important they are, that they cannot support these groups such as Animals Australia and cannot support what they're doing. These people are vandals. These people are akin to terrorists. (ABC 2013a)

In preparation for the release of the new bill, the minister highlighted the importance of the legislation as a corrective to the limits of trespassing laws in preventing activists from accessing farms (Hodgkinson 2014). Previously, such trespass could incur a penalty of $550 (*Inclosed Lands Protection Act 1901*).

Significantly, the minister's press release included a statement of support from the RSPCA NSW,[30] putting this organisation at odds with the national body's stated position on this type of law. To some extent this reflects a tension between some state societies and activists. In jurisdictions where the RSPCA has enforcement responsibilities, criticism of the existing monitoring of welfare standards can be seen as a de facto criticism of the performance of the society.

The timing of the NSW legislation was significant. It followed closely on the highly successful promotion of open rescue by Animal Liberation NSW in 2013, overlapped with the *Four Corners* special on live baiting in greyhound training, and was introduced at a time when the federal government was actively pushing a wide range of legislation focused on terrorism and terror-related offences.

---

30 The CEO is quoted as saying, 'If people have legitimate animal welfare concerns they should contact the RSPCA NSW, NSW Police or the Animal Welfare League NSW and they will investigate them, as the independent enforcement agencies for the *Prevention of Cruelty against Animals Act*'.

7 Animal-using industry

The former minister for agriculture's comparison of animal activists with terrorists reflects three important cultural and political factors. First, it expressed frustrations over the intrusion of animal protectionists into the agricultural policy domain, a space traditionally seen as an 'iron triangle' of industry, rural politicians and agricultural public servants (this is explored further in Chapter 8). Representatives of the pork industry, which has increasingly been subject to direct action by activists, talk about the sense of 'violation' felt by farmers upon discovering unauthorised entry (interview: A. Spencer, 23 June 2014). Second, it represented a response by rural-based politicians and their parties to an issue over which they risked losing support to minor parties (interview: R. Brown MLC, Shooters and Fishers Party, 18 March 2014). Third, it took place within a general climate of security fears, which have been used to justify a wide range of legislative changes (Gleeson 2014, 89). As Gleeson observes, security discourse and legislation[31] often take place in the context of a real or perceived existential conflict. Thus, those AIOs most supportive of such regulations tend to be those that see activists as an essential threat to their existence.

New trespass restrictions are not the only legal challenge activists face. The Coalition Against Duck Shooting is subject to specific restrictions on rescue activities under legislation that limits non-shooters' access to proscribed areas at particular times under the Wildlife (Game) Regulations 2012 (Victoria). Supported by both the Coalition and Labor parties, the regulations were ostensibly introduced

---

31 This type of legal restraint on disruptive political activism is not unique to the area of animal protection activism. Under the Abbott Coalition government (2013–2015), laws were proposed to limit environmental litigation, following the success of environmental activists in delaying the development of a major mining facility in Queensland (Cox and Lee 2015). Similarly, the decade to 2015 was a high-water mark for laws from both major political parties that have restricted or criminalised political protests at the state level (in Western Australia, laws have proscribed 'dangerous behaviour'; in Victoria, police have been given increased powers to move protesters along; Queensland has introduced temporary exclusion zones; et cetera). What these laws have in common is that they are intended to reduce the impact of political activism on major economic interests and/or provide police with elective powers in policing 'unpopular' and non-mainstream political protest.

to prevent the accidental shooting of protesters (as occurred in 2011), but have the effect of proscribing rescue actions. As with the NSW biosecurity laws, protesters have not seen this as a significant barrier so much as an opportunity to re-frame their struggle; they are no longer merely battling a dwindling number of hunters, but are now engaged in a David and Goliath struggle against the state. As one activist explained:

> Three years of court cases. It wore the government out before it wore us out. And they realised that, even [though] two rescuers have received $10,000 in fines and costs, they're back on the wetland a month later. It hasn't stopped us. They suddenly realised that going to court was a long-running issue and rescuers were still [coming] back, and that's been going on for years ... Different governments as they come in have to learn that lesson. But I think it has helped us because it's given us new angles to run on, new media angles. (Interview: L. Levy, 30 August 2013)

Others have been willing to engage in illegal actions due to a belief that they are unlikely to be significantly punished (Mark 2001). Activists have shown a willingness over several decades to accept prosecution, and media organisations have often been willing to broadcast material collected illegally.[32] At times, this has led to legal victories using public-interest justifications of trespass (for example, in a trespass case involving Parkwood eggs in 1997). This is a problem for industry, particularly when activists are not prohibited from using the 'proceeds' (usually video footage) of their crimes (interview: R. Cox, 2 October 2013).

In South Australia, attempts to prohibit the use of covert surveillance devices have been made twice in the last decade (2012 and 2014).[33] This legislation would have criminalised the publication of

---

32 This said, there is clearly a visibility bias in evaluating the decisions of journalists, as there is no systematic data on what proportion of illegally obtained footage is deemed not to be in the public interest and is turned down by media organisations. In this way, the conduct of journalists, acting as proxies of the public, is invisible in the legal discussion of 'ag-gag'.
33 The Surveillance Devices Bill 2014 was defeated in the upper house by the Opposition and the South Australian Greens. The 2012 bill lapsed due to the prorogation of Parliament.

material gathered covertly without court approval (which would only be granted if it was deemed in the public interest). The legislation is interesting in that its potential effect on APOs was only identified after it was developed and it is doubtful that industry expressed an interest in such legislation before it was underway (interview: T. Franks MLC, 26 September 2014). The bill was opposed by a variety of social interests, including the Law Society of South Australia (White 2013), activist organisations and, most significantly, media organisations and journalists (Dobbie 2015).

The mobilisation of media organisations in opposition to this legislation was not only fatal to its passage, but also served to undermine key justifications for the bills. Feeling the legislation would impinge on the work of journalists, media organisations pushed back strongly against the new laws. In doing so, they made the same criticisms of such legislation commonly made by activists: the laws would restrain free speech, increase costs associated with litigation, and encourage the abuse of court processes. Journalists have been drawn into legal disputes between agricultural interests and activists on a number of occasions in Australia. When this happens, the involvement of the media often strengthens the public-interest defence of invasive activism. This was the case with *Australian Broadcasting Corporation v Lenah Game Meats* (2001), in which a Tasmanian-based producer of possum meat had obtained an injunction against the ABC broadcasting footage obtained by Animal Liberation members. In this case, the injunction was overturned on public-interest grounds (Little 2014, 260–1). The media's involvement or endorsement can create a 'halo effect' for activists, whose work becomes associated with investigative journalism. In July 2014, an episode of *Today Tonight Adelaide* (Channel 7) featured footage of animal mistreatment obtained by activists, interposed with hidden-camera footage filmed by the program's own crew. Investigations into animal mistreatment – 'defenceless animals at the mercy of factory farms and puppy breeders', in the words of the voiceover (Archer 2014) – was afforded moral equivalency with the human victims usually featured on the program. The activists did not appear in the show, but the reporter adopted their argot. In some cases, media organisations have even 'commissioned' footage from activists, thereby blurring the boundaries between activists and journalists and increasing the scepticism agricultural producers feel about parts of the media.

Thus, while some AIOs see the explicit or implicit use of anti-activist laws as a useful tool against activist campaigns, the evidence to date tends to demonstrate that in adopting this strategy, the industry risks being seen to be associated with heavy-handed or repressive laws. During the debate about new legislative measures, Voiceless brought out a prominent American critic of 'ag-gag' to attack the intent and legitimacy of new laws, while reiterating the idea that industry must have 'something to hide' (O'Sullivan 2015d).

APOs, meanwhile, have pre-emptively adjusted their messaging strategies in anticipation of the new laws. Activists engaged in live rescue have been photographed and filmed wearing protective attire, highlighting their adherence to biological security measures (Sacre 2013). However, this seems to be more of a publicity tactic than a consistently adopted change in practice,[34] and the effectiveness of such footage as a legal defence remains uncertain.[35] Strategic lawsuits against public participation (or SLAPPs) are comparatively rare in Australia, and are sometimes the result of poor legal forethought by activists (interview: a lawyer involved in animal law, 13 May 2014).

The Abbott Coalition government's decision to de-fund the national Australian Animal Welfare Strategy and abolish its advisory committee, which included both industry and APO representatives and technical experts (discussed further in Chapter 8), could be interpreted as a sign of sympathy with industry groups who have proposed more aggressive measures to limit the capacity of APOs. However, suggestions from industry that the Commonwealth investigate and remove the charity status of Animals Australia were not heeded (Bettles

---

34 For example, in 2012, Animal Liberation Victoria staged a demonstration in Federation Square, Melbourne with over a hundred supporters wearing disposable clean suits (Webb 2012). In a publicised open rescue in 2015, however, activists were shown *in situ* wearing street clothing with latex gloves (Carney 2015).

35 As Gotsis and Roth (2015) observe of the civil trespass suit *Windridge Farm Pty Ltd v Grassi* (2011, 254 FLR 87), claims by the defendant that they adhered to biosecurity measures akin to those seen on Animal Liberation NSW's *60 Minutes* appearance failed to satisfy the judge, who awarded additional costs for the veterinary inspection of animals on the property.

2013),[36] and the federal government has not formally supported overtly ag-gag national legislation (the Criminal Code Amendment [Animal Protection] Bill 2015 was introduced as a private member's bill by a Liberal senator from Western Australia).[37]

Thus, AIOs have won, on a very uneven basis, some legal tools with which to confront the APOs' strategic challenge. To some extent, this mirrors the similar successes of farming organisations in the 1970s and 1980s in expanding exemptions from potential cruelty prosecutions by changing legislation to provide blanket exemptions for accepted and normal farming practice (that is, exemptions for the status quo). These exemptions prevented aggressive calls for the use of state power against primary producers, a significant legislative win against a new set of challenging organisations with a very marginal political status.[38] Forty years later the legislative victories against APOs are far more modest. The likelihood of a significant impact on invasive trespass and filming is, however, limited, although the high penalties theoretically possible under the 2015 Act may have a strong deterrent effect on activists in NSW. Overall, however, the industry's lobbying has achieved a quasi-policy solution at best: while the laws have real potential, their effect is largely a symbolic service to a beleaguered industry's stakeholders. APOs are likely both to challenge the constitutionality of the laws, and to carry on undeterred by existing legal sanctions. If anything, the prospect of prosecution under the new laws increases the newsworthiness of future APO actions in NSW, and provides APOs with a connection to other social movements similarly targeted by 'anti-protesting' provisions.

---

36 This may indicate learned wariness of this aggressive tactic. During the Howard Coalition government (1996–2007) attempts were made to delist organisations that were seen as being political in nature from the register of charities; registration provides legitimacy, as well as taxation advantages, to organisations and their donors (Hamilton and Maddison 2007). These changes were subject to a successful legal challenge.
37 Senator Chris Back, previously a large-animal veterinarian.
38 However, even at this time these changes were contained within wider 'modernisation' of legislation, so do not represent unalloyed anti-activist measures. This is discussed in more detail in the next chapter.

Conclusion

The response of animal-using industry in Australia to issues of animal welfare has shifted over the last few decades. Having long been in a privileged position as protected insiders, animal agriculture maintains an advantage relative to activists in incremental policy processes, but this advantage is not automatically shared by other animal industry groups, and has not prevented producers and retailers from voluntarily adopting higher welfare standards, putting pressure on other commercial actors. The shift towards more open public communication has been slow but noticeable, and has included co-operative, communicative and combative approaches. In the latter case, AIOs have shown that they maintain important and enduring relations with policy-making elites. We will examine the role of these elites in the next chapter.

8
Political and administrative policy elites

In this final chapter we examine the relationship between animal welfare and protection policy and the political and policy elites in Australia. We have established in preceding chapters that animal protection and welfare issues tend not to be 'driven' centrally by the state. Unlike policy areas such as education and human welfare, in the animal protection domain governments are not the central determinants of what happens 'on the ground', nor of the formulation of the key regulations that guide private behaviour. This is not to say that the state is insignificant. Its significance lies in a number of areas: the 'choice' policy-makers make to leave many animal issues to the world of private governance reflects an ongoing satisfaction with the status quo, but also non-decision-making: the active choice not to act. The government still provides the context in which private governance occurs, by authorising private regulation or by developing general regulatory instruments. And finally, in some cases the state make direct interventions in this policy area.

Understanding the decision-making processes behind non-decisions, delegation and action is therefore critical if we are to understand the role of the state in animal welfare and protection policy in Australia. These issues are explored here from three perspectives: from the view of political elites in government charged with overseeing these areas of policy (especially the relevant minister); from the perspective of non-government or backbench politicians who are active in protection and welfare debates; and, finally, from the perspective of public servants who work in the areas of policy development and service delivery most closely associated with welfare and protection.

The view from the minister's desk

As animal welfare and protection policy is essentially a form of political choice, we need to ask what this choice looks like for authoritative decision-makers in Australia. Is it a form of executive management, where discrete executive decisions are guided by well-established criteria and norms (Davis 1995)? Or is it a less structured area where problems are unpredictable and decision-making situational? The answer is both, but, compared with many policy areas, disproportionately the latter.

Animal welfare and protection policy is a problematic area of policy-making because it lacks the unification of an overarching policy paradigm to provide policy-makers with a point of reference when choice is required. Policy paradigms are sets of coherent and well-established policy ideas that guide the development of specific policy (Daigneault 2014). They have a number of functions: they provide a decision heuristic, a means of justifying decision-making, and a way to calibrate decisions across and between policy domains (Hall 1993). The power of paradigms can be seen in areas such as illicit drug policy, where competing paradigms (such as law enforcement and public heath) present very different policy responses to the same social phenomena. Shifts between different paradigms are fundamental discontinuities and 'punctuations'; change within a paradigm tends to be incremental and to involve more slight adjustments to policy 'settings'.

The lack of a paradigm for animal welfare and protection stems from two causes. Political decision-makers are like most Australians in this area: they lack a unified and coherent political philosophy regarding human–animal relations. The relationship between humans and animals remains a significantly neglected area of public ethics, which means there is less guidance available for political elites than in other policy areas. The lack of a shared discourse with the public also means that when elites talk about the issue, their capacity to communicate

8 Political and administrative policy elites

effectively with the community is limited. Thus the paradigm problem affects both policy decision-making and political conversation.

At a more structural level, animal welfare and protection policy lacks a neat institutional home in the policy space. Different regulations and laws governing welfare and protection policy fall under the responsibility of a range of departments. Perhaps the clearest division of labour is the split between production animals (generally the responsibility of departments of agriculture) and companion animals (local governments). But the number of relevant state agencies involved in the development of animal protection policy can be broad, particularly where marginal cases are concerned or when more than one jurisdiction is involved. Even within a single state or territory, animal welfare and protection are dispersed: wild and pest animals are also considered by environmental departments; research and teaching draws in the education and health departments; commercial issues may necessitate consideration by the departments for business; treasury and finance will want to consider regulatory impacts; and the attorney-general will have an interest in legal implications.

As we can see in Appendix F, this is reflected in the large number of legislative instruments that govern animal treatment in Australia. While this could be seen as the source of the paradigmatic gap – and atomisation is significant in retarding unification to some degree – the existence of a unified policy model is one way that even dispersed policy development can be harmonised and made consistent. Overall, this quantum of legislation has developed largely without any single apex of oversight, allowing idiosyncratic variations (intentional and otherwise) to be retained in law and regulation.

As a result, policy co-ordination is often absent when animals are involved, with drivers for policy change and development coming from a range of sources. As the former NSW minister for primary industries observed:

> Animal welfare issues tended to come up not so much as a holistic picture of animal welfare, but as issues arose. So . . . it came from different angles. There were obviously some national initiatives around the way at the time on national standards, on sort of animal husbandry and things like that, which came out through ministerial

councils, and there were other issues which came up, for instance when there was an incident which required some sort of attention or some discussion with the people involved. (Interview: S. Whan MLC, 19 March 2014)

Because of this, the personal and party priorities of individual ministers are significant in driving issues along. Each of the ministers interviewed for this volume reported particular issues that attracted their attention in office, often stemming from personal interests (interview: B. Green MP, 22 September 2014), party programs or priorities (interview: S. Rattenbury MLA, 23 July 2013), or the sense that long-running processes needed to be 'forced' along (interview: S. Whan MLC, 19 March 2014). None reported a strong interest in rationalising this area of policy-making given the effort this would require compared with the low salience of the issue.

Even for ministers with animal welfare as a core part of their portfolios, these issues tended to be less significant than other activities, and were often left to be driven by departmental or other (i.e. intergovernmental) processes. Each of the major legislative reviews of animal cruelty legislation discussed with interviewees was triggered by regular legislative-review processes, so the introduction of new legislative requirements or practices tended to reflect longer-term concerns about the 'pent-up' need for modernisation, clarification or harmonisation (interview: I. Cowie, 27 August 2014): that is, incremental and settings-oriented policy-making. (This also makes it difficult at times to associate particular legislative changes with specific governments.)

When soliciting input or advice, ministers generally prefer to work with those organisations they perceive as authoritative, such as industry peak bodies and national APOs (interview: B. Green MP, 22 September 2014). Decision-making is largely based on cost–benefit calculations, but policy modifications may also be made in response to particular circumstances or to the needs of particular constituencies; political considerations are highly important and have not been replaced by a purely technocratic decision-making. In general, the default response of policy-makers is that of 'a hard-headed appreciation of economic realities' (Beilharz 1988). This favours those stakeholders who are able to articulate their concerns in the language of economic costs and benefits.

As an example, the Victorian director of the Bureau of Animal Welfare outlined a policy development process involving the modification of traps for dogs and foxes (such traps are used to reduce predatory attacks on sheep). As this was a comparatively minor agenda matter affecting a 'pest' species, the bureau acted as both advisor and protector of animal welfare concerns. The two primary stakeholders considered politically were hunters and farmers. The farmers' interest was to ensure no reduction in the eradication of pest animals, and this concern formed a minimum requirement in the development of any policy change in the bureau's policy calculus. While the bureau's recommendation for optimal welfare was that traps should be cleared daily to prevent undue suffering by reducing the time each animal spent in the trap, the practical realities of a small trapping industry necessitated a three-day standard. This was based on advice from the trappers about their capacity to survey remote areas. A back-and-forth policy development process resulted in changes to the standards, with the addition of a poison-delivery mechanism to the traps, as the bureau judged a three-day timeframe between capture and death to be a cruelty. Each modification increased the regulatory impact, leading to a secondary policy development and the development of a scheme to negate the cost of implementation (involving trap buyback and replacement by the state) (interview: 21 August 2013). In this case the entire cost of welfare improvement was borne by the state.

Issue salience and agenda setting

Even in (or particularly in, as they may have multiple portfolios to oversee) the smallest Australian jurisdictions, a minister for the Crown faces an arduous task. Ministers, directly and through their various bureaucratic and political gatekeepers, ruthlessly ration time to tasks they feel are important either personally or politically (Tiernan and Weller 2010). While some ministers display an almost active lack of interest in animal welfare issues because of a low concern for animal welfare (interview: M. Parke MP, 4 September 2014), their perception of the significance of the issue in their constituencies is important in determining the level of engagement they have with issues that arise in their portfolio.

	Vote		
	Labor	Coalition	Greens
Which of the following statements comes closest to your view about the treatment of animals? (2012)			
Deserve the same rights as people to be free from harm and exploitation	30%	28%	40%
Deserve some protection from harm and exploitation, but it is still appropriate to use them for the benefit of humans	61%	66%	55%
Don't need much protection from harm and exploitation since they are just animals	4%	3%	2%
Don't know	5%	3%	3%
Do you believe that . . . climate change is happening and caused by human activity or do you believe that the evidence is still not in and we may just be witnessing a normal fluctuation? (2015)			
Is happening and is caused by human activity	72%	42%	88%
We are just witnessing a normal fluctuation	20%	48%	8%
Don't know	8%	11%	4%

Table 8.1. Partisan attitudes to animal protection and climate change. Essential Media Communications (2012; $n = 1,000$) (2015; $n = 1,012$). Original survey questions edited for length.

The unstructured and volatile nature of popular opinion makes it difficult for policy-makers to gauge what the public's response to any given issue will look like. Australians have a strong interest in the wellbeing of animals, but this interest is moderated by long periods of complacence due to the social and physical distance between humans and most animals. As discussed in Chapter 4, prior to 2011, regular media reporting of animal-welfare policy problems highlighted individual cruelty cases. This explains why policy change most commonly focuses on the actions of individuals, such as increased penalties for and policing of individual cruelty acts,[1] and the regulation of

---

[1] Whether administratively (e.g. the 2005 formation of a police taskforce to investigate a string of attacks on cats) or legislatively (e.g. increasing the capacity

8 Political and administrative policy elites

companion-animal owners (Instone 2011). Media 'outrages' are therefore important in opening windows of opportunity into areas marked by policy network closure, and the willingness of the public to actively petition government for action on a wide range of issues associated with animals is important in driving elite action in the short term.

In focusing on the role of media shocks in altering the political agenda, we implicitly accept a non-partisan view of the policy domain: that is, that systematic policy change does not generally occur with changes in government. In considering differences between different political parties, it is important to note that popular attitudes to animal welfare are not significantly skewed towards a particular partisan position. Building on the data presented in Chapter 3, Table 8.1 shows that both Coalition and Australian Labor Party voters share the same fundamental beliefs about animal ethics, while Australian Greens voters are more likely to endorse a strong rights perspective, but only moderately more so than the average elector. Fundamental attitudes towards animals, particularly when compared with clearly partisan policy issues (illustrated here using fundamental beliefs about climate science), are not predictable based on the tendency of the individual to vote for one major party or another. The exception to this may be the smaller constituency of National Party voters, which I discuss below.[2]

The length of the window for change opened by media shocks largely depends how long the issue 'runs' in the press. Political elites are aware that popular interest in welfare issues tends to be cyclical; the benefits of action are generally short term (e.g. increased popular support, the mitigation of public concerns, and a public perception that their politicians are responsive), while the costs are long term (e.g. impacts on stakeholders, and the costs of implementation and/or regulation). Issues may appear and disappear from the public stage in successive peaks. A good example is the treatment of greyhounds by the racing industry in Australia. The cruelty and corruption in this industry

---

to record the identity of individuals prosecuted for cruelty offences) (Boom and Ellis 2009).
2 The combination of Liberals and Nationals in Table 8.1 obscures this, but the small size of this subset within the overall sample is a reason the market researchers combined this group.

were highlighted by successive reports throughout the 2000s (McEwan and Skandakumar 2011), only for a scandal to erupt in 2014–2015.[3] This cycling can lead to a variety of outcomes, including simple reaction:

> There's a level of nervousness about going into this review, and that's more because we wonder . . . we definitely wonder what's going to drive this review, and what's going to be the primary thing. Is it bird welfare? Or is it people getting, you know, bureaucrats getting driven by ministers driven by letters that are driven by whatever else? And honestly, in a lot of the discussions we've had, coming from government, I've hardly ever heard the words, 'Well, we're seeking to improve bird welfare.' It's all about getting people off your back, and that's a really frustrating thing for industry because it signals . . . it makes you think . . . what the hell are we doing this for? (Interview: a representative of the chicken industry, 31 January 2014)

This can also lead elites to adopt a strategy of 'waiting out' a temporary spike in popular concern or undertaking symbolic actions. In this way animal protection and welfare issues are seen by many policy-makers in terms of 'issue-attention cycle'. Following Downs (1972), this reflects a political paradox whereby the concentrated costs of addressing public concern are not 'remunerated' by ongoing public support for elite action.

Outside of comparatively simple and pain-free policy choices – for example, the ban on importing exotic animal trophies introduced by the Commonwealth minister for the environment in 2015 (Cox 2015) – a perception that there is not sustained support for change leads to a degree of non-decision-making – that is, to actively avoiding making decisions and attempting to stop issues from coming onto the political agenda (Bachrach and Baratz 1970). To some extent, this is a natural result of policy in areas such as animal agriculture being contained largely in the closed policy networks of administrative politics. If a potential change in policy will have a negative impact on an enduring stakeholder group, the costs of implementing it are magnified. This also explains why some areas of animal welfare regulation, such as the

---

3 In that trainers who use live bait to train their dogs do so in the belief that it will make their animals more competitive.

8 Political and administrative policy elites

regulation of companion animals in public spaces, or in reviews of strata legislation (Thomson 2013), are not subject to agenda closure: the policy space is not institutionally and historically closed, and the costs of action are socially diffused.

This non-decision-making approach can appear as a reluctance to take the first move on policy issues, and encourages excessive indexing of the minister's preferences against the policy positions of other jurisdictions. Where a collective norm exists, elites are far more willing to express and reaffirm it. Where no such norm exists, governments often run dead, which can be frustrating to advocates for change as well as defenders of the status quo. This is not the result of a lack of technical capacity, but rather a lack of legitimacy for more dramatic changes to existing policy settings:

> The government has got [the] human capital [to introduce new policies] but they're not going to do it because it's a contentious policy issue. They're happy to enforce a regulation after it's been decided. A classic example would be GM [genetically modified food]. Western [Australia]'s government's policy position on GM? Don't know. Cautious. What's the government's policy position on using lime on acidic soils? 'Yeah, you should use lime on acidic soils.' Every agricultural department in Australia will say that. But when it comes to something [that] has some social implications, all of a sudden, they don't want to have a position. (Interview: I. Randles, 30 September 2013)

This would be more problematic for industrial animal use if acceptable farm practice was defined against social, as opposed to industrial, norms.

Managing the electorate

While Table 8.1 indicated a low variation in attitudes towards animals by supporters of the four largest political parties, there are considerable differences between the parties' formal policy positions on animal protection, and the parties have different approaches to dealing with animal welfare and protection issues.

As we can see in Table 8.2, the scope and comprehensiveness of formal, publicised policy from the major Australian political parties varies considerably. This variation exists both in the willingness of each party to develop and promote a policy at all, and the extensiveness of those policies that do exist. Of these parties, the Greens (at both national and state level) have the most extensive explicit policies for animal welfare and protection, with a national animal welfare spokesperson (Senator Lee Rhiannon) and, in some states, an animal welfare portfolio (although the latter appears to be more driven by personal interest; interview: T. Franks MLC, 26 September 2014). The next most extensive policy is that of the ALP, which has a national policy and some specific jurisdictional statements. The Coalition parties rarely include these issues in their policy programs and when they do, their policies tend to be generalised statements rather than comprehensive policies, or focused on very specific issues.

Although the depth of a party's policy has implications for policy-making, it may not be significant at an electoral level. This is because animal issues do not tend to feature in election campaigns or debates. While elections are 'focusing events' that are conceived of as activating popular interest in policy and politics, mediatisation and low public attention tends to narrow the range of issues covered considerably (Maisel and Brewer 2012, 318). All but a small set of key issues and themes are squeezed out. And as we recall from Table 3.14, only 4 percent of Australians rank animal welfare as a top-priority issue.

State support for welfare APOs does sometimes feature in election campaigns (interview: M. Beatty, 16 April 2013), in part because they are well-known organisations with positive associations in the general community. A party may promise increased funding for the RSPCA, for example, or support for a specific welfare facility. Unsurprisingly, major parties tend to avoid association with 'radical' organisations or positions during elections. If more specific policy issues do arise, they tend to be 'narrowcasted' (that is, directed at small specific groups of voters, increasingly using social media), and treated as second- and third-order issues seen to be significant to particular populations or demographic groups but not to the electorate as a whole.

8 Political and administrative policy elites

Party	Jurisdiction	Date	Policy	Distinct policy?	Specific elements?	Scope
Labor	ACT	2015	Yes	Yes	Yes	Medium
	NSW	2013	No			
	NT	n.d.	No			
	Queensland	2015	No			
	SA	2014	Yes	Yes	Yes	Medium
	Tasmania	2013	Yes	No	No	Brief
	Victoria	2014	No			
	WA	2014	Yes	Yes	Yes	Medium
	National	**2015**	**Yes**	**Yes**	**Yes**	**Brief**
Greens	ACT	2012	Yes	Yes	Yes	Short
	NSW	2015	Yes	Yes	Yes	Long
	NT	n.d.	No			
	Queensland	2014	Yes	Yes	Yes	Short
	SA	n.d.	National			
	Tasmania	n.d.	No			
	Victoria	2014	Yes	Yes	Yes	Long
	WA	2013	Yes	Yes	Yes	Long
	National	**2013**	**Yes**	**Yes**	**Yes**	**Long**
Liberals	ACT	n.d.	No			
	NSW	2015	No			
	SA	2013	No			
	Tasmania	2014	No			
	Victoria	2002	No			
	WA	2013	Yes	No	No	Brief
Liberal-National	NT (CLP)	2012	No			
	Qld (LNP)	n.d.	No			
	National	**2013**	**No**			
Nationals	NSW	n.d.	Yes	Yes	Yes	Brief
	SA	2014	No			
	Victoria	2014	No			
	WA	2013	No			

Table 8.2. Published animal welfare and protection policies of Australian political parties.

Some APOs have attempted to run both electoral and public-awareness campaigns in marginal seats in an attempt to wring concessions from the candidates. Marginal seat campaigns are perceived as effective only in very close electoral contests given the comparatively low level of significance of animal protection issues to most voters (interview: L. Levy, 30 August 2013), but smaller APOs do find that they get greater access to policy-makers during election campaigns, as candidates attempt to target specific groups in the community who may be electorally useful. Oscar's Law, for example, has found the Victorian ALP receptive to concerns about intensive pet breeding in the lead-up to elections (interview: D. Tranter, 22 September 2014). During campaigns, normally closed policy-making networks can be circumvented by reaching future decision-makers through their party machines, as opposed to formalised, bureaucratic consultative structures.

Finally, animal welfare and protection policy is actively promoted as the primary agenda of the Animal Justice Party (AJP). This party, modelled on the Dutch *Partij voor de Dieren* (Party for the Animals, established in 2002 and with 23 MPs as of 2015)[4] was formed in 2009 and registered by the Australian Electoral Commission in 2011.[5] In 2015 it elected its first member of parliament, Mark Pearson MLC, to the upper house of the NSW state parliament. Pearson was formerly the executive director of Animal Liberation NSW, reflecting the party's closeness to this particular APO, as well as the fact that social movement organisations may hold on to some tactics and strategies over long periods of time (Animal Liberation first engaged in electoral politics in the 1980s). As of mid-2015, the AJP had 4,500 members nationally (Elliott 2015), making its membership approximately one-tenth the size of major parties like the ALP.

The origins of the party are complex, but involve a number of factors:

- the successful electoral model of the *Partij voor de Dieren* communicated through transnational activist networks

---

4 These include 22 national MPs (two upper-house, two lower-house and eighteen provincial) and one EU parliamentary seat.
5 Suggesting it took over a year for the party to acquire the 500 members necessary for registration.

- perceptions of increased issue salience and therefore a greater likelihood of electoral success (particularly after 2011)
- conflict between Animal Liberation NSW and ACT and the ACT Greens over a kangaroo cull in that jurisdiction (interview: S. Rattenbury MLA, 23 July 2013).

Regardless of the first two points, the party faced scepticism from some APOs who thought the strategy unlikely to succeed, a distraction from local campaigning, and likely to run the risk of alienating those existing parties that had 'good' animal policies (interview: M. Pearson, 5 June 2013). While animal protection issues have a strong catchment in the community that could be a valuable source of votes, major welfare-providing APOs with large mailing lists generally avoid direct electoral politics for fear of reprisals from political elites and a loss of popular support. Further, the historical distance between Animal Liberation and other APOs limited the ability of the party to mobilise this base.

To some extent the AJP reflects tensions over the 'ownership' of animal protection politics. The Australian Greens actively compete with APOs over the issue of animal welfare for supporters and donors. The AJP therefore reflects a serious tension between political and social movement organisations:

> When they found out it was being formed, the Greens and the Democrats wrote to us saying, 'What the hell are you doing?', and I thought, 'Okay, why are they reacting?' ... They think it's their baby, this animal issue. (Interview: M. Pearson, 5 June 2013)

The decision by the AJP to preference the Greens last in the 2013 federal election in the ACT, although seemingly odd given the comparative closeness of the two organisations' likely base of support, reflects the intensity of the conflict between Animal Liberation and the ACT Greens over the issue of culling (both in the ACT specifically and in general) and a basic tension between Animal Liberation and the Greens on the issue of individual animal protection versus habitat conservation. The specific decision to cull Canberra kangaroos, made by a Greens minister on advice from his department, was extremely significant in the formation of the AJP, causing as it did frustrations within Animal Liberation over their inability to shift Greens policy on the issue.

To date, the AJP has not bled support from the Australian Greens. The 2013 federal election saw the AJP attract less than 1 percent of the primary vote in the senate in the ACT, a jurisdiction in which the Greens have limited likelihood of winning a quota because of the small number of senators afforded each territory.[6] Overall, the party's impact remains small (Table 8.3), with its biggest success to date the winning of a NSW upper-house seat with 1.73 percent of the primary vote, thanks to the preference-harvesting system promoted by 'preference whisperer' Glenn Druery and his alliance of minor parties (Aston 2014a). The best individual result to date was in the seat of Swansea in the same election, where Joshua Agland received 2.91 percent of the primary vote.[7] The party, however, considers these results significant enough to influence the policies of other parties, particularly in close electoral contests.

Year	Election	Area	Primary vote
2013	Senate	National	0.70
	House of Representatives	National	0.01
2014	Legislative Council	Victoria	1.70
	Legislative Assembly	Victoria	0.23
2015	Legislative Council	NSW	1.73
	Legislative Assembly	NSW	0.12
	House of Representatives, by-election	WA, Canning	1.41

Table 8.3. Animal Justice Party, electoral results.

Left or right? Town or country?

Following the analysis of voter attitudes to animal welfare and protection, and the analysis of formal party policy on this issue, it is possible to conclude that animal protection and welfare policy sits on a continuum across the standard ideological spectrum: that increased

---

6   At the time of writing, the next ACT election will be held on 15 October 2016.
7   Swansea is a coastal electorate approximately 100 kilometres north of Sydney, in the Hunter region of NSW.

8 Political and administrative policy elites

interest in these issues, and a willingness to make positive policy (as opposed to non-decision-making), are aligned with the political 'left', while non-decision-making and an oppositional stance towards APO activism comes from the political 'right'. This assessment would align with the ideological dominance research discussed in Chapter 3.

Interviewees offered mixed opinions on this question, but most felt that policies on animal welfare and protection by the major parties did generally follow this left–right spectrum (interviews: M. Parke MP, 4 September 2014; R. Brown MLC, 18 March 2014; L. Levy, 30 August 2013; a South Australian MP, 25 September 2014; an animal welfare advocate, 5 September 2014). This is often matched by corresponding levels of APO access to political elites on the left of the political spectrum (interview: D. Campbell, 30 January 2014). This view was shared by representatives of Oscar's Law, who see policy responses as precisely indexed to the ideological spectrum:

> This year, I've been at Parliament House every week with meetings, with the Labor Party and the Greens. The Liberal Party's uninterested in meeting with me. That's alright, but ... Labor is not going to come out and ban puppy farms, so what we're trying to do is use a code of practice as a way of shutting down puppy farms, so making it financially unviable. (Interview: D. Tranter, 22 September 2014)

Some respondents expressed a view that elite attitudes to animal protection reflect a lack of interest or an ignorance about the issues and organisations involved; others observed hostility from parties or individuals who see themselves as conservative or as occupying the middle ground:

> There's still the attitude – well, particularly from [former Liberal National Party premier] Campbell Newman – he seems to lob us all together. He seems to think we're all just in one camp and we're all a whole bunch of lefties. (Interview: M. Beatty, 16 April 2013)

The extent to which comparatively disengaged political elites share this view is unclear, but it highlights one of the risks of the excessive closeness of some APOs discussed in Chapter 6.

Some industry actors, particularly those engaged in regularised relationships with policy-makers, reject simple delineations along party lines, citing their capacity and willingness to work with any party of government (interview: general manager [policy], NFF, 14 November 2014). For some, this reflects a belief that standard policy-making processes will apply regardless of who is in office, while for others it reflects the quite different competencies of different parties:

> Labor governments have been easier for us to work with in the past because generally their ministers have not had an agricultural background and are willing to open their hearts and minds to what we suggest. That's a very general statement. But then along comes the Coalition now, and individual ministers... The current one, [National Party MP Barnaby] Joyce, is very, very good to work with because he understand the industry; he listens to us as well. (Interview: J. Toohey, 4 July 2014)

A knowledgeable minister can be an impediment for industry, if he or she is able to challenge the views of advisors and industry representatives. National Party MPs are often seen as having high technical competency in this area (interview: a senior public servant, Primary Industries, 29 July 2013), making them sometimes more amenable to the views of agricultural producers, but also sometimes unpredictable and unwilling to uncritically wave through departmental and other advice.

Perceived higher levels of partisan support does not automatically mean that that this reflects organisational closeness. One APO observed that a former ALP health minister was 'trouble' and:

> wouldn't respond to any request for meetings. She responded to our cosmetics issue by saying that we actually need to test on animals, so really dismissed our concerns. Until just prior to the last election when she announced that they would ban animal testing on cosmetics if they were elected[8]... As frustrating as it was that she wouldn't meet with us before and she wouldn't... push for a ban on cosmetic testing, even though [she was] no longer in government,

8 Political and administrative policy elites

I think the fact that has she has said this publicly gives a precedent . . . (Interview: H. Marston, 23 September 2013)

There is also some scepticism among the animal protection community about the ALP's commitment to protection issues; there is a perception that the ALP is willing to take these issues on strongly from opposition, but is likely to weaken its views when in government (see below). This reflects an electoral calculus that parties can gain electoral benefits by supporting selected parts of the animal welfare agenda without having to work with APOs themselves. In 2013, the ALP campaigned to younger people on the basis of its animal-testing policy (Image 10).

While ideology – a tendency to resist social change through conservatism, a belief in the primacy of humans over non-human animals, or one's place on the social dominance scale – can explain much of this spread of opinion, important variations exist. Members of a political party may have different positions based on their personal backgrounds and philosophies. One key source of this variation is rural background, and particularly rural background with a family history in animal agriculture (interview: S. Whan MLC, 19 March 2014).[9] These political elites are more likely to support the status quo and to resist changes to animal welfare, particularly radical changes that would alter industrial norms. These individuals are found in all political parties, but disproportionately in the National Party, where issues of animal welfare and protection have both economic and cultural significance.

The fact that so many liberation, strong-rights and abolitionist animal protectionists are urban-based sits badly with National Party MPs. This plays into a sensitivity amongst these politicians, who are alert to the tendency for rural interests to be overlooked by the city-based media and political system (Chapman 2013, 69). For some,

---

8 As Ellis (2009, 354–5) observes, the minister in question, Tanya Plibersek, had previously framed this issue as somewhat zero-sum, suggesting concern for animal welfare must come at the expense of concern for human welfare.
9 This is not a universal observation. The Australian Greens spokesperson on animal welfare, Senator Lee Rhiannon (NSW), grew up in dairying (O'Sullivan 2015e). Many active proponents of increased animal protection have rural but non-animal-industry backgrounds. An example is the ALP's Melissa Parke, federal MP for Fremantle, Western Australia between 2007 and 2016.

welfare campaigns are simply an example of urban know-nothings interfering in rural life. This interference affects rural people directly, through the economic impacts of regulation, and indirectly, through the regulation and cultural dismissal of traditional country sporting pursuits such as hunting, racing and rodeos. In this area National Party MPs have played a role in supporting and/or expanding hunting across Australia, and are quick to point out that duck hunting bans have been successfully introduced only under Labor administrations (in WA, NSW and Queensland; interview: L. Levy, 30 August 2013).

APOs who attempt to engage with these MPs directly may find themselves denied access to the policy debate. The CEO of the RSPCA Victoria recounts a conversation with the former National Party minister for agriculture (2010–2014):

> So, we know each other well. But we have very clear differences of opinion. And when we talk about subjects like duck hunting, jumps racing, restricted breed legislation . . . he just says, 'Nope, don't agree.' And it's that simple. There's no discussion. No, you know, like, 'I'm interested to hear your point of view, can we talk about it?' It gets to the point of, 'Nope, don't agree, next.' (Interview: M. Mercurio, 4 June 2013)

Symbolically, politics in this area can become discursively angry, as seen in the characterisation of some APOs and activists as terrorists in the previous chapter. This can reflect other tropes of the political right in Australia. For example, the use of nationalist rhetoric to refute animal protectionists, a strategy that has tended to focus on PETA (USA) rather than local APOs (Marohasy 2005). Significantly, the strength of feeling of these MPs often leads to them holding key ministries (including agriculture) when in government. They also have opportunities to shape the policy approach of the Liberal Party, thanks to formal coalition agreements and a tendency by the Liberal Party to defer to its junior partners on issues affecting rural Australia.

8 Political and administrative policy elites

A national policy approach?

Our discussion to this point has focused on the role of the states and territories. We have, however, noted the tendency for policy to be pushed upwards towards national bodies (both government and non-government). The significance of the Commonwealth in animal protection and welfare policy is traditionally limited constitutionally to issues of border control (the original and dominant zone of biosecurity policy for most of Australia's history), the expenditure of money, and issues associated with the use of general powers, such as the regulation of corporations and inter-state trade. Previously we observed that centripetal *and* centrifugal policy drivers were important in recasting the role of the Commonwealth government in this area of policy-making. This is particularly evident in two long-term policy processes, the first being the dramatic change in overarching industry policy affecting agricultural producers from the 1970s onwards, and the second being attempts after the 1980s to harmonise animal welfare standards through the Council of Australian Governments (COAG) intergovernmental policy process. Each has important implications for policy and political opportunity structures, and tells us something about incrementalism and punctuated incrementalism.

Australia, remarkably for a nation famed for its historical dependence on agriculture, has spent the last half a century making policy to reduce state intervention in agricultural practice. While, as discussed in Chapter 1, farming was heavily promoted as a nation-building activity in the colonial and post-war periods, the role of the state in agricultural regulation significantly declined with the wholesale adoption of neo-liberal economic policies from the 1970s onwards: namely, a preference for free markets and the deregulation of industry to promote flexibility and reduce regulatory costs. Unlike their US counterparts, Australian farmers lack the complex and enduring network of subsidies and subventions, a network that in the USA both supports the sector and provides policy levers with which governments can attempt to regulate farmers' behaviour.

As Smith and Pritchard (2014) argue, the move towards a global free-trade environment followed the abrupt external shock of the UK entering the European common market in 1973. Following this event Australia experienced a revolution in policy thinking, which saw the

Commonwealth government reduce state intervention in industry policy and move towards a greater focus on economic growth via free- and bilateral trade negotiations. In the agricultural sector, farmers were conceptually re-classified from yeomen to business-people, with the state adopting the meta-objective of microeconomic reform aimed at overall agricultural efficiency to allow farm enterprises to compete globally.

Agricultural policy in Australia, therefore, tends to be characterised by the following:

- It is focused at the Commonwealth level, partially due to path-dependency (a legacy of pre-1970s nation-building) and partially due to its association with the Commonwealth's monopolisation of external affairs and the role of international treaty-making in promoting free markets and economic deregulation.
- The Commonwealth government, regardless of which party is governing, continues to pursue free-trade opportunities for Australian agricultural products, institutionalising this objective into the diplomatic service.
- National, non-industry-specific regulatory bodies have become more significant as other forms of regulation have declined. The use of mechanisms such as competition law (as embodied in institutions like the ACCC; see Chapter 6), for example, have become increasingly important as neo-liberalism values trustworthy regulatory environments that support this ideology of 'free contracting' (Martin and Ritchie 1999, 120).
- Where state intervention is required to meet the meta-objective, it often takes the form of indirect support of the industry aimed at improving productivity and competitiveness relative to rivals (such as subsidies of rural industry research schemes; Price 2014), or the periodic restructuring of non-competitive industries through adjustment schemes, usually based on the principle of 'get big or get out' (such as incentive payments for farmers to leave their industry) (Wheller 2014). The extent to which industrial concentration has occurred reflects a range of factors, but the role of large investment in plant and equipment has played a role. Thus egg production, for example, saw dramatic concentration post-deregulation (that is,

8 Political and administrative policy elites

from the 1980s onwards) because of the dominance of intensive and expensive production systems (Hunton 1997).
- The use of other policy mechanisms outside of economic policy and direct intervention to adjust for the negative impacts of economic restructuring on rural communities through a wide range of general and specific policies (the former may include general welfare policies; the second environmental assistance, emergency funding and subsidised services) at both the Commonwealth and state levels.

This general orientation towards agricultural policy-making is supported by the NFF, born of a commitment to free trade, which it continues to promote. As Marangos observes, 'The NFF family of agricultural interest groups has played a central role in facilitating the free-market approach to Australian agricultural policy and co-generating the discourses that support it' (2009, 46). It is this orientation that puts some distance between the NFF and those more traditional parts of the National Party of Australia that retain their agrarian-socialist roots.

This wholesale change in agricultural policy, slowly implemented over decades, has implications for the rise of the second wave of animal protectionist concerns that has coincided with it. The major impact was reducing the significance of the Commonwealth as a potential direct regulator outside of its direct sphere of constitutional power. However, as the significance of the micro-economic reform agenda has played out over 40 years, new institutional actors have become powerful meta-regulators of commercial actors. The greater interest in the role of labelling schemes, for example, fits within this approach to welfare issues, because it is seen to empower consumers and allows conflict to be pushed outside of the 'political' sphere and into the world of jurisprudence (consumer law), and also because government regulation to increase consumer information is acceptable under the free-contracting model of neo-liberal policy-making (Bruce 2012c). However, the growth of unofficial standards presents new regulatory compliance issues if and when government decides to harmonise regulation to protect consumers and ensure that they are accurately informed. Government's lack of a policy response in this area has created a policy vacuum that has been filled by a range of ad hoc industry standards and practices, both domestic and international.

The Commonwealth government of Australia has sustained a limited interest in animal welfare policy-making over decades and has focused most of its policy-making efforts on the reactive management of crises such as the live-export scandal (which I will discuss further below). However, the most significant structural developments in national policy-making over the last 30 years are interlinked processes: the establishment of the Senate Inquiry into Animal Welfare (1983–1991), largely driven by political outsiders (the Australian Democrats), the resultant formation of a National Consultative Committee on Animal Welfare (NCCAW) in 1989, and the conversion of this process into a formal, if voluntary, standards-making process through the Australian Animal Welfare Strategy (AAWS) in 2004 (Bartlett 2009). In the establishment of the AAWS, the Commonwealth reached agreement with the states and territories to oversee the development of optional national welfare codes, effectively taking the determination of what could be considered appropriate commercial conduct into the COAG system of intergovernmental working and consultative groups. It also demonstrated how policy outsiders can be important in pushing for initial changes to policy-making structures that develop incrementally over time.

This transition is significant in the way it moved the development of advisory standards from the CSIRO into an arena with wider representation and oversight provided though the Advisory Committee to AAWS (Dale and White 2013). This reflected a recognition of the essentially political nature of decisions about welfare settings, and the problem that the preceding NCCAW used a comparatively closed process (Neumann 2005). Significantly, while the CSIRO enjoys high levels of public trust, its closeness to animal-using industry and its focus on industry development have some similarities to the 'capture' of departments of agriculture discussed above. Thus for proponents of a national model with greater representative input (APOs), this was a positive development, even if major contributors to the standards process were still aligned with industry (through the organisation that contributed technical expertise to the standards process, Animal Health Australia).[10]

Botterill (2007, 195) argues that the restructuring of the intergovernmental consultation and co-ordination structures around ministerial agricultural councils has not led to increased influence for the states over national policy-making (either via the Commonwealth, or through harmonisation), but has instead permitted greater top-down influence by the Commonwealth over the states. This was aided by the comparatively voluntary nature of the standards-development process, its slowness, and the quick depoliticisation of welfare and protection issues into AAWS and out of sight (indeed, as both the ALP and Coalition were involved in the evolution from senate inquiry into AAWS, this also served to depoliticise the body). In Botterill's analysis of ten years of agenda items from ministerial councils (190), animal welfare issues overall make up a small part of the intergovernmental agenda (about 5 percent).

This example of national structural change, however, demonstrates the difficulties of attempts to institutionalise APOs into standards development. In a review of the AAWS processes undertaken for the Commonwealth before the 2013 change of government, Pricewater-houseCoopers (PwC) (2013) concluded that the process of standards development was overly long and did not produce standards specific enough for simple implementation. In recommending the AAWS model continue in a revised form, however, the consultants observed that the inclusiveness of the process was its core strength, that stakeholder consultation should be expanded (particularly to directly represent public opinion in standards-making through social-science research of the type discussed in Chapter 3), and that conflict resolution be improved to speed decision-making and expedite the mediation of stakeholders' views.

Importantly, PwC noted the lack of an overarching paradigm or meta-policy for animal welfare as problematic in resolving disputes.

---

10 Animal Health Australia (AHA) is a non-profit company owned by the Australian Commonwealth and state governments, livestock industry peak bodies, the Australian Veterinary Association and the CSIRO. Thus, the orientation of AHA remains aligned to welfare standards that sustain or promote profitability via its strategic priority to 'maintain and increase market access through effective partnerships for livestock welfare and production, and disease policy development and implementation' (Animal Health Australia 2010). Standards development in this process is undertaken with the direct participation of representatives of affected industries (Dale and White 2013, 163).

While this may reflect a solid technical assessment, the reporters clearly overestimated the willingness of key stakeholders to see a fundamentally political process be bureaucratised or subject to greater public involvement. To have an overarching meta-policy would be to resolve the inherent conflict between participants in some way (Dale 2009, 187). Governments of all stripes have consistently lacked the willingness and capacity to achieve this, and so have used the AAWS process to contain conflict.

The containment largely worked for eight years, as codes were developed and slowly and unevenly adopted (or not) into state legislative regimes as the measure of 'acceptable industry practice' (the standard defence against cruelty charges). The best example of this is in the area of stock transport, a longstanding welfare issue that predates federation. At times, jurisdictions would pre-empt the stock code and the industry's voluntary standards for domestic political reasons (for example in the ACT, as discussed, there was a strong local drive against caged-egg production), and/or to seize commercial advantages by 'branding' their own state production systems as meeting higher welfare standards than others.

Tasmania, for example, in pre-empting other jurisdictions in the phasing out of battery-hen and sow stalls (a policy announced in 2012 for implementation by 2017), was willing to 'annoy' other agricultural ministers and to cop, in the words of Primary Industries Minister Bryan Green:

> an enormous amount of pressure from the national bodies when it came to the sow stall decision because effectively it stuffed the whole national timeframe up that was in place for a transition away from sow stalls at a national level, and people made all sorts of overtures with respect to the way that Tasmania was operating. But I knew that it was important from Tasmania's point of view, particularly when it came to marketing. It was interesting that the big supermarkets came on board almost straight away, as soon as we had effectively forced a significant change nationally, with respect to the timing. (Interview: B. Green MP, 22 September 2014)

This reflected the desire for the state to secure a strategic advantage, as well as a response to the need of the minority ALP government to sustain the support of the Tasmanian Greens, who were sitting as cabinet members under an 'alliance' agreement (rather than a formal coalition) between 2010 and 2014.

The AAWS was abolished following the 2013 election of the Abbott Coalition government, marking an end to the process of national consultative standards development (interview: D. Kelly, 25 August 2014). While the abolition of the AAWS can be seen in the context of attempts to reduce the significance of Animals Australia – both by curtailing Animal Australia's participation in standards-making, and by removing the funding it received as a participant in AAWS – in response to their role in the live-export ban of 2011, the AAWS was just one of a large number of bodies abolished by the incoming government, a decision justified on the grounds of cost-reduction. While the minister for agriculture observed that 'In my discussions with people who have a stake in the process, they're quite at ease with this' (Vidot 2013a), he was mistaken. Animals Australia was very critical of the loss of access to this national forum, and some industrial actors had found the AAWS to be useful because of the involvement of APOs (particularly the RSPCA) and because of the project funding it provided to programs other than standards-making, such as education and training (interview: J. Toohey, 4 July 2014).[11] Overall, the decision to abolish the AAWS reflected the weakness of support for animal welfare policy to some extent, but it must also be viewed in the context of a government that was notable for its use of high-handed executive decisions without input from either external or backbench stakeholders (the so-called captain's picks that eventually undermined Abbott's leadership).[12]

---

11 Australia Pork Limited (APL), on the other hand, was more positive about the decision (interview: A. Spencer, 23 June 2014). The differences between APL and the Cattle Council of Australia are considerable in terms of the degree to which APL is an integrated organisation with a small membership that covers most producers. Cattle producers are less likely to be members of their SFOs (interview: J. Toohey, 4 July 2014).

12 The decision may also represent a shift towards 'competitive federalism', an ill-defined concept promoted by Abbott but possibly including greater devolution

The NFF's stated position was that the abolition of the AAWS was a positive outcome aligned with the minister's messaging about regulatory reduction, but this is problematic in that the AAWS had the potential to significantly reduce regulatory complexity for industries that operate across state and territory borders. At the time of writing, however, it is unclear if national harmonisation will be taken up from the bottom, or if another AAWS-like structure will be reinstated by a future government.

The abolition of AAWS and its advisory committee, therefore, is an example of externally imposed network closure: the AAWS advisory structure provided a point of access to the bureaucratised and closed policy-making environment of agricultural standards-development. It developed out of a perceived need to incorporate industrial critics and increase the legitimacy of standards processes by using APOs as proxies for popular opinion. Over time, however, this exchange of resources (that is, of access for legitimacy) did not sustain these ties, in part because of the willingness of governments in 2013–2015 to take strong actions to constrain APOs, a willingness related to an increase in conflict in the policy domain driven by APO campaigns. This conflict, in turn, slowed standards-making, but can also be attributed to some degree to the slowness of standards-development. For APOs, the susceptibility of the AAWS to closure demonstrates that animal welfare issues have failed to generate strong network ties at the national level that would sustain and defend this small institutional foot-hold against arbitrary executive action, whether driven by a specific desire to reduce APOs' access to the policy space, or by a more general policy of purging bureaucratic structures.

This has a number of implications. The first is that we are likely to see a shift in APO advocacy away from the Commonwealth and back to the state governments (off a comparatively low base: survey data showed that less than 20 percent of advocacy focus was directed towards the Commonwealth). Over time, this may motivate state governments to replace the AAWS, or to call for the reincorporation of the AAWS Advisory Committee model at the federal level, both

---

and an exiting of the Commonwealth from harmonisation activities to encourage laboratory federal tendencies.

to reduce conflict in their jurisdictions and to cost-shift policy development back to the Commonwealth.[13]

Second, the dismantling of the AAWS process has significantly reduced the capacity of state agencies to engage in complex policy-making around welfare and protection issues. This is due to the small size (both in absolute terms, and relative to regulated industry) of the technical capacity in Australian state governments in this area, particularly in the interface between welfare settings and regulatory costs (particularly the cost of developing regulatory impact statements; interview: a director of a bureau of animal welfare, 21 August 2013). The upshot of this is that, in addition to the loss of co-ordination and harmonisation, states are more likely to defer to regulated industries due to a lack of capacity.

Third, there are industrial implications. An example is the regulation of dog breeding. For the Pet Industry Association of Australia (PIAA), dog breeding represents a significant risk because the majority of its activities fall outside of organisations regulated by their members' code:

> Now, of the 650,000 dogs that are sold in Australia every year, we know that somewhere between 10 and 12 percent only are sold through retail. The great majority are sold over the internet or [through] a newspaper. And we have grave concerns with that for a number of reasons, but the most important of which is that very infrequently would the purchaser have any idea of where . . . that dog came from, where it was bred and how it was bred, who its parents are, and under what conditions it was bred, and often it won't be micro-chipped, which is now the law. Often it won't have had its proper injections, and often, typically, they'll meet in a Woolworths or a McDonald's car park and hand the dog over for cash. (Interview: R. Perkins, 24 March 2014)

For the PIAA, national companion animal regulations would be useful for its members. Accredited PIAA members would strengthen the peak

---

13 Both economic costs, and the political costs of having a somewhat intractable conflict addressed by another jurisdiction.

organisation's brand, but would also regulate out of the market casual un- and under-regulated traders (a similar concern was expressed by the Australian Professional Rodeo Association about under-regulated competitions in remote areas; interview: S. Bradshaw, 5 May 2014). The current debate in jurisdictions including NSW and Victoria has the potential to further undermine the role and influence of the PIAA, by regulating industrial breeders and pet shops out of the supply of puppies and kittens.

The view from the benches

As we have seen with the politics of accommodation within the Liberal–National Coalition, lobbying and agitation for policy change also comes from inside the political class. In animal welfare and protection this includes interactions between individuals and minor parties, as well as the work of interest groups within parties of government to change government and party policy.

The Greens

The most significant example is that of the Australian Greens. Poised on the bridge between a minor party continually locked out of government and one able to form coalitions (formally and informally) with other major parties (realistically limited to the ALP), the Greens influence policy both from 'permanent opposition' and as members of government (the role of the Greens in governments in the ACT and Tasmania has been noted above). The Greens' interest in animal protectionism is to a degree unsurprising, given the slightly higher level of ethical concern for animals expressed by its membership, but other factors also play a role in the Greens' more extensive policy positions on these issues:

- *Ideology*: In keeping with the left–right conceptualisation of animal protection, the Greens are widely considered 'of the left' and so are likely to be associated with animal protectionism. Concern for animal wellbeing fits within the party's core desire to 'cultivate a global, ecological consciousness and long-range perspective in order

to safeguard the interests of both existing and future generations and non-human species' (Australian Greens 2014).
- *Origins*: Born from a social movement, the Australian Greens still retain some movement characteristics, in both attitudes and behaviours (an example of the latter is members' engagement in traditional movement activities such as rallies), and many of its members remain active participants in other social movement organisations and campaigns (Jackson 2011). Unlike the increasingly careerist path of MPs from other major parties, many Greens in government and party roles come from an activist background and have been active in social movement organisations (interview: I. Esguerra, senior advisor to Shane Rattenbury MLA, 23 July 2013).
- *Rational choice*: The comparative scarcity of formal engagement with APOs and animal issues by other political parties since the disappearance of the Australian Democrats has been identified by Greens activists as an opportunity to raise the party's profile and impact (O'Sullivan 2015e).
- *Inheritance*: Significantly, the Greens are the inheritors of an interest in animal protection policy following the decline of the Australian Democrats at the end of the 20th century. Some key figures from the Democrats (notably former senator Andrew Bartlett, who was the president of Animal Liberation Queensland before being elected to the Senate and discussed his vegetarianism in his maiden speech in 1997) joined the Greens, and other active Greens MPs were directly influenced by Bartlett's work (interview: T. Franks MLC, 26 September 2014).

However, Miragliotta (2006) observes that the Greens' embrace of electoral professionalism is a significant counter-balance to previous radicalism, and this may make for more human-centric and materialist policies. Specific to the issue of animal protection, the Greens face internal tensions over the position of animals in their ideological schema. As Jackson (2016) notes, this has led to disputes within the party as to how to frame their policy, and how to handle trade-offs between animal protectionism and concern for preservation of wider ecological systems (bioregionality) associated with both conventional and radical environmentalism. The former discounts the value of individual non-human animals to the health of the wider ecosystem, while the latter discounts all animals (including collective human interests) to this meta-objective.

This can lead to MPs occasionally being blindsided by 'people whose values I care about'. As Shane Rattenbury MLA observed about tensions between conservationism and animal protectionism in the ACT:

> We had these people in recently who are opposed to the cull and they want to do a translocation. So we had a chat to them about that. And I was putting the view that ultimately I'd like to not have to cull and if we can find good alternatives, such as translocation or fertility control, that will be great. Because I don't like shooting kangaroos; I'd rather not. And we had one person there who just – his stated role in the group was as 'the ethicist' – who said: 'We can't do fertility control on kangaroos, that interferes with the individual choice on how to reproduce, or not.' Which was a bit of an eye opener for me because I sort of – I didn't – animal welfare theory and philosophy is not one of my big areas. I have a broad interest in it, but not – I've not studied it in great detail. And I was quite surprised by that in the first instance and then thought, 'Wow, that's really, that's a very purist approach to this.' (Interview: 23 July 2013)

Ultimately, the Greens position nationally has been to incorporate the type of language many APOs object to in the construction of animal welfare and protection laws: an explicit acceptance of a degree of 'necessary animal cruelty' to achieve other human and ecological ends by focusing on the elimination of cruelty that is 'unnecessary' (Australian Greens n.d.). This puts the national policy at odds with that of some of its state branches (particularly NSW, the home state of its animal welfare spokesperson).

The anti-Greens: the Shooters and Fishers Party

An exemplar for the AJP in influencing policy as a minor party is the Shooters and Fishers Party (SFP). This party was formed in response to increased regulation of firearms in NSW in the early 1990s, and was energised following the introduction of increased national regulation of guns after the 1996 Port Arthur massacre in Tasmania (Singleton et al.

2012, 359). The SFP has, under a variety of party names, held one or two seats in the NSW upper house since 1995 and, where it has been able to affect the passage of government legislation, won concessions from the government of the day. These windows of opportunity are small, but the SFP's presence in parliament has given the party resources and visibility, sustaining the NSW arm relative to other states, where their electoral success is considerably more limited.[14]

The policy focus of the SFP in NSW is broad, but its core interests remain the liberalisation of gun laws, the expansion of hunting rights, the promotion of hunting, and opposition to ideological opponents such as conservationists and the Australian Greens (one member of the SFP described this as a 'counter-punching policy'; interview: R. Brown MLC, 18 March 2014). Major achievements relevant to animal protection and welfare debates have occurred when the party has held the balance of power (Flannery 2012; Sartor 2011), such as the establishment of the NSW Game Council (see below) in 2002, expanded hunting into NSW national parks in 2012 (McKee 2013), and the promotion of the concept of 'conservation hunting' through the elimination of pest animals by recreational hunters.

The ALP: live export's near miss

Labor's relationship with APOs, at both the state and national levels, is less expansive and less explicit. While the Greens are publicly willing to engage with small APOs in the development of their policy, the ALP's major interface with welfare is large commercial interests and their representative bodies, and only the largest APOs. Smaller APOs are less likely to gain access to ALP ministers (although shadow ministers are often more approachable), but do have interactions with the party via some backbenchers. Voiceless summarises this degree of access well:

> We go with sort of the assumption that, I don't care what party you are, if you want to help animals, we want to go with you, we want to

---

14 In addition, the single electorate model of the NSW Legislative Council makes it most tractable to minor parties obtaining seats because of its comparative low quota.

help you write laws, and make it easy for you to introduce something or support something ... which is going to be difficult now ... [with the] Liberals in office. But yes, we do what we can with the Greens. With Labor, we did have a lot of support from some Labor members as well on the national [level] and in [a] couple [of] different states. (Interview: D. Campbell, 30 January 2014)[15]

While this might suggest that APOs have only a marginal influence on the ALP, recent history indicates this is not the case. Labor backbenchers have been active when policy windows open that allow them to disrupt the normal pattern of closed, incremental policy development.

The case of live exports over the last 30 years demonstrates this. For the vast majority of Australians, the live export of sheep, cattle, and (to a very small extent) camels and horses is an invisible part of the agricultural export sector. Only really apparent to people in the industry, and the few city-dwellers located near major live export port facilities, live export has been a small but growing part of the agricultural sector in Australia. The industry has expanded considerably in response to increased living standards in surrounding regions, especially where distance previously made agricultural production for domestic consumption less economic (for instance in the Northern Territory).

The live-export trade, like all exports, is constitutionally regulated by the state governments while the animals are within Australia, but responsibility shifts to the Commonwealth once they are selected for export. Historically, the national government has been happy for the peak industry body (currently LiveCorp) to grant export licenses based on industry self-regulation and standards-making. Since 2000, however, live exports have burst onto the national stage on two occasions: first, following the 2003 death of 5,500 sheep aboard the MV *Cormo Express* after Saudi officials refused to land the shipment due to suspected infection in the flock; and second, in 2011, when the ABC broadcast the *Four Corners* episode 'A bloody business'.

---

15   This quotation has been restructured to aid in clarity. The original text discussed specific party relationships first.

In each case, the government of the day responded to popular concern rapidly, ratcheting up regulation with new requirements aimed at increasing existing welfare oversight and standards, but focused on other issues of immediate concern. Thus, in legislating new standards in 2004, the Howard Coalition government focused on aligning welfare tests to the standards of destination countries, and improving veterinarian access to animals en route (Caulfield 2009). This was intended to prevent the kind of situation that had caused the deaths, where animals were cleared for export but then denied approval to land at their destination. Following the temporary suspension of trade to Indonesia in June and July 2011, the Commonwealth introduced another focused response: the Exporter Supply Chain Assurance System (ESCAS). ESCAS built on existing export licensing arguments to produce a regulatory system for most live-exported animals. This required that exporters (Poppi 2014):

- prove compliance with World Organisation for Animal Health welfare standards
- introduce systems to trace individual animals through the supply chain
- demonstrate control of the animals' treatment through the supply chain (post-export) against the standard; and
- report and audit processes and compliance.

Importantly, ESCAS suited the political mood of Australians not opposed to live export per se but looking to export Australian ideas about appropriate welfare standards (see Table 8.4). The temporary suspension of trade and the introduction of this expanded welfare model, incorporating a radical expansion of responsibility over exported animals, appears to have quieted public concerns, and the popular outrage expressed in 2011 was not repeated when investigations showed that the new system had not prevented further welfare problems. The inability of ESCAS to meet public expectations was anticipated by observers, given the difficulties of extraterritorial regulation and the new system's reliance on industry oversight (Hastreiter 2013). Significantly, ESCAS has created a new opportunity for APO activism, in overseeing the system and measuring its performance against its stated goals. As Lyn White observes:

Animals Australia has become a de facto government agency, providing the only oversight of live export regulations on the ground in importing countries. Some two-thirds of all investigations undertaken by the Department of Agriculture into breaches by export companies are based on Animals Australia's evidence. (Interview: 24 September 2014)

ESCAS has been the subject of criticism and there have been proposals from government and industry to wind back the system (Cawood 2014) where destination nations refuse to permit the operation of Australian regulation (Bettles 2015).

The development and implementation of ESCAS, while consistent with the incremental and reactive nature of much animal welfare policy-making, also highlighted a serious policy debate within the ALP that led to the development of its current national policy platform at the 2011 national conference. This move, driven by Western Australian MP Melissa Parke and a group of individual backbenchers, aimed to adopt a policy to phase out live exports in Australia (Willingham 2011). This was not a unique position. New Zealand had made a similar decision (since reversed) to ban live sheep exports in the 1980s. Importantly, the ad hoc interest group[16] brought together members of the left faction with individuals from the right of the party, gaining strong support from elements of the union movement who would prefer to see local slaughter and chilled meat export replace the live trade (interviews: M. Parke MP, 4 September 2014; K. Thomson MP, 26 June 2014).

The motion to phase out the trade was lost at the conference (215 votes to 175 in favour) (Beef Central 2011). Importantly, this move reflected frustrations among these MPs with the way the response to the live-export crisis had been developed within the caucus process: they felt that the process had been controlled too closely by the minister for agriculture's staff, who had used delays to wait out popular concerns about the crisis. In the end, this strategy proved effective and the moment in which a complete ban might have been achieved passed. Overall, the ESCAS story is unusual in the degree of public engagement

---

16 The ALP also has a formal interest-group system within the party, of which Labor for Refugees is an example.

Australia should	Total	Labor	Coalition	Greens
Not export live animals	25%	25%	24%	35%
Only export to countries that guarantee animals will be treated humanely	54%	53%	55%	58%
Export to any country that wants them	15%	15%	19%	5%
Don't know	6%	7%	3%	1%

Table 8.4. Community attitudes to live sheep and cattle exports. Essential Media Communications (2012); n = circa 1,000.

with the issue, but the tendency towards incremental reform (and later re-deregulation) follows a quite traditional policy arc whereby a rapid decline in public attention puts the policy back under control of agricultural interests within the public sector.

Institutional solutions

The 2011 ALP national conference did provide those with an interest in animal protection in the ALP with some policy wins. Labor policy was changed to commit to the AAWS process, resist 'ag-gag', and – importantly – establish an independent office of animal welfare. These last two items demonstrate the influence of major APOs including the RSPCA Australia, Voiceless and Animals Australia (some ALP policy-writers have a background in these organisations; interview: M. Parke MP, 4 September 2014). The concept of an independent office of animal welfare is promoted by many APOs as a means of resolving the essential conflict of interest in line departments engaged in both industry promotion and welfare oversight. This view has been embraced by the Australian Greens, and its inclusion in ALP policy initially filled APOs with confidence that this model could be implemented within years (Animals Australia 2012).

This confidence has been short-lived. The Australian Greens have included the independent office model in private members' bills,[17] but the ALP backed away from its implementation when in government. During the peak of concern about live exports, the minister for agriculture proposed the alternative model of an inspector-general of animal welfare and live animal exports based within his department, but this was not realised before the change of government in 2013 (Vidot 2013b). There have been moves to have the commitment removed from the national policy altogether. This demonstrates the weakness of attempts to establish policy advocacy bodies within the existing structure of the public service: regardless of discussions about the 'politicisation' of the public service during the past 50 years, such organisations often have difficulties finding purchase; even if they are established, they may face hostility and resistance from within the public sector. Strong external stakeholders and elite protection is needed to sustain such bodies.

Another example of such a structural advocate-cum-regulator is the NSW Game Council. The council was established in 2002 under the Carr Labor government. The inability of the government to control the upper house of parliament following the 1999 election (Bennett 1999) led to negotiations with a number of small minor parties and the provision of concessions in exchange for supporting major elements of the government's legislative agenda. The Shooters and Fishers Party, aware of the opportunity this presented, developed the idea of the council as a statutory authority regulating and promoting hunting. As with the proposed independent office, this model served both to institutionalise regulation of hunting in an autonomous agency away from direct departmental control, and to incorporate an advocate for the general policy orientation of the SFP within government.

The council served as an alternative source of policy advice to relevant ministers dealing with hunting regulation and environmental management. This led to clashes with other agencies over technical advice promoted by the council, for example, over the efficacy of conservation hunting in limiting the impact of invasive species (Booth and Low 2009). Over its lifetime, however, the council met its designers' intentions: favourable regulation and the active promotion of hunting. Its impact, however, tended to be limited by its small size and limited funding, as anticipated in an agency with no advocate in cabinet.

---

17 Voice for Animals (Independent Office of Animal Welfare) Bill 2015 (Commonwealth).

The abolition of the NSW Game Council came about, ironically, thanks in part to its effectiveness. This occurred in 2013, following increased scrutiny of hunting regulation and regulators with the expansion of hunting into NSW national parks. In December 2012 the acting chief executive of the council participated in an illegal goat hunt on private lands; he was later convicted, as was another council volunteer (Aston 2014b). A review of the council by government found serious limitations in the governance of the organisation, and the council was abolished shortly after. This had significant implications for the then premier, Barry O'Farrell, to whom the SFP personally attributed this decision (interview: R. Brown MLC, 18 March 2014).

The implications of this example are significant. The capacity for minor parties or pressure groups within parties to institutionalise advocates for their concerns exists, and – as with the case of the Game Council in NSW – can have a considerably long lifespan. These bodies, however, can be orphans of the political process, with little resistance to abolition if the political tide turns against them. For the NSW Game Council, its advocacy role led it to engage in practices not normally associated with the public sector, and it became 'further and further isolated from mainstream government administration' (Dunn et al. 2012).

This type of problem is predictable, with Shapiro (1997) noting the tendency for such bodies to experience problems of co-ordination with cognate arms of government, as well as challenges to their political legitimacy. 'Unloved' agencies involved in the regulation of conduct are common, however, and include many ombudsmen and bodies responsible for freedom of information. These agencies tend to persist where they have a combination of demonstrated effectiveness, strong support from influential stakeholders, bipartisan approval from within the political elite, and co-operation with other agencies. There are serious doubts that an independent office of animal welfare would meet all or most of these criteria.

The view from the public service office

Given the comparatively low significance of animal protection and welfare policy in the wider political agenda of many policy elites, the role of public servants in the policy process is extremely important. Portfolio management, stakeholder relations, regular policy reviews and legislative changes tend to be driven at the junior and mid-levels of the public service within a context of routine public-sector management (interviews: M. Hyman, 22 July 2013; I. Cowie, 2 August 2014). In large jurisdictions, many of the key public officials in the development and management of policy are insulated from their ministers by levels of intervening management (interview: D. Kelly, 25 August 2014).

This creates a degree of autonomy at both levels of the executive-administrative structure: bureaucrats largely manage their work within the processes of the public sector, and ministers are necessarily constrained by having direct intervention in their policy decisions by expert staff. It also has implications for trust between these two policy-making partners: the lack of interaction does not build trust, which is important when political elites have to respond to crises or make dramatic policy changes. Overall, the conduct of public servants in this process is informed by two 'positions': their information base and their structural location.

The knowledge position

Public servants' capacity to manage policy and to provide policy advice is contained by their level of knowledge. Knowledge in this case can be divided into two types:

- Technical knowledge, including an understanding of animals and animal welfare, husbandry, industry, economics and policy; and
- Political knowledge, including an understanding of external stakeholders, their influence, and their likely reactions and responses to policy changes and how to manage them, as well as an awareness of the views of key decision-makers within government, including but not limited to the minister and cabinet. Political knowledge also includes an understanding of public opinion.

8 Political and administrative policy elites

For the management of animal welfare policy this presents some difficulties, for a number of reasons. As we have seen, the policy orientation of many elites can be ambiguous: non-decision-making and politically expedient ambiguity provide limited guides for action by public servants. This encourages conservatism and risk avoidance. Conservatism in this context means a default towards existing 'meta-policy': those grand narratives about general policy instruments that are employed by governments as general principles of policy development and administration. Even this presents some problems for public servants. If we consider agricultural animals, the meta-policy orientation of agricultural policy has been towards efficiency and reduced direct public financial support for farming. In moving away from direct capture by rural interests following the neo-liberal paradigm shift of the 1970s, Zhou has argued, agriculture bureaucrats have widened their sense of responsibility from 'farmers' to 'taxpayers' (2013, 44). This might suggest that public servants would be increasingly interested in public opinion. However, while this major change to agricultural policy represented a complete change in the policy paradigm for rural communities, the impact on welfare regulation by public servants remains extremely narrow.

This is the case for two reasons. First, the shift in focus towards more efficient production has not significantly changed the role of departments of agriculture in regulating animal welfare. While the state now intrudes less frequently than it once did into production systems, the basic tendency of departments to support industrial activity has not changed. Where high welfare coincides with improved productivity, departments are likely to regulate for high welfare standards. Where productivity and welfare clash, productivity is usually prioritised (Goodfellow 2012).

Second, the capacity for public servants in this area to understand the expectations of the general public is limited. Welfare policy and administrative units, in particular, tend to be focused on technical capacity rather than social science, and have limited resources to engage in environmental scanning. As a result, they report a limited understanding of public preferences (interview: a senior public servant, Primary Industries, 29 July 2013). This is reinforced by a tendency to favour AIO sources of information over APOs. Animals Australia and Voiceless report better relationships with individual MPs than with government departments, which has implications for the flow of information from these groups and their constituencies (interviews: L. White, 24 September 2014; D. Campbell, 30 January 2014).

The reasons for this are diverse, but include a limited capacity to engage in stakeholder management, the greater capacity of AIOs to be available than smaller APOs, and issues of legitimacy and credibility. For some public servants focused on sustaining their reputation as evidence experts, public participation in regulatory discussions is counterproductive, generating large amounts of 'spam' and little content of technical use given the high cost of administrating consultations (interview: director of a bureau of animal welfare, 21 August 2013), and, it must be observed, the lack of political elite support for funding this type of extensive and expensive community engagement. As a result, the agencies' potential role as a trusted conduit between the community and either primary producers or their ministers is limited.

Culturally and professionally, this group is more engaged with other technical experts, as well as with individuals and organisations within industry. This is reinforced by the movement of staff between industry and the public sector, a tendency that reduces the willingness for dialogue between departments and APOs (interview: D. Campbell, 30 January 2014). Prior to the abolition of the AAWS process, horizontal exchange of policy expertise and innovation (through the jurisdiction reporting process in this model) was supported, something that will become more ad hoc and limited with the removal of the AAWS 'bridge'. Overall, these public servants are in a weak position to speak authoritatively on animal protection outside of their technical foci.

The structural position

Debates about the creation of bodies such as an independent office of animal welfare highlight a second key influence on the role of public servants: the primary source of animal welfare policy development pertaining to agricultural animals is commonly contained within departments of primary industries, and these departments have an inherent conflict of interest in setting welfare standards.

8 Political and administrative policy elites

This view, the so-called Miles' Law or 'where you stand depends on where you sit' perspective (Berman et al. 1985), is commonly held by both APOs and AIOs (Flint 2015a). For the former, an independent office would offer a solution to this problem; for the latter, there are strategic reasons for preferring that policy-making take place in the context of such structures. This can been illustrated in the decision by the state of Western Australia to shift animal welfare out of the department of local government and into the department of agriculture (following this, only the Northern Territory retained agricultural animal welfare in local government, but it too has since moved responsibility for welfare to the primary industries portfolio). This resulted from active lobbying from the SFO and other industry groups (interview: I. Randles, 30 September 2013) over a considerable period of time (the local government department resisted a similar proposal during the redevelopment of key welfare legislation in 2002; interview; I. Cowie, 27 August 2014), based on a range of concerns, including that welfare regulators had been overly influenced by APOs and were being excessively vigorous in their activities. With the shift, a better 'fit' between regulators and industry was achieved:

> I think moving the matter, moving around the jurisdiction of the department of agriculture, there's a lot more empathy and understanding of livestock production and a lot of people are happy about that. But I think that's been quite a practical move. (Interview: R. Cox, 2 October 2013).

This illustrates the prioritisation of one type of knowledge over another, but also an interest in finding an empathetic fit between industry and those who oversee it.

A debate continues about the role of non-state regulation in this area of law. As we can see in Table 8.5, while departments of primary production are key welfare policy-makers, a mixed pattern of enforcement exists around production animals. A majority of jurisdictions retain quasi-private enforcement, with RSPCA inspectors being appointed as special constables under various acts. In this way the societies retain a link to their 19th-century origins as institutional agitators for enforcement of cruelty laws, but the enforcement model can be

Jurisdiction	Government department	RSCPA
Commonwealth	Department of Agriculture, Fisheries and Forestry	No
ACT	Territory and Municipal Services	Yes
NSW	Department of Primary Industries	Yes
Northern Territory	Department of Agriculture and Fisheries	No
Queensland	Department of Agriculture and Fisheries	No
South Australia	Department of Environment, Water and Natural Resources	Yes
Tasmania	Department of Primary Industries, Parks, Water and Environment	Yes
Victoria	Department of Economic Development, Jobs, Transport and Resources	No
Western Australia	Department of Agriculture and Food	Yes

Table 8.5. Institutions responsible for agricultural animal welfare enforcement. Updated from Goodfellow (2013), 195.

ambiguous and changeable. In Western Australia, RSPCA decisions to prosecute have changed, from prosecuting only in extremis, in line with departmental policy (Flint 2015b), to a more autonomous approach to prosecution; this shift followed the decision to move responsibility for animal welfare from the department of local government to the department of agriculture discussed above. In 2015 this became the subject of a parliamentary inquiry into the RSPCA, exploring the appropriateness of its enforcement activities. Similar concerns have been raised in South Australia, where there is some pressure to remove responsibility for agricultural enforcement from the RSPCA (interview: a South Australian MP, 25 September 2014). In both cases critics have questioned the vigour and accuracy of the societies' enforcement, and have raised concerns that the organisations are opposed to contemporary industrial farming practices or that they are inherently 'anti-farming' (Flint 2015c).

The regulation of regulators, both state and non-state, is complex. While RSCPA inspectors may be viewed suspiciously by those they regulate (both in primary production, but also in commercial non-agricultural animal contexts), moves against them tend to be comparatively rare because of their high level of popular support.

Governments also have both direct and indirect means to 'rein in' the societies when they elect to do so. The most direct way involves funding: the financing of local welfare and inspection organisations by state and territory governments is variable, and welfare organisations are sensitive to maintaining good relations with government (Fidler 2015), both because of the financial support the state provides and in order to ensure that situations such as the Western Australian inquiry do not arise. (Some organisations, however, receive enough private revenue not to require a state subvention.) The periodic public 'blow-ups' experienced by the various RSPCA organisations over the years (often involving disputes within their boards and/or between staff and management) can be either a headache for governments, who find themselves without a key service provider (interview: B. Green MP, 22 September 2014), or an opportunity to clip the organisations' wings. Which party is in government often determines which response occurs. When RSPCAs do lose investigative powers over production animals, they are unlikely to regain them, pointing to a slow shift towards a policy norm that no longer tolerates autonomous policing.

Less directly, the dependence on co-operation with state departments of agriculture in the enforcement of anti-cruelty provisions shapes the conduct of RSPCAs. While the distribution of powers and responsibilities is governed by formal agreements with government, these are subject to informal influences at the 'street level', as departmental staff work closely with external enforcement officers. Like all complex relationships, the memoranda of understandings employed to regulate these practices are not exhaustive, and informal agreements and understandings, as well as in-field ad hoc negotiation, determine how they are applied in practice (interview: M. Beatty, 16 April 2013).

At times this can lead to maladministration. Enforcement officers have been accused of tipping off the targets of their investigations before planned site inspections. For instance, during an investigation into the systematic use of live baiting by greyhound trainers in NSW in 2015, internal documents obtained by the ABC suggested that trainers subject to inspection were provided prior notification by Greyhounds

NSW regulators, giving them an opportunity to conceal criminal conduct (Meldrum-Hanna and Clark 2015). This appears an important determinant in the 2016 decision, released after the finalisation of this manuscript, for the state of NSW to phase out greyhound racing. Former RSPCA inspectors have claimed that industrial producers subject to cruelty investigations have been informed in advance by their state-government counterparts (Fidler 2015). Furthermore, individual regulators and enforcement units who are seen as too vigorous may be the subject of direct complaints to the relevant ministry by industry, which commonly results in them being encouraged to moderate their conduct in future. This results from an unequal level of access to regulators, and from the direct access to government enjoyed by many AIOs. Thus, industry relationships exist up and down the administrative-political structure, and allow for intervention by commercial actors and peak bodies on a routine basis to shape policy formation (and non-decision-making) as well as policy implementation and the administration of public administration.

Conclusion

We have seen that policy-making, particularly in the area of animal welfare, involves both the allocation of resources and the mobilisation of values. While international ideas and transnational relationships are significant in this process, there are unique and defining aspects of Australian culture, geography and constitutional arrangements that shape how this contest of interests and ethics plays out. This has implications for our understanding of this increasingly contested area of policy development, but also for our understanding of Australian policy-making more generally. In this volume I have sought to build on the work of many other scholars to present – I hope – a more holistic view of this multifaceted policy domain than we have seen before.

In reviewing the preceding chapters, several wider observations emerge.

The first concerns how history shapes contemporary public policy, and the importance of understanding the historical context of contemporary policy debates. Past policy decisions in a range of areas have had a powerful impact on today's policy terrain. The initial, unnerved reactions of Europeans to the oddity of native species in the 18th century found expression in 19th-century colonial land clearing and marsupial extermination acts, and have echoes in the kangaroo culls of the 20th and 21st centuries. Early decisions to structure particular industries, such as dairying, to advance nation-building objectives remain politically potent, despite dramatically changed production and economic conditions. At a wider level, the notion that history is naturally or inevitably 'progressive' is undermined by the observation that social movements can be effectively demobilised, sometimes for long periods, if internal weaknesses combine with state action to depoliticise particular issues.

A second important observation is that there is a clear dissensus over issues of animal treatment and welfare, both between and within the political elite and the general public. The Australian public, due to a wide range of social and economic factors, has become urban and urbane. Once a nation that famously 'rode on the sheep's back', contemporary Australia is pet-loving and squeamish about the realities of animal production systems. Political and economic elites have an interest in ensuring that issues of animal welfare remain subordinated to other concerns, especially macro- and micro-economic performance. While many issues are subject to this type of misalignment between popular and elite opinion (the privatisation of public assets is a classic example), this makes for a volatile political climate. The public's comparatively unstructured knowledge and fleeting interest can produce semi-predictable 'shocks' that are not easily handled using normal risk management tactics. What this process of periodic issue management conceals, however, is that the public is moving towards an expanded circle of compassion, and increasingly expects that producers will incorporate these concerns into their production processes.

A third interesting observation is the way animal advocates, in challenging the status quo, have not simply worked to create a new discourse around human–animal relations, but have also attacked traditional policy-making as a closed space or 'iron triangle'. This has taken a variety of forms, first (circa the 1980s), in attempts to gain representation in advisory settings and policy networks, and second (in the 21st century) a shift towards exploring ways to effect change through 'private governance' and via systems and structures outside of direct state regulation. In recent years, the deregulation of farming and the move towards neo-liberalism across the economy have reduced the opportunities to use state agencies to achieve new regulatory outcomes in many areas. In adapting to this situation, activists have shown a new pragmatism and a recognition that change can come about in other ways, including changes in cultural norms and expectations, and by harnessing the power of economic systems in constraining and directing consumer preferences.

Conclusion

Innovation and change, therefore, have been recurring themes of the analysis. While the rise of new animal advocacy organisations in the late 1970s and early 1980s was a catalyst for new debates and policy change, each of the major actors in the policy space has been, to some extent, examining new ways to advance their political interests. Australian activists have been creative in their use of media and direct action to promote their cause, within a comparatively conservative political culture. In response, industry organisations have recognised that their natural advantages as 'owners' of animal production systems are increasingly contested. Within a complex policy network, relationships have been significantly reconfigured in recent decades in ways that would not have been conceivable throughout most of Australia's modern history. New technologies have expanded the capacity of welfare organisations and activists to recruit support and form alliances, while organisations and industry are increasingly working together, albeit in uneasy and pragmatic relationships.

In this reshaped policy domain, there is an ongoing dispute over who has the least power and influence, with both industry and activist groups competing for the title of most beleaguered. When it comes to influencing public opinion, both groups face challenges. Although proponents of change may be able to mobilise public support, they must operate within the strictures of community norms that value some animals (especially companion animals) above others, and that tend to favour a modest, weak-rights framework of concern. Meanwhile, few industry actors have the capacity or resources to significantly restructure public opinion, and many are trapped within nostalgic notions of agricultural production that are comforting to the wider community but also completely unrealistic. Industry has tended to burrow into those areas of policy-making where it has traditional strengths. Agricultural policy-making generally remains strongly committed to the status quo, but the industry has a narrowing power base; although it may be able to defend the status quo on a day-to-day basis, it is vulnerable to negative publicity and to issues that cannot be contained in a single portfolio area.

Overall, my analysis has tended to conclude that political elites are not key to the story of change in this policy area. However, while the rise of private governance and non-state regulation is important in explaining how policy adjustment has occurred without the intervention of the state, it is important to recognise that political non-decision-making is not sustainable when it comes to animal welfare. While debates of this type are often subject to strong political avoidance (issues including abortion-law reform, euthanasia and same-sex marriage are recent examples), any area of public policy involving conflicts over basic values will, inevitably, be driven onto the public agenda as participants attempt to force a resolution through decisive action. This 'crisis' model of activism has been adopted both by activists who have used the media to mobilise public opinion, and by industrial actors who have called for protection from intrusive direct action. The Commonwealth government's decision in 2013 to eradicate formal policy development processes can be seen as a form of active 'non-decision-making' intended to starve policy challengers of a platform for their grievances. However, these grievances are unlikely to subside without the type of active co-option and neutralisation seen in the early 20th century. As agricultural interests do not retain the type of political or economic influence of a century ago, it is unlikely this trick can be pulled off twice in the history of animal welfare policy debates in Australia.

This leads inevitably to the observation that issues of animal welfare will move back onto the public agenda in the near term. If stakeholders and observers are to effectively make sense of these policy debates when they occur, a systematic analysis of the type offered here will hopefully add value to those debates.

Appendix A
Research methods

Three primary research approaches have been employed to expand on, or supplement, the secondary material. This reflects a commitment to mixed-methods research, as advocated by Weishaar et al. (2014), to understand complex social phenomena. This does come at the cost of eclecticism. These methods are summarised below.

The primary research method was the use of in-depth semi-structured interviews. Undertaken during 2013–2014, 60 interviews were completed, the majority of which were conducted face to face (a list of interviewees is provided following the reference list). Each interview lasted, on average, one hour, and was transcribed. One of the interviews comprised eight participants in a focused discussion. The majority of interviewees were purposively sampled as informants about the policy-making process in their respective jurisdiction, geographic area, industry or field. Some difficulties presented themselves in the recruitment process, leading to under-representation of government ministers, and of executives from certain animal industries. Where possible this gap has been addressed using additional sampling, but it remains the key limitation of the primary method employed; this is a known problem in political science, and can lead to a reliance on retired ministers and their associates to infer and triangulate.

While this volume includes a discussion of direct action and illegal activities, the collection of any information related to criminality was explicitly excluded from the research methodology for this project. Discussion of these topics in this volume is limited to secondary data sources and literatures.

Throughout the book, interview responses have been used as direct evidence about behaviour, policy-making and processes. Where appropriate and with permission, direct quotations from interviewees have been included to enliven the text. In addition, interview evidence was combined with survey data from NGOs (see below) to map out the policy domain and to create an expanded edge list (that is, a graph of relationships between organisational actors). This permitted the use of social network analysis to understand and describe interactions between policy process participants and activists. This analysis was produced using the open-source Gephi analysis package (http://gephi.github.io/).

Three content analyses were undertaken:

- A systematic analysis of newspaper articles from 2005 through 2014. Drawing on material sampled from the ProQuest database of Australian newspaper articles, one in ten articles from this ten-year period was randomly sampled for analysis ($n = 657$).[1] Manifest coding of article content was undertaken using the Nvivo qualitative analysis package.
- An analysis of free-to-air television content was undertaken in 2015 to identify the extent of, and different kinds of, representations of animals on Australian television screens. Nineteen hours of content were assessed. This comprised:
  - A baseline survey. Using a sample of peak viewing periods (7–10pm; Nielsen 2011), each of the major networks primary channels (ABC1, SBS1, 7, 9, 10) was assessed against a manifest and latent coding frame, and;
  - Deliberate sampling of the representation of non-mainstream diets on popular cooking television programs. Content was analysed descriptively, looking at narrative treatments of these diets.
- An analysis of the representation of animals and farming on Australian supermarket shelves was undertaken in 2015. Using a major national supermarket chain, visible (that is, customer-facing)

---

1 Searches were produced using the search strong ('animal welfare' OR 'animal rights' OR 'animal cruelty') AND ftany(yes)) AND (at.exact('News') AND stype.exact('Newspapers'))

Appendix A

packaging of dry goods and refrigerated products was systematically inspected and analysed to examine the representation of animals, farms and farmers. Of the total store content, 195 items were identified for analysis.

Three surveys were conducted as part of the research for this book:

- In late 2013 a survey of non-government organisations (NGOs) concerned with animal protection was conducted. Following the construction of a mailing list of 126 organisations, 50 responses were received (39.7 percent) and subject to analysis. This mailing list included all identifiable organisations at the time, including advocacy, service-provision and mixed organisations across Australia. The survey instrument included 14 open and closed questions.
- In 2014 a survey of animal-welfare officers associated with university research institutions was undertaken. From a mailing list of 39 individuals, 18 responses were received (46.1 percent) and subject to analysis. The survey instrument included 22 open and closed questions and was based on a modified version of the instrument employed by van Luijk et al. (2013).
- In 2015 a survey of protest participants was conducted at the Ban Live Export National Rally organised by Animals Australia in Sydney. The estimated attendance at the rally was 650 individuals; 350 survey requests were distributed and 57 responses received (representing approximately 8.8 percent of attendants, and a response rate of 16.3 percent). The survey instrument included 18 open and closed questions and was identical to that used in a wider research project of street protest participants as part of ongoing research (see: Jackson and Chen 2015).

Appendix B

Major ethical positions regarding animals

Cartesian materialism

Associated with: René Descartes
Applies to: All non-human animals.

Animals are soulless automata and require no ethical consideration; they can be regarded purely as property. Their status as objects makes their use no different from that of other inanimate objects.

Constrained materialism

Associated with: Immanuel Kant
Applies to: All non-human animals. They cannot use symbolic language and therefore are not rational moral agents.

Animals lack rationality, the test of moral concern. In that care should be taken regarding animals it should be indexed against animals that display human-like behaviours (e.g. the productive labour of a working animal). Cruelty to animals is 'bad' in that it promotes cruelty to humans.

Religious duty

Associated with: Various
Applies to: Varies depending on religion. Prohibitions on animal use may be temporal, i.e. applicable only on certain days or in certain contexts.

Animals are available for human use, within specified *a priori* limits derived from scripture.

Appendix B

Speciesism

Associated with: the critiques of Richard Ryder (who coined the term), Peter Singer (who elaborated)
Applies to: All non-human animals. Comparative moral worth is distributed arbitrarily and idiosyncratically.

A speciesist society is one in which the interests of humans are arbitrarily given higher value than that of animals, and which takes an 'us and them' approach to ethical decision-making. This preference for human interests is not based on a philosophical position, but on a prejudice in favour of one's own species.

Carnism / status quo

Associated with: Michael Leahy, Roger Scruton
Applies to: All animals. Comparative moral worth is determined through statute and relationships with individual human actors.

Humans are distinct from animals because language and society allow us to develop moral agency. Human interests have priority over the interests of animals, who are primitive beings. Animal welfare concerns reflect 'natural impulses of affection and solidarity', which are refined into statute and law through democratic processes and institutions. This process tests claims against the status quo, which is demonstrably right as it has survived political and legal challenge from outlier groups.

Omnivorous reactionary

Associated with: Michael Pollan, Simon Fairlie
Applies to: All 'higher' animals. Comparative moral worth is determined by the extent of suffering experienced before use. Small farms are likely to deliver better welfare standards.

Humans are omnivores evolutionarily, biologically and culturally. Food norms have evolved to ensure health, environmental sustainability and social cohesion. Industrial food manufacturing undermines these norms. Understanding the origins of our food encourages more ethical choices, including when consuming animals.

Virtue ethics

Associated with: Rosalind Hursthouse

Applies to: All non-human animals. Comparative moral worth is avoided in exchange for a 'common sense' understanding of the differences between animals.

The treatment of animals should be based on consideration of what a 'virtuous agent' would do. Action should be taken according to the individual's capacity to effect change.

Ethics of care (weak)

Associated with: Nel Noddings
Applies to: All animals. Comparative moral worth is determined by the animal's proximity to human carer(s) and its ability to form relationships.

Animals deserve care based on their proximity to, and relationships with, humans; within in these relationships between moral agents, our focus should be the wellbeing of care-givers and care-receivers. Animals without a relationship to humans have no moral status. Animal use is permissible.

Ethics of care (strong)

Associated with: Carol Adams, Josephine Donovan
Applies to: All animals. Comparative moral worth should not be determined by similarity, but by weakness.

Humans already care about non-human animals, but the full manifestation of this care is often circumvented by social and economic forces. The use of animals is often associated with patriarchal power relations and ethical feminism would abstain from participation in these practices (e.g. meat eating) as part of a wider break with the practice and performance of male domination.

Animal liberation / utilitarianism

Associated with: Peter Singer
Applies to: All sentient animals. Comparative moral worth is determined by the capacity to suffer.

Animals deserve equal consideration of their welfare, but are different from people, particularly with regards to the capacity of humans to anticipate the future. Animals may, therefore, be subject to human use based on purely utilitarian calculations, as their capacity for suffering is often (but not always) less than that of humans. Suffering in animals, if mitigated, reduces humans' moral concern for their life.

Appendix B

Weak animal rights

Associated with: Mary Ann Warren
Applies to: All animals. Comparative moral worth is determined by cognitive complexity.

Animals deserve protection, but are different from humans. The inappropriateness of mistreating animals is in direct relationship to their mental sophistication. Humans are fundamentally different from animals as humans exhibit complex rationality. Animals have some rights, not because they are moral agents but in order to interdict human mistreatment. Animals can be used, if they are treated humanely in the process.

Strong animal rights

Associated with: Tom Regan
Applies to: All sentient animals. Comparative moral worth is determined by the individual's psychological identity and their future life opportunities.

Animals are 'subjects of a life' with intrinsic moral value irrespective of their capabilities. All subject of a life deserve respect (including freedom from harm) because they have complex psychological states (including emotions, beliefs and self-awareness). Choices may be made that privilege an individual or group over another based on the relative impact on their future opportunities, but only in rare cases. The systematic use of animals by people is unnecessary and should be abolished.

Abolitionism

Associated with: Gary Francione
Applies to: All sentient animals. Moral worth is not based on similarity of sentience to humans.

A radical change in human behaviour is needed to abolish the use of animals by humans. Animal-welfare measures promote animal slavery by normalising the status of animals as property. The use or 'ownership' of animals by humans is not morally acceptable in any form.

Appendix C
Australian animal protection organisations – a sample

19th century–pre-WWII

Colonial/state-based RSPCAs

Type: Charity
Ideological focus: Welfarism/weak rights
Core activity: Welfare services

Lord Smith Animal Hospital

Type: Charity
Ideological focus: Welfarism/weak rights
Core activity: Welfare services
(Now part of the Animal Welfare League federation)

World League for the Protection of Animals (Australia)

Type: Abeyance structure
Ideological focus: Abolition (anti-vivisectionist)
Core activity: Community education

Post-WWII

Animal Welfare League New South Wales

Type: Charity
Ideological focus: Welfarism/weak rights
Core activity: Welfare services

Anti-Vivisection Union of South Australia

Type: Abeyance structure
Ideological focus: Abolition

Appendix C

Core activity: Community education

Blue Cross Animals Society of Victoria

Type: Charity
Ideological focus: Welfarism/weak rights
Core activity: Welfare services

Cat Protection Society of New South Wales

Type: Charity
Ideological focus: Welfarism/weak rights
Core activity: Welfare services

Tasmanian Canine Defence League

Type: Charity
Ideological focus: Welfarism/weak rights
Core activity: Welfare services
(Now the Dogs' Homes of Tasmania)

1970s–1990s ('Second wave')

Animal Liberation New South Wales

Type: SMO (first 'second wave' organisation)
Ideological focus: Liberationist
Core activity: Protest
(First 'second wave' organisation)

Animal Liberation Queensland

Type: SMO
Ideological focus: Liberationist/abolition
Core activity: Direct action, protest

Animal Liberation Victoria

Type: SMO
Ideological focus: Abolition
Core activity: Direct action

Animals Australia

Type: Hybrid
Ideological focus: Mixed rights
Core activity: Lobbying (outsider)

Choose Cruelty Free

Type: Interest group
Ideological focus: Abolition
Core activity: Community/consumer education

Domestic Animal Birth-control Society (DABS)

Type: Charity
Ideological focus: Welfarism/weak rights
Core activity: Welfare services

RSPCA Australia

Type: Interest group (federal structure)
Ideological focus: Welfarism/weak rights
Core activity: Lobbying (insider)

Wildlife Information and Rescue Service

Type: Charity
Ideological focus: Welfarism/weak rights
Core activity: Welfare services, with crossover into conservation movement

21st century

Animal Justice Party

Type: Hybrid, political party
Ideological focus: Liberation/strong rights
Core activity: Electoral

Animal Welfare League Australia

Type: Interest group ('capstone' peak organisation)
Ideological focus: Welfarism/weak rights
Core activity: Lobbying (insider)

Edgar's Mission Farm Sanctuary

Type: Charity
Ideological focus: Abolition
Core activity: Welfare services

PETA Australia (previously PETA Asia-Pacific)

Type: SMO
Ideological focus: Abolition
Core activity: Protest

Appendix C

Sea Shepherd Australia

Type: SMO (local branches of US-based organisation)
Ideological focus: Environmentalism
Core activity: Direct action

Voiceless

Type: Interest group
Ideological focus: Strong rights
Core activity: Legal, capacity building

Vegan Australia

Type: SMO
Ideological focus: Abolition
Core activity: Dietary advocacy

Appendix D

Animal-using industry in Australia – representative bodies and their relationships with policy-makers

The names of specific organisations are italicised.

Agriculture

Subcategory National organisation	State or subsidiary organisation	Policy goals: primary	Policy goals: secondary
Primary production			
National Farmers Federation	State farmers' organisations	Economic efficiency / productivity	Rural community welfare
National commodity councils	State commodity council		
	Commodity service organisations		
	Independent SFOs		
Independent national commodity councils	Independent state commodity councils		
Non-primary production, services to industry			
National industry peak	State industry peak	Economic efficiency / productivity	Generic industry regulation
	Professional practices areas (law, finance, etc.)		

Appendix D

Subcategory National organisation	State or subsidiary organisation	Policy goals: primary	Policy goals: secondary
Non-primary production, 'downstream' supply chain			
National industry organisation	Sectoral industry associations	Economic efficiency / productivity	Generic industry regulation
	Large, individual corporations		

Animal entertainment

Subcategory National organisation	State or subsidiary organisation	Policy goals: primary	Policy goals: secondary
Racing, equestrian, and recreational riding			
Racing Australia	State-based legislated racing peaks	Economic efficiency / productivity	Anti-corruption / gambling
	Individual racing clubs		
Equestrian Australia	State equestrian associations	Sports	Leisure
National non-horse racing associations	State racing animal associations	Animal health	
National riding associations	State and local riding associations		
	Breed-specific riding associations		
Rodeo			
National rodeo associations	Local rodeo organisations	Tourism	Welfare
Hunting			
Shooters and outdoor recreation parties	State and local shooters clubs	Risk management / gun laws	Varies: Tourism Cultural maintenance Pest control
National Shooters Association			

Animals in education and research

Subcategory National organisation	State or subsidiary organisation	Policy goals: primary	Policy goals: secondary
Exhibited			
Zoo and Aquarium Association	Major organisations	Public good	Welfare
Research			
National Health and Medical Research Council		Intellectual property	Education provision
Universities Australia	Individual universities		
Laboratory Professionals Association		Workforce provision	Technical standards
Education			
	State departments of education	Education provision	Educational standards
Australian Science Teachers Association	State teachers organisations		Workforce provision/ standards

Companion animals

Subcategory National organisation	State or subsidiary organisation	Policy goals: primary	Policy goals: secondary
Companion animals			
Companion animal industry peak bodies	Breeders associations	Generic industry regulation	Welfare
	Major retailers		Consumer protection
	Animal services orgs		

Appendix D

Breed-specific organisations

Subcategory National organisation	State or subsidiary organisation	Policy goals: primary	Policy goals: secondary
Commercial animals			
Breed associations, species	Breed and sub-breed associations	Productivity	Resilience
Companion animals			
Breed associations, species	Breed and sub-breeds associations	Urban management	Dangerous breeds

Professional workers

Subcategory National organisation	State or subsidiary organisation	Policy goals: primary	Policy goals: secondary
Professional workers			
Australian Veterinary Association	AVA local groups	Workforce provision	Technical capacity

Appendix E
Timeline of animal welfare policy in Australia

Year	Event
c40,000 BCE	First human settlement of Australian continent
c8,000 BCE	Introduction of the dingo to Australia
1788	European settlement of the Australian content, arrival of first beef cattle and greyhounds Establishment of first colonial government
1791	Arrival of founding sheep flocks
1804	Privy Council Committee on *Trade and Foreign Plantations* recommends a wool industry be established in the Australian colonies
1805	Sydney's first commercial dairy established in Ultimo
1807	First commercial-grade wool exported
1810	First formal horse race in Australia (NSW)
1822	Passage of Richard Martin's *Cruel Treatment of Cattle Act* (UK), Britain's first animal cruelty legislation
1824	Formation of the Society for the Prevention of Cruelty to Animals (UK)
1827	Bigge Commission recommends large joint stock companies and expanded land grants to encourage increased investment
1835	Wool overtakes seal products as the major Australian export
1837	First anti-cruelty legislation in Australia (Tasmania)

Appendix E

Year	Event
1840	Society for the Prevention of Cruelty to Animals (UK) becomes a Royal Society (RSPCA)
1846	Opening of first Australian meat cannery (NSW)
1850	Australia provides 50 percent of British wool imports
1853	Passage of the *Act for the Regulation and Licensing of Public Conveyances and to Prevent the Wanton Ill-treatment of Horses and Cattle* (SA) Cessation of convict transportation to Australia
1854	Formation of the Humane Society (Melbourne)
1856	Bessemer process for producing steel wire leads to reduced fencing costs and the increased enclosure of lands
1859	'Successful' acclimatisation of rabbits in Victoria
1860	Introduction of camels to Australia First running of the Melbourne Cup
1864	First known dog show in Australia (Melbourne) Formation of Victoria Racing Club
c1865	First commercial greyhound coursing in Australia
1865	Passage of the *Police offences statute* (Victoria), including a general prohibition of cruelty to cattle
c1870	Establishment of Australia's first meat-freezing works (NSW)
1871	Formation of the SPCA (Victoria)
c1872	Formation of the SPCA (Tasmania)
1873	Formation of the SPCA (NSW)
1875	Formation of the SPCA (SA)
1876	Formation of a precursor to the SPCA (Queensland), although it becomes inactive before 1883
c1880	Introduction of mechanical butter-production technology
1881	Passage of the *Protection of Animals Act* (Victoria) Arrival of the vegetarian Seventh-Day Adventist Church in Australia Introduction of milk separators
1883	Formation of the SPCA (Queensland)
c1885	Formation of the Theosophical Societies in Australia

Animal welfare in Australia

Year	Event
	Formation of the Women's Christian Temperance Unions in Australia
1885	First live export of animals from Australia (to Hong Kong)
1886	Formation of the Amalgamated Shearers' Union of Australia, representing shearers from NSW, Victoria and South Australia Formation of the Vegetarian Society (Melbourne) First vegetarian restaurant opened (Melbourne)
c1887	Formation of the Band of Mercy Australia (promoting animal welfare to children)
1888	Formation of the Band of Mercy (Junior SPCA) Queensland
1889	Formation of the International Vegetarian Union (UK)
c1890	Formation of the Australian Vegetarian Society Establishment of a branch of the Vegetarian Society in Ballarat RPSCA Queensland's charter expanded to include protection of children Introduction of milking machines
1890	SPCA (SA) falls into inactivity Formation of the Pastoralists' Union of NSW, the South Australian Farmers' Federation and the United Pastoralists' Association of Queensland
1891	Shearers' strike Formation of the NSW Vegetarian Society Formation of the Pastoralists' Federal Council
1893	Formation of the Farmers' and Settlers' Association Formation of the Queensland Vegetarian Society
1892	Formation of the SPCA (Western Australia) Passage of the *Police Act* (Western Australia), including general protection for animals
1895	Formation of the Animal Protection Society of NSW
1896	Establishment of first dogs' home in Victoria Closure of the NSW Vegetarian Society
1897	Passage of the *Police Act* (SA), including a general prohibition against cruelty and neglect of animals, punishable by a fine of up to £5 or imprisonment of two months
1898	Formation of the South Australian Vegetarian Society Publication of the first Australian vegetarian cookbook

Appendix E

Year	Event
1898	Establishment of the Sanitarium Food Co. (Melbourne) by the Seventh-Day Adventist Church
1901	Federation Passage of the *Animals Protection Act* (Queensland) Construction begins on the first rabbit-proof fence in Western Australia (completed 1907)
1904	SPCA South Australia re-established
c1908	No Australian vegetarian societies any longer in operation
1909	Formation of the Wildlife Preservation Society of Australia (Sydney) First large-scale butter exports from Australia
1910	First Australian animal ambulance established by the SPCA South Australia
1912	Formation of the Western Australian Farmers' Federation Passage of the *Prevention of Cruelty to Animals Act* (Western Australia)
1913	SPCA South Australia permitted to contribute directly to government school publications
c1915	Formation of the Purple Cross League (Victoria), concerned with the welfare of battlefield horses, after many military horses taken to war with the Australian Imperial Force were not returned to Australia
1916	Adelaide slaughterhouses begin using stunning
1919	Establishment of horse 'rest homes' in Western Australia and Victoria
c1920	Introduction of sheep mulesing Emergence of the Australian merino breed of sheep
1920	Formation of the League of Kindness (Junior SPCA Victoria) Establishment of an animal rest reserve in Queensland SPCA Western Australia inspectors are formally recognised in legislation
1921	Formation of the Australian Veterinary Association
1922	Closure of the Purple Cross League
1923	SPCA South Australia opens the first free veterinary clinic SPCA Victoria begins advocating use of the 'humane killer' gas bolt for livestock
c1925	Development of the Kelpie breed of cattle dog First commercial greyhound racing in Australia

Year	Event
1925	Legal recognition of SPCA Queensland inspectors *Bernard v Evans* (UK) defines cruelty as 'causing unnecessary suffering'
1926	Introduction of dairy subsidies Establishment of the Theosophist-owned radio station 2GB (Melbourne), promoting vegetarianism Formation of the Council for Scientific and Industrial Research (CSIR)
1927	Formation of the SPCA Tasmania
1928	Formation of the Animal Welfare League Victoria
1929	Commonwealth introduces partial prohibition on live exports of merino sheep
c1930	Introduction of first cattle feed-lots
1931	Unemployed men riot over the removal of beef from their ration in South Australia
1932	Military personnel deployed to control emus in Western Australia (the 'Emu War')
1935	Establishment of the Lord Smith Animal Hospital by the Animal Welfare League Victoria Formation of the World League for the Protection of Animals (WLPA) (NSW)
1936	Electrocution of pigs introduced in South Australia (the 'electro-leathaller') Formation of South Australian Dairyfarmers' Association
c1940s	SPCA NSW campaigns for 'country killing' in rural abattoirs to reduce stock travel and related suffering
1942	Formation of the Australian Dairy Farmers Federation
1946	Tractors outnumber horses in Australia for the first time
1947	Banning of hare coursing (NSW)
1948	Re-establishment of the Vegetarian Society
1949	Establishment of Queensland and Western Australian branches of the Vegetarian Society
1950	Formation of the Tasmania Canine Defence League Removal of intentionality requirement for cruelty prosecutions in Victorian law

Appendix E

Year	Event
	Re-establishment of Victorian and South Australian branches of the Vegetarian Society
	First major rabbit population control measure achieved via the Myxoma virus
1951	Formation of the Anti-Vivisection Union of South Australia
	Establishment of Equestrian Australia
1955	Establishment of the SPCA ACT
1956	Australian SPCAs become royal societies
1957	First animal welfare television program, *Animal Orphanage*, screened (Victoria)
1958	Formation of the Animal Welfare League NSW
	Formation of the Cat Protection Society of NSW
1959	Formation of the Animal Welfare League Queensland
	Establishment of CHOICE (Australian Consumers' Association)
	Banning of trapshooting using live birds in Victoria
c1960	Beginning of the contemporary live sheep export industry
1960	Joy Adamson publishes *Born free*, popularising wild animal conservation
1962	Formation of Vegetarian and Vegan Society (SA)
1963	Formation of the Hunt Saboteurs Association (UK)
1964	Ruth Harrison publishes *Animal machines* (UK)
	Formation of the Animal Welfare League South Australia
	Establishment of the Australian Chicken Meat Federation
	In Victoria, new legislation restricts the right of offenders to own animals, and regulates private zoos
	Live sheep exports to the Middle East
c1963	First national meeting of Australian RSPCAs
1965	Formation of the SPCA Northern Territory
1966	Animal coursing banned in Victoria
	Film adaptation of *Born free* released
	Formation of the Blue Cross Animals Society of Victoria
1967	Last overland cattle droving
1968	Passage of the *RSPCA Act* (Victoria)

Year	Event
	Passage of the *Agriculture (Miscellaneous Provisions) Act* (UK), introducing duty-of-care provisions for animals in agricultural production (this was later extended to other animals)
1969	Formation of the Australian Wildlife Protection Council
1970	Banning of steel-jawed traps in municipal areas in South Australia Introduction of the Commonwealth reserve price scheme for wool Establishment of the Kangaroo Protection Committee NSW
1971	Constance Bienvenu (critic of the RSPCA Victoria) declared a vexatious litigant Formation of the Australian Animal Protection Society
c1972	Arrival of the International Society of Krishna Consciousness in Australia
1973	Formation of the Vegan Society of Victoria
1975	Peter Singer publishes *Animal liberation* (UK)
1977	Donald Griffin publishes *The question of animal awareness: evolutionary continuity of mental experience* (USA) Formation of Animal Liberation NSW
1978	Vegan Society becomes a national organisation
1979	Formation of Animal Liberation Victoria Formation of the Animal Societies Federation of NSW Formation of Greenpeace Australia Formation of the World Wildlife Fund, Australian branch Anti-Vivisection Union of Australia renamed the Australian Association Against Painful Experiments on Animals (AAAPEA)
1980	Passage of the *Prevention of Cruelty to Animals Act* (NSW) (current governing act) Formation of Animal Liberation Brisbane (later Animal Liberation Queensland) Formation of the Cattle Council of Australia Formation of Humane Research Australia (Australian Association for Humane Research Inc) Formation of the Fund for Animals in Australia Establishment of the National Farmers' Federation Establishment of the Pet Industry Joint Advisory Council (Pet Industry Association of Australia)
1981	Formation of Animal Liberation South Australia

Appendix E

Year	Event
	Formation of the Australian Federation of Animal Societies (AFAS, later ANZFAS and Animals Australia)
	Formation of RSPCA Australia, a national merger of individual RSPCAs (replacing a federal secretariat)
	Formation of People for the Ethical Treatment of Animals (USA)
1982	Formation of Animal Liberation (SA)
	Formation of the Vegan Society of NSW
	Formation of the World Society for the Protection of Animals Australia
1983	Formation of Australians for Animals
1984	Establishment of the Senate Committee on Animal Welfare, and initiation of the Senate Inquiry into Animal Welfare
	Tom Regan publishes *The case for animal rights* (USA)
1986	Passage of the *Animal Welfare Act* in South Australia (current governing act)
	Passage of the *Research Animals Act* in NSW
	Banning of live animal coursing in South Australia
	National Farmers' Federation establishes the Australian Farmers' Fighting Fund
1987	Passage of the *Prevention of Cruelty to Animals Act* in Victoria (current governing act)
	Formation of Avian Rights (NSW)
	Formation of the Coalition Against Duck Shooting (CADS) (Victoria)
	Formation of the Humane Society (NSW)
	Formation of Wildlife Information and Rescue Service (WIRES) (NSW)
	AFAS introduces individual memberships and accepts New Zealand organisational members (becomes ANZFAS)
	Formation of the Australian and New Zealand Council for the Care of Animals in Research and Teaching
1988	Release of Model Code of Practice – Sea Transport of Livestock
	Introduction of national food labelling laws
1990	RSPCA inspector Stuart Fairlie murdered while investigating a reported case of animal cruelty (Victoria)
	Establishment of the National Consultative Committee on Animal Welfare
1991	Formation of the Vegetarian/Vegan Society of Queensland
	Formation of Animals Australia
1992	Completion of Senate Inquiry into Animal Welfare

Year	Event
1993	Release of Model Codes of Practice covering: animals at sale yards, farming of deer, feral livestock animals, goat, intensive farming of rabbits, sheep Termination of the Wool Price Reserve Scheme 25,000 people rally in Sydney for the 'Day for Animals' organised by the International Fund for Animal Welfare Passage of the *Animal Welfare Act* in the ACT (current governing act) Start of Animal Liberation campaign against conditions at Prime Minister Paul Keating's PM Piggery Release of *Model Code of Practice – Cattle* Formation of the Australian Vegetarian Society (NSW) Inc. Formation of the Queensland Farmers' Federation Formation of the Shooters, Farmers and Fishers Party (later the Shooters Party)
1994	Passage of the *Animal Welfare Act* in Tasmania (current governing act), including the first duty of care provisions in Australian legislation Animal Liberation Victoria forms an open rescue group Release of Model Code of Practices for: domestic poultry, rail transport of livestock, road transport of livestock
c1995	Peter Singer runs for federal parliament for the Australian Greens The first RSPCA Million Paws Walk is held in Queensland
1995	Formation of People Against Cruelty in Animal Transport (WA) (later Stop Live Exports)
1996	Establishment of first Animal Liberation Front cells in Australia Calicivirus, used to control rabbit populations, escapes and spreads to the Australian mainland after testing on Wardang Island in South Australia
1997	RSPCA Million Paws Walk becomes a national event Senator Andrew Bartlett (Australian Democrats) advocates vegetarianism in his maiden speech to federal parliament
c1998	NSW bans jumps racing Formation of the National League for the Protection of Horses Establishment of a Senate inquiry into animal experimentation
1998	Formation of the Australian Livestock Exporters' Council New Zealand leaves ANZFAS; ANZFAS becomes Animals Australia
1999	Formation of the Australian Racing Board (Racing Australia) Formation of Vegetarian Victoria (formally the Vegetarian Network Victoria)

Appendix E

Year	Event
2000	Formation of AgForce Queensland
	Passage of the *Animal Welfare Act* in the Northern Territory (current governing act)
	RSPCA inspector Jason Nichols is shot during an inspection and survives (Victoria)
	Release of Model Codes of Practice covering: husbandry of captive bred emus, land transport of cattle
2001	Passage of the *Domestic Animals Act* (ACT), introducing mandatory de-sexing and micro-chipping of dogs and cats
	Formation of Australian Pork Limited
	Formation of the Medical Advances Without Animals (MAWA) Trust
	Formation of the People and Animal Welfare Society (WA)
	Termination of subsidies for the dairy industry
2002	Passage of the *Animal Care and Protection Act* in Queensland (current governing act)
	Release of *Model Code of Practice – Livestock at Slaughtering Establishments*
2003	Passage of *Animal Welfare Act* in Western Australia (current governing act)
2004	Death of 5,500 sheep on the MV *Cormo Express* en route between Fremantle and Saudi Arabia, leading to the establishment of the Keniry Livestock Export Review (Commonwealth)
	Passage of *Agriculture, Fisheries and Forestry Legislation Amendment (Export Control) Act* (Commonwealth)
	Formation of Animals Tasmania (later Against Animal Cruelty Tasmania)
	Formation of Edgar's Mission Inc. (Victoria)
	Establishment of World Vegan Day Melbourne as an annual event
2005	Establishment of the Australian Animal Welfare Strategy
	PETA USA campaign against mulesing begins
	Development of the RSPCA model animal legislation for co-ordinated national legislative advocacy
	Formation of Animal Management in Rural and Remote Indigenous Communities (AMRRIC)
	Establishment of Sentient: The Veterinary Institute for Animal Ethics
	Establishment of Voiceless
	Animal Liberationists throw paint at the president of RSPCA Victoria in protest against RSPCA's handling of egg farms
2006	Publication of the Neumann Report (NCCAW review)

Year	Event
	First dedicated animal law course taught in Australia (at the University of New South Wales, by Geoffrey Bloom)
	Formation of the Centre for Animal Welfare and Ethics at the University of Queensland
	Establishment of the Cruelty Free Festival (Sydney) as an annual event
	Formation of Lawyers for Animals (Melbourne)
	Formation of Stop Tasmanian Animal Cruelty
2007	Formation of the Australian and New Zealand Laboratory Animal Association
2008	Formation of the Animal Welfare League Australia
2009	Lewis Report into greyhound racing industry (Victoria)
	Passage of the *Animal Management (Cats and Dogs) Act* in Queensland, dealing with unwanted animals
	Scott Review into the greyhound racing industry in NSW
2010	Russia suspends kangaroo meat imports (until 2012)
	Formation of PETA Australia
2011	Formation of the Animal Justice Party (AJP)
	Formation of Oscar's Law (Victoria)
	Formation of Human-Animal Research Network (HARN) at the University of Sydney
2012	AAWS produces the Australian Horse Welfare Protocol
	Airing of 'A bloody business' on *Four Corners* (ABC TV)
	Federal government suspends live exports to Indonesia for four weeks
	ALP National Conference votes to establish an Independent Office of Animal Welfare
	Duck hunt protester shot and injured in Victoria
2013	Formation of Vegan Australia
	Introduction of Exporter Supply Chain Assurance System (ESCAS)
2014	Abolition of the Australian Animal Welfare Strategy Advisory Committee
	Formation of the Animal Defenders Office (ACT)
	Formation of the Human Rights and Animal Ethics Research Network (University of Melbourne)
	Establishment of a NSW Legislative Council inquiry into greyhound racing
2015	AAWS produces Australian Horse Welfare Protocol
	ACT bans cages in chicken and pig industries

Appendix E

Year	Event
	Russia suspends kangaroo meat imports for a second time
	Release of the Newgate Report into agricultural advocacy structures in Australia
	Airing of 'Making a killing' on *Four Corners* (ABC-TV), documenting cruelty in the greyhound industry
	Election of Animal Justice Party candidate Mark Pearson to the NSW Legislative Council
	Establishment of NSW parliamentary inquiry into companion animal breeding
	Establishment of Tasmanian parliamentary inquiry into greyhound racing
	Establishment of WA parliamentary inquiry into the RSPCA WA
	Indonesia reduces live cattle quota from Australia, relaxes import restrictions from other nations
	Australia reaches live cattle export agreement with China as part of ongoing free-trade talks
	Productivity Commission begins review of agriculture, including animal protection regulation
2016	NSW passes legislation banning greyhound racing

Appendix F
Significant legal instruments

Compiled from Eadie (2009), Bruce (2012a), Cao (2010), Sankoff et al. (2013) and primary sources.

National

Main legal instruments: Constitutional powers over: quarantine, fisheries, trade and commerce, and treaties. Power to develop model codes. *Australian animal welfare strategy* 2005 (status remains uncertain at the time of writing)

Agriculture and food
  Game
  National code of practice for the humane shooting of kangaroos and wallabies for commercial purposes (regulates the welfare of kangaroos killed for commercial purposes)
  Live export
  Australian Meat and Livestock Industry Act 1997 (requires licensing of exporters; requires compliance with industry standards to receive an export permit)
  Export Control Act 1982
  Navigation Act 1912 (regulates animals while on ships)

Slaughter
  Food regulation standing committee Australian standard for the hygienic production and transportation of meat and meat products for human consumption 2007 (adopted nationally through various food regulations; requires animals be stunned before they are killed; includes exemptions for religious, eg halal and kosher, practices)
  Export Control Act 1982 (provides for halal slaughter of exported meat)

Research and education
  Australian code of practice for the care and use of animals for scientific purposes 2002

Appendix F

NHMRC Australian code of practice for the use of animals for scientific purposes 1969 (encourages the '3 Rs': replacement, reduction and refinement of research methods using animals; established animal ethics committees in licensed institutions; is made binding through its bundling with research grants)

Wildlife protection

Whaling

Seas and Submerged Lands Act 1973 (Australia claims an exclusive economic zone adjacent to the Australian Antarctic Territory)
Convention on international trade in endangered species of wild fauna and flora 1973

Antarctic treaty 1959
International convention for the regulation of whaling 1945

Other wildlife

Environmental Protection and Biodiversity Conservation Act 1999 (regulates the welfare of imported exotic animals; protects animals of national environmental significance; protects threatened native species in Commonwealth areas)

Indigenous Australians

Native Title Act 1993 (removed restrictions on traditional animal hunting and use by native-title holders)

ACT

Main legal instrument: *Animal Welfare Act* 1992 (prohibits acts of cruelty and unnecessary pain; adherence to an approved code is a defence)
Definition of an animal: all animals excluding human beings
Enforcement: inspections by the RSPCA ACT

Agriculture and food

No specific farm act. Poultry covered by the *Poultry model code of practice*

Companion animals

Domestic Animals Act 2000 (all cats and dogs to be micro-chipped at point of sale)

Entertainment

Circus

Animal Welfare Act 1992 (regulates circus animals; prohibits some species of exotic animals)

Horse Racing

Animal Welfare Act 1992 (jumps racing banned)

Hunting[1]

Firearms Act 1996 (licensed hunting of vermin on private land permitted with permission)

Rodeos
Animal Welfare Act 1992 (prohibits rodeos)

Zoos
Animal Welfare Act 1992 (regulates travelling zoos; prohibits some species, e.g. bears)

Media
Voluntary code for animals used in film and photography
Animal Welfare Act 1992 (requires adherence to the national code)

Invasive Animals
Pest Plants and Animals Act 2005

New South Wales

Main legal instruments: *Prevention of Cruelty to Animals Act* 1979 (prohibits acts of cruelty; prohibits failure to prevent acts of cruelty, alleviate pain or provide necessary treatment); *Crimes Act* 1900 (prohibits serious animal cruelty; provides exemption for routine animal husbandry practices)
Definition of an animal: excludes cephalopods
Enforcement: inspection by the RSPCA New South Wales and the Animal Welfare League

Agriculture and food
No specific farm act. Stock animals exempted from some anti-cruelty measures (e.g. concerning exercise and caging). Poultry covered by the *Poultry Meat Industry Act* 1986 and the *Prevention of Cruelty to Animals Act* 1979

Companion animals
Companion Animals Act 1998 (regulates dangerous breeds; all cats and dogs to be micro-chipped at point of sale)

Entertainment
Circuses
Exhibited Animals Protection Act 1986

Hunting
Game and Feral Animal Control Act 2002 (licenses hunting for game animals on private and public land; hunting licence not required for hunting feral animals on private land with the owner's permission; hunters must be aged 12 or over; permits use of hunting dogs; requires compliance with *Game council code of practice*, which includes welfare provisions)

---

1 The classification of hunting under entertainment is contested by some hunters on the grounds that they consume the animals they kill.

Prevention of Cruelty to Animals Act 1979 (hunting animals exempted)

Horse Racing
Protecting the welfare of horses competing in bush races in NSW 2003 (voluntary code of practice)
Prevention of Cruelty to Animals Act 1979 (jumps racing banned)

Rodeos
NSW code of practice for the welfare of animals used in rodeo events 1988 (compliance provides exemption from the *Prevention of Cruelty to Animals Act* 1979)
Prevention of Cruelty to Animals Act 1979 (prohibits animal fighting; exempts rodeos)

Zoos
Exhibited Animals Protection Act 1986 (regulates zoos and marine parks)
Zoological Parks Board Act 1973

Theatre
Prevention of Cruelty to Animals Act 1979 (requires code compliance for animals used in theatrical performances)

Research and education
Animal Research Act 1985 (requires adherence to national code; specifically regulates private businesses and individual researchers)

Invasive animals
Game and Feral Animal Control Act 2002
Threatened Special Conservation Act 1995
Rural Lands Protection Act 1998 (eradication orders cannot contravene *Prevention of Cruelty to Animals Act* 1979)
Local Government Act 1993
Environmental Planning and Assessment Act 1979
National Parks and Wildlife Act 1974

Wildlife protection
Threatened Special Conservation Act 1995
Environmental Planning and Assessment Act 1979
National Parks and Wildlife Act 1974 (cruelty exemption granted for killing animals for crop protection)

Indigenous Australians
Game and Feral Animal Control Act 2002
National Parks and Wildlife Act 1974

Northern Territory

Main legal instrument: *Animal Welfare Act* 1999 (prohibits acts of cruelty; defence granted where there has been adherence to the relevant code; exemption for use of electrical devices on farm animals. The Northern Territory is the only Australian jurisdiction that specifically states that cultural or religious practices are not a defence)

Definition of an animal: excludes cephalopods
Enforcement: inspection by government department(s) and police
Agriculture and food
No specific farm act. Poultry covered by the *Poultry model code of practice*

Companion animals
Law Reform (Misc. Provisions) Act 1956
Summary Offences Act 1923 (imposes fines against owners of dogs that attack)

Entertainment
Horse Racing
Animal Welfare Act 1999 (jumps racing banned)
Hunting
Territory Parks and Wildlife Conservation Act 2006 (permits can be issued for collection of live animals, e.g. as companion animals; permits can be issued for the hunting of pigs and waterfowl in specified seasons and locations; hunters must be aged 12 or older)

Research and education
Animal Welfare Act 1999 (requires adherence to the national code)

Invasive animals
Territory Parks and Wildlife Conservation Act 2001 (permits can be issued to take or interfere with problem animals)

Indigenous Australians
Territory Parks and Wildlife Conservation Act 2001 (exemption from permit requirement for traditional hunting)
Animal Welfare Act 1999 (traditional hunting excluded from definition of cruelty)

Queensland

Main legal instrument: *Animal Care and Protection Act* 2001 (prohibits acts of cruelty; defence granted where adherence to relevant code; the person in charge of an animal has a duty of care; some prohibited practices (e.g. tail docking) may be carried out by veterinarians if in the animal's interest); Criminal Code (as at 2014) (criminalises 'serious animal cruelty')
Definition of an animal: all animals excluding human beings
Enforcement: inspection by the RSPCA Queensland for companion animals and State Department for livestock

Appendix F

Agriculture and food

No specific farm act. Game covered by the adoption of national kangaroo and wallaby shooting code as delegated legislation. Poultry covered by the *Animal Care and Protection Act* 2001 and a voluntary poultry code

Companion animals

Animal Management (Cats and Dogs) Act 2008 (delegates power to councils to enforce dangerous animals prohibitions; all cats and dogs to be micro-chipped at point of sale)

Entertainment

Circuses
Animal Care and Protection Act 2001 (regulates circus animals via a mandatory code of practice)

Horse racing
Animal Care and Protection Act 2001 (bans jumps racing)

Hunting
Nature Conservation Amendment Bill 2006 (bans duck and quail hunting)

Rodeos
Animal Care and Protection Act 2001 (cruelty exemption where necessary to protect a human competitor or spectator)

Zoos

Land Protection (Pest and Stock Route Management) Act 2002
Animal Care and Protection Act 2001 (regulates zoo animals)
Nature Conservation Act 2001 (allows use of exotic animals under permit)

Media

Animals used in film and television are protected by a voluntary code

Research and education

Animal Care and Protection Act 2001 (requires adherence to national code)

Invasive Animals

Land Protection (Pest and Stock Route Management Act) 2002
Animal Care and Protection Act 2001 (cruelty exemption for feral and pest animals)

Wildlife

Nature Conservation Act 1992 (killing of animal for damage mitigation to commercial activities allowed via permit)

Indigenous Australians

Animal Care and Protection Act 2001 (conditional exemption for traditional hunting where pain is minimised)

South Australia

Main legal instrument: *Animal Welfare Act* 1985 (prohibits acts of ill-treatment; defence granted where adherence to prescribed code; electrical devices may be used on some farm animals)
Definition of an animal: excludes fish, reptiles, crustaceans and cephalopods
Enforcement: inspection by the RSPCA South Australia

Agriculture and food

No specific farm act. Pork covered by required compliance with the *Model code of practice for the welfare of animals: pigs* 2008. Poultry covered by the *Guidelines for the establishment and operation of poultry farms in South Australia* 1998, and by the *Animal Welfare Act* 1985 (which recommended a Poultry Model Code of Practice)

Companion animals

Dog and Cat Management Act 1985 (delegates power to councils to enforce dangerous animals prohibitions)

Entertainment

Circuses

Animal Welfare Act 1985 (regulates circus animals via mandatory code of practice)

Hunting

National Parks and Wildlife Act 1972 (requires hunting licence to hunt unprotected species during specified seasons; permits hunting on private land, with permission)

Rodeos

Animal Welfare Act 1985 (regulates animals to be used in rodeos)
Calf Roping (Rodeos) Prohibited Animal Welfare Act 1985 (requires adherence to the national code)

Invasive Animals

National Resource Management Act 2004
Plant and Animal Control (Agricultural Protection and Other Purposes) 1986 (suffering not considered)

Wildlife

National Resource Management Act 2004
National Parks and Wildlife Act 1972 (prohibits the taking of native animals and eggs; hunting licence exemption for non-protected species damaging crops and property)

Indigenous Australians

National Parks and Wildlife Act 1972 (exemption for traditional hunting, excluding prohibited species)

Appendix F

Tasmania

Main legal instrument: *Animal Welfare Act* 1993 (prohibits acts of unreasonable and unjustifiable pain; person in charge of animal has a duty of care)
Definition of an animal: excludes cephalopods
Enforcement: inspection by the RSPCA Tasmania
Agriculture and food
No specific farm act. Poultry covered by the *Animal Welfare Act* 1993 (which recommended a Poultry Model Code)

Companion animals
  Cat Management Act 2009
  Dog Control Act 2000 (delegates power to councils to enforce dangerous animal prohibitions)

Entertainment
  Circuses and zoos
  Nature Conservation Act 1992 (licences the exhibition of undefined 'wildlife' undefined)
  Horse racing
  Animal Welfare Act 1993 (jumps racing banned)
  Hunting
  Nature Conservation Act 2002 (licences hunting of specific species, and specifies permittable seasons, weapons, and bag limits; prohibits the use of dogs in hunting)

Rodeos
  Animal Welfare Act 1993 (requires rodeo operators to comply with the NCCAW standards for the care and treatment of rodeo livestock)
  Animal Welfare Act 1993 (requires adherence to national code)

Invasive animals
  Vermin Control Act 2000 (animals specified as vermin, e.g. rabbits, hares and foxes, may be hunted at any time on Crown land or, with the permission of landowners, private lands)
  Animal Welfare Act 1993 (allows declaration of pest species)

Indigenous Australians
  Nature Conservation Act 2002 (conditional exemption for traditional hunting)

Victoria

Main legal instrument: *Prevention of Cruelty to Animals Act* 1986 (prohibits acts of cruelty, exemption for farm workers where adhering to a code, exemption for self-defence)
Definition of an animal: excludes cephalopods
Enforcement: RSPCA Victoria

Agriculture and food
No specific farm act. Poultry covered by the *Code of accepted farming practice for the welfare of poultry* 2003 and the *Prevention of Cruelty to Animals Act* 1986. Slaughter covered by the *Meat Industry Act* 1993

Companion animals
Domestic Animals (Dangerous Dogs) Act 2010 (delegates power to councils to enforce dangerous animal prohibitions)
Domestic Animals Act 1994 (regulates animal hoarding; all cats and dogs to be micro-chipped at date of registration)

Entertainment
Circuses
Code of practice for the public display and exhibition of animals 2001 (voluntary code)
Hunting
Wildlife Act 1975 (provides licences for game hunting, regulates permissible seasons, locations permissible and bag limits, prohibits the use of lead (toxic) shot, hunters must be aged 12 or older, permits harrying, i.e. dog tracking of sambar deer)

Rodeos
Prevention of Cruelty to Animals Act 1986
Zoos
Code of practice for the public display of exhibition of animals 2001 (voluntary code)
Zoological Parks and Gardens Act 1995
Media
Prevention of Cruelty to Animals Act 1986 (specifies a voluntary code for animals used in film)

Research and education
Prevention of Cruelty to Animals Act 1986 (requires adherence to national code)

Invasive Animals
Catchment and Lands Protection Act 1994
Flora and Fauna Guarantee Act 1988 (may require land owner to eradicate listed species)

Indigenous Australians
Wildlife Act 1975 (allows the issuing of licences to hunt or take wildlife for cultural purposes)

Western Australia

Main legal instrument: *Animal Welfare Act* 2002 (prohibits acts of cruelty; exemptions for self-defence, accepted veterinary and farm practices, and acts authorised by law)
Definition of an animal: excludes fish, reptiles, crustaceans and cephalopods

Appendix F

Enforcement: inspection by the RSPCA Western Australia, local government and state departments

Agriculture and food
No specific farm act. Poultry covered by the *Code of practice for poultry in Western Australia* 2003

Companion animals
Cat Act 2011 (all cats to be microchipped by six months of age)
Dog Act 1976 (delegates power to councils to enforce dangerous animal prohibitions)

Entertainment
Circus and Zoos
Animal Welfare Act 2002 (regulates exhibited animals via mandatory code of practice; cruelty exemptions for zoos and wildlife parks)

Horse racing
Animal Welfare Act 2002 (jumps racing banned)

Hunting
Firearms Act 1973 (hunting limited to feral species on private land with the owner's permission; duck hunting is prohibited)

Rodeos
Animal Welfare Act 2002 (provides a defence against prosecution if there has been compliance with the *Code of practice for the conduct of rodeos in Western Australia* 2003)

Research and education
Animal Welfare Act 2002 (requires adherence to national code)

Invasive animals
Animal Welfare Act 2002 (cruelty offence exemption for proscribed pests)

Indigenous Australians
Wildlife Conservation Act 1970 (allows taking of fauna for customary purposes)

Appendix G

Top Google queries relating to the 10 most frequently searched-for animals

1. Dog or puppy

Dog
1. Dog
2. Dogs
3. Dog breeds
4. Dog training
5. Dog names
6. Dog food
7. Cat
8. Black dog
9. Red Dog [movie]
10. Dog rescue

Puppy
1. Dog
2. Puppy dog
3. Puppies
4. Puppy training
5. Dogs
6. Puppy dogs
7. Puppy for sales
8. Puppy names
9. Puppy school
10. Cute puppy

2. Chicken or bird

Chicken
1. Chicken recipe
2. Chicken recipes
3. Recipes
4. Chicken soup
5. Curry chicken
6. Roast chicken
7. Chicken salad
8. Chicken pox
9. Chicken pasta
10. Fried chicken

Bird
1. The bird
2. Flappy Bird [game]
3. Birds
4. Early bird
5. Black bird
6. Blue bird
7. Bird cage
8. Little bird
9. Mockingbird
10. Free bird

Appendix G

3. Fish
1. Fish and chips
2. Plenty of fish
3. Fish tank
4. Big fish
5. Fish oil
6. Fish games
7. Fish shop
8. Fishing
9. Fish market
10. Fish recipes

4. Pig, pork or bacon

Pig
1. Peppa Pig [TV show]
2. Peppa
3. Guinea pig
4. Pigs
5. Peppa Pig Youtube
6. Peppa Pig games
7. Pig dog
8. Pig hunting
9. Guinea pigs
10. Teacup pig [breed]

Pork
1. Pork recipe
2. Roast pork
3. Pork belly
4. Recipes
5. Pork recipes
6. Pulled pork
7. Pork ribs
8. Cooking pork
9. Pork belly recipe
10. Pork chops

Bacon
1. Bacon recipe
2. Egg and bacon
3. Kevin Bacon [actor]
4. Chicken bacon
5. Bacon recipes
6. Bacon soup
7. Bacon pasta
8. Egg bacon pie
9. Chicken and bacon
10. Francis Bacon [artist]

5. Horse
1. The horse
2. Horse racing
3. Horse riding
4. Horses
5. Horse deals [website]
6. Horse games
7. Horse for sale
8. Horse results
9. White horse
10. Dark horse

6. Cat or kitten

Cat
1. Cats
2. Cat dog
3. Dog
4. Black cat
5. Funny cat
6. Cat Empire [band]
7. Cat games
8. Cat Stevens [musician]
9. Grumpy Cat [meme]
10. Nyan cat [meme]

Kitten
1. Cat
2. Kittens
3. Kitten Cannon [band]
4. Kitten names
5. Kitten for sale
6. Cute kitten
7. Kitten games
8. Ragdoll kitten
9. Atomic Kitten [band]
10. New kitten

7. Beef, cow or cattle

Beef
1. Beef recipe
2. Recipes
3. Beef recipes
4. Roast beef
5. Slow cooker beef
6. Beef stroganoff
7. Beef salad
8. Corned beef
9. Beef curry
10. Beef stew

Cow
1. Cash cow
2. Sunrise Cash Cow [TV segment]
3. Sunrise [TV show]
4. Mad cow
5. Cow milk
6. Cows
7. Mad cow disease
8. Blue cow
9. Cow girl
10. Cow horse

Cattle
1. Cattle dog
2. Cattle for sale
3. Beef cattle
4. Cattle station
5. Cattle dogs
6. Australian cattle dog
7. Cattle breeds
8. Cattle farm
9. Cattle sales
10. Sheep

8. Lamb or sheep

Lamb
1. Lamb recipe
2. Lamb roast
3. Lamb recipes
4. Recipes
5. Lamb shanks
6. Lamb slow cooker
7. Lamb chops
8. Slow cooked lamb
9. Lamb shank
10. Leg of lamb

Sheep
1. Black sheep
2. Shaun Sheep [TV show]
3. Shaun the Sheep
4. Sheep dog
5. Sheep games
6. Home Sheep Home [game]
7. Sheep for sale
8. Albino Black Sheep [website]
9. Game sheep
10. Dorper sheep [breed]

9. Shark

1. Shark attack
2. The shark
3. Great white shark
4. Shark Bay [place]
5. Sharks
6. Groove Shark [website]
7. Whale shark
8. Sydney shark
9. Shark attacks
10. Shark tank

10. Spider

1. Spider Man [movie]
2. Amazing Spider Man [movie]
3. White spider
4. Spider bite
5. Spider web
6. Spider Man 2 [movie]
7. Spider Solitaire [game]
8. Solitaire
9. Spiders
10. Spiderman

Works cited

AFP and Bloomberg (2015). Google loses search share, Yahoo rises. *Sydney Morning Herald*. 12 January. http://tinyurl.com/hrbzmb9.
Allen M (2013). The temperance shift: drunkenness, responsibility and the regulation of alcohol in NSW, 1788–1856. PhD thesis, University of Sydney. http://hdl.handle.net/2123/9521.
Allen M W, M Wilson, S H Ng and M Dunne (2000). Values and beliefs of vegetarians and omnivores. *Journal of Social Psychology* 140(4): 405–22.
Ammon R J (2001). *Global television and the shaping of world politics: CNN, telediplomacy, and foreign policy*. Jefferson: McFarland & Company.
Animal Health Alliance (2013). *Pet ownership in Australia 2013*. Canberra: Animal Health Alliance.
Animal Health Australia (2010). *Strategic plan: 2010–2015*. Canberra: Animal Health Australia.
Animal Liberation ACT (2012). Parkwood Eggs vigil. http://tinyurl.com/jr548tn.
Animals Australia (2012). Victory! Labor votes animals into office. http://tinyurl.com/hdy67sb.
Ankeny R A (2008). The moral economy of red meat in Australia. In S R Friedland (ed.). *Food and morality: proceedings of the Oxford symposium on food and cookery 2007* (pp20–8). Blackawton, Devon: Prospect Books.
Anti-vivisection Union of Australia (1978). The AV review.
Archer G (2014). Surveillance devices. *Today Tonight Adelaide*. Channel Seven. 9 July.
Arendt H (1953). Understanding and politics. *Partisan Review* 20(4): 377–92.
Arluke A and C Sanders (1996). *Regarding animals: animals, culture, and society*. Philadelphia: Temple University Press.
Armstrong S J and R G Botzler (eds) (2008). *The animal ethics reader*. 2nd edition. London: Routledge.

Asen R (2000). Seeking the 'counter' in counterpublics. *Communication Theory* 10(4): 424–46.

Asimov I (1965). *A short history of biology*. London: Thomas Nelson & Sons.

Aston H (2014a). Number crunching: micro-party candidates place their hopes in Glenn Druery, the preference whisperer. *Sydney Morning Herald*. 15 March. http://tinyurl.com/zeb3pdv.

Aston H (2014b). Game council boss convicted on hunting, gun charges. *Sydney Morning Herald*. 14 February. http://tinyurl.com/gvpvudy.

Atkinson M (2003). The civilizing of resistance: straightedge tattooing. *Deviant Behavior* 24(3): 197–220.

Australia Chicken Meat Federation (2011). *The Australian chicken meat industry: an industry in profile*. Sydney: Australian Chicken Meat Federation Inc.

Australian Associated Press (2014). Western Australia shark cull condemned as futile after attacks fall. *Guardian*. 18 February. http://tinyurl.com/zoekdk6.

Australian Associated Press (2011b). I'll be back: shot duck hunt protester. *Sydney Morning Herald*. 21 March. http://tinyurl.com/4kwtsrw.

Australian Associated Press (2011a). Live exports to Indonesia suspended as Jakarta calls for calm. *Sydney Morning Herald*. 31 May. http://tinyurl.com/3t9lhp6.

Australian Associated Press (2004). Cormo Express disaster haunts industry. *Age* (Melbourne). 29 October. http://tinyurl.com/z2fja8b.

Australian Automobile Association (n.d.). About us. http://www.aaa.asn.au/about-us/.

Australian Broadcasting Corporation (2015a). Bali Nine: Australia makes official complaint to Indonesia over photos of police chief with Andrew Chan and Myuran Sukumaran. *ABC News*. 6 March. http://tinyurl.com/jdmg9pb.

Australian Broadcasting Corporation (2015b). Jumps racing to continue at Morphettville in Adelaide despite SA Jockey Club opposition. *ABC News*. 17 February. http://tinyurl.com/k5kmc52.

Australian Broadcasting Corporation (2014). WA shark cull: thousands rally at Cottesloe Beach as catch-and-kill protests ramp up. *ABC News*. 1 February. http://tinyurl.com/lfljgsk.

Australian Broadcasting Corporation (2013a). Animal rights activists 'akin to terrorists', says NSW Minister Katrina Hodgkinson. *ABC News*. 18 July. http://tinyurl.com/gq5pu94.

Australian Broadcasting Corporation (2013b). Coles ditches Animals Australia bags opposing factory farming conditions. *ABC News*. 6 June. http://tinyurl.com/kc6b6av.

Australian Broadcasting Corporation (2011). Saffin welcomes live export ban as a first. *ABC North Coast NSW*. 8 June. http://tinyurl.com/j5pwmby.

Works cited

Australian Broadcasting Corporation v. Lenah Game Meats Pty Ltd (2001). HCA 63. http://eresources.hcourt.gov.au/showCase/2001/HCA/63.
Australian Bureau of Statistics (2014). *Livestock products, Australia, December 2013*. Canberra: Australian Bureau of Statistics.
Australian Bureau of Statistics (2012). *4102.0 – Australian social trends, Dec 2012*. Canberra: Australian Bureau of Statistics.
Australian Bureau of Statistics (2000). *Apparent consumption of foodstuffs, Australia, 1997–98 and 1998–99*. Canberra: Australian Bureau of Statistics.
Australian Bureau of Statistics (1997). *Interest groups Australia 1995–96*. Canberra: Australian Bureau of Statistics.
Australian Egg Corporation Limited (2014). *Egg industry overview June 2014*. Sydney: Australian Egg Corporation Limited.
Australian Greens (2014). The charter and constitution of the Australian Greens. Australian Greens. http://greens.org.au/charter.
Australian Greens (n.d.). Animals (policy statement). http://greens.org.au/policies/animals.
Australian Institute of Company Directors (2015). Gender diversity on boards. http://tinyurl.com/jkc52eb.
Australian Pork (2012). *Australian pig annual: 2011–2012*. Canberra: Australian Pork Limited.
Australian Professional Rodeo Association (n.d.). Livestock welfare overview. http://www.prorodeo.com.au/Livestock-Welfare-Overview-32/.
Australian Racing Board (2013). *2012/13 Australian racing fact book*. Sydney: Australian Racing Board.
Australian Research Review Panel (2014). The use of restricted drugs and the conduct of restricted acts of veterinary science in animal research. http://tinyurl.com/z2yymu9.
Australian Veterinary Association (1997). Animal welfare societies. http://tinyurl.com/zfvrbcy.
Bachrach P and M Baratz (1970). *Power and poverty*. New York: Oxford University Press.
Backus P and D Clifford (2013). Are big charities becoming more dominant? Cross-sectional and longitudinal perspectives. *Journal of the Royal Statistical Society: Series A (Statistics in Society)* 176(3): 761–76.
Bailey C (2011). Kinds of life: on the phenomenological basis of the distinction between 'higher' and 'lower' animals. *Environmental Philosophy* 8(2): 47–68.
Baines S, J Powers and W J Brown (2007). How does the health and well-being of young Australian vegetarian and semi-vegetarian women compare with non-vegetarians? *Public Health Nutrition* 10(5): 436–44.

Baker S (1993). *Picturing the beast: animals, identity, and representation.* Manchester: Manchester University Press.

Bandura A (1997). *Self-efficacy: the exercise of control.* New York: W H Freeman & Company.

Bang H (2004). Everyday makers and expert citizens: building political not social capital (working paper). https://digitalcollections.anu.edu.au/handle/1885/42117.

Bartlett A (2009). Animal welfare in a federal system: a federal politician's perspective. In P Sankoff and S White (eds). *Animal law in Australasia: a new dialogue* (pp376–88). Leichhardt, NSW: Federation Press.

Basney L (2000). *An earth-careful way of life: Christian stewardship and the environmental crisis.* Vancouver: Regent College Publishing.

Bastian B, S Loughnan, N Haslam and H R M Radke (2012). Don't mind meat? The denial of mind to animals used for human consumption. *Personality and Social Psychology Bulletin* 38(2): 247–56.

Baudrillard J (1994). *Simulacra and simulation.* Ann Arbor: University of Michigan Press.

Beamish T D and A J Luebbers (2009). Alliance building across social movements: bridging difference in a peace and justice coalition. *Social Problems* 56(4): 647–76.

Becker L B and T Vlad (2009). News organizations and routines. In K Whal-Jorgensen and T Hanitzsch (eds). *The Handbook of Journalism Studies* (pp59–72). New York: Routledge.

Beef Central (2011). ALP conference rejects live export ban push. *Beef Central.* 4 December. http://tinyurl.com/zno4c3v.

Beggs D S, A D Fisher, E C Jongman and P H Hemsworth (2015). A survey of Australian dairy farmers to investigate animal welfare risks associated with increasing scale of production. *Journal of Dairy Science* 98(8): 5330–8.

Behrend K (2015). The role sanctuaries play in animal advocacy and digital storytelling. Paper presented to the Animal Activists Forum, Melbourne, 10–11 October.

Beilharz R (1988). Science and the politics of animal use in food production: the situation in Australia. *Applied Animal Behaviour Science* 20: 143–50.

Belot H and M Inman (2015). United Patriots Front leader given circus tickets for ripping animal rights posters. *Sydney Morning Herald.* 23 October. http://tinyurl.com/jh2o3a8.

Bennett S (1999). *New South Wales election 1999.* Canberra: Department of the Parliamentary Library. Research paper no. 22.

Bentham J (1907). *An introduction to the principles of morals and legislation.* 2nd edition. Oxford: Clarendon Press.

Works cited

Berger A A (2011). *Ads, fads, and consumer culture: advertising's impact on American character and society*. 3rd edition. Lanham: Rowman & Littlefield Publishers.

Berman D, L Martin and L Kajifez (1985). County home rule: does where you stand depend on where you sit? *State and Local Government Review* 17(2): 232–34.

Berry J (1997). *The interest group society*. 3rd edition. New York: Longman.

Bettles C (2015). Push for new Saudi live-ex trade. *Land*. 25 June. http://tinyurl.com/hzqzltz.

Bettles C (2014). United we stand, says NFF. *FarmOnline*. 20 October. http://tinyurl.com/hzk54xj.

Bettles C (2013). Activists stripped of government funds in MYEFO. *FarmOnline*. 19 December. http://tinyurl.com/zfrh3ap.

Bezzina C and B Collins (2011). *The job: fighting crime from the frontline*. Docklands, Vic.: Slattery Media Group.

Boom K and E Ellis (2009). Enforcing animal welfare law: the NSW experience. *Australian Animal Protection Law Journal* 3: 6–32.

Booth C and T Low (2009). The conservation hunting con. *Pacific Conservation Biology* 15(4): 235–37.

Borren M (2013). 'A sense of the world': Hannah Arendt's hermeneutic phenomenology of common sense. *International Journal of Philosophical Studies* 21(2): 225–55.

Botterill L (2007). Managing intergovernmental relations in Australia: the case of agricultural policy cooperation. *Australian Journal of Public Administration* 66(2): 186–97.

Botterill L (2006). Soap operas, cenotaphs and sacred cows: countrymindedness and rural policy debate in Australia. *Public policy* 1(1): 23–36.

Botterill L (2005). Policy change and network termination: the role of farm groups in agricultural policy making in Australia. *Australian Journal of Political Science* 40(2): 207–19.

Botterill L (2003). Government responses to drought in Australia. In L Botterill and M Fisher (eds). *Beyond drought: people, policy and perspectives* (pp49-66). Canberra: CSIRO Publishing.

Boucher G and M Sharpe (2008). *The times will suit them: postmodern conservatism in Australia*. Crows Nest, NSW: Allen & Unwin.

Bourdieu P (1979). Public opinion does not exist. In A Mattelart and S Siegelaub (eds). *Communication and class struggle* (pp124–30). New York: International General.

Bourdieu P (1990). *The logic of practice*. Stanford: Stanford University Press.

Bowmar R (2009). Alternative strategic responses to animal welfare advocacy: a case study of merino wool and mulesing. Master of Science thesis, Michigan State University.

Brand Story (2012). Project equilibrium: qualitative research to determine consumer perceptions of free-range stocking densities. Report prepared for the Australian Egg Corporation Ltd. https://www.aecl.org/dmsdocument/463.

Brennan G, L Eriksson, R E Goodin and N Southwood (2013). *Explaining norms*. Oxford: Oxford University Press.

Bril B, E Hombessa-Nkounkou, J Bouville and C Ocampo (2001). From milk to adult diet: a comparative study on the socialization of food. *Food and Foodways* 9(3–4): 155–86.

Brown B (1980). *Animal welfare in agriculture: a special study*. Sydney: Livestock and Grain Producers' Association of NSW.

Browne E (2012). Clowning around: why has the NSW Parliament failed to abolish exotic animal circuses? *Australian Animal Protection Law Journal* 7: 82–106.

Browne W P (1999). Studying interests and policy from the inside. *Policy Studies Journal* 27(1): 67–75.

Bruce A (2012a). *Animal law in Australia: an integrated approach*. Chatswood: LexisNexis.

Bruce A (2012b). Labelling illogic? Food animal welfare and the Australian consumer law (Part 2). *Australian Animal Protection Law Journal* 8: 6–59.

Bruce A (2012c). Labelling illogic? Food animal welfare and the Australian consumer law (Part 1). *Australian Animal Protection Law Journal* 7: 5–47.

Bruno S, N Lutwak and M A Agin (2009). Conceptualizations of guilt and the corresponding relationships to emotional ambivalence, self-disclosure, loneliness and alienation. *Personality and Individual Differences* 47(5): 487–91.

Bruns F (2014). Medical ethics and media research on human beings in National Socialism. In S Rubenfeld and S Benedict (eds). *Human subjects research after the Holocaust* (pp39–50). Geneva: Springer.

Bryman A (2004). *The Disneyization of society*. Thousand Oaks: Sage Publishers.

Budd W B (1988). *Hear the other side: the RSPCA in South Australia 1875–1988*. Horthorndene, SA: Investigator Press.

Bullo S (2014). *Evaluation in advertising reception: a socio-cognitive and linguistic perspective*. Houndmills: Palgrave Macmillan.

Burke P F, C Eckert and S Davis (2014). Segmenting consumers' reasons for and against ethical consumption. *European Journal of Marketing* 48(11/12): 2237–61.

Works cited

Burstein P (1991). Policy domains: organization, culture, and policy outcomes. *Annual Review of Sociology*, 17: 327–50.

Butler D (2005). Security guards hired as RSPCA Chief fears for life. *Herald Sun* (Melbourne), p3. 17 June.

Callicott J B (1994). Conservation values and ethics. In G Meffe and C R Carroll (eds). *Principles of conservation biology* (pp24–49). Sunderland, Mass.: Sinauer Associates.

Cao D (2010). *Animal law in Australia and New Zealand*. Pyrmont, NSW: Lawbook Co.

Capano G (2012). Policy dynamics and change: the never-ending puzzle. In E Araral, S Fritzen, M Howlett and M Ramesh (eds). *Routledge handbook of public policy* (pp451–61). Oxon: Routledge.

Carney J (2015). Horrific images show the shocking state inside Victoria hen farm. *Daily Mail Australia*. 2 April. http://tinyurl.com/nboovdw.

Carter A (2012). *Direct action and liberal democracy*. London: Routledge.

Castles A C, Farrell L (1983). *Compendium of human rights courses in Australian tertiary institutions*. Canberra: Human Rights Commission. Occasional Paper No. 4.

Caulfield M (2009). Live export of animals. In P Sankoff, and S White (eds). *Animal law in Australasia: a new dialogue* (pp153–73). Leichhardt, NSW: Federation Press.

Cawood M (2014). Changes to the Exporter Supply Chain Assurance System. *Stock and Land*, p40. 27 April.

Chapman S (2013). *Over our dead bodies: Port Arthur and Australia's fight for gun control*. Sydney: Sydney University Press.

Chen P J (2015). The virtual party on the ground. In M Miragliotta, A Gauja and R Smith (eds). *Contemporary Australian political party organisations* (pp127–39). Melbourne: Monash University Publishing.

Chen P J (2013). *Australian politics in a digital age*. Canberra: ANU Press.

Cicero M T (1896). *On the nature of the gods*. London: Methuen.

Clark C (2013). Animals Australia under the microscope. *Landline*. ABC Television. 16 June.

Clemons R and K Day (2015). Free-range eggs. CHOICE consumer report. http://tinyurl.com/h5vl36w.

Cobbe F P (1884). *The future of the lower animals*. London: International Association for the Total Suppression of Vivisection.

Cockfield G and L C Botterill (2013). Rural and regional policy: a case of punctuated incrementalism? *Australian Journal of Public Administration* 72(2): 129–42.

Coghlan S (2014). Australia and live animal export: wronging nonhuman animals. *Journal of Animal Ethics* 4(2): 45–60.

Cohen J E (1997). *Presidential responsiveness and public policy-making: the public and the policies that presidents choose.* Ann Arbor: University of Michigan Press.

Coleman G (2007). Public perceptions of animal pain and animal welfare. Presented at the Australian Animal Welfare Strategy Science Summit on Pain and Pain Management. Melbourne. 18 May.

Coleman G, M Hay and S Toukhsati (2005). *Effects of consumer attitudes and behaviour on the egg and port industries.* Report to Australian Pork Ltd and Australian Egg Corporation Ltd.

Compston H (2009). Networks, resources, political strategy and climate policy. *Environmental Politics* 18(5): 727–46.

Considine M (1994). *Public policy: a critical approach.* South Melbourne: Macmillan Education Australia.

Cowling D (2012). Google – 94% of Australian web searches. *Social Media News.* 28 March. http://tinyurl.com/zgryp9j.

Cowling D (2010). Australian search engine market update October 2010. *Social Media News.* 29 October. http://tinyurl.com/2cvhq85.

Cox L (2015). Government bans importation of African lion trophies from hunting. *Sydney Morning Herald.* 13 March. http://tinyurl.com/hq2ltso.

Cox L and J Lee (2015). Abbott government to change environment laws in crackdown on 'vigilante' green groups. *Sydney Morning Herald.* 18 August. http://tinyurl.com/onzeee6.

Cribb A and S Gewirtz (2015). *Professionalism.* Chichester: Wiley.

Croft D (1991). The relationships between people and animals: an Australian perspective. In D Croft (ed.). *Australian people and animals in today's dreamtime: the role of comparative psychology in the management of natural resources, advances in comparative psychology.* New York: Praeger.

Croley S P (2008). *Regulation and public interests: the possibility of good regulatory government.* Princeton, NJ: Princeton University Press.

Crook E (2008). *Vegetarianism in Australia: a history.* Canberra: International Vegetarian Union.

Crossman D (2011). *The animal code: giving animals respect and rights.* North Melbourne: Arcadia.

Crowson R A (1970). *Classification and biology.* London: Heinemann Educational.

Daigneault P M (2014). Puzzling about policy paradigms: precision and progress. *Journal of European Public Policy* 21(3): 481–84.

Dairy Australia (2015). Dairy facts at a glance. http://tinyurl.com/j9mo9lb.

Works cited

Dale A (2009). Animal welfare codes and regulations: the devil in disguise? In P Sankoff and S White (eds). *Animal law in Australasia: a new dialogue* (pp174–211). Leichhardt, NSW: Federation Press.

Dale A and S White (2013). Codifying animal welfare standards: foundations for better animal protection or merely a facade? In P Sankoff, S W White and C Black (eds). *Animal law in Australasia: continuing the dialogue* (pp151–82). Leichhardt, NSW: Federation Press.

Dale E and S Waterhouse (2015). *Women on boards: 2015 charities board room diversity index*. https://www.womenonboards.net/Resources/Boardroom-Diversity-Index.

Darwin C (1871). *The descent of man, and selection in relation to sex.* London: John Murray.

Davidson B R (1981). *European farming in Australia: an economic history of Australian farming.* New York: Elsevier Scientific Publisher.

Davis G (1995). A government of routines: executive coordination in an Australian state. South Melbourne: Macmillan Education Australia.

Davis M (2014). Neoliberalism, the culture wars and public policy. In C Miller and L Orchard (eds). *Australian public policy: progressive ideas in the neo-liberal ascendency* (pp27–44). Bristol: Polity Press.

Dawtrey Z (2012). RSPCA Tasmania facing its demise. *Mercury* (Hobart). 7 November. http://www.themercury.com.au/article/2012/11/07/365464_tasmania-news.html.

de Brito S (2014). Confessions of a vegan. *Sydney Morning Herald*. 3 August. http://tinyurl.com/jc62gry.

della Porta D and M Diani (2006). *Social movements: an introduction.* 2nd edition. Malden: Blackwell Publishing.

Department of Families, Housing, Community Services and Indigenous Affairs (2007). Volunteering in Australia: changing patterns in voluntary work 1995–2006. Canberra: Department of Families, Housing, Community Services and Indigenous Affairs.

Descartes R (2007). From the letters of 1646 to 1649. In F Kalof and A Fitzgerald (eds). *The animals reader: the essential classic and contemporary writings* (pp59–62). Oxford: Berg.

Devine M (2009). Roads are for cars, not Lycra louts. *Sydney Morning Herald*, p17. 20 October.

Diani M (2000). The concept of social movement. In K Nash (ed.). *Readings in contemporary political sociology* (pp155–76). Oxford: Basil Blackwell.

Divine K (2011). *Vegans are cool: a delicious collection of essays, interviews and articles by cool vegans from around the planet.* Fremantle: Vivid Publishing.

Dobbie M (2015). *Going after whistleblowers, going after journalism: a report into the state of press freedom in Australia 2015.* Sydney: Media, Entertainment and Arts Alliance.

Donovan J and R T Coupe (2013). Animal rights extremism: victimization, investigation and detection of a campaign of criminal intimidation. *European Journal of Criminology* 10(1): 113–32.

Downs A (1972). Up and down with ecology: the issue-attention cycle. *Public Interest* 28: 38–50.

Duckworth J (2009). *Not every dog has his day: the treatment of dogs in Australia.* Melbourne: Axiom Creative Enterprises.

Dunayer J (1995). Sexist words speciesist roots. In C J Adams and J Donovan (eds). *Animals and women: feminist theoretical explorations* (pp11–31). Durham: Duke University Press.

Dunleavy P and B O'Leary (1989). *Theories of the state: the politics of liberal democracy.* New York: New Amsterdam.

Dunn S, S Corrigan and R Watkinson (2012). *Governance review of the Game Council of NSW.* Report prepared for the NSW Department of Primary Industries. Sydney: IC Independent Consulting.

Dunwoody S (1999). Scientists, journalists, and the meaning of uncertainty. In S M Friedman, S Dunwoody and C L Rogers (eds). *Communicating uncertainty: media coverage of new and controversial science* (pp59–80). New York: Routledge.

Dwyer L (2011). A late-life epiphany for Michael Kirby. *Sydney Morning Herald.* 17 December. http://tinyurl.com/82kvlca.

Eadie E (2009). *Animal suffering and the law: national, regional and international.* West Lakes: Seaview Press.

Ebdrup N (2012). Weird 'plant-animal' baffles scientists. *ScienceNordic.* 19 January.

Economics References Committee (2015). *Third party certification of food.* Canberra: Australian Senate.

Edwards F and D Mercer (2013). Food waste in Australia: the freegan response. In S Evans, H Campbell and A Murcott (eds). *Waste matters: new perspectives on food and society, the sociological review monographs* (pp174–91). Malden: Wiley-Blackwell.

Elliott C D (2012). Packaging fun: analyzing supermarket food messages targeted at children. *Canadian Journal of Communication* 34: 303–18.

Elliott K (2015). Animal Justice Party and the NSW election – Mark Pearson. *Freedom of species.* 3CR Community Radio (Melbourne). 5 April. http://tinyurl.com/znpzaot.

Ellis E (2013). The animal welfare trade-off or trading-off animal welfare? In P J Sankoff, S W White and C Black (eds). *Animal law in Australasia: continuing the dialogue* (pp344–66). Leichhardt, NSW: Federation Press.

Ellis E (2009). Collaborate advocacy: framing the interests of animals as a social justice concern. In P Sankoff and S White (eds). *Animal law in Australasia: a new dialogue* (pp354–75). Leichhardt, NSW: Federation Press.

Epstein L and H A Segal (2000). Measuring issue salience. *American Journal of Political Science* 44(1): 66–83.

Essential Media Communication (2015). *Essential Report: 24 March 2015.* Melbourne: Essential Research.

Essential Media Communication (2012). *Essential Report: 19 November 2012.* Melbourne: Essential Research.

Fairholme E G and W Pain (1924). *A century of work for animals: the history of the RSPCA, 1824–1924.* London: John Murray.

Fairlie S (2010). *Meat: a benign extravagance.* White River Junction, Vt: Chelsea Green Pub.

FarmOnline (2013). Coles withdraws AA bags. *FarmOnline.* 5 June. http://tinyurl.com/zcmgzzb.

Farrer K T H (2005). *To feed a nation: a history of Australian food science and technology.* Collingwood, Vic: CSIRO Publishing.

Fawcett A (2013). Euthanasia and morally justifiable killing in a veterinary clinical context. In J Johnston and F Probyn-Rapsey (eds). *Animal death* (pp205–19). Sydney: Sydney University Press.

Festinger L (1957). *A theory of cognitive dissonance.* Evanston: Row & Peterson.

Fidler, Richard (2015). Interview with Frank Bingham. *Conversations with Richard Fidler.* ABC Radio National. 16 January. http://tinyurl.com/huof2p2.

Field J (2003). *Social capital, key ideas.* London: Routledge.

Filippi M, G Riccitelli, A Falini, F Di Salle, P Vuilleumier, P Comi and M A Rocca (2010). The brain functional networks associated to human and animal suffering differ among omnivores, vegetarians and vegans. *PLoS ONE* 5(5): e10847.

Finch N, P Murray, J Hoy and G Baxter (2014). Expenditure and motivation of Australian recreational hunters. *Wildlife Research* 41(1): 76.

Fitzgerald K J and D M Rodgers (2000). Radical social movement organizations: a theoretical model. *Sociological Quarterly* 41(4): 573–92.

Flannery T (2012). *Quarterly Essay 48: After the future – Australia's new extinction crisis.* Collingwood, Vic.: Black Inc.

Flemming A (2013). Antifa notes. *Slackbastard* blog. 26 September. http://slackbastard.anarchobase.com/?p=34844.

Flesher Fominaya C (2010). Collective identity in social movements: central concepts and debates. *Sociology Compass* 4(6): 393–404.

Flint J (2015a). RSPCA inquiry: Department of Agriculture and Food WA 'not suited' to animal welfare role. *PerthNow*. 22 September. http://tinyurl.com/h6qzy3c.

Flint J (2015b). Former president of the RSPCA in WA says charity has lost its way. *PerthNow*. 10 May. http://tinyurl.com/hhokm3c.

Flint J (2015c). RSPCA seen as 'anti-farming' by producers, peak groups tell inquiry. *PerthNow*. 2 August. http://tinyurl.com/hyzjyp2.

Flükiger J M (2008). The radical animal liberation movement: some reflections on its future. *Journal for the Study of Radicalism* 2(2): 111–32.

Fox K (2015). *Vegan ventures: start and grow an ethical business*. Sydney: Vegan Business Media.

Fox M A (1986). *The case for animal experimentation: an evolutionary and ethical perspective*. Berkeley: University of California Press.

Fozdar F and B Spittles (2014). Of cows and men: nationalism and Australian cow making. *Australian Journal of Anthropology* 25(1): 73–90.

Francione G L (2008). *Animals as persons: essays on the abolition of animal exploitation*. New York: Columbia University Press.

Francione G L (2000). *Introduction to animal rights: your child or the dog?* Philadelphia: Temple University Press.

Franklin A (2007). Human–nonhuman animal relationships in Australia: an overview of results from the first national survey and follow-up case studies 2000–2004. *Society and Animals* 15: 7–27.

Franklin A (2006). *Animal nation: the true story of animals and Australia*. Sydney: UNSW Press.

Franklin A, B Tranter and R White (2001). Explaining support for animal rights: a comparison of two recent approaches to humans, nonhuman animals, and postmodernity. *Society and Animals* 9: 127–44.

Fraser N (1990). Rethinking the public sphere: a contribution to the critique of actually existing democracy. *Social Text* 25/26: 58–80.

Freedman C (1997). A survey of manufacturing industry policy: from the Tariff Board to the Productivity Commission. *Economic Record* 73(2221): 169–83.

Gamson W (1990). *The strategy of social protest*. 2nd edition. Belmont, Calif.: Wadsworth.

Garner R (1993). *Animals, politics and morality*. Manchester: Manchester University Press.

Gartrell A (2015). Cory Bernardi takes aim at Australian Institute of Sport over dining hall halal. *Sydney Morning Herald*. 1 August. http://tinyurl.com/hcm2dd4.

Works cited

Gauja A (2012). Participation and representation through political parties. In R Smith, A Vromen and I Cook (eds). *Contemporary politics in Australia: theories, practices and issues* (pp166-76). Port Melbourne: Cambridge University Press.

Gerbner G and L Gross (1976). Living with television: the violence profile. *Journal of Communication* 26(2): 172-99.

Giddens A (1986). *The constitution of society: outline of the theory of structuration*. Berkeley: University of California Press.

Giugni M (2004). *Social protest and policy change: ecology, antinuclear, and peace movements in comparative perspective*. Lanham: Rowman & Littlefield.

Glasgow D (2008). The law of the jungle: advocating for animals in Australia. *Deakin Law Review* 13(1): 181-210.

Gleeson K (2014). *Australia's 'war on terror' discourse*. Farnham, Surrey: Ashgate.

Godden D (2006). *Agricultural and resource policy: principles and practice*. Sydney: Sydney University Press.

Godlovitch S, R Godlovitch and J Harris (eds) (1971). *Animals, men and morals: an inquiry into the maltreatment of non-humans*. London: Victor Gollancz Ltd.

Goldner M (2001). Expanding political opportunities and changing collective identities in the complementary and alternative medicine movement. In P G Coy (ed.). *Political opportunities, social movements and democratization, research in social movements, conflicts and change* (pp69-102). Amsterdam: JAI.

Goodfellow J (2013). Animal welfare law enforcement: to punish or persuade? In P J Sankoff, S W White and C Black (eds). *Animal law in Australasia: continuing the dialogue* (pp183-207). Leichhardt, NSW: Federation Press.

Goodfellow J (2012). Captured by design: the story of farm animal welfare regulation in Australia. Presentation to the Future of Animal Law conference, Macquarie University, 18 October. http://tinyurl.com/groau53.

Goodsir D (2015). Mankind diminished by barbarism in the cause of political expediency. *Sydney Morning Herald*. 29 April. http://tinyurl.com/zl8wqse.

Gotsis T and L Roth (2015). Farm trespass, surveillance and the Biosecurity Bill 2015. Ebrief no. 08/2015. Sydney: NSW Parliamentary Research Service.

Graham V (1983). Farmers to battle the animal liberationists. *Land*. 6 October.

Grant W (2001). Pressure politics: from 'insider' politics to direct action? *Parliamentary Affairs* 54(2): 337-48

Greenebaum J (2012). Managing impressions: 'face-saving' strategies of vegetarians and vegans. *Comparative Biochemistry and Physiology* 36(4): 309-25.

Greyhounds Australasia (n.d.). Australasian stats. http://www.galtd.org.au/industry/australasian-statistics.

Gross K (2008). Framing persuasive appeals: episodic and thematic framing, emotional response, and policy opinion. *Political Psychology* 29(2): 169-92.

Guither H D (1998). *Animal rights: history and scope of a radical social movement.* Carbondale, Ill.: Southern Illinois University Press.

Gulbin M (2015). Unholy alliance: meatworkers join fight against live export. *Northern Star* (Lismore). 4 June. http://tinyurl.com/jcmyhrh.

Guppy D (2015). Live baiting greyhounds: the woman who revealed the scandal. *Courier-Mail* (Brisbane). 15 June. http://tinyurl.com/z2mqopu.

Guthrie S and F Akindoyeni (2014). *The Newgate review of the future of Australian farm sector representation.* Sydney: Newgate Communications.

Habermas J (1989). *The structural transformation of the public sphere: an inquiry into a category of bourgeois society.* Cambridge, Mass.: MIT Press.

Haenfler R (2004). Collective identity in the straight edge movement: how diffuse movements foster commitment, encourage individualized participation, and promote cultural change. *Sociological Quarterly* 45(4): 785-805.

Hall P A (1993). Policy paradigms, social learning, and the state: the case of economic policymaking in Britain. *Comparative Politics* 25(3): 275-96.

Halpin D (ed.) (2005a). *Surviving global change? Agricultural interest groups in comparative perspective.* Hampshire: Ashgate, Aldershot.

Halpin D (2005b). 'Digging deep to keep their clout': agricultural interest groups in Australia. In D Halpin (ed.). *Surviving global change? Agricultural interest groups in comparative perspective* (pp141-63). London: Ashgate.

Halpin D (2004). Transitions between formations and organisations: a historical perspective on the political representation of Australian farmers. *Australian Journal of Politics and History* 50(4): 469-90.

Hamilton C and S Maddison (2007). *Silencing dissent how the Australian government is controlling public opinion and stifling debate.* Crows Nest, NSW: Allen & Unwin.

Hampson I (1997). The end of the experiment: corporatism collapses in Australia. *Economic and Industrial Democracy* 18(4): 539-66.

Harrison R (1964). *Animal machines: the new factory farming industry.* London: Vincent Stewart.

Harrison R, T Newholm and D Shaw (eds) (2005). *The ethical consumer.* London: Sage.

Harwood D (1928). *Love for animals and how it developed in Great Britain.* New York: Columbia University.

Hastreiter M (2013). Animal welfare standards and Australia's live exports industry to Indonesia: creating an opportunity out of a crisis. *Washington University Global Studies Law Review* 12(1): 181–203.

Hatch P H, H R Winefield, B A Christie and J Lievaart (2011). Workplace stress, mental health, and burnout of veterinarians in Australia. *Australian Veterinary Journal* 89(11): 460–68.

Haug C (2013). Organizing spaces: meeting arenas as a social movement infrastructure between organization, network, and institution. *Organization Studies* 34(5–6): 705–32.

Hayek A (2004). Epidemiology of horses leaving the racing and breeding industries. Bachelor of Science (Veterinary science) thesis, University of Sydney. http://kb.rspca.org.au/afile/235/37/.

Haynes, R P (2008). *Animal welfare: competing conceptions and their ethical implications*. New York: Springer.

Hayward S (2011). *Mere environmentalism: a biblical perspective on humans and the natural world*. Washington: American Enterprise Institute for Public Policy Research.

Headey B (2006). Socially responsible pet ownership in Australia: a decade of progress. Melbourne: Melbourne Institute of Applied Economic and Social Research, University of Melbourne.

Heath T J (2002). Longitudinal study of veterinarians from entry to the veterinary course to ten years after graduation: career paths. *Australian Veterinary Journal* 80(8): 468–73.

Heckscher C and J McCarthy J (2014). Transient solidarities: commitment and collective action in post industrial societies: transient solidarities. *British Journal of Industrial Relations* 52(4): 627–57.

Hefford R (1985). *Farm policy in Australia*. St Lucia: University of Queensland Press.

Hemsworth P H and Coleman G (2001). Animal welfare in the dairy industry and public perception. *Australian Journal of Dairy Technology* 56(2): 130.

Henry A D, M Lubell and M McCoy (2011). Belief systems and social capital as drivers of policy network structure: the case of California regional planning. *Journal of Public Administration Research and Theory* 21(3): 419–44.

Henzell T (2007). *Australian agriculture: its history and challenges*. Collingwood, Vic.: CSIRO Publishing.

Herman E S and N Chomsky (2002). *Manufacturing consent: the political economy of the mass media*. New York: Pantheon Books.

Herzog H A, N S Betchart and R Pittman (1991). Gender, sex-role identity and attitudes toward animals. *Anthrozoos* 4: 184–91.

Hodgkinson K (2014). Media release: new measures to protect farmers. NSW Department of Primary Industries. 9 October. http://tinyurl.com/zg7dfa4.

Holland P (2011). *The animal kingdom: a very short introduction*. Oxford: Oxford University Press.

Holyoke T T, H Brown and J R Henig (2012). Shopping in the political arena: strategic state and local venue selection by advocates. *State and Local Government Review* 44(1): 9–20.

Hudson H (1914). *The red road: a story by a roan bullock on the wrongs suffered by animals at the hand of man*. Sydney: Animals' Protection Society.

Humane Research Australia (2014). Statistics of animal use in Australian research and teaching. http://www.humaneresearch.org.au/statistics/.

Humane Research Council (2014). *Animal tracker Australia: baseline survey results*. Olympia, Wash.: Humane Research Council.

Hunton P (1997). Australia's egg industry eight years after de-regulation. *World Poultry* 13(6): 14–5.

Hursthouse R (2006). Applying virtue ethics to our treatment of the other animals. In J Welchman (ed.). *The practice of virtue: classic and contemporary readings in virtue ethics* (pp136–55). Indianapolis: Hackett Pub.

Hutchings V L (2003). *Public opinion and democratic accountability: how citizens learn about politics*. Princeton: Princeton University Press.

Institute for Critical Animal Studies (2015). About. http://www.criticalanimalstudies.org/about/.

Instone L (2011). Regulating rover: legislating the public place of urban dogs. *Australian Animal Protection Law Journal* 6: 75–90.

Iyengar S (1991). *Is anyone responsible? How television frames political issues*. Chicago: University of Chicago Press.

Jabour J and M Iliff (2009). Theatre sports in the southern ocean: engagement options for Australia in whale research protest action. *Australian Journal of International Affairs* 63(2): 268–89.

Jackson L M, L M Bitacola, L M Janes and V M Esses (2013). Intergroup ideology and environmental inequality: intergroup ideology. *Analyses of Social Issues and Public Policy* 13(1): 327–46.

Jackson S (2011). The Australian Greens: between movement and electoral professional party. PhD thesis, University of Sydney. http://hdl.handle.net/2123/7858.

Jackson S (2016). *The Australian Greens: from activism to Australia's third party*. Melbourne: Melbourne University Press.

Jackson S and P J Chen (2015). Rapid mobilisation of demonstrators in March Australia. *Interface: A Journal for and about Social Movements* 7(1): 98–116.

Janda S and P Trocchia (2001). Vegetarianism: toward a greater understanding. *Psychology and Marketing* 18(12): 1205–40.

Jasper J (1997). *The art of moral protest*. Chicago: Chicago University Press.

Johnston J and S Baumann (2010). *Foodies: democracy and distinction in the gourmet foodscape*. New York: Routledge.

Joint Select Committee on Companion Animal Breeding Practices in New South Wales (2015). *Inquiry into companion animal breeding practices in New South Wales*. Sydney: Parliament of New South Wales.

Jopson D (2012). The end of the sheep's back. *Globe and Mail* (Sydney). 20 December. http://tinyurl.com/zl2x433.

Jordan G and W A Maloney (1997). Accounting for sub governments: explaining the persistence of policy communities. *Administration and Society* 29(5): 557–83.

Joy M (2010). *Why we love dogs, eat pigs, and wear cows: an introduction to carnism, the belief system that enables us to eat some animals and not others*. San Francisco: Conari Press.

Judd S M, J D Newton, F J Newton and M T Ewing (2014). When nutritional guidelines and life collide: family fruit and vegetable socialisation practices in low socioeconomic communities. *Journal of Marketing Management* 30(15–16): 1625–53.

Jupp J (2007). *From White Australia to Woomera: the story of Australian immigration*. 2nd edition. Cambridge: Cambridge University Press.

Kalof L (2007). *Looking at animals in human history*. London: Reaktion Books.

Kant I (1963). *Lectures on ethics*. New York: Harper Torchbooks.

Kazarov E (2008). The role of zoos in creating a conservation ethic in visitors. Study abroad thesis, Washington University in St Louis.

Keane J (2009). *The life and death of democracy*. New York: W W Norton & Co.

Kemmerer L (2012). *Animals and world religions*. New York: Oxford University Press.

Kendall H, L Lobao and J Sharp (2006). Public concern with animal wellbeing: place, social structural location, and individual experience. *Rural Sociology* 71(3): 499–28.

Kingdon J W (1995). *Agendas, alternatives, and public policies*. New York: Longman.

Knaus C (2013). Feathers fly over egg raid. *Canberra Times*. 14 March. http://tinyurl.com/hakhxc7.

Knight A (2013). *The costs and benefits of animal experiments*. Houndmills: Palgrave Macmillan.

Knoke D (2011). Policy networks. In J Scott and P J Carrington (eds). *The SAGE Handbook of Social Network Analysis* (pp210–22). London: SAGE.

Kurland N B and S J McCaffrey (2016). Social movement organization leaders and the creation of markets for 'local' goods. *Business and Society* 55(7): 1017–58.

La Barbera C (2012). *States of nature: animality and the polis.* New York: Peter Lang.

Lally P, N Bartle and J Wardle (2011). Social norms and diet in adolescents. *Appetite* 57(3): 623–27.

Langley S and A Hogan (2015). Research survey reveals more Australian grocery shopping habits. *Australian Food News.* 18 May. http://tinyurl.com/gvcejbc.

Larson J A (2013). Social movements and tactical choice. *Sociology Compass* 7(10): 866–79.

Law J (2014). Advertising Standards Bureau reveals 10 most complained-about commercials for 2014. *News.com.au.* 1 July. http://tinyurl.com/h56d8p9.

Lea E and A Worsley (2003). Benefits and barriers to the consumption of a vegetarian diet in Australia. *Public Health Nutrition* 6(5): 505–11.

Leach D K (2005). The iron law of what again? Conceptualizing oligarchy across organizational forms. *Sociological Theory* 23(3): 312–37.

Leahy M P T (1994). *Against liberation: putting animals in perspective.* London: Routledge.

Leifeld P and V Schneider (2012). Information exchange in policy networks. *American Journal of Political Science* 56(3): 731–44.

Leynse W L H (2008). *Lunchtime in Loireville: learning to become a culturally competent member of French society through food.* New York: New York University.

Lipsky M (2010). *Street-level bureaucracy: dilemmas of the individual in public services.* 30th anniversary expanded edition. New York: Russell Sage Foundation.

Little J (2014). Tracks to advocacy: journalism studies, animal rights and Australian media law. *Asia Pacific Media Educator* 24(2): 257–68.

Lloyd S and A G Woodside (2013). Animals, archetypes, and advertising: the theory and the practice of customer brand symbolism. *Journal of Marketing Management* 29(1–2): 5–25.

Locke S (2015). Wool brokers seek wool from non-mulesed sheep for a premium in European and US markets. ABC Rural. 7 October. http://tinyurl.com/gme42h8.

Loomis B and A J Cigler (2015). The changing nature of interest groups politics. In A J Cigler, T Nownes and B Loomis (eds). *Interest group politics.* Washington: CQ Press.

Louw P E (2010). *The media and political process.* 2nd edition. Los Angeles: SAGE.

Luke B (2007). *Brutal: manhood and the exploitation of animals.* Urbana: University of Illinois Press.

Works cited

Lundby K (ed) (2009). *Mediatization: concept, changes, consequences.* New York: Peter Lang.

Lupton D (1996). *Food, the body, and the self.* London: Sage Publications.

Lyle J and G Henry (2002). Survey of recreational fishing in New South Wales. Sydney: Department of Primary Industry NSW.

MacDonald M (2012). Social media: is it a golden opportunity or a steamroller? *The Australian Holstein Journal*, June–July: 59–61.

Mackinger C (2009). AETA, paragraph 278 and conspiracy to . . . conspiracy laws and the repression of animal liberation activism. *Interface: A Journal For and About Social Movements* 1(2): 244–9.

Maguire A (2015). Barbaric and futile: world must do away with state-sponsored killing. *Conversation.* 9 August. http://tinyurl.com/hqln4ss.

Maher J (2012). It's called fruit juice so it's good for me right? An exploratory study of children's fruit content inferences made from food brand names and packaging. *Journal of Applied Business Research* 28(3): 501–13.

Mahoney C (2008). *Brussels versus the beltway: advocacy in the United States and the European Union, American governance and public policy.* Washington: Georgetown University Press.

Maisel L S and M D Brewer (2012). *Parties and elections in America: the electoral process.* 6th edition. Lanham: Rowman & Littlefield Publishers.

Malamud R (2013). Service animals: serve us animals: serve us, animals. *Social Alternatives* 32(4): 34–40.

Maloney WA, G Jordan G and A M McLaughlin (1994). Interest groups and public policy: the insider/outsider model revisited. *Journal of Public Policy* 14(1): 17–38.

Mann C (2015). What to say when you don't know everything. *Freedom of species.* 3CR Community Radio (Melbourne). 25 October. http://tinyurl.com/jofrzby.

Mann S, J Nolan and B Wellman (2003). Sousveillance: inventing and using wearable computing devices for data collection in surveillance environments. *Surveillance and Society* 1(3) 331–55.

Marangos J (2009). An institutional and economic complexity approach to the development of agricultural interest groups in Australia. *Journal of Economic Issues* 43(1): 43–68.

Mark P (2001). To free a hen. *The Animals' Agenda* 21(4): 25–6.

Markham A (2009). Animal cruelty sentencing in Australia and New Zealand. In P Sankoff and S White (eds). *Animal law in Australasia: a new dialogue* (pp289–306). Leichhardt, NSW: Federation Press.

Marohasy J (2005). Campaigning against our cultural heritage. *IPA Review*, March: 16–17.

Marsh S and D Pannell (2000). Agricultural extension policy in Australia: the good, the bad and the misguided. *Australian Journal of Agricultural and Resource Economics* 44(4): 605–27.

Marshall A M (2010). Environmental justice and grassroots legal action. *Environmental Justice* 3(4): 147–51.

Marston H (2014). *Leo escapes from the lab: based on a true story*. Melbourne: Humane Research Australia.

Martin P and H Ritchie (1999). Logics of participation: rural environmental governance under neo-liberalism in Australia. *Environmental Politics* 8(2): 117–35.

Martin W (1989). *Australian agricultural policy, 1983–1988*. Canberra: Centre for Economic Policy Research, Australian National University.

McAllister I (2011). *The Australian voter: 50 years of change*. Sydney: UNSW Press.

McDonald T (2012). Greyhound racing euthanasia rates slammed. *ABC News*. 10 November. http://tinyurl.com/jyaxecr.

McEwan A and K Skandakumar (2011). The welfare of greyhounds in Australian racing: has the industry run its course? *Australian Animal Protection Law Journal* 6: 53–74.

McGregor-Lowndes M and E Pelling (2013). *An examination of tax deductible donations made by individual Australian taxpayers in 2010–11*. Working paper ACPNS 60. Brisbane: Australian Centre for Philanthropy and Nonprofit Studies, Queensland University of Technology

McInerney J (2004). *Animal welfare, economics and policy*. London: Department for Environment, Food and Rural Affairs.

McKee J (2013). No hunting in national parks: the campaign one year on. *Nature New South Wales* 57(2): 24.

McKillop C (2014a). Coles' new grass-fed beef brand accused of undermining cattle accreditation system. *ABC Rural*. 21 October. http://tinyurl.com/hzgxqzk.

McKillop C (2014b). Woolworths beef deal brings grass-fed premiums. *ABC Rural*. 1 April. http://tinyurl.com/zvted73.

McLeod A (2008). Quality control: the origins of the Australian Consumers' Association. *Business History* 50(1): 79–98.

McManus P, D Montoya and G Albrecht (2012). Jumping to conclusions? Media coverage of jumps racing debates in Australia. *Society and Animals* 20(3): 273–93.

McNair B (2015). Judicial murder is meat and drink for the media. *Conversation*. 3 May. http://tinyurl.com/hszqodl.

McNiven I and D Bell (2010). Fishers and farmers: historicising the Gunditjmara freshwater fishery, western Victoria. *La Trobe Journal* 85: 83–91.

Works cited

Meat and Livestock Australia (2013a). *Fast facts 2013: Australia's beef industry*. Sydney: Meat and Livestock Australia Limited.

Meat and Livestock Australia (2013b). *Fast facts 2013: Australia's sheepmeat industry*. Sydney: Meat and Livestock Australia Limited.

Meldrum-Hanna C and S Clark (2015). Greyhound live baiting: internal documents reveal cover-ups, tip-offs and mismanagement inside NSW racing regulator. *ABC News*. 31 August. http://tinyurl.com/jh5ps8d.

Meng J (2009). *Origins of attitudes towards animals*. Brisbane: Ultravisum.

Miller P (2007). Swarm theory: the genius of swarms. *National Geographic*, July. http://tinyurl.com/6dspg2.

Milligan T (2013). *Civil disobedience protest, justification and the law*. New York: Bloomsbury.

Milner A, H Niven, K Page and A LaMontagne (2015). Suicide in veterinarians and veterinary nurses in Australia: 2001–2012. *Australian Veterinary Journal* 93(9): 308–10.

Mintrom M and S Vergari (1996). Advocacy coalitions, policy entrepreneurs, and policy change. *Policy Studies Journal* 24(3): 420–34.

Miragliotta N (2006). One party, two traditions: radicalism and pragmatism in the Australian Greens. *Australian Journal of Political Science* 41(4): 585–96.

Moore S A and S F Rockloff (2006). Organizing regionally for natural resource management in Australia: reflections on agency and government. *Journal of Environmental Policy and Planning* 8(3): 259–77.

Morell V (2014). Court slams Japan's scientific whaling. *Science* 344(61–79): 12.

Moskowitz H R, M Reisner, J B Lowlor and R Deliza (2009). Packaging research in food product design and development. Ames: Wiley-Blackwell.

Munro L (2012). The animal rights movement in theory and practice: a review of the sociological literature. *Sociology Compass* 6(2): 166–81.

Munro L (2005a). *Confronting cruelty: moral orthodoxy and the challenge of the animal rights movement*. Leiden: Brill.

Munro L (2005b). Strategies, action repertoires and DIY activism in the animal rights movement. *Social Movement Studies* 4(1): 75–94.

Munro L (2001a). *Compassionate beasts: the quest for animal rights*. Westport, Conn.: Praeger.

Munro L (2001b). Caring about blood, flesh, and pain: women's standing in the animal protection movement. *Society and Animals* 9(1): 43–61.

Munro P (2008). Animal cruelty linked to economy. *Sydney Morning Herald*. 12 October. http://tinyurl.com/jrhhtbr.

Munson Z W (2008). *The making of pro-life activists: how social movement mobilization works*. Chicago: University of Chicago Press.

Murrie G (2013). 'Death-in-life': curare, restrictionism and abolitionism in Victorian and Edwardian anti-vivisectionist thought. In J Johnston and F Probyn-Rapsey (eds). *Animal death* (pp253–76). Sydney: Sydney University Press.

Nason J (2015). *Four Corners* exposés of animal cruelty lack context. *Beef Central*. 13 March.

Neale R J, C H Tilston, K Gregson and I Stagg (1993). Women vegetarians: lifestyle considerations and attitudes to vegetarianism. *Nutrition and Food Science* 93(1): 24–7.

Neales S (2014). Cattle class suit against live export ban could top $1bn. *Australian*. p6. 29 October. http://tinyurl.com/neales2014.

Neumann G (2005). *Review of the Australian Model Codes of Practice for the welfare of animals, final report*. Adelaide: Geoff Neumann & Associates Pty Ltd.

New South Wales Department of Primary Industries (2008). *Biosecurity strategy: what is biosecurity?* Sydney: NSW Department of Primary Industries.

Newmyer S T (2011). *Animals in Greek and Roman thought: a sourcebook*. Oxon: Routledge.

Nielsen (2011). What hour puts the prime in primetime for Asia-Pacific viewers. *Nielsen Newswire*. 11 September. http://tinyurl.com/zypfmoa.

Noelle-Neumann E (1984). *The spiral of silence: public opinion, our social skin*. Chicago: University of Chicago Press.

Nordenskiold E (1946). *The history of biology: a survey*. New York: Alfred A Knopf.

Noszlopy L, K Sen, I N D Putra and G MacRae (2006). The Schapelle Corby show: drugs, media and society. *Australian Journal of Anthropology* 17(1): 70–85.

O'Brien N (2014). Destruction of greyhounds distresses vet students. *Sun-Herald* (Sydney). 2 February.

O'Sullivan S (2015a). Protecting animals 4: Di Evans from RSPCA South Australia. *Knowing Animals* podcast. 29 October. http://knowinganimals.libsyn.com/.

O'Sullivan S (2015b). Protecting animals 3: Christine Townend from Animal Liberation and help in suffering. *Knowing Animals* podcast. 2 October. http://knowinganimals.libsyn.com/.

O'Sullivan S (2015c). Protecting animals 5: Shatha Hamade from Animals Australia. *Knowing Animals* podcast. 14 November. http://knowinganimals.libsyn.com/.

O'Sullivan S (2015d). Protecting animals 1: Emmanuel Giuffre from Voiceless. *Knowing Animals* podcast. 12 September. http://knowinganimals.libsyn.com/.

O'Sullivan S (2015e). Protecting animals 2: Senator Lee Rhiannon from the Australian Greens. *Knowing Animals* podcast. 29 September.

Works cited

O'Sullivan S (2011). *Animals, equality and democracy*. Houndmills: Palgrave Macmillan.

Oogjes G (2005). *22 Years: Australia's animal welfare laws, industry/government alliances, attitudes and government processes*. Melbourne: Animals Australia.

Orrell-Valente J K, LG Hill, W A Brechwald, K A Dodge, G S Pettit and J E Bates (2007). 'Just three more bites': an observational analysis of parents' socialization of children's eating at mealtime. *Appetite* 48(1): 37–45.

Pachirat T (2013). *Every twelve seconds: industrialized slaughter and the politics of sight*. New Haven: Yale University Press.

Parbery P and R Wilkinson (2013). Victorians' attitudes to farming. Melbourne: Department of Primary Industry.

Pariser E (2011). *The filter bubble: what the internet is hiding from you*. New York: Penguin Press.

Park M (2006). Opening cages, opening eyes: an investigation and open rescue at an egg factory farm. In P Singer (ed). *In defence of animals: the second wave* (pp174–80). Malden: Blackwell Publishers.

Parks R and B Evans (2014). Dietary identities in higher education. *College and University* 89(3): 12–23.

Paxton G K (1994). Should feminists be vegetarians? *Signs* 19(2): 405–34.

Pearson M and Lennon J (2010). *Pastoral Australia fortunes, failures and hard yakka: a historical overview 1788–1967*. Collingwood: CSIRO Publishing, Department of the Environment, Water, Heritage and the Arts and the Australian Heritage Council.

Peel L (1973). *The pastoral industries of Australia*. Sydney: Sydney University Press.

Pellegrin P (1986). *Aristotle's classification of animals: biology and the conceptual unity of the Aristotelian corpus*. Berkley: University of California Press.

Pendergrast N (2015). Live animal export, humane slaughter and media hegemony. *Animal Studies Journal* 4(1): 99–125.

Perry D and G Perry (2008). Improving interactions between animal rights groups and conservation biologists. *Conservation Biology* 22(1): 27–35.

Pertzel B (2006). *For all creatures: a history of RSPCA Victoria*. Burwood East, Vic.: RSPCA Victoria.

Philips C and A Philips (2011). Attitudes of Australian sheep farmers to animal welfare. *Journal of International Farm Management* 5: 1–26.

Phillips C and A Phillips (2012). *Animal welfare in Australia: a tour of cattle and sheep properties*. Brisbane: Clive & Alison Phillips Publishing.

Pierson P (2000). Increasing returns, path dependence, and the study of politics. *American Political Science Review* 94(2): 251–67.

Pieters R, M Wedel and R Batra (2010). The stopping power of advertising: measures and effects of visual complexity. *Journal of Marketing* 74(5): 48–60.

Pollan M (2006). *The omnivore's dilemma: a natural history of four meals.* New York: Penguin Books.

Polletta F and J M Jasper (2001). Collective identity and social movements. *Annual Review of Sociology* 27(1): 283–305.

Poppi DP (2014). Live cattle export industry. In D J Cottle and L Kahn (eds). *Beef cattle: production and trade* (pp235–49). Collingwood, Vic.: CSIRO Publishing.

Posłuszna E (2015). *Environmental and animal rights extremism, terrorism, and national security.* Burlington, Mass.: Elsevier Science.

Potard G and M Keogh (2014). *Opportunities to improve the effectiveness of Australian farmers' advocacy groups: a comparative approach.* Sydney: Australian Farm Institute.

Potter W (2011). *Green is the new red: an insider's account of a social movement under siege.* San Francisco: City Lights Books.

Pratto F, J Sidanius, L M Stallworth and B F Malle (1994). Social dominance orientation: a personality variable predicting social and political attitudes. *Journal of Personality and Social Psychology* 67(4): 741–63.

Price R (2014). Rural research and regional innovation: are past and present research funding policies building future resilience in the bush? In A Hogan and M Young (eds). *Rural and Regional Futures* (pp226–46). London: Routledge.

PricewaterhouseCoopers (2013). *Review of the animal welfare standards and guidelines development process.* Canberra: Department of Agriculture, Fisheries and Forestry.

Primary Industries Ministerial Council (2006). *Model code of practice for the welfare of animals: the sheep.* 2nd edition. Canberra: CSIRO Publishing.

Probyn-Rapsey F (2015). Dingo maybe. *Animal Studies Journal* 4(2).

Probyn-Rapsey F (2013). Nothing to see – something to see: white animals and exceptional life/death. In J Johnston and F Probyn-Rapsey (eds). *Animal death* (pp239–52). Sydney: Sydney University Press.

Prothero D R (2007). *Evolution: what the fossils say and why it matters.* New York: Columbia University Press.

Queensland Dairyfarmers' Organisation (2009). *Queensland Dairyfarmers' Organisation industry survey results 2009.* Brisbane: Queensland Dairyfarmers' Organisation.

Raggatt M (2015). Parkwood farm accepts final payment for barn egg conversion. *Canberra Times.* 23 May. http://tinyurl.com/raggatt2015.

Raggatt M, N Towell and T McIlroy (2013). Canberra RSPCA chief executive Michael Linke resigns. *Canberra Times* (Canberra). 14 October. http://tinyurl.com/raggatt2013.

Works cited

Rahbek Pedersen E (2009). The many and the few: rounding up the SMEs that manage CSR in the supply chain. *Supply Chain Management: An International Journal*, 14(2): 109–16.

Regan T (2004). *The case for animal rights, updated with a new preface*. Berkeley: University of California Press.

Rhodes R A W (2007). Understanding governance: ten years on. *Organization Studies* 28(8): 1243–64.

Rhodes R A W (1996). The new governance: governing without government. *Political Studies* 44(4): 652–67.

Rinfret S R and Pautz M C (2014). *US environmental policy in action: practice and implementation*. New York: Palgrave Macmillan.

Ritter E, K Lutz and M Levine (2008). When humans and sharks meet. In FM Olsson (ed.). *New developments in the psychology of motivation* (pp45–52). New York: Nova Biomedical Books.

Rivis A and P Sheeran (2003). Descriptive norms as an additional predictor in the theory of planned behaviour: a meta-analysis. *Current Psychology* 22(3): 218–33.

Robinson K (2003). One vote, one value: the WA experience. In G Orr, B Mercurio and G Williams (eds). *Realising democracy: electoral law in Australia* (pp100–13). Leichhardt, NSW: Federation Press.

Rose D B (2011). *Wild dog dreaming: love and extinction*. Charlottesville: University of Virginia Press.

Rose D B (1996). *Nourishing terrains: Australian Aboriginal views of landscape and wilderness*. Canberra: Australian Heritage Commission.

Rose J D, R Arlinghaus, S J Cooke, B K Diggles, W Sawynok, E D Steven and C D L Wynne (2014). Can fish really feel pain? *Fish and Fisheries* 15(1): 97–133.

Rosemary B (2012). National RSPCA urged to resolve conflict. *Examiner* (Launceston). 14 November. http://tinyurl.com/j2jbb8d.

Roslyn W (2013). Live export jumps onto the election agenda. *SBS News*. 19 August. http://tinyurl.com/zdka7tz.

Roth L (2014). *Public opinion on sentencing: recent research in Australia* (ebrief no. 08/2014). Sydney: NSW Parliamentary Research Service.

Rout M and D Crowe (2012). I understand your distress, PM tells backbenchers. *Australian*. 8 November. http://tinyurl.com/rout2012.

Roy Morgan Research (2015). Is Australia getting gayer – and how gay will we get? http://tinyurl.com/zr25mgp.

Roy Morgan Research (2014a). Australian women 14+ who have ever used cosmetics. http://tinyurl.com/jptjbjp.

Roy Morgan Research (2014b). Market share narrows between Coles and Woolworths, while ALDI makes important gains. http://tinyurl.com/ow92t33.

Roy Morgan Research (2013). Meat-free, health-conscious and a little bit anxious: Australia's vegetarians. http://tinyurl.com/hhe6u5q.

Rozin P (1996). Sociocultural influences on human food. In E D Capaldi (ed.). *Why we eat what we eat: the psychology of eating* (pp233–63). Washington, DC: American Psychological Association.

RSPCA Australia (2015). RSPCA Australia national statistics 2014–2015. Canberra: RSPCA Australia.

Rubin H J and I Rubin (2008). *Community organizing and development.* 4th edition. Boston: Pearson/Allyn & Bacon.

Ruby M B (2012). Vegetarianism: a blossoming field of study. *Appetite* 58(1): 141–50.

Ruse K, A Davison and K Bridle (2015). Jump horse safety: reconciling public debate and Australian thoroughbred jump racing data, 2012–2014. *Animals* 5(4): 1072–91.

Sabatier P (1997). Top-down and bottom-up approaches to implementation research. In M J Hill (ed). *The policy process: a reader* (pp266–96). Harlow: Prentice Hall/Harvester Wheatsheaf.

Sacre H (2013). Roam free. *60 Minutes.* Nine Network Australia. 31 March.

Sandøe P and S B Christiansen (2008). *Ethics of animal use.* Oxford: Blackwell.

Sankoff P, S White and C Black (eds) (2013). *Animal law in Australasia: continuing the dialogue.* Leichhardt, NSW: Federation Press.

Santich B (1995). *What the doctors ordered: 150 years of dietary advice in Australia.* Victoria: Hyland House.

Sartor F (2011). *Fog on the hill: how NSW Labor lost its way.* Melbourne: Melbourne University Press.

Schudson M (1998). *The good citizen: a history of American civic life.* New York: Free Press.

Scott L R and P D Carter (1996). The role of veterinarians on animal experimentation ethics committees. *Australian Veterinary Journal* 74(4): 309–11.

Sefton and associates (2013). *Blueprint for Australian agriculture 2013–2020.* Canberra: National Farmers' Federation.

Shapiro M (2010). Sea Shepherd's Paul Watson: 'You don't watch whales die and hold signs and do nothing'. *Guardian.* 21 September. http://tinyurl.com/gly8f4z.

Shapiro M (1997). The problems of independent agencies in the United States and the European Union. *Journal of European Public Policy* 4(2): 276–77.

Works cited

Shell E R (2009). *Cheap the high cost of discount culture*. New York: Penguin Books.
Shevelow K (2008). *For the love of animals: the rise of the animal protection movement*. New York: Henry Holt & Co.
Shiffman D (2014). Keeping swimmers safe without killing sharks is a revolution in shark control. *Animal Conservation* 17(4): 299–300.
Signal T and N Taylor (2006). Attitudes to animals in the animal protection community compared to a normative community sample. *Society and Animals* 14(3): 265–74.
Singer P (2009). *Animal liberation: the definitive classic of the animal movement*. Updated edition. New York: Ecco Books/Harper Perennial.
Singer P, B Dover and I Newkirk (1991). *Save the animals! 101 easy things you can do*. North Ryde, NSW: Angus & Robertson.
Singleton G, D Aitkin, B Jinks and J Warhurst (2012). *Australian political institutions*. Sydney: Pearson Higher Education.
Skocpol T (1999). Advocates without members: the recent transformation of American civic life. In T Skocpol and M Fiorina (eds). *Civic engagement in American democracy* (pp461–509). Washington, DC: Brookings Institution Press.
Smith E and B Pritchard (2014). Australian agricultural policy: the pursuit of agricultural efficiency. In A Hogan and M Young (eds). *Rural and regional futures* (pp58–70). London: Routledge.
Smith F B (1965). Spiritualism in Victoria in the nineteenth century. *Journal of Religious History* 3(3): 246–60.
Smith M J (1991). From policy community to issue network: salmonella in eggs and the new politics of food. *Public Administration* 69(2): 235–55.
Smith S (2007). Constance May Bienvenu: animal welfare activist to vexatious litigant. *Legal History* 11: 31–61.
Soroka S (2002). *Agenda-setting dynamics in Canada*. Vancouver: University of British Columbia Press.
Southwell A, A Bessey and B Baker (2006). Attitudes towards animal welfare: a research report. Canberra: TNS Consultants.
Spahn P (2006). Contract federalism. In E Ahmad and G Brosio (eds). *Handbook of fiscal federalism* (pp182–97). Northampton: Edward Elgar.
Spedding C R W (2000). *Animal welfare*. London: Earthscan Publications.
Splichal S (2012). Public opinion and opinion polling: contradictions and controversies. In C Holtz-Bacha and J Strömbäck (eds). *Opinion polls and the media: reflecting and shaping public opinion* (pp25–46). Houndmills: Palgrave Macmillan.
St John G (1997). Going feral: authentica on the edge of Australian culture. *Australian Journal of Anthropology* 8(3): 167–89.

Staggenborg S (2016). *Social movements*. 2nd edition. New York: Oxford University Press.

Stallwood K (2012). Animal rights: moral crusade or social movement? Paper presented at the 9th Annual MANCEPT Workshops in Political Theory, University of Manchester, 5–7 September.

Stark T, T Signal and N Taylor (2006). Australia domestic violence, child abuse and companion animal harm: service provision. *Journal of the Home Economics Institute of Australia* 13(1): 2–5.

Stern C (1999). The evolution of social-movement organizations: niche competition in social space. *European Sociological Review* 15(1): 91–105.

Stewart J, D Hedge and J Lester (2008). *Public policy: an evolutionary approach*. 3rd edition. Belmont: Thomson/Wadsworth.

Stolle D, M Hooghe and M Micheletti (2005). Politics in the supermarket: political consumerism as a form of political participation. *International Political Science Review / Revue internationale de science politique* 26(3): 245–69.

Stone DA (2002). *Policy paradox: the art of political decision making*. Revised edition. New York: Norton.

Stryker S, T J Owens, R W White and S Stryker (eds) (2000). Identity competition: key to differential social movement participation? In *Self, identity, and social movements, social movements, protest, and contention* (pp21–40). Minneapolis: University of Minnesota Press.

Sutton D E (2010). Food and the senses. *Annual Review of Anthropology* 39(1): 209–23.

Tait P (2013). Caught: sentimental, decorative kangaroo identities in popular culture. In M Boyde (ed.). *Captured: the animal within culture* (p175). London: Palgrave Macmillan UK.

Tait P and R Farrell (2010). Protests and circus geographies: Exotic animals with Edgley's in Australia. *Journal of Australian Studies* 34(2): 225–39.

Tallman I, R Marotz-Baden and P Pindas (1983). *Adolescent socialization in cross-cultural perspective: planning for social change*. New York: Academic Press.

Tapp V (2014). Russia bans kangaroo meat due to unacceptable levels of E. coli. *ABC Rural*. 18 August. http://tinyurl.com/j3fohx5.

Tarrow S (1994). *Power in movement*. Cambridge: Cambridge University Press.

Taylor G and T Osborne (2015). Dog owner guilty of assaulting RSPCA inspectors tasked with euthanasing 'emaciated' animal. *ABC News*. 19 August. http://tinyurl.com/hbgbvaj.

Taylor K, N Gordon, G Langley and W Higgins (2008). Estimates for worldwide laboratory animal use in 2005. *Alternatives to Laboratory Animals* 36(3): 327–42.

Works cited

Taylor N (2004). In it for the nonhuman animals: animal welfare, moral certainty, and disagreements. *Society and Animals* 12(4): 318–39.

Taylor N and T Signal (2009a). Pet, pest, profit: isolating differences in attitudes towards the treatment of animals. *Anthrozoos* 22(2): 129–35.

Taylor N and T Signal (2009b). Lock 'em up and throw away the key? Community opinions regarding current animal abuse penalties. *Australian Animal Protection Law Journal* 3: 33–52.

Taylor N, E Richards and T Signal (2013). A different cut? Comparing attitudes toward animals and propensity for aggression within two primary industry cohorts – farmers and meatworkers. *Society and Animals* 21(4): 395–413.

Taylor V (1989). Social movement continuity: the women's movement in abeyance. *American Sociological Review* 54(5): 761–75.

Tham J C (2010). *Money and politics: the democracy we can't afford*. Sydney: UNSW Press.

Thirict D (2010). Flying fox conservation laws, policies and practices in Australia: a case study in conserving unpopular species. *The Australasian Journal of Natural Resources Law and Policy* 13(2): 161–94.

Thompson R C (2002). *Religion in Australia: a history*. Melbourne: Oxford University Press.

Thomson J (2013). Pet owners rejoice at new NSW strata model by-law. *Sydney Morning Herald* (Domain section). 4 November. http://tinyurl.com/z2yzzj7.

Thorne T (2012). *Creeping death: the rise of the animal welfare lobby and the fall of the cattle industry*. Brisbane: McCullough Robertson Lawyers.

Tiernan A and P Weller (2010). *Learning to be a minister: heroic expectations, practical realities*. Carlton, Vic.: Melbourne University Press.

Tiffen R and R Gittins (2009). *How Australia compares*. 2nd edition. Port Melbourne: Cambridge University Press.

Tilly C (1999). *From interactions to outcomes in social movements*. In M Giugni, D McAdam and C Tilly (eds). *How social movements matter, social movements, protest, and contention* (pp253–70). Minneapolis: University of Minnesota Press.

Tindall D B, H Harshaw and J M Taylor (2011). The effects of social network ties on the public's satisfaction with forest management in British Columbia, Canada. In Ö Bodin and C Prell (eds). *Social networks and natural resource management: uncovering the social fabric of environmental governance* (pp147–79). Cambridge: Cambridge University Press.

Tiplady C (ed.) (2013). *Animal abuse helping animals and people*. Wallingford, UK: Centre for Agriculture and Bioscience International.

Tiplady C, Walsh D and Baulch M (2013). Human/animal abuse. In C Tiplady (Ed). *Animal abuse: helping animals and people* (pp93–103). Wallingford, UK: Centre for Agriculture and Bioscience International.

Townend C (1981). *A voice for the animals: how Animal Liberation grew in Australia*. Kenthurst, NSW: Kangaroo Press.

Tribe A (2008). *Zoos and animal welfare*. Heidelberg: Springer.

Truman D (1951). *The governmental process: political interests and public opinion*. New York: Knopf.

Tuchman G (1978). *Making news: a study in the construction of reality*. New York: Free Press.

Turner J (n.d.). *Animal breeding, welfare and society*. London: Earthscan Publications.

Twine R (2010). *Animals as biotechnology: ethics, sustainability and critical animal studies*. London: Earthscan Publications.

Tyler T and M Rossini (eds) (2009). *Animal encounters*. Leiden: Brill NV.

Van Biezen I, P Mair and T Poguntke (2012). Going, going ... gone? The decline of party membership in contemporary Europe. *European Journal of Political Research* 51(1): 24–56.

van Luijk J, Y Cuijpers, L van der Vaart, T C de Roo, M Leenaars and M Ritskes-Hoitinga (2013). Assessing the application of the 3Rs: a survey among animal welfare officers in the Netherlands. *Laboratory Animals* 47(3): 210–19.

Vegan Australia (n.d.). Welcome to Vegan Australia: love life, live vegan. http://www.veganaustralia.org.au/.

Vegetarian/Vegan Society of Queensland (2010). *A pound of flesh: a survey of 1202 Australians about whether they're vegetarian or vegan and what their attitudes to animals are*. Brisbane: Vegetarian/Vegan Society of Queensland.

Verrinder J M and C J C Phillips (2014). Identifying veterinary students' capacity for moral behavior concerning animal ethics issues. *Journal of Veterinary Medical Education* 41(1): 358–70.

Victorian Farmers' Federation (2014). About membership. http://tinyurl.com/vff2014.

Vidot A (2013a). Federal government scraps welfare advisory group. *ABC Rural*. 8 November. http://tinyurl.com/ozkv94q.

Vidot A (2013b). Labor to appoint independent animal welfare inspector. *ABC Rural*. 31 July.

Vromen A (2015). Campaign entrepreneurs in online collective action: GetUp! in Australia. *Social Movement Studies* 14(2): 195–213.

Waddell J (2004). *But you kill ants: answers to 100 objections to vegetarianism and veganism*. Brookvale, NSW: BA Printing and Publishing Services.

Works cited

Wallis J and R Gregory (2009). Leadership, accountability and public value: resolving a problem in 'new governance'? *International Journal of Public Administration* 32(3-4): 250-73.

Walmsley D J (1993). The policy environment. In T Sorensen and R Epps (eds). *Prospects and policies for rural Australia*. Melbourne: Longman Cheshire.

Walters K S and L Portmess (eds) (2001). *Religious vegetarianism: from Hesiod to the Dalai Lama*. Albany: State University of New York Press.

Warner M (2010). *Publics and counterpublics*. New York: Zone Books.

Warren M A (1987). Difficulties with the strong animal rights position. *Between the Species* 2: 161-173.

Webb S (2012). Australian Animal Liberation members stage macabre demonstration, cradling 100 dead animals in Melbourne city square. *Daily Mail Australia*. 10 October. http://tinyurl.com/jbx3yju.

Webster J (ed.) (2011). *Management and welfare of farm animals: UFAW farm handbook*. 5th edition. Wheathampstead: Universities Federation for Animal Welfare.

Weishaar H, A Amos and J Collin (2014). Capturing complexity: mixing methods in the analysis of a European tobacco control policy network. *International Journal of Social Research Methodology* 18(2): 1-18.

Wells A E D, J Sneddon, J A Lee and D Blanche (2011). Farmers' response to societal concerns about farm animal welfare: the case of mulesing. *Journal of Agricultural and Environmental Ethics* 24(6): 645-58.

Wells A E D, J Sneddon, J A Lee and D Blanche (2010). Understanding Australian farmers' intentions to change practices in response to calls from animal welfare groups: The case of mulesing. *Agricultural Science* 22(2): 25-6.

Whateley G (2012). *Black Caviar: the authorised story*. Sydney: HarperCollins Publishers.

Wheller S (2014). Commonwealth employment and welfare policies in post-war regional Australia. In A Hogan and M Young (eds). *Rural and regional futures*. London: Routledge.

White E (1937). *Lesser lives*. Brisbane: W R Smith & Paterson Pty Ltd.

White J (2013). *Inquiry into surveillance devices*. Adelaide: The Law Society of South Australia.

White R (2008). Regulation of animal welfare in Australia and the emergent Commonwealth: entrenching the traditional approach of the states and territories or laying the ground for reform. *Federal Law Review*, 35(3).

White S (2012). Animal law in Australian universities: towards 2015. *Australian Animal Protection Law Journal* 7: 70-81.

Wiese A and W Toporowski (2013). CSR failures in food supply chains – an agency perspective. *British Food Journal* 115(1): 92-107.

Williams A (n.d.). *Evaluation of tooth grinding as a method for improving economic performance in flocks with premature incisor tooth loss ('broken mouth')*. Final report (no. 5), Project DAV. Melbourne: Wool Research and Development Corporation.

Williams L and J Germov (2011). Devouring the social appetite. *Australian Humanities Review* 51: 167–74.

Williams R (1976). *Keywords: a vocabulary of culture and society*. New York: Oxford University Press.

Williams V (2002). Conflicts of interest affecting the role of veterinarians in animal welfare. *ANZCCART News* 15(3): 1–3.

Willingham R (2011). ALP conference will tackle live export trade. *Sydney Morning Herald*. 17 November. http://www.smh.com.au/national/alp-conference-will-tackle-live-export-trade-20111116-1nj6w.html.

Wilson F G (2013). *A theory of public opinion*. New Brunswick, NJ: Transaction Publishers.

Wong L, E A Selvanathan and S Selvanathan (2013). *Changing pattern of meat consumption in Australia*. Brisbane: Griffith University.

Wrenn C (2012). Abolitionist animal rights: critical comparisons and challenges within the animal rights movement. *Interface: A Journal For and About Social Movements* 4: 438–58.

Xue B, R W Williams, C J Oldfield, G Goa, K Dunker and V N Uversky (2012). Do viral proteins possess unique features? In V N Uversky and S Longhi (eds). *Flexible viruses: structural disorder in viral proteins*. Hoboken, NJ: Wiley.

Yaziji M and J P Doh (2013). The role of ideological radicalism and resource homogeneity in social movement organization campaigns against corporations. *Organization Studies* 34(5–6): 755–80.

Yoho J (1998). The evolution of a better definition of 'interest group' and its synonyms. *Social Science Journal* 35(2): 231–43.

Young D (2005). *Sporting island: a history of sport and recreation in Tasmania*. Hobart: Sport and Recreation Tasmania.

Young SA (2011). *How Australia decides: election reporting and the media*. Cambridge: Cambridge University Press.

Zambrano C (2013). Unwanted pets: time to change. *Pet Industry News* 23(2): 8–10.

Zhou ZY (2013). *Developing successful agriculture: an Australian case study*. Wallingford, UK: Centre for Agriculture and Bioscience International.

List of Interviewees

Position descriptions were correct at the time of interview but may since have changed. Anonymous interviewees appear at the end of the list.

Mr Michael Beatty, Media and Community Relations, RSPCA Queensland, 16 April 2013
Mr Stephen Bradshaw, Animal Welfare Representative, Australian Professional Rodeo Association, 5 May 2014
The Hon. Robert Brown MLC (NSW), Shooters and Fishers Party, 18 March 2014
Ms Dana Campbell, CEO, Voiceless, 30 January 2014
Ms Maureen Collier, Secretary, Vegetarian/Vegan Society of Queensland, 17 April 2013
Mr Ian Cowie, Former Director, Department of Local Government, Western Australia, 27 August 2014
Mr Russell Cox, Executive Officer, Western Australian Pork Producers' Association, 2 October 2013
Ms Debbie Dekker, President, Queensland Horse Council Inc., 17 April 2013
Ms Lara Drew, Animal Liberation ACT, 23 July 2013
Ms Indra Esguerra, Senior Advisor to Shane Rattenbury MLA, 23 July 2013
Mr Neil Ferguson, Chairman, Agricultural Produce Commission, Pork Producers' Committee, Western Australia, 3 September 2013
Dr Eliot Forbes, Executive Director of the Australian Racing Board and Chairman of the ARB Retirement of Racehorses Committee; CEO of Tasracing Pty Ltd, 9 April 2014
Mr Malcolm France, founder, Australian and New Zealand Laboratory Animal Association, 19 May 2014
Ms Tammie Franks MLC, South Australian Greens, 26 September 2014
General Manager Policy, National Farmers' Federation, 14 November 2014

Ms Tracy-Lynne Geysen, Brisbane Lawyers Educating and Advocating for Tougher Sentences, 19 April 2013
The Hon. Bryan Green MP (Tasmania), Australian Labor Party, 22 September 2014
Ms Elizabeth Hill, President, University of Melbourne Animal Protection Society, 20 August 2013
Mr Mark Hyman, Chair, Animal Welfare Advisory Committee, 22 July 2013
Ms Deb Kelly, Manager, Animal Welfare, Department of Environment, Water and Natural Resources, South Australia, 25 August 2014 (by correspondence)
Mr Wes Judd, Director, Queensland Dairyfarmers' Organisation Ltd, 19 April 2013
Mr Laurie Levy, founder, Coalition Against Duck Shooting, 30 August 2013
Ms Patty Mark, founder, Animal Liberation Victoria, 3 June 2013
Ms Helen Marston, CEO, Humane Research Australia, 23 September 2013
Mr Greg McFarlane, Chair, Vegan Australia / Vegan Society of NSW, 17 May 2013
Ms Maria Mercurio, CEO, RSPCA Victoria, 4 June 2013
Mr Chay Neal, President, Animal Liberation Queensland, 16 April 2013
The Hon. Melissa Parke MP, Australian Labor Party, 4 September 2014
Mr Mark Pearson, Executive Director, Animal Liberation NSW, 5 June 2013 (as of 2015, Member of the Legislative Council NSW for the Animal Justice Party)
Mr Roger Perkins, CEO, Pet Industry Association of Australia, 24 March 2014
Mr Ian Randles, Policy Officer, Western Beef and Sheep Producers Committee, Pastoralists and Graziers Association of Western Australia, 30 September 2013
The Hon. Shane Rattenbury MLA, ACT Minister for Territory and Municipal Services, Corrections, Housing, Aboriginal and Torres Strait Islander Affairs, and Ageing, 23 July 2013
Mr Andrew Spencer, CEO, Australian Pork Ltd, 23 June 2014
Mr Kelvin Thomson MP, Australian Labor Party, federal member for Wills, 26 June 2014
Mr Justin Toohey, Animal Welfare Officer, Cattle Council of Australia, 4 July 2014
Ms Debra Tranter, Founder, Oscars' Law, 22 September 2014
Ms Sharyn Watson, Executive Director, Medical Advances Without Animals Trust, 25 June 2014
The Hon. Steve Whan MLC, NSW Shadow Minister for Resources and Primary Industries, Shadow Minister for Tourism Major Events Hospitality and Racing, and Shadow Minister for Rural Water, 19 March 2014
Ms Lyn White, Animals Australia, 24 September 2014 (by correspondence)
Animal welfare advocate, 5 September 2014
CEO, Queensland Farmers' Federation, 16 April 2013
CEO, RSPCA Australia, 24 June 2014

List of Interviewees

Director, Victorian bureau of animal welfare, 21 August 2013
Eight individuals associated with the Sydney veg*n community, 8 May 2014
Executive officer, animal welfare organisation, 9 October 2014
Former officer, animal welfare department, 1 August 2014
Lawyer involved in animal law, 13 May 2014
Member of Parliament, South Australia, 25 September 2014
Policy officer, Queensland Farmers' Federation, 16 April 2013
Representative of the chicken industry, 31 January 2014
Representative of the grocery industry, 9 April 2014
Representative of the retail industry, 22 April 2014
Senior public servant, primary industries, 29 July 2013

Index

abattoirs 6, 89, 260, 342
Abbott, Tony 272, 299
abeyance structures 187, 220
abolitionism (strong animal rights) 125, 136, 170, 171, 173, 178, 188, 213, 218, 291, 329
activism
 animal rights xx, 31
 anti-activist legistlation 182, 267, 272, 273
 anti-vivisection 16
 Blackbird, The (anonymous activist) 211–212
 direct action 173, 190, 211–218
 in the media 96–97, 119, 265–273
 organisations 11, 127, 132
 political 117, 151–221
Adams, Carol 79, 374
advertising 104–106, 200, 219, 259, 264
'ag-gag' legislation *see* activism: anti-activist legistlation
agricultural shows 111, 116
agriculture
 animal agriculture xix, 6, 17, 65, 69, 73, 96, 214, 291
 media depictions of 111–117
 methods 4
 trade 223–273, 307–318

Animal Activists Forum 172, 179, 187
Animal Attitude Scale (AAS) 47, 70, 80, 169–171, 179, 213
Animal Defenders Office 162
Animal Health Australia 296
Animal Justice Party 286–288
animal law 135, 162, 198, 201, 220
Animal Liberation Front (ALF) 212
Animal Liberation (organisation) 36, 136, 157, 178, 181, 216, 271
 ACT 136, 162, 183, 211
 NSW 186, 189, 199, 214, 217, 268, 286
 Queensland 184, 303, 331
 Victoria 159, 183, 200, 203, 209
Animal Protection Organisation (APO) 10, 11, 152–222, 223–224, 228, 232–235, 239, 241, 245, 247, 251–267, 271–273
animal rights 17, 34, 48, 73, 99, 109, 155, 170, 173, 178, 213, 329; *see also* abolitionism (strong animal rights)
animal shelters 15, 180–181, 197, 214
Animal Welfare League 185, 228, 330
animal welfare policy 10, 10, 14, 17, 124, 126, 128, 161, 219, 223, 231, 234, 239, 275–318
 history 3–19

animals as property 29, 33, 326, 329
Animals Australia 51, 91, 128, 129, 158–162, 173, 179–185, 187, 201, 206, 233, 268, 272, 299, 308, 309, 313, 325
animal-using industry organisation 223–274, 313–315, 318
animal-welfare officers 215, 247, 250, 325
anthropocentrism 28, 30–33, 48–50, 105, 111, 112, 117
Anti-Vivisection Union of South Australia 118, 188, 220
anti-vivisectionist *see* vivisection
Australia Pork Limited 299
Australian and New Zealand Council for the Care of Animals in Research and Teaching (ANZCCART) 251
Australian and New Zealand Laboratory Animal Association (ANZLAA) 252
Australian Animal Welfare Strategy (AAWS) 229, 296–301, 309, 314
Australian Broadcasting Corporation (ABC) 89, 91–95, 96, 98, 181, 268, 271, 306
Australian Chicken Meat Federation (ACMF) 42
Australian Competition and Consumer Commission (ACCC) 201–201, 294
Australian Democrats 296, 303
Australian Labor Party (ALP) 193, 284, 291, 297, 299, 302, 305–309, 309
Victorian Labor Party 286
Australian Racing Board 43, 53
Australian Veterinary Association 228, 247, 297, 337; *see also* veterinarians

Bacon Week 183
Bartlett, Andrew 303
Beef Riot 7
behaviourism 23, 31, 32, 34, 48, 78, 169
Bienvenu, Constance May 186, 267
Biosecurity Act 2015 (NSW) 266–269
birds 46, 105, 110, 112, 203, 210, 282, 360; *see also* chickens
British Union for the Abolition of Vivisection (BUAV) 11

capitalism 77, 194, 219
Cartesian materialism 28, 326
cats 45–46, 90, 106, 192, 362
Cattle Council of Australia 58, 92, 230
chickens xvi, xvi, 62, 71, 105, 110, 259, 261, 360
chicken meat 9, 42, 134, 214, 225, 231
chicken cages 102, 239
CHOICE (consumer advocacy organisation) 61, 201
Choose Cruelty Free 188
Christianity 11, 12, 27–28
circuses 44, 232, 252
Coalition Against Duck Shooting 203, 210, 269
Coalition, The *see* Liberal–National Party (LNP)
codes of practice 247, 264, 296, 298
cognitive capacity of animals 30, 32, 49, 329
commodity councils 225–234, 258–264, 334
companion animals *see* birds, cats, dogs, fish
consciousness of animals 5, 24
conservation 10, 27, 188–193, 287, 304; *see also* environmentalism
conservation hunting 305, 310
consumer activism 57–62, 76, 254–256
cosmetics 58, 290

Index

Council of Australian Governments (COAG) 293, 296
counter-publics 117–121
cows 10, 42, 60, 94, 98, 362
  mad cow disease 129
Crossman, Danny 192
Cruel Treatment of Cattle Act (1822) 10, 125
cruelty 16, 17, 27, 29, 54–57, 90–95, 102, 193, 198, 280
  anti-cruelty 11, 11, 14, 98
CSIRO 6, 296

Darwin, Charles 23, 28, 30
Descent of man 30
de Brito, Sam 121
Deakin, Alfred 12, 13, 83
Descartes, René 28, 48, 326, 373
diet xvii, 4, 7, 12–14, 41, 109–110, 172
  carnism xvii, xviii, 34, 327
  religious aspects 26, 27, 99, 350
  veganism 77, 190
  vegetarianism xviii, 80
dogs 45, 46, 90, 106, 111, 181, 192, 209, 246, 301
  dog racing 43, 64, 227, 257
  live baiting 268, 282, 317
  working dogs 44
Donovan, Josephine 79, 214, 328, 374, 374
duck hunting 160, 203, 292

education 63, 119, 121, 156, 199, 221, 252, 299, 336
eggs *see* chickens
entryism 186
environmentalism 4, 27, 65, 80, 162, 188–194, 199, 234, 269, 303; *see also* conservation
ethics 21–36

euthanising animals 44, 181, 197, 248
evolutionary theory 22, 23, 30, 327
experimentation on animals *see* cosmetics, education, vivisection
Exporter Supply Chain Assurance System (ESCAS) 93–94, 307–309

factory farming 17, 73, 265
far right 99–100
farm animals 51, 51, 69–74, 115; *see also* chickens, cows, pigs
farming *see* agriculture
federalism 6, 162, 299, 300–302
feminism 12, 33, 328
feminist ethics of care 33, 178, 328
fish 45, 105, 110, 113, 361
fishing 4, 41, 44
flexitarian diet 77
Four Corners see Australian Broadcasting Corporation (ABC)
Francione, Gary 30, 33, 48, 80, 155, 329
free-range eggs 59, 59, 60, 201, 214, 233

genetic modification 250, 283
graffiti 120
Greens, The xv, 191, 280, 281, 284, 287–291, 302–304, 305, 309, 309
greyhounds *see* dogs: dog racing

Harrison, Ruth 17, 58
Animal machines 17, 73
horses 15, 16, 53, 110, 111, 192
  horse racing 43, 160, 227, 232, 257, 265
Howard, John 273, 307
Humane Research Australia 44, 52, 188
Humane Research Council 48, 59, 62, 67, 82, 206

hunting 4, 44, 292, 305, 310; *see also* conservation: conservation hunting, duck hunting
Hursthouse, Rosalind 31, 327

Indigenous Australians 4–5
Indonesia xv, xix, 89–95, 307
industrial animal use *see* agriculture: animal agriculture, agriculture: trade
insects 24, 112
Institute for Critical Animal Studies (ICAS) 95, 171, 221
Islam 27, 99, 100

Joyce, Barnaby 290

kangaroos 10, 90
  kangaroo cull 190, 287, 287, 304
  kangaroo meat 90, 98
Kant, Immanuel 27, 48, 326
King, Martin Luther Jr 217
Kirby, Michael 161

labelling schemes 58, 200, 295
laboratory animals 43, 52, 119, 214, 247–258, 336
labour movement *see* Australian Labor Party (ALP), union movement
language of animal welfare 17, 49, 65, 118, 173, 179, 214
Lawrence, W.R. 186
Leahy, Michael 34–36, 48–49, 327
  Against liberation 34
Liberal–National Party (LNP) 8, 99, 273, 285, 289, 292, 302, 306
liberation, strong rights, abolition (LSRA) 155, 170, 177, 187, 190, 213, 219

live exports xv–xvi, xix, 66, 89–106, 127, 130, 159, 179–194, 230, 253, 265, 296, 305–310, 325

Mark, Patty 157, 209
Martin, Richard 10, 125
masculinity 72, 82, 108, 179
Meat and Livestock Australia Ltd 81, 226
meat eating 4–7, 27, 34, 35, 41–42, 64, 70–82, 106–110, 113–121
mediatisation 204–215
media 29, 36, 72, 75, 85–122, 194, 281; *see also* online media, print media, social media, television
Medical Advances Without Animals (MAWA) 161, 220
Million Paws Walk 209
mulesing xv, 56, 71, 72, 134, 216–218, 237, 263

National Farmers' Federation (NFF) 8, 225, 229–235, 239, 263, 295, 300
nationalism 7, 258, 292
Nationals, The *see* Liberal–National Party (LNP)
native animals 10, 56, 105, 210, 319
neo-liberalism 243, 293–295, 320

O'Farrell, Barry 311
online media 110–111; *see also* social media
open rescue 209, 212, 214, 215; *see also* activism: direct action
Oscar's Law 209, 286, 289

pain and suffering 30, 32, 72–72, 237
Parke, Melissa 291, 308
Pearson, Mark 157, 207, 217, 286

Index

People for the Ethical Treatment of Animals (PETA) xvi, 167, 205, 206
PETA (USA) xv, 90, 162, 216, 232, 237, 263, 292
pescetarian diet 77
pest animals 10, 112, 257, 277, 279
Pet Industry Association of Australia (PIAA) 246, 301–302
pet shops 60, 302
pets *see* companion animals
pigs 57–58, 72, 110, 117, 134, 200, 268
Plibersek, Tanya 291
policy domain xxi, 40, 122, 123–138, 173, 188–193, 269, 276, 281, 321
policy network 124–133, 136, 161, 174, 223–224, 229, 243–245, 281
Pollan, Michael 35, 327
The omnivore's dilemma 35
print media 87–91
protests xvi, 99, 102, 179, 190, 191, 209, 269
public opinion 39–84, 297, 321
and public servants 312

Queensland Farmers' Federation 225, 230

Regan, Tom 31, 33, 34, 48, 80, 155, 329
religious duty xviii, xxi, 12, 36, 64, 83, 326
retailers 62, 75, 112–115, 128, 200, 207, 231, 233, 254–256, 259, 265, 274
Rhiannon, Lee 284, 291
rodeos 44, 292, 335
Australian Professional Rodeo Association 44, 227, 235, 302
Royal Society for the Prevention of Cruelty to Animals (RSPCA) 11–15, 91, 132, 152–220, 246, 268, 315–318
ACT 183, 186

New South Wales 183, 268
Queensland 15, 95, 180
Tasmania 186, 206
Victoria 11, 183, 217, 292
Western Australia 186
Ryder, Richard 48, 327

Scruton, Roger 34, 327
Animal rights and wrongs 34
Scully, Carl 84
Sea Shepherd Conservation Society 189, 215
sentience xx, 22, 28, 32, 328–329
sharks xvi, 111, 190
Shooters and Fishers Party (SFP) 61, 116, 269, 304–305, 310
Singer, Peter xx, 36
Animal liberation 17, 31, 155
slavery 33–34, 329
social media 195, 208, 209, 209, 263–265, 284
social movement organisations 163, 164, 175–178, 186, 208
Societies for the Protection of Animals (SPCA) 11–15; *see also* Royal Society for the Prevention of Cruelty to Animals (RSPCA)
speciesism 32, 33, 179, 327
state farming organisations 225, 229, 233, 240, 260, 299, 315, 334
suffering *see* pain and suffering
supermarkets *see* retailers
supply chain 75, 128–128, 133–135, 200–201, 217, 227, 254–256, 307

Tasmania 88, 186, 187, 206, 271
television 87, 91–95, 103–110
terrorism 212, 268–269, 292
tourism 105, 111
Townend, Christine 185, 189

Tranter, Debra 209
trapping 279

union movement 6, 151, 193–194, 308
universities *see* education
urbanisation 14–15, 61, 111, 116, 242, 263, 292
utilitarianism 4, 29, 30, 33, 36, 195, 328

veganism 83, 109, 118, 172, 190; *see also* diet: veganism
vegetarianism 12, 27, 81–83, 108, 119, 303; *see also* diet: vegetarianism
veterinarians 71, 158, 228, 247–252, 307, 337
virtue ethics 29, 31, 327
vivisection 12, 25, 33–34, 50, 187

Voiceless 135, 161, 185, 208, 219, 220, 234, 262, 305, 309, 314
volunteerism 153, 167, 173

Warren, Mary Ann 48, 49, 79, 329
welfarism xiii, 29–33, 94, 154–155, 170, 174, 213, 330–332
Western Australia 190, 203, 269, 292, 315, 316
whaling 190, 215, 351
women 4, 12, 50, 80–81, 178–180
wool 5, 8, 90, 134; *see also* mulesing
World League for the Protection of Animals (WLPAA) 188

zoos 16, 44, 252